MUSCLE CAR INTERIOR Restoration Guide

Daniel Strohl

S-A DESIGN

CarTech®

CarTech®

CarTech®, Inc.
39966 Grand Avenue
North Branch, MN 55056
Phone: 651-277-1200 or 800-551-4754
Fax: 651-277-1203
www.cartechbooks.com

Edit by Paul Johnson
Layout by Monica Bahr

ISBN 978-1-61325-039-6
Item No. SA167P

Library of Congress Cataloging-in-Publication Data

Strohl, Daniel.
Muscle car interior restoration guide / by Daniel Strohl.
p. cm.
ISBN 978-1-932494-98-3
1. Muscle cars—Interiors—Conservation and restoration. I. Title.

TL152.2.S75 2009
629.2'6—dc22

2009006442

Title Page:
An accurate, original restoration will provide enormous pride and years of faithful service on the road. This 1964 GTO convertible has been restored to pristine condition.

Back Cover Photos

Top Left:
When the headliner is fastened to the top, it is stretched and smoothed. A razor blade is used to trim the excess headliner material from the edges.

Top Right:
The door panels in our 1968 Camaro had a long service life and now it's time for replacement. Removal starts by unscrewing the armrest. New panels will soon replace the old ones.

Middle Left:
The Camaro bucket seat is being disassembled because it needs a full restoration, which includes new foam, hog rings, and vinyl covers.

Middle Right:
A restored set of gauges provides a striking upgrade in appearance. Refacing the speedometer requires removing and reinstalling the needle, which needs to be done carefully to avoid damaging the speedometer's internals.

Bottom Left:
The entire dash lifts off the interior with the removal of a few screws. The wires for climate control and the other gauges need to be carefully detached before you proceed.

Bottom Right:
The rear window is inserted at the right height for this convertible top. A chalk mark was made at the bow to indicate that height, then just the center of the rear window piece was stapled to the rail, avoiding sending a staple through the bolt holes in the rail.

OVERSEAS DISTRIBUTION BY:

Brooklands Books Ltd.
P.O. Box 146, Cobham, Surrey, KT11 1LG, England
Telephone 01932 865051 • Fax 01932 868803
www.brooklands-books.com

Brooklands Books Aus.
3/37-39 Green Street, Banksmeadow, NSW 2019, Australia
Telephone 2 9695 7055 • Fax 2 9695 7355

CONTENTS

ACKNOWLEDGMENTS

I knew this would be a tough book to write from the get-go, if only because of my location (Bennington, Vermont) and the lack of interior and upholstery shops in my area that focus on older cars, let alone muscle cars specifically. And I didn't want the entire book to have photos of just one hand holding a part and the other hand holding the shutter release button on my camera, so I needed to step out of my garage.

Fortunately, I've made plenty of friends and contacts while working at *Hemmings Motor News*, and I was able to call on several of them for assistance. While most people in the hobby won't recognize the name, Jeff Reeves, the technical editor for the American Motors Owners Association, provided the most valuable assistance for this book, opening my eyes to less expensive, alternative methods of doing things and providing instructions for some of the techniques with which I was less familiar. Even though we share the AMC sickness, he knows just as much about the Big Three products as well.

Some of the hands you'll see in this book that aren't mine belong to a few upholstery shop guys and specialists who, again, aren't necessarily widely known on the national scene, but do great work and deserve a nod. Among them are Jerry Ambrosi of Master Upholstery in Newton, New Jersey; Kurt Reiche and Gil Monge of Gillin Custom Design in Middletown, New York; John Yannone of Newburgh Auto Glass in Walden, New York; and Conrad Zukowski of Conrad's Radio Service in Worcester, Massachusetts. Melvin Benzaquen of Classic Restoration Enterprises in Pine Island, New York, also assisted on that front. To the owners of the various cars and parts under restoration at each of those shops, I thank you as well.

For some of the projects that I did myself for this book, I'd like to thank John Sloane of the Eastwood Company, and Scott Whitaker from Dynamic Controls, for the materials and supplies. You'd be surprised how many companies refuse to help out an author working on a book like this, but John and Scott answered my calls and my questions.

My fellow editors at *Hemmings Motor News* have been good for suggestions and advice throughout the process of putting this book together. I've never before worked with a more professional and talented group of guys. In particular, my editor-in-chief, Richard Lentinello, has been a constant source of inspiration and motivation since he hired me at *Hemmings*.

And, of course, I can't leave out my wife, Heather, who provided the support I needed while working on this book. We both knew this book would require an insane amount of time and energy, and so I only agreed to write it when she gave the project her blessing. I promise I'll finish that bathroom renovation now, dear.

INTRODUCTION

Most guys dread it. They do anything to avoid it. They put it off as long as possible. They pay specialists big money to take care of it for them.

While these guys have absolutely no problem plunging elbow deep in grease to solve a transmission problem, gleefully spending hours preparing their car's bodywork for a perfect paint job, or eking another tenth on the quarter-mile from their traction setup, they tend to view interior work with apprehension. "It's just not my thing," they say, trying to rationalize that sizeable check to the interior and upholstery shop. Or worse, they ignore their interior completely, figuring that nobody will notice a few rips in the seat, a few cracks in the dash, or the headliner tacked up with pushpins nabbed from the office supply room.

But interior restoration shouldn't cause grown men to run and hide and act as if they're about to break out in hives. Nor should it remain a mystery to those who haven't attempted it. Considering the interior represents about 95 percent of what you see and 100 percent of what you touch when driving your muscle car (and what fun is a muscle car if you can't drive it?), you'll probably want to make sure you enjoy and appreciate that aspect of your muscle car. And with the prices of muscle cars now fluctuating between Wall Street investment and auction fodder, a quality restored interior, or one tastefully modified, will mean the difference of thousands, if not tens of thousands of dollars when it comes time to put the car up for sale. Sure, handing your muscle car's interior over to a shop accomplishes that, and plenty of quality interior shops make a robust living nowadays off muscle car guys who view themselves as too manly to tackle their own interiors. But by doing it yourself, you not only could save a good chunk of money, but you also have the satisfaction of knowing just what level of effort went into your muscle car's interior, you can customize it as you see fit, and you earn bragging rights over your buddies who simply signed a check for their interiors.

However, the intrepid muscle car owner setting out to restore his interior won't find much in the way of instruction—maybe a magazine article here or there about recovering bucket seats, perhaps a handful of aftermarket suppliers that specialize in carpet kits or interior trim pieces and have how-to videos on their websites. But what happens when it comes time to figure out the power seat wiring or replace the sagging and torn headliner?

That's where this book comes in. While factory service manuals and magazine articles might cover bits and pieces of how to remove and replace interior components, and most marque-specific books only concern themselves with what makes an interior correct, this book aims to give the muscle car restorer all the information necessary to perform a basic hands-on interior revival.

To gain the most from this book, however, view it more as a guide rather than a manual. Each muscle car certainly has its own unique attributes both inside and out, but their interiors tend to be products of their eras and thus have a lot in common, from the preponderance of vinyls and plastics rather than cloth and chromed metals, to the appearance of bucket seats and consoles in anything considered cool in that era. For that reason, this book will take a wide view of 1964–1974 muscle cars and include information and tutorials on muscle cars from all the Big Three plus AMC.

Rather than focus on what's correct for each individual muscle car, this book will instead help you decide whether to replace, refurbish, or repair your interior components and then detail the techniques, tools, and materials involved in returning your muscle car's interior to its former glory. On the other hand, while I will mention little ways in which you can customize your interior, I won't go hog wild and present Ed Roth- or George Barris-style custom interiors.

Along the way I'll include tips on how to make the most out of your interior restoration funds. At the end of this book, there is a listing of many of the key vendors and suppliers for muscle car interiors who should be able to help you find the materials and parts you'll need, along with a handful of shops who might be able to offer advice on your particular restoration. Feel free to look up your local automotive upholsterer and pick his brain for tips and tricks.

Keep in mind, too, that there's always more than one way to skin a cat, so the methods and techniques shown here may not be the same as what you have tried or seen other people use. What I tried to do was present some of the most basic and most cost-effective techniques while avoiding shortcut techniques that impair your muscle car's safety, ergonomics, and aesthetics. Yet in some cases, an inclination for one technique over another may simply come down to personal preference.

The same goes for the products and companies mentioned in this book. The restoration aftermarket is a multi-billion-dollar industry, and it didn't become that large with just one product or one company offering a solution to every need; instead, you'll have several to choose from, and I have mentioned only some of the more cost-effective or better-known products and companies, rather than exhaustively listed every product and company that serves the interior restoration slice of the aftermarket.

As for the products themselves, you'll soon notice that a lot of chemicals figure into an interior restoration. Many of those chemicals are flammable and hazardous, so take care when using them around open flames, and use them only in well-ventilated areas, preferably while wearing a respirator and latex gloves to reduce skin irritation.

What this book won't focus on is stitch counts, or even stitching at all. A heavy-duty upholstery-type sewing machine will not only set you back a few grand and require years of experience to adequately operate, the use of one isn't necessary for probably 95 percent of your interior work. Because of muscle cars' wide support in the restoration aftermarket, much of what you need, from the carpet set to the seat covers, will come pre-stitched. Buying the specialized tools and developing the specialized techniques necessary for stitching up an occasional interior just doesn't make sense, so you can view this book as Interior Restoration 101, and leave the stitching to the pros.

Individual muscle car owners aren't the only ones who will benefit from this book, either. Restoration shop owners who outsource their interior restorations surely feel the pinch on their operations every time they add up the bills for interior shops at the end of the month. By bringing those tasks in-house, they can realize a little more cost-efficiency and thus a healthier profit margin.

And if you do end up cutting that check to a restoration shop, this book will still show you what to expect from your resto shop, so you can rest assured you spent that money well and picked the shop that didn't cut corners or choose inferior materials or methods.

So grab your steering wheel puller and hog ring pliers and face your fear of interior restoration. Your muscle car will thank you.

CHAPTER 1

GETTING STARTED: PLANS AND TOOLS

Pop quiz. You've just bought your first muscle car. You saved your pennies for years to buy the exact car you've dreamed about, stripes, scoops, and all. To the consternation of your wife, you cleared out a spot in the garage just for it while the transporter hauled it halfway across the country. Your coworkers can't wait for it to arrive, if only so you'll shut up about it around the water cooler.

It finally arrives, bumpers gleaming, Hurst shifter beckoning from between the bucket seats. You roll it off the truck, sign the papers with the transporter, and finally, it's all yours. If it runs, you put the plates on it, grab the wife, and take it for a quick spin around the block, rapping the throttle so all your neighbors hear it. You then give it a good wash and wax and back it into the garage.

While admiring it and ignoring the wife's calls to come to dinner, which of these do you do? a) open up the resto catalogs you've accumulated and start ordering every little part you'll need to whip this muscle car into tip-top shape, b) yank the nasty seats and headliner and toss them to the curb, c) sell off the original parts in anticipation of new reproduction parts, d) pull and pile the original parts in the corner of the garage, or e) none of the above.

Putting the Plan Together

As difficult as it may be to restrain yourself from actually starting the project (because, let's face it, they're all projects, even the ones that are supposedly 100 percent restored), the only thing you should touch at this point is to put pen to paper. Interior restoration is no light project, and you can easily jump in over your head while trying to restore your interior. It's the type of project that's made up of dozens of different tasks, all of which require varying skill sets, and when you finish each task, nothing else in the car looks quite as nice, so you might as well replace the carpet and the seats and the headliner and, oh, the dash has a crack in it... And before you realize it, you're either cutting corners just to put it all back together, or you're down to bare floorboards and an upturned paint bucket for a seat. You don't want that. Your muscle car doesn't want that.

The way to avoid coming to that point is through proper planning and organization. It may feel as if you're not making any progress at all during this phase, but you have plenty of tasks ahead of you in this project, and (at least for most of us) the distractions of everyday life to prevent you from devoting all of your resources—financial, mental, and physical—to this project. So if you take the time now to develop a plan, your interior restoration will progress much smoother when it actually comes time to turn wrenches.

So what do I mean by planning and organization? I mean, simply, methods for keeping you from overrunning your budgeted resources, methods for keeping you on track and focused on your time lines, and methods for keeping your project from devolving into an absent-minded or even forgotten affair. Everybody has their own organizational methods, based on how well they've worked in the past. Those same organizational skills should be put to use here.

That said, a number of decisions need to be made before you crack open the toolbox. First and foremost, just how much work are you willing to do yourself and how much will you farm out? As I hinted in the introduction, one of the aims of this book is to familiarize yourself with the techniques so you have an understanding of not only how to restore an interior, but also how much outside help you want to rely on. Maybe you want to do only some of it yourself, but leave other tasks to dedicated interior shops. Maybe you feel comfortable with most of the tasks, but feel an experienced shop will better take care of one or two specific tasks. Maybe you want to leave the work to the shops, but make the purchasing decisions yourself.

If, after reading this book, you still have questions about how much work you can realistically accomplish on your own, speak with an interior shop. Ask around for one locally, consult the various shops mentioned in this book, or look up a reputable shop listed in the Services section of *Hemmings Motor News*. Ask them how much a beginner can do and how many tasks require an expert's touch.

If you really want to do it all yourself, but find yourself lacking the experience, then perhaps diving into a one-of-one Hemi Mopar or Super Duty Pontiac isn't the best beginner project. Instead, push the high-dollar muscle car to the side and replace the interior in a six-cylinder Falcon. The practice won't hurt, and show judges won't count stitches on a basic commuter the same way they would on a supercar. After figuring out what works and what doesn't, then you can tackle your dream car.

Just as important as answering the question of who will do the work, is answering the question of what work will be done. The first part of this question concerns the approach you're going to take with your car.

Is it in original, untouched, unmolested condition? Consider leaving as much of it original as possible. Yeah, that advice goes against the purposes of this book, but original interiors—down to their fasteners and build sheets—are a highly prized commodity, if only for the fact that they offer insight into how the factories built these cars, information that 100-point restorers hold precious. Original interiors also sometimes include more durable materials than what some aftermarket restoration companies provide, and they also include details that aftermarket companies neglect to include, either for the sake of manufacturing costs or for the purpose of appealing to a more universal subset of restorers.

More likely, your muscle car's interior has suffered a few decades of abuse. Let's face it: Muscle cars, for the most part, were built as cheap amusement for youth, so the manufacturers weren't going to install premium-quality interior materials. Nor were the cars going to escape the rough hands of young drivers. The reason we love muscle cars is that we could beat on them, thrash on them, drive them hard and put them away wet. Throughout the 1970s and 1980s, the second-hand and third-hand owners of these cars respected them even less and subjected them to fashions we consider obscene today. Pioneer tape decks? Chain-link steering wheels? Shag carpet?

Elements of Restoration

Some choose to further customize their car at this point, and it's certainly possible to end up with a quality custom interior nowadays. Some guys deliberately set out to replicate the late 1960s/early 1970s street machine vibe, down to the Green Line gauges, eight-ball shifter knob, and questionable contents of the ashtray. Some muscle car owners have even started applying modern street rod interior fashions and techniques to their 1960s and 1970s muscle cars, including digital dashes, electronic transmission shifters, and fancy chrome steering columns. Far be it from me to criticize those choices, but tastes change over time and fashions come and go, as they always will. An entirely restored interior, however, remains stylish no matter what the era, and tends to increase resale value while a customized interior tends to lower resale value.

Even among the restore-it enthusiasts, there remain some shades of distinction. Are you going to restore it exactly as it came from the factory? Are you going to restore it using only New Old Stock (NOS) or original parts? Are you going to restore it, but add the options you would've liked had you bought this car new? Are you going to restore it as a clone of another car? Or are you going to mildly customize it—perhaps add some modern materials and technology that were unavailable when this car was new, but not interfere with the aesthetics of the muscle car era?

Answering these questions will in turn help you determine how much of this project you can accomplish with the budget and time

New Old Stock

NOS\en-oh-ess\, noun:

1. Acronym for New Old Stock, describes parts built by the factory as replacements or spares for assembled cars.
2. To be considered New Old Stock, the part must have never been installed on a vehicle.
3. Is not pronounced "noss" and has nothing to do with nitrous oxide or young punks in foreign cars in L.A.

The Problem with NOS

You'll hear a lot of guys proudly say they built their cars using only NOS parts, but restorers tend to have one of two mind-sets regarding NOS parts.

On the one hand, NOS parts came straight from the factory of the company that built the car or from the supplier that manufactured the part. Thus, you can be pretty sure it was manufactured from the same exact materials, in the same exact methods, and to the same exact tolerances. Plus, there is that pride of owning a car that contains only parts that were manufactured by that one company.

But on the other hand, many restorers believe that NOS parts are the parts that didn't quite make the cut. Maybe they had some blemish or defect that wasn't serious enough to warrant them being tossed, but still wasn't minor enough to allow it to pass on through to the assembly line. Much of that theory is based on anecdotal evidence, however, as well as on the different procedures among the different manufacturers.

Pricewise, the market doesn't guarantee stability in the cost of NOS parts, and the laws of supply and demand, when applied to a finite and dwindling supply, dictate that the cost will inevitably increase.

But the real reason to look askance at NOS parts is the simple concern of shelf wear. Larger parts that don't easily fit into boxes are tossed around–on the factory floor, in and out of storage, in and out of the parts vendor's van. Even smaller parts that do fit into boxes aren't treated with kid gloves, and thus often show nicks and scratches. Nor were the materials in the parts designed to last forever. Plastics become brittle over time, and rust is not uncommon on NOS sheetmetal, depending on the storage environment.

So while it's cool to brag about the NOS content of your muscle car, NOS parts may not turn out to be as wonderful as they sound.

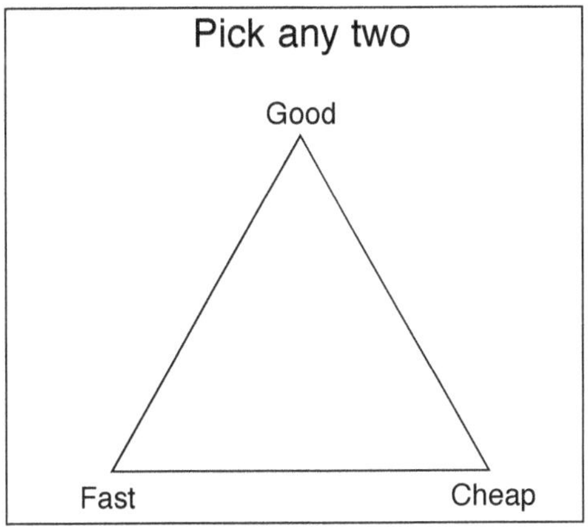

The project triangle visualizes the inability to complete a project quickly and to a high standard of quality with minimal resource outlay. In this classic project triangle, you can pick two aspects, but you can't have them all. You're thus encouraged to eliminate either speed, quality, or frugality from your project planning.

you've allotted for it. Experienced restorers have a bit of advice they like to offer their first-time customers: "You can have it done fast and cheap, but not good; you can have it done fast and good, but not cheap; or you can have it done good and cheap, but not fast."

In the field of business and IT, project managers have visualized the previous advice as a triangle, with fast at one angle, good at another, and cheap at the third. You're then encouraged to pick any two.

Thus, if you have cash falling out of your pockets, if you don't care how the interior of your car looks, or have all the time in the world, then you have no problem. The rest of us, meanwhile, need to reserve some of the budget for other aspects of the restoration, like paint, an engine rebuild, and wheels and tires, and we would rather not leave the car looking like a hillbilly circus just had its way with the interior. Time tends to give way for most of us, then, which is another reason why, barring logistical reasons, the interior tends to be

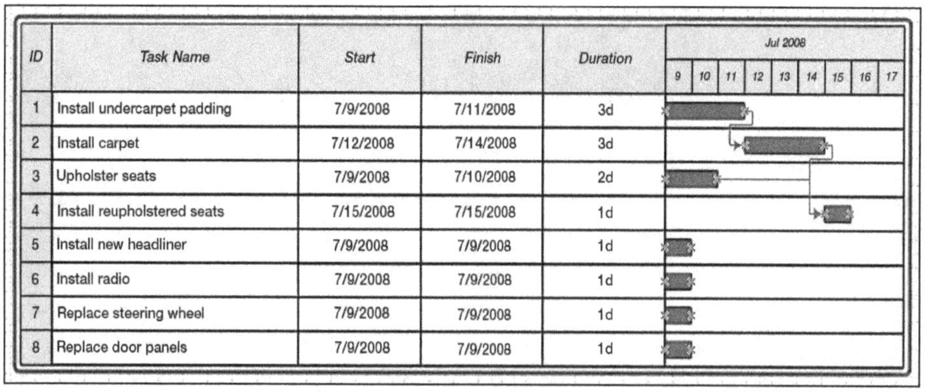

ID	Task Name	Start	Finish	Duration	Jul 2008 (9–17)
1	Install undercarpet padding	7/9/2008	7/11/2008	3d	
2	Install carpet	7/12/2008	7/14/2008	3d	
3	Upholster seats	7/9/2008	7/10/2008	2d	
4	Install reupholstered seats	7/15/2008	7/15/2008	1d	
5	Install new headliner	7/9/2008	7/9/2008	1d	
6	Install radio	7/9/2008	7/9/2008	1d	
7	Replace steering wheel	7/9/2008	7/9/2008	1d	
8	Replace door panels	7/9/2008	7/9/2008	1d	

In a typical Gantt chart, each task is laid out as a horizontal bar spanning the amount of time that task is expected to last. You can then draw relationships (the little blue lines with arrows) between the tasks to determine the order the tasks should follow each other.

the very last task holding up a complete restoration.

Fortunately, interiors don't require a complete top-to-bottom restoration all at once. For the most part you can take a modular approach—that is, you can pick and choose what requires immediate attention and what can wait. Returning to project management references, if you were to map out your interior restoration project on a Gantt chart that clearly shows a project schedule, you'd find very few task dependencies and thus a very stunted critical chain. You'll probably want to install undercarpet padding before the carpet, and both before the seats, but the rest can be completed in any order and, really, at any time.

Priority List and Budget

Here's where you need to prioritize, then, with the absolute worst aspects of the interior (those that require the most resources to complete) at the top of your list. It may be fun and gratifying to peck away at smaller tasks that don't require huge resources—replacing $3 switches rather than recovering seats for $300—but the danger to the project lies in expending all your resources on the quick-and-easy stuff, leaving little or nothing for the significant and resource-intensive parts.

You need to actually make a list—write it out. Go sit in the car with your pen and paper and jot down everything you see. Make sure all your gauges are working, make sure the steering wheel rim has no cracks in it, fully extend the seat belts, peel back the carpet. Next to everything you've jotted down, write a number, with 1 for the most egregious offenses and 10 for the least. Start a folder for all of your car's paperwork and stick the list in it. That way when you think of something else, you'll be able to keep all your ideas in one place rather than on a thousand notes spread all over the garage.

Hand-in-hand with prioritization, you should also formalize your available resources by creating a

Restoration Priorities

Looking at the entire restoration project in the same terms of project management, interior restoration should probably come after rust repair, bodywork, and paint on the critical chain, if only because a thorough and proper paint job should include the interior body surfaces: the floors, the door jambs, any exposed interior metal. "We're usually the last," said Jerry Ambrosi, owner of Master Upholstery in Newton, New Jersey. However, if you're planning a custom interior–especially one that involves drilling new holes or filling existing holes–it might be wise to move up at least the fitment of those custom interior pieces in the critical chain to a point just after the bodywork, but before the paint work. Actual installation of the custom interior can then wait until after the paint has dried.

Critical chain placement of the mechanical work can come either before or after the interior, keeping in mind the operation of the gauges and the input controls (pedals, steering column, knobs, and switches). Again, you should probably make sure the gauges and controls are all in working order before removing the interior, at a point in the critical chain before or during the restoration budget and a schedule. Figure out how much time and how much money you can allocate to this project. Do you need it done before the next show season? Do you need it done for less than what you inherited from Aunt Gertrude? Or is this a "Whenever I get it done, I get it done" kind of project? And be realistic here too. Only you know how capable you are of accomplishing these tasks within your given budget and timetable, only you know exactly how much money you'll be able to devote to this project, and only you know how much time you can spend on it.

Experienced restorers also advise novices that the actual budget and schedule tends to conflict with the planned budget and schedule. They suggest settling on a realistic amount of time and money for the project, then multiplying those figures by some factor, usually one-and-a-half or two. Indeed, unplanned and unforeseen expenses and tasks can quickly add up.

So how do you plan for the unknown? You can either do as the expert restorers suggested and adjust your expectations—maybe the interior will be done in eight months rather than four—or you can adjust the tasks that require immediate attention—maybe you only need to recover the front seats for now; the back seats are good enough to wait until later.

Research

Thorough research and organization also helps combat the unknown. Beside each item on the priority list, figure out approximately how much that item will cost. Familiarize yourself with the reproduction parts available for your car's interior, not just from the more well-known aftermarket companies, but also from the cottage industry guys who might offer a quality reproduction of a specific part that the big companies don't offer. See if an abundant supply of NOS parts still exists for your vehicle and decide whether you want to go that route. Whether doing the task yourself or relying on a shop, ask that shop how long they tend to spend on that task. They may very well give you two different totals, one of them the number of hours they would bill a customer for that task, the other the number of hours it would take to do it yourself.

Most of the research you conduct for this restoration should take place now. If performing a concours, factory-correct restoration, first obtain the judging guidelines for the relevant club or organization. Befriend one or more judges from that organization and start picking their brains. Go to club events and shows, camera in hand, and photograph cars like yours (or like you wish your car would end up). Speaking to the owners of those cars will not only net you valuable information about parts sources and restoration techniques, but the owner of the car may also allow you to further inspect the car, to sit in it, and to feel the different materials that owner used. It will also give you insight as to how the judging guidelines are applied on a case-by-case basis. Joining the relevant clubs or registries and subscribing to their newsletters often yields otherwise unavailable information about cottage industry parts sources and group buys of hard-to-reproduce items. The Internet-savvy restorer can also find plenty of marque-specific—even model-specific—assistance through web forums and mailing lists.

Of course, not everything can be found on the Internet. Two incredibly useful tools for your research are assembly manuals and fabric swatch books. The former are important simply because they show you exactly how your car was put together (and should be taken apart) and in what steps. The latter, used by dealerships when these cars were new to help customers choose a color and interior scheme for their cars, include every type of material in every color available for that year in sample form attached to the pages of the book. Just as a painter wouldn't attempt to reproduce a factory color without a paint chip chart, an upholsterer wouldn't attempt to reproduce seats or carpeting without a fabric swatch book. Neither assembly manuals nor fabric swatch books are particularly easy to find or inexpensive, if only because factories and

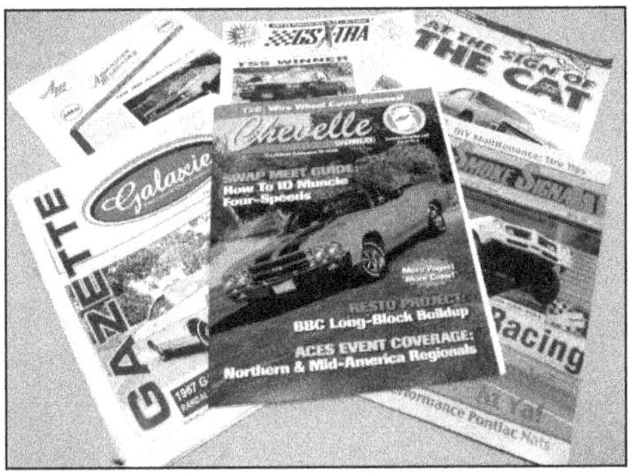

No matter the type of muscle car, there's a club out there for it, with members who've been down the same road as you're planning to travel. Check out the club's publication and website for helpful tips and restoration information particular to your car.

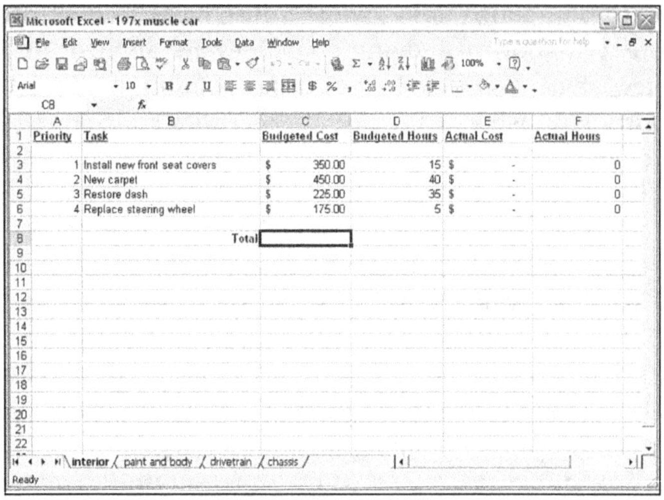

To keep track of expenses, both chronological and financial, you'll want to use a spreadsheet. Create columns for Priority, Task, Budgeted (or expected) Cost, Budgeted Hours, Actual Cost, and Actual Hours.

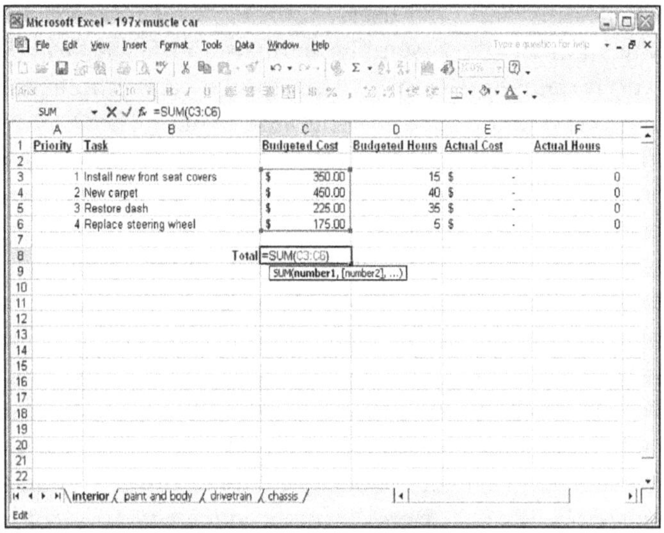

Once you've filled in a few figures, create a row for Totals below the last row of the table. Then use the AutoSum function (the sigma in the tool bar) to calculate the total. The program will automatically recalculate any rows you insert above the Total row.

Using a Spreadsheet

A spreadsheet is useful not just for the restoration of your muscle car's interior, but also for other aspects of your restoration project as a whole. Rather than making a copy of the entire spreadsheet file and modifying it for your engine build, for your paint and bodywork, and for your chassis restoration, compress all those different sheets into one overall restoration project file for that car.

dealerships tended not to retain such voluminous references for too long, but they do turn up from time to time. Check with literature dealers such as McLellan's or Bob Johnson's to track down pertinent assembly manuals and swatch books.

Magazines can prove useful with their tech stories, though interior tech stories tend not to be as numerous as tech stories on engine or suspension components. The greater benefit to magazines often lies in their advertisements, which can alert you to new products and restoration materials. The granddaddy of all car magazines, *Hemmings Motor News,* is chock-full of advertisements that can assist in your research.

Finally, restoration company catalogs and certain books prove to be worthwhile resources; the former for finding tools, parts, and materials and their pricing and the latter for researching exactly how your muscle car was built.

Your research will likely inspire ideas about your interior that you hadn't thought of before. Now is the time to go back to your priority list and add those ideas.

Eventually, your priority list will contain enough information to warrant placing it on a spreadsheet on your computer, which is a perfect way to keep track of your resources. Ideally, you would create six columns: Priority, Task, Budgeted Cost, Budgeted Hours, Actual Cost, Actual Hours. The first, Priority, requires just a number to determine where in the list each task lies, and will help if you need to adjust your priorities. The second, Task, requires a brief description of the specific part of the interior restoration. Budgeted Cost and Budgeted Hours are what you expect to devote here at the beginning of this project, whether you're completing that task yourself or whether you're assigning it to a restoration shop. Actual Cost and Actual Hours are for a running tally once you've begun the project.

At the bottom of the last four columns, reserve a space for totaling the costs and hours, using the spreadsheet program's AutoSum function to do that automatically.

You may also want to set up another section underneath the main spreadsheet section to keep track of any income you make from this car. The most likely source of income comes from selling off old

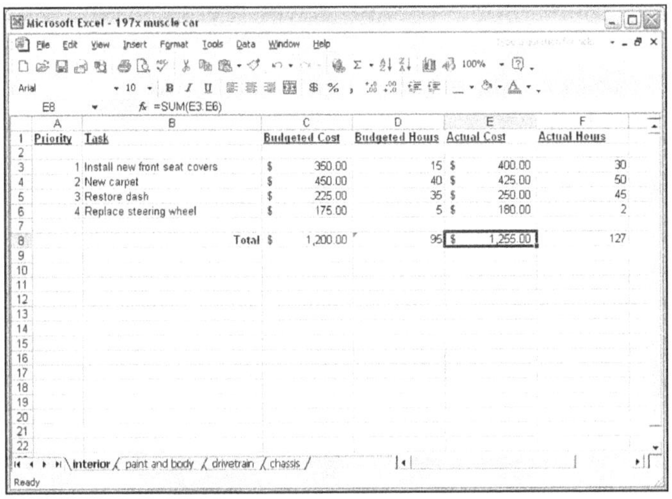

Priority	Task	Budgeted Cost	Budgeted Hours	Actual Cost	Actual Hours
1	Install new front seat covers	$ 350.00	15	$ 400.00	30
2	New carpet	$ 450.00	40	$ 425.00	50
3	Restore dash	$ 225.00	35	$ 250.00	45
4	Replace steering wheel	$ 175.00	5	$ 180.00	2
	Total	$ 1,200.00	95	$ 1,255.00	127

After totaling the budgeted resources and the actual resources, you can compare the two and decide whether to reduce the number of tasks in the project or adjust your expectations for the project's end date and total cost.

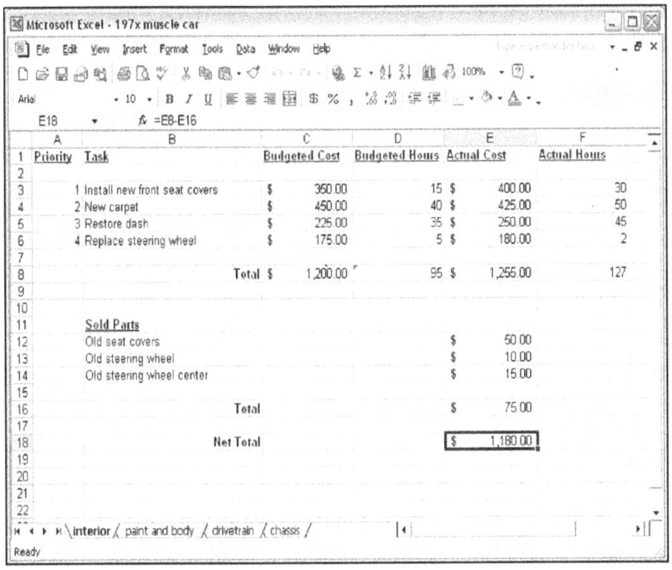

Priority	Task	Budgeted Cost	Budgeted Hours	Actual Cost	Actual Hours
1	Install new front seat covers	$ 350.00	15	$ 400.00	30
2	New carpet	$ 450.00	40	$ 425.00	50
3	Restore dash	$ 225.00	35	$ 250.00	45
4	Replace steering wheel	$ 175.00	5	$ 180.00	2
	Total	$ 1,200.00	95	$ 1,255.00	127
	Sold Parts				
	Old seat covers			$ 50.00	
	Old steering wheel			$ 10.00	
	Old steering wheel center			$ 15.00	
	Total			$ 75.00	
	Net Total			$ 1,180.00	

By adding more rows below the Total row, you can also keep track of the parts sold to finance this project. After adding up the money generated by any sales, you can then subtract it from the total amount spent on the project to discover the Net Total amount that the project costs.

parts, in which case, you would want to describe the part sold in the Task column, enter the price you sold it for in the Actual Cost column, and then use the AutoSum function to total the sales. Subtract that total from your previous total and you'll have a more realistic accounting of your project's financial situation.

This spreadsheet approach not only allows you to reshuffle your priority list quickly, it encourages you to consider any tasks that you may have overlooked. It also allows you to budget your time and money more realistically if you budget from the bottom up rather than from the top down. That is, for a moment ignore any estimates you've already made of the total budget for this project and focus only on what each task will require, letting the AutoSum function calculate what the project will cost. By comparing the total cost derived from the spreadsheet to your estimated total cost, you can see how much more or how much less time and money you will likely spend than you first thought.

However, even the budgeted cost in both time and money is still just a guess, which is why you have columns for actual dollars and actual time spent on each task. As long as you remain honest (and really, who would you be fooling if you didn't?), these allow you to quickly and easily chart your progress and help you to keep on schedule and on budget. And when it comes to completely unexpected expenditures (for example, you accidentally put an elbow through your NOS center console lid. Not as if anybody we know did anything like that...), the spreadsheet allows you to simply add a row and fill in the actual cost and time to cover that expenditure. In the interest of keeping honest, you should leave the Budgeted Cost and Budgeted Hours columns blank for those unexpected tasks.

Of course, you may find that your estimated totals are actually stiffly defined upper limits on the time and money you can spend on the interior of your car. Here again, by using the spreadsheet you can quickly and easily determine what tasks to knock off your priority list until it falls in line with your budget.

Just as important a question as the above is how you're going to come up with the money for this restoration. As with the amount of money you're spending on your interior, the source of your funding is up to you. Nowadays, you'll likely purchase many of the parts and supplies online or through a catalog. Whether you put your purchases on a credit card or debit card, be sure to include any interest charges and shipping charges on your budget spreadsheet. Finally, many car clubs arrange discounts for club members with certain aftermarket companies. Ask around within your club to see if any such discounts exist.

Organization

So with a plan in place, a budget decided upon, priorities defined, and credit card warmed up and ready, you're probably thinking now comes the part where you bust out the tools. Not just yet. One common mistake derails many interior restoration projects: throwing parts out immediately after removing them from the car.

Every part still has a function until you declare the project complete, whether as a reminder of reproduction parts that you still need to purchase, as a comparison for quality and correctness against new reproduction parts, or as a materials donor for repairing other parts. Even if you don't intend to reinstall a part, you'll want to keep it for reference. You can tell a lot about how parts are supposed to go back together by their shapes and sizes and even by their quantities.

Here's why you should stay organized: In this picture of my garage, the car's bucket seats are toward the back of the garage, behind the stack of tires, behind the boxes of new parts, and behind the mounds of old parts. Moving everything out of the way will take at least half an hour, whereas if everything were rationally organized or stored out of the way, getting to the seats wouldn't take any time at all.

If you do throw a part out or sell it before you're done using it as a reference, then inevitably minutes afterward, you'll have a question about how the new part is installed that only the old part can answer. Finding an answer through other means then ends up becoming a huge waste of time.

And as you'll soon find out, a car takes up way more space when it's apart versus when it's all together. In particular, molded interior panels, seats, and dashboards require a whole lot of room when they're out of a car, and none of them fit on your standard garage shelving with much ease. So consider leaving those large, ungainly parts where they're designed to belong—installed in the car—until it becomes necessary to remove them. While not mentioned earlier, space is just as precious a commodity as time and money, and should be at least considered through the course of an interior restoration, if not budgeted in the same manner as your time and money.

This is where good physical organizational skills become an asset. If your garage or basement resembles a thrift store, then maybe it's time to spend a weekend tidying up. If it's a lost cause, companies actually exist that will come in and organize your garage and set you up with the shelf and rack space you need to avoid "Level One Disaster Area" status.

And as with the time and money necessary for a restoration, figure out exactly how much storage space you'll need for your interior, then double it. Invest in bins of all sizes or simply pluck plastic and glass containers—and their lids—from the recycling. Resealable sandwich baggies, especially the ones with a strip for easy marking, make great screw, nut, and bolt containers. In a pinch, you could push screws through a

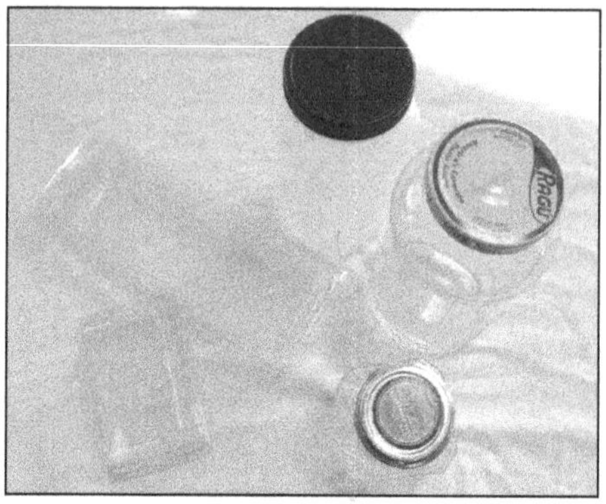

Parts stores package some things in clear plastic containers nowadays, which are worth holding on to for small-parts storage. Clear glass and plastic containers saved from the recycling bin also make great, cheap small-parts storage.

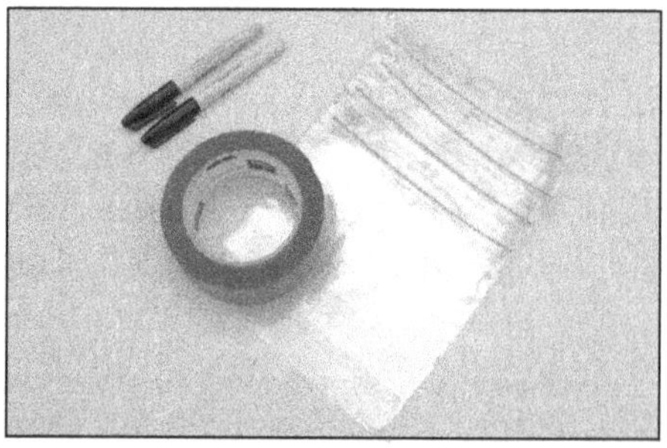

To store and organize fasteners, use sandwich bags or larger storage bags that zip close. Label the bags with strips of masking tape and a marker that won't rub off the masking tape. You'll need plenty of these bags, so consider them a regular garage supply instead of borrowing them from the kitchen.

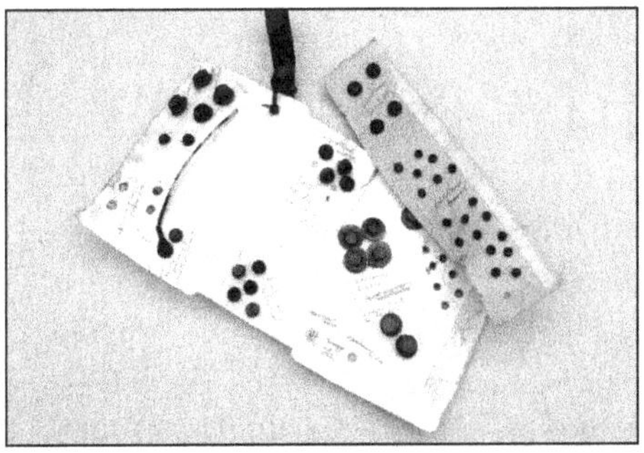

Boxboard is that thin cardboard that cereal boxes are made from and, when broken down, makes for an excellent place to temporarily store all the screws that come out of your interior. Just push the screws through, then label them with a pen directly on the boxboard. The boxboard also provides space to jot down notes about the fasteners.

section of boxboard or run a zip-tie through a group of nuts that must remain together; all three methods offer quick labeling and quick-glance identification of the contents. Invest in a roll of masking tape and a couple felt-tip markers in order to label your containers. On larger parts that don't fit into containers, you can still apply the masking tape directly to the surface of the part for identification (many parts are easily confused, left for right and vice versa) or for notes regarding the condition and fate of the parts.

Properly Store Your Parts

Clear off as much shelving space as possible, or even build additional shelving, for all the parts that will come out of your car's interior. Try to keep different types of parts on different shelves. For instance, keep interior trim parts grouped together on one shelf and dash items grouped together on another shelf. This will help you not only more effectively keep track of your total inventory, but will free up an entire shelf once you've completed that particular task. Try to put the lighter, more fragile parts on higher shelves and heavier parts on lower shelves, both to reduce potential breakage of the parts and to save your back when lifting the parts on and off the shelves.

Bigger items, such as seats and headliners, tend not to fit on shelves very well, but don't just clear some garage floor space for them. Instead, if you have to, build a small platform to get every interior part up off the floor. Garages and basements (especially basements) flood without warning. Suspension parts and body panels can survive a flooding; interior parts, made of fabrics, soft backing boards, and foam, do not easily survive water damage.

Garages and basements also tend to become habitats for rodents, which make beelines (mouselines? ratlines?) for the soft stuff of an interior, where they can inflict the most damage. So when setting up your storage area, consider mouseproofing the storage area and setting it up away from suspected rodent habitats already in existence.

Do not rely on your workbench for storage. All too soon, the workbench becomes crowded and you find yourself using the hood of your car as a substitute—not something you want to do if you value the paint on your car. And speaking of your workbench, make sure you have a large, flat surface for many of the tasks in this book; large enough for an entire bench seat. Many interior and upholstery shops prefer to cover their workbenches not in plywood, which is very rough and can catch and tear fabric easily, but in something smoother, like linoleum. In a pinch, an old, clean blanket is still better than bare plywood. And if you're building a workbench, for the sake of your back muscles, build it to a comfortable height.

Another storage-related tip: Do not buy any parts or materials until you need them. This frees up your cash flow for the parts and materials you need immediately, and just as important, it frees up the storage space for the parts and materials you need immediately. Even Henry Ford, 85 years ago, realized the benefit to this approach when he wrote in *My Life and Work,* "We have found in buying materials that it is not worthwhile to buy for other than immediate needs. We buy only enough to fit into the plan of production... That would save a great deal of money, for it would give a very rapid turnover and thus decrease the amount of money tied up in materials." His thoughts on that topic eventually inspired Toyota to develop the Just In Time inventory strategy that has since become an important management style for nearly every goods manufacturer, distributor, and retailer around the world.

Then again, if you can come up with the shelf space and can locate and pay for all the parts and supplies you need, then go ahead and buy everything before diving into the project. Aftermarket companies have a tendency to discontinue, modify, or increase the price of an item without notice, and NOS supplies never increase, so it sometimes doesn't hurt to make an exception to this rule and hoard the parts you need when they're available.

At any time up to the time you need them, however, is a perfect time to buy tools.

Mouseproofing

Almost any car guy you ask has both a story about how much damage mice caused to his collector car and a remedy for said mouse problem. Mice can climb practically anything, jump like an NBA star, and chew through wiring, turning your precious muscle car into a rolling fire hazard. In a hardtop, they may destroy the headliner, and in a convertible, they tend to target either the seats or the convertible top. In addition, mice have been known to spread the hantavirus, rabies, and other infectious diseases, which makes their presence a health hazard.

You could go with the dizzying array of poisons at any hardware store or grocery store, but mice tend to return to their nests when dying, which usually results in a hide-and-seek game with a rotting mouse corpse in your car.

Inexpensive, classic mousetraps effectively kill the mice away from your muscle car. Unfortunately, they require disposal of the mouse corpse and do little to deter additional mice. The humane-style mousetraps work well, but require taking the time to release the mice far away from your garage, and the mice inevitably return to their preferred nesting spots.

Sacrificial paper towels are often suggested, along with the line of thought that the mice will shred the paper towels instead of your interior. Even if it works, however, the method does nothing to deter mice and may actually encourage them to nest in your muscle car.

Instead, you want to persuade them to vacate the premises, for which a number of country remedies have cropped up, including the use of mothballs, dryer sheets, peppermint oil, a pan of gasoline, and shavings of Irish Spring soap. Some of the remedies reportedly work, while some don't; they seem to depend on the preferences of your local mouse population. And when the weather turns cold enough, mice seem to withstand just about any effort to deter them from reaching a warm shelter.

Still, a couple simple tips can reduce the likelihood of mice setting up shop in your muscle car. First, when storing your car for any extended period of time, flip down the sun visors. Otherwise, the visors make an inviting platform for mice to rest on while destroying your headliner. Second, close all the cabin vents, especially the fresh air vents. Leaving those open is like sending out an engraved invitation to every mouse in the area to come hang out inside your muscle car for the winter.

One surefire way to ensure you have no mice may not be that palatable to some. Kurt Reiche, an upholsterer at Gillin Custom Design in Middletown, New York, said he only encounters two other pests inhabiting old cars: spiders and snakes. "And whenever we see snakes, we never see mice," he said.

But everybody seems to agree that the most organic method for rodent removal is still the best: Get yourself a cat.

Tools

Henry Ford offered a lot of good advice to live by. One of his lesser-quoted lines, however, has to do with the importance of tools: "If you don't buy the tool you need, you will eventually pay for it, but not have your tool."

He knew that, whatever the task, it's going to take a tool to complete it, and you won't complete that task without that tool. Refuse to buy the tool, and you'll just have to pay somebody who has the tool to do it for you, then pay that person again and again every time you need to use that tool.

Henry obviously didn't borrow tools from his neighbors, but then again, good neighbors share a six-pack of brew in exchange for borrowing tools. But the bright side of Henry's advice is that he's giving you permission to go buy tools, and not many guys are going to refute that advice.

Interior restoration requires some of the same tools as most other restoration projects: screwdrivers, wrenches, ratchets, pliers, and sometimes hammers. But interior restoration also requires many specialty tools due to the nature of the projects. Compared to the undersides of muscle cars, interiors tend not to feature as many exposed fasteners, for safety reasons and perhaps in an effort not to interrupt the aesthetics that the interior designers had in mind. Interiors also tend to feature much softer materials, which require vastly different fasteners in some cases, and vastly different tools designed not to damage those softer materials.

For that reason, one good rule of thumb to follow when restoring your interior: Don't use a screwdriver unless you're actually driving screws. We've all used screwdrivers as pry tools, poke tools, or as general substitutes for some specialty tool we don't have. The danger of using screwdrivers for other than their intended purpose inside a car comes when the screwdriver slips and then gouges your console or rips your seat cover. And, of course, Murphy's Law dictates that the seat cover you rip will be the brand-new one you just bought for $350. So keep them out of the interior until they're called for. Nor do I have to remind you not to carry your screwdrivers in the back pocket of your jeans.

I've already discussed one tool you likely won't find in your garage. Your computer is useful not only in organizing your project through spreadsheets (and project management software, if you're that ambitious), it's useful for ordering parts on the Internet, researching the correctness of your interior, and gathering advice on the parts and methods that work best for your particular car. A laptop, of course, would be infinitely easier to take out to the garage, but would then be infinitely more susceptible to dirt, dust, and overspray.

One of the most versatile tools I've found, regardless of the task, is the rotary tool, also known as the Dremel, after the brand that has dominated the household rotary tool business over the last couple decades. With the right attachments, it can become a router, a planer, or even a reciprocating saw, but you'll be most interested in the various bits that are available for it that allow you to effortlessly cut plastic, shape materials, or polish metals, among many other tasks.

Unlike air-powered tools that rely on torque, electric rotary tools rely on speed and high RPM—sometimes up to 35,000 rpm—to do the job. While cordless rotary tools offer greater portability, you'll want to use the corded types and an extension cord; battery-powered rotary tools just don't provide enough oomph for the intensive tasks that an interior restoration demands. Invest in a multi-speed rotary tool; different materials require different speeds. Invest in the widest variety of bits you can afford, and buy the flexible collet extensions for greater maneuverability around tight spots.

Another all-purpose tool I recommend obtaining is a heat gun, useful here for softening plastics, softening rubber undercoating, activating heat shrink tubing, and quick-drying paint. If possible, find one with multiple settings, and always start with the lowest heat range and work your way up until you find a heat range that works.

Remember, when using any device that produces heat in a garage filled with oily rags and other combustibles, always keep a fire extinguisher handy. Two if possible, one on either side of the garage, in case a fire blocks your access to one extinguisher. A cell phone that dials 9-1-1 is also a good idea.

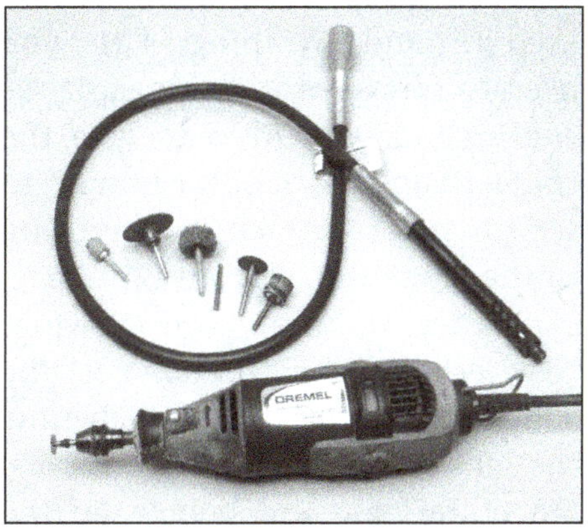

The real value of rotary tools such as this Dremel Multi-Tool is in their flexibility. You can rapidly change out a plastic cutting wheel for a sanding bit, a drill bit, or a polishing wheel. Even more flexibility comes from the collet extension that allows you to get into tighter spaces.

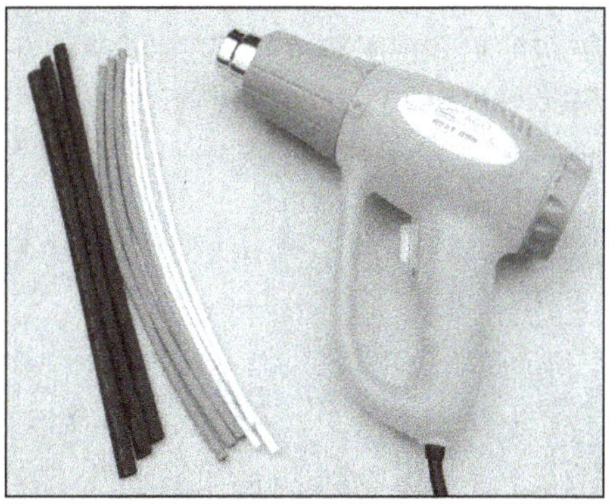

Heat guns should be in every car guy's toolbox, and not just for their ability to activate heat shrink wire coverings (shown here with the heat gun). They're also useful for removing adhesives, softening plastics, and quick-drying paint.

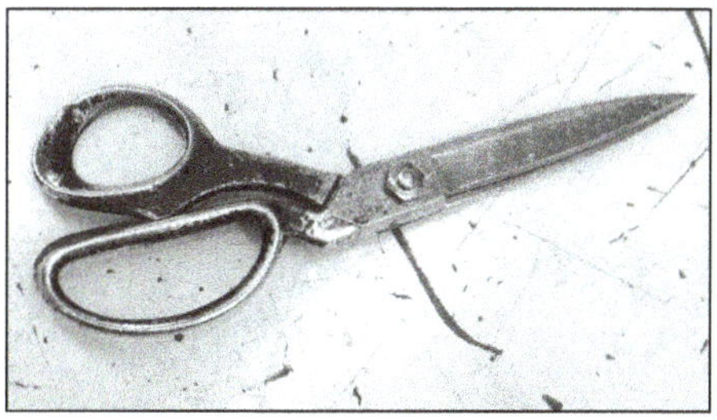

Even if you don't plan on stitching your interior, a good pair of shears comes in handy for all sorts of tasks, from making patterns, to trimming the headliner or carpet, to cutting noise and heat barriers. Don't just borrow your kid's grade-school scissors; buy a professional set and keep them sharp.

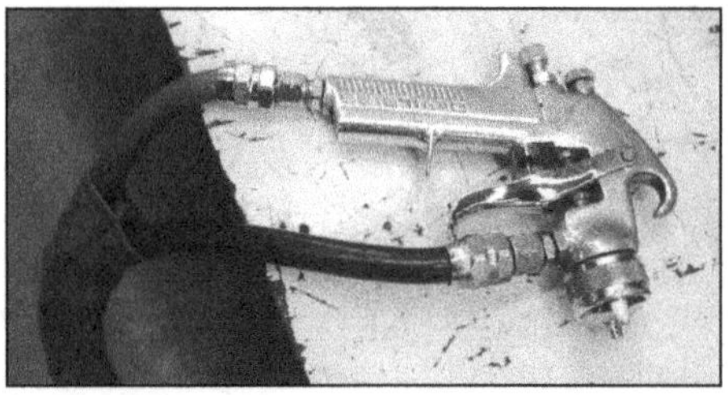

Even though it says DeVilbiss, this is not simply a paint spray gun pressed into service to shoot adhesive. DeVilbiss, among other manufacturers, makes a dedicated adhesive spray gun designed for easy cleanup and low adhesive buildup. While most home restorers won't find such a gun necessary, pros use them all the time.

An air compressor supplies the air pressure for the adhesive spray gun, but the adhesive itself is delivered to the gun from a pressure pot, which can range in size from a 1-liter pot attached directly to the gun to a 30-gallon pot for larger, industrial uses. This one is typical and holds about 2½ gallons.

Though not considered an all-purpose tool, a good set of shears come in handy for a number of different tasks in an interior restoration. Don't cheap out and get a pair of scissors at the office supply store, however; you'll be cutting more than just paper. Instead, any upholstery supply store or craft/fabric store will have heavy-duty fabric shears, the heavier duty the better. Make sure to keep the pivot oiled and the blades sharp.

Throughout your interior restoration, you're going to use a lot of fabric adhesive or contact cement, and after you use it a couple times, you're going to find a lot more uses for it than you would have expected. The stuff comes in aerosol cans, so buying a pressure pot and a spray gun dedicated to spraying contact cement may not be necessary for somebody doing just a few touch-ups here and there on their own car, but any upholstery shop worth its salt will have a pressure pot or two.

Even if using contact adhesive from an aerosol can, you need to keep in mind two things: First, you need to spray both mating surfaces, and second, you need to give the contact adhesive about a minute to set up before attaching anything to the glued surfaces. Jerry Ambrosi, of Master Upholstery in Newton, New Jersey, said if you don't let the adhesive set up, during which time the glue releases its solvent vapors, "then the glue will bubble up the minute the car hits the sun."

Along with contact adhesive, use a stiff piece of cardboard or press-board as a shield to prevent overspray on the rest of your interior or glass. Should you squirt overspray on the rest of your interior, some restorers recommend using a short length of duct tape—adhesive side out—to pick up any excess adhesive. Any wax or grease remover, including 3M's dedicated adhesive remover, will also eliminate oversprayed adhesive.

Like it or not, your muscle car interior will contain some plastic parts, and it's likely that not all of them are reproduced. I'll go over the repair of plastics in Chapter 2, but you should consider purchasing a

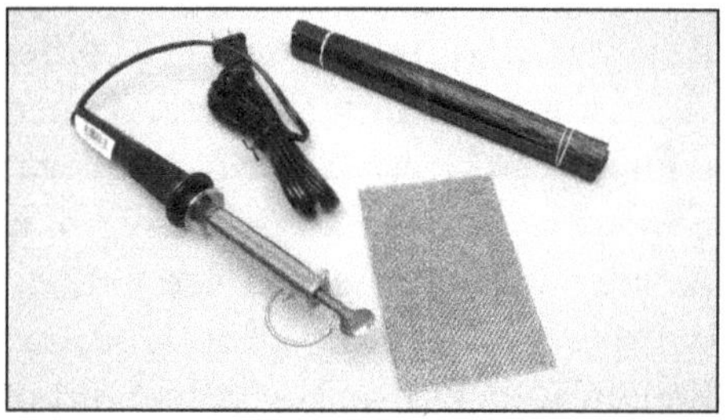

You've probably tried to melt two pieces of plastic together with a soldering iron. A plastic welder works on the same principle, but includes plastic welding rods designed to add material and strength to the weld. Reinforcing wire mesh sheets add more strength to thinner pieces of plastic.

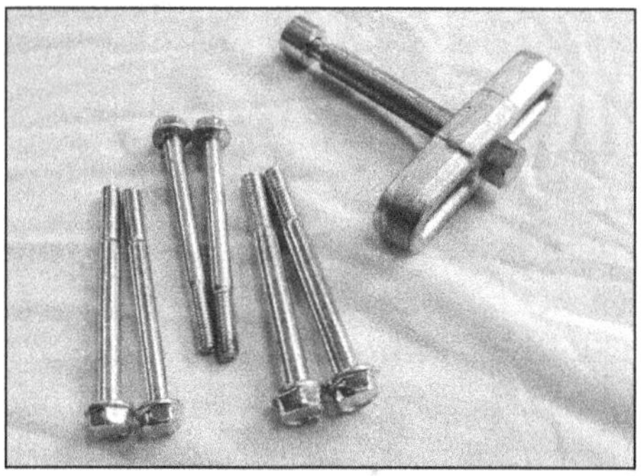

Steering wheels are held tightly to the columns for a reason; you don't want yours coming off the column while driving down the street. This means that when you do want to remove the steering wheel from the column, it won't be easy unless you have a steering wheel puller, a simple machine that uses screwing action to force the steering wheel off its splines.

plastic welding kit. Most of them work on most types of plastics, which can often mean the difference between a seamless repair and one that looks like booger-welded steel.

A number of specialty tools should also inhabit your toolbox for interior restorations. Much like a harmonic balancer puller, a steering wheel puller will do that job quickly and effectively without the need to resort to brute strength or some odd combination of pry bars.

Hog ring pliers and stretching pliers really only come into use when installing seat covers. However, both are essential in keeping the seat fabric pristine and free from tears.

Finally, a good set of trim tools should take the place of your screwdriver-and-clawhammer method of removing trim, door panels, window cranks, and about anything else with hidden fasteners or clips. Try to find a set of trim tools made out of nylon or some other type of plastic—they're generally hard enough to pop the fasteners, but soft enough not to scratch, dent, or puncture the trim itself.

Do you need to invest in a sewing machine? Here's where a lot of guys are put off by interiors, thinking they'll suddenly become women if they touch a sewing machine, let alone own one. The

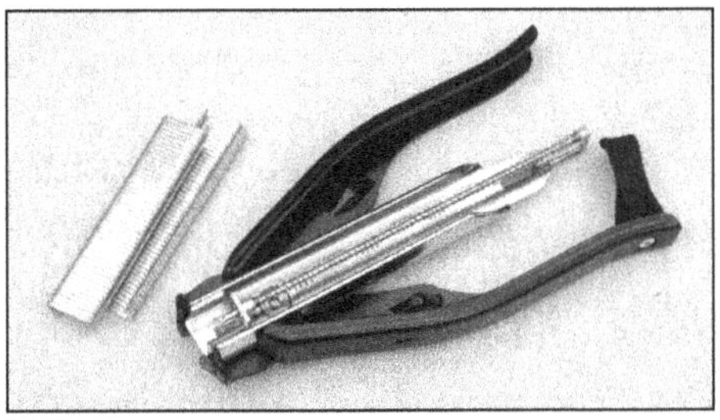

Most people have heard of hog ring pliers, but never seen one in action. These professional one-handed hog ring pliers load hog rings like a desktop stapler loads staples. When the handles are squeezed, the jaws at the front slice a ring off the stack and bend it to shape in one motion.

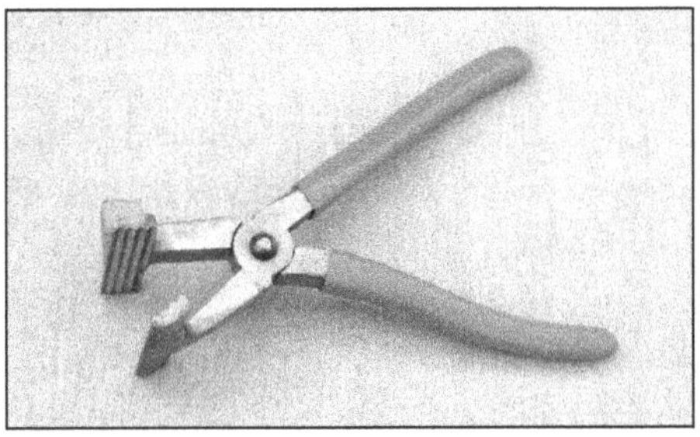

Stretching pliers stretch seat covers over seat frames and foam, and pull the fabric or vinyl tight so you can put a hog ring around the edge of the cover and secure it. Imagine trying to use your fingers or any other type of pliers, and you'll instantly see the value of stretching pliers.

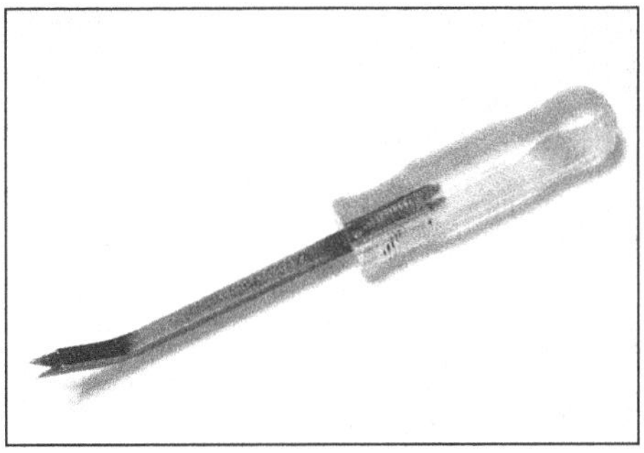

Staples are a cheap and effective way to secure fabric and vinyl in many areas of the interior. To properly remove them, you need a staple remover, which looks like a flathead screwdriver with a deformed head. A staple remover pries out the staples as a flathead screwdriver would, but a staple remover is lithe enough to get under the staples and do no damage.

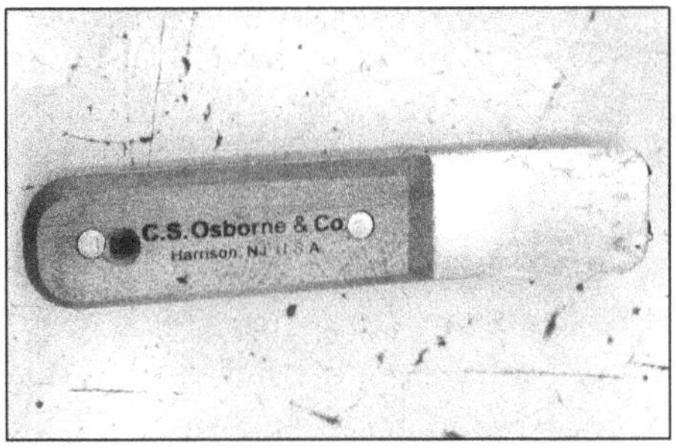

A tuck tool comes in handy for many phases of interior restoration, and is designed to be thin enough to tuck or push fabric or vinyl into places your fingers can't reach. Note its rounded edges, designed to keep the tool from puncturing or otherwise damaging fabric, vinyl, and trim. In a pinch, a clean plastic spreader used for bodywork can be used instead of a dedicated tuck tool.

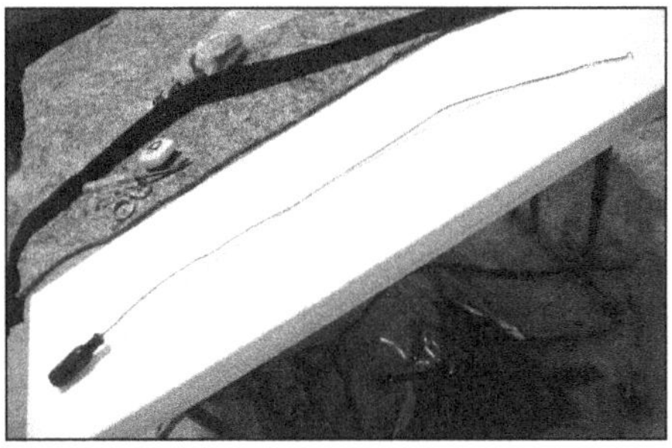

One of the specialty tools you may want to invest in is this one, used for fishing the cables (that keep convertible tops taut) through their fabric pockets in the convertible tops. A length of coat hanger or welding rod serves the same purpose, but the tool could conceivably be used for also fishing electrical wiring around dashboards and under carpet.

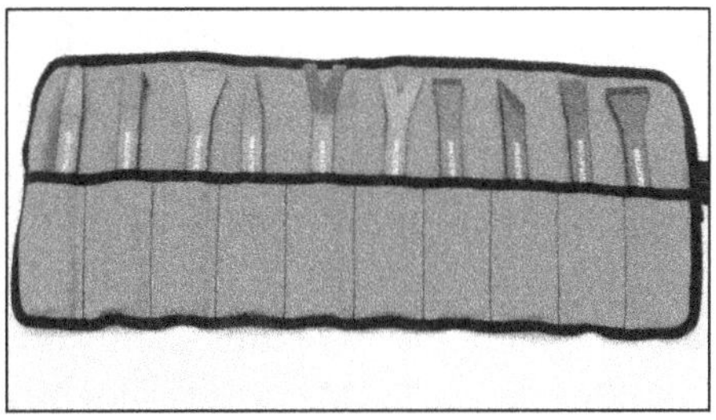

Eastwood sells a kit of nylon pry tools designed not to mar the soft plastics and vinyls of most muscle car interiors the way screwdrivers and metal pry tools do. Just remember, though, if the item you're prying still isn't budging, there may be additional screws you didn't initially see.

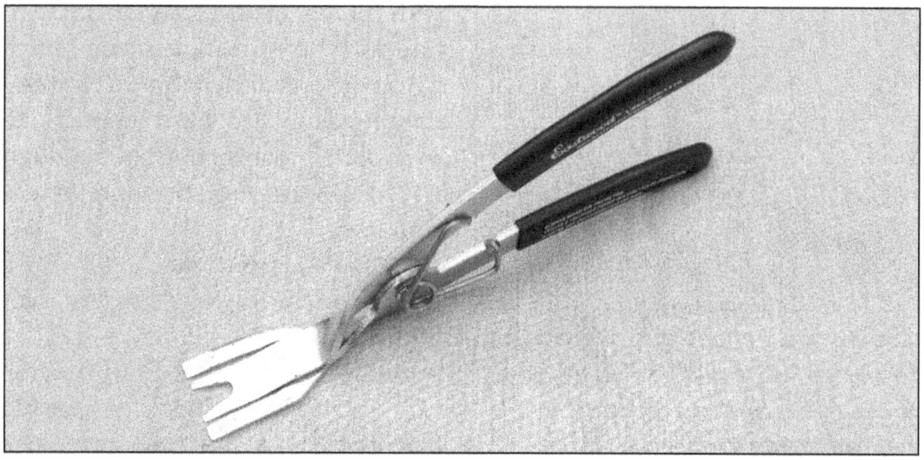

A little more specialized than the nylon pry tools, these panel clip removal pliers, also from Eastwood, work in reverse of most pliers. You slip them behind a panel, usually a door panel, and around the clips holding the panel to the sheet metal behind it. You then squeeze the handles to separate the jaws, popping the clips without ruining the panel.

reality is that a good sewing machine intended for heavy materials such as canvas, vinyl, and automotive fabrics can cost more than most guys figure on spending on their entire interior restoration, and unlike the previous tools mentioned, the proper operation of a sewing machine requires quite a bit of training and practice. Add to that the fact that many reproduction seat covers, carpets, and headliners come prestitched nowadays, and most average home restorers likely will not need to invest in a sewing machine.

On the other hand, you want to do it all, or perhaps your particular seat covers aren't available in reproduction. Or you just have a cool custom concept in your head for your muscle car. In that case, following Henry's advice, you're going to want to look for an industrial sewing machine, preferably one with a long arm, able to sew heavier materials such as canvas and leather. To choose a brand and model of industrial sewing machine, ask your local upholstery shop, awning maker, or sailboat supply and repair shop.

Finally, figure out how you'll go about refinishing your fasteners. While interior screws, nuts, and bolts tend not to suffer rust the same way their external brethren do, they are not immune from the ravages of time. Several companies make interior fastener kits for some of the more popular muscle cars, but not all, so many restorers must work with what they have. Hardware stores inevitably don't carry anything close to what the original manufacturer specified, and fastener-specific outlets like Fastenal and Au-ve-co can provide fasteners that do the job, but may not look the part.

The simplest method only requires you to box up the fasteners, ship them to a replater, and write a check. Unfortunately plating has become a scarce and expensive business thanks to environmental regulations. So it may come down to your own preferred method of refinishing.

Using a wire wheel effectively cleans the fasteners, but also effectively removes fingerprints if you're not careful. If you have a small-parts wire basket, media blasting will certainly do the trick, but may try your patience. Tumblers make a great alternative, especially for small parts, but often require lengthy tumble times. Electrolysis and chemical

The aftermarket has made things much simpler for muscle car guys, and as a result, it's entirely possible to restore your interior without once touching a sewing machine. If it becomes necessary to buy a sewing machine, invest in an industrial-grade machine and consider the models with deeper throats for stitching bulkier pieces.

strippers can work quickly and effectively, but leave residues if you're not careful. Once you've stripped the fasteners of rust, paint, or any other unwanteds, replating is actually possible for the home restorer using kits from Caswell Inc. or Eastwood.

So you've now memorized every catalog that you requested, you've created the most detailed priority list known to man, you've charged the battery in your digital camera, and you've stocked your tool chest with these funny-looking nylon pry bars. It's now time to tackle that interior, task by task. Take a deep breath and keep in mind yet another Henry Ford quote: "If you think you can do a thing or think you can't do a thing, you're right."

Photographing the Project

A camera will help immensely with documenting the disassembly and reassembly of your interior. You'll want to photograph parts before, during, and after removal, especially parts that require specific orientations, adjustments, or assembly procedures. Digital cameras make this documentation much easier than film cameras—not only can you see immediately whether you properly photographed the parts and processes, you can take many more pictures, thanks to memory cards that grow cheaper and larger all the time. If you don't already have a digital camera, try to find one in the 5- to 8-megapixel range, then stuff it with the largest memory cards you can afford. Keep its batteries continually charged.

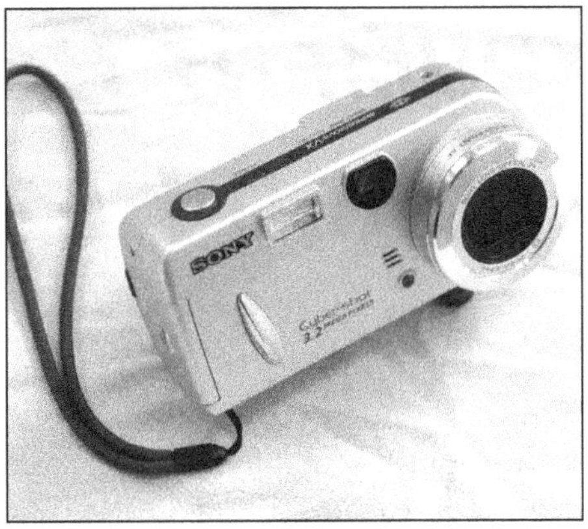

A typical point-and-shoot digital camera will help you document the disassembly process so you're not finding yourself scratching your head when it comes time to reassemble everything. Look for one with a few more megapixels than the older camera pictured.

When photographing your interior, first make sure you're focusing on the part you're documenting. Try not to use your on-camera zoom and instead move as close to the part as possible. Light up the area as brightly as possible with work lights, but if your camera has multiple flash settings, set it to the lowest. This may seem contradictory, but a bright flash may overexpose your photo (especially close-up objects) and cast harsh shadows that make it difficult to discern important details.

Try to download the photos to your computer sooner rather than later and keep them organized according to task. When it comes time to reassemble your interior, you can then print out the photos that you think will best help and take those printouts to the garage.

Here's an improperly lit photograph, with harsh light from the flash blowing out details close to the camera lens, harsh shadows elsewhere, and soft focus on everything in the background. When photographing your car for reference, pictures like this don't convey much information.

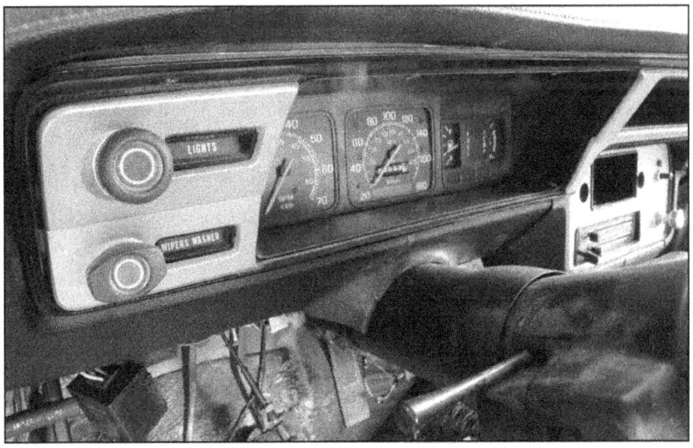

A more evenly lit and sharply focused photograph, however, does convey useful information for your restoration. If possible, use a small tripod for your camera, turn off (or turn down) the flash, and use additional lighting to obtain a better picture. And take multiple pictures from different angles for a better idea of how everything goes together.

Instrument Panel and Dashboard Restoration

As mentioned earlier, the interior is about 95 percent of what you'll see of your muscle car while driving it. Most of the interior that you'll see while driving is right in front of you: dashboard, instrument cluster, center stack, and console. Your car's designers carefully chose the layout to serve several functions. The entire assembly has to be pleasing to the eye without being distracting. The dash itself has to have the right materials to prevent glare. The instruments have to convey sometimes complex and rapidly changing information at a quick glance. So when something's just not right with any of those components—when a gauge isn't responding, for instance—your eye tends to focus on that and not on the road.

The good thing is that you can now convince your wife that you need to have the dash recovered because it's a safety issue, not just an aesthetics issue. The bad thing is that dashboard restoration is a rather complex task, which becomes tougher the more complicated your dash is, and many muscle cars had increasingly intricate dashboards with multiple contours and angles. Gauge restoration is even more involved, and precise gauge calibration requires oscilloscopes, signal generators, and other electronic equipment most guys won't have in their garage. Oftentimes, your best bet is to send gauges and dashes out to specialists who have the right equipment to do the job.

Still, it's worth watching these specialists not only to settle your curiosity, but also to gain an appreciation for what goes into instrument and dashboard restoration and to take away tips on how best to take care of your instruments and dashboards.

Instrument Panel Refurbishment

Obviously, the best time to address your instruments is while you're addressing your dashboard. After all, if you're going to have to remove your dashboard to have it recovered, you will also have to remove the instrument cluster to lift the dashboard out anyway, so why duplicate your efforts by removing the instrument cluster again at a later date?

You'll find once you do remove the instrument cluster on your muscle car that this is a complex part of the restoration. While cars of the 1930s through the 1950s had an integrated look and feel to their instrument clusters, with everything flowing into an art-deco or space-age theme, the instruments in muscle cars had a real back-to-basics appearance. This made it seem as though each circular gauge were its own individual component, just as in the rally and race cars that Detroit wanted the youth of America to believe they were piloting. Why else would the manufacturers start to install tachometers at this period, when they'd barely done so in the five decades prior?

All the aftermarket gauges that speed shops peddled over the years helped reinforce the concept of individual components. Yet pulling a muscle car's instrument cluster out from its dash shows that the gauges remained just as integrated as in previous decades. Of course, the integration can be a good thing. Were it not for that printed circuit board on which everything mounts, the tangle of wires behind the dash would be greater and far more complicated.

When actually removing the instrument cluster from the dash, loosen the nuts that hold up the steering column and let the column hang a little lower, or remove the column altogether. If keeping the column in the car while you're removing the gauges, make sure to drape a towel or rag over it so the instrument cluster doesn't nick the paint on the column if you accidentally drop the cluster.

Even though the printed circuit board eliminated a lot of wiring mess, you'll still encounter a good number of wires on the back side of the cluster, so don't just yank the cluster out of the dash once you've loosened all the screws holding it in. Instead, carefully feel around the back of the cluster for the connector from the wiring harness and any wires for the dash lamps. You'll also need to feel around for the speedometer cable and unscrew it from the cluster. Now would be a good time to unscrew the other end of the speedometer cable, clean the old grease off the cable insert, and apply new grease. The more grease the better.

LEDs vs. Incandescent Dash Lamps

LEDs are everywhere nowadays–in your cell phone, in your Christmas lights, in traffic lights, on your toaster oven. And they're even starting to show up not only in new car tail lamps, but in their headlamps as well. That's because LEDs offer a number of advantages over traditional Thomas Edison-tech incandescent light bulbs. And a lot of car enthusiasts have been sprinkling LEDs throughout their interiors. The question is: Do you want to do the same with your muscle car?

LED stands for light-emitting diode. A diode is basically a one-way valve for electricity, and by manipulating the diode's construction, it can produce a useable amount of light. Unlike filament-type bulbs, LEDs use a fraction of the energy (and thus produce a fraction of the heat), can shine much brighter, provide quicker on/off switching, and last much longer. You can also buy them in a wide variety of colors, so you'd no longer be stuck with the stock hue behind your instruments. A number of retailers, such as SuperBrightLEDs.com, now sell LED bulbs designed to replace most automotive exterior and interior light bulbs.

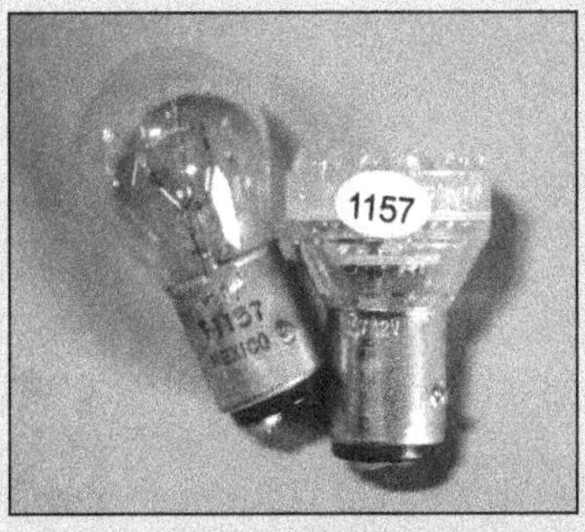

Whether your dashboard uses the larger 1157-size bulbs, shown here, or the smaller 194-size bulbs, you can find LED-based bulbs designed to replace your incandescents. The LED-based bulbs last longer, produce less heat, and consume less energy, but with the trade-off of a higher price.

The downside, however, comes mostly in the cost–at least twice that of incandescent bulbs–but also in a few other subtleties. First, some LEDs shine at wavelengths that are hard for the human eye to process. Blue LEDs are the worst. Second, most older circuits aren't set up to properly dim LEDs, so you're basically left with two states–on and off–instead of the infinitely variable adjustment afforded by a rheostat and a filament-type bulb. Finally, LEDs are narrowly directional, unlike incandescents, which spread light everywhere. This may be an advantage in certain locations, but in others, it's a distinct disadvantage, and the easiest solution is to add multiple LEDs to the same bulb, which increases the cost.

So converting to LEDs makes sense if you have a problem with light-bulb lenses or housings melting from the heat given off an incandescent bulb. Or if your stock alternator can't keep up with the loads of running your car's engine and all of its lights and electrical accessories. They also make sense if you have your dashboard and instrument cluster apart for the restoration and don't want to go through re-disassembly just to replace burned-out light bulbs (speaking of which, with the dashboard apart, now is a good time to replace all the bulbs back there, regardless of whether you decide on incandescents or LEDs). And if you consider how long LEDs last versus regular incandescents, their higher price may very well pay for themselves in the long run.

Next, you need to figure out if you want to send your gauges out for restoration and recalibration, or if you simply want to replace or reface them. On our 1965 GTO, with gauges that worked perfectly but looked a little aged, I decided on the latter route using parts supplied by Original Parts Group.

First, I did research on 1965 GTOs and discovered that the tachometer, with a green band all the way around the face, was used only on the GTO from early in the 1965 model year. Late 1965 GTOs used a different tachometer face, in which the green band becomes yellow and then red. And for you trivia buffs, 1965 was the only year GTOs had the checkered-flag graphic on the face of the speedometer.

Three Phillips-head screws along the top of the instrument panel and three along the bottom secure this GTO's panel to the dash. The screws for most muscle cars' instrument panels are usually inserted from beneath, so if you find that you can't remove your panel, squeeze underneath your dashboard and look up to find any less-than-obvious screws. Don't try to pry the panel away from the dashboard with brute strength; you'll usually find the hidden screw that way, but only after you've cracked your instrument panel. Some instrument panels use plastic or metal clips instead of screws in some places; check with your car's assembly manual to see if that's the case.

With the instrument panel free from the dashboard, we were able take the assembly over to the workbench, where we removed the GTO's cluster from the panel and then removed the gauge assemblies from the cluster. To reface the speedometer, we had to remove the needle

Instrument Panel Restoration

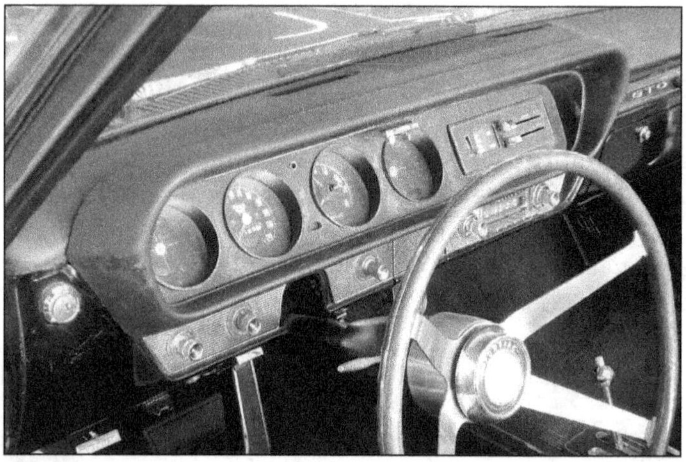

1 ***The instrument panel in our 1965 GTO had seen better days. At some point, it lost its veneer facing and was down to the bare plastic, which looked rather dingy. The lenses in front of the instruments had gone a little hazy, and the instruments themselves had become a little sun bleached. Fortunately, we were able to find reproduction parts to help spruce up our dashboard and only needed to set aside an afternoon to do so.***

2 ***After removing a few screws, we were able to separate the instrument panel from the dashboard. Here, you can see the cables for the climate control, which need to be disconnected before removing the instrument panel entirely. Also, disconnect the wiring harness that plugs into the instrument panel, any dash lamp wires, and the speedometer cable.***

3 ***With the instrument panel removed, now is a good time to grease the speedometer cable and check the behind-the-dash wiring for frays, cracks, and bad grounds. Also, replace the bulbs in the dash lamps.***

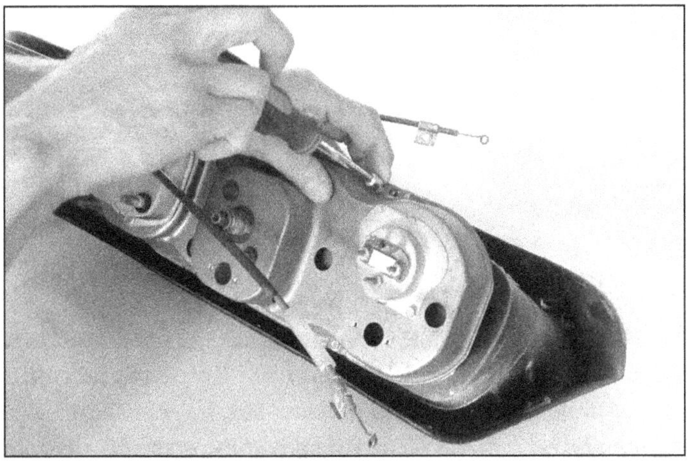

4 *With the instrument panel out of the car and on a workbench, we were able to separate the metal chassis of the instrument cluster from the plastic panel. Note where or if any instruments ground to the chassis. If dealing with a circuit board, look for discoloration between the circuits that would indicate a short circuit.*

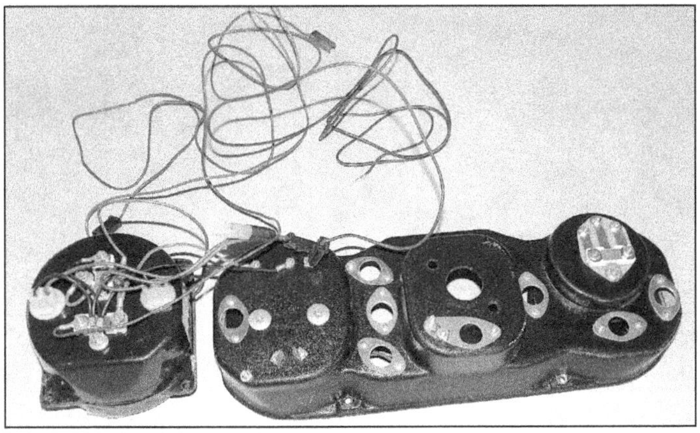

5 *Though we used a reproduction instrument cluster chassis, most such chassis were well protected from any rust or damage throughout the years, so it wouldn't take much to clean one up. If you will be painting your chassis, make sure not to paint over ground connections.*

6 *New faces for the gauges alone will make the dashboard look ten times better. Refacing the speedometer requires removing and reinstalling the needle, which needs to be done carefully to avoid damaging the speedometer's internals. Note how we modified the dash lamps to merge all of the lamps' grounds into one.*

first, done by carefully turning the needle clockwise completely around the dial until it came loose from its mounting post. We could then easily replace the speedometer face by removing a couple screws.

If your plans include sandblasting and painting your instrument cluster at this point, make sure to consider whether your gauges are normally grounded through the metal chassis of the instrument cluster and, if so, to leave at least a little bit of the metal exposed where they go to ground. A dab of dielectric grease in those spots on reassembly will help prevent corrosion.

One thing I decided to do at this point was to join all the ground wires for the dash lamps into one common ground wire. This way, should I ever have grounding issues for the dash lamps in the future, I'll only have to trace down that one ground wire instead of half a dozen or so to find the trouble area and fix it. Any corroded or dirty contacts on the circuit board can be cleaned with fine sandpaper, emery cloth, or even a rubber eraser, depending on the level of corrosion.

Finally, should you find the acrylic lens in front of the gauges fogged, scratched, or hazed, most restorers recommend using Novus Plastic Polish to bring back the acrylic's transparency. While it's possible to use a buffing wheel set at very low speeds—less than 1,000 rpm is what Novus recommends—smaller instrument lenses should be done by hand using a disposable lint-free cotton cloth. Novus markets three grades of plastic polish: #3 is meant for heavy scratches, #2 for light scratches, and #1 for final dressing. Start with #3 or #2 and work your way down to #1.

With everything cleaned, refaced, or replaced, reassembly is simply the reverse of disassembly. Just be careful when tightening the screws going into the plastic; over-tightening them will often lead to cracks or other damage, especially on older plastic. Only tighten the screws until they're snug; no tighter.

With the instrument panel back in the car, I thought it looked a little plain and realized something was missing—the wood-grain appliqué that was originally glued to the face of the panel. Pontiac used two versions of the wood-grain dash in 1965, apparently interchangeably with each other. One version used real wood veneer on an aluminum backing, while the other used a paper-backed imitation grain. I wanted the real wood veneer, so I ordered a veneer dash kit, available from most restoration parts houses that deal in GTO parts. The kit allows you to install the veneer either by itself or with the aluminum backing.

The veneer, aluminum-backed just like the original, required a bit of trimming with a rotary tool to fit the instrument panel, and to more closely replicate the original stain, I treated the wood to a coat of boiled linseed oil. Using contact cement, I was then able to secure the veneer to the instrument panel. As I did this, I realized that it wouldn't be too tough to source either thin veneer or thin aluminum to craft something similar to dress up an otherwise plain muscle car dash panel.

When you've finished reinstalling the gauges and hooking everything back up, make sure to test all the gauges for correct operation—especially the speedometer. I recommend making sure the

Instrument Panel Restoration *CONTINUED*

7 ***Being careful not to overtighten the screws going into the plastic face of the instrument panel (freshly cleaned, you may notice), we reassembled the whole shebang and reinstalled it in the GTO. Yet something was still missing.***

8 ***We bought a real-wood veneer kit, trimmed it, stained it to the right shade, and glued it to the dash panel surface with contact cement. We chose to leave the aluminum backing off the veneer, though it would hurt nothing to leave it on.***

9 ***Sure, it looks much better than how it started out, but refreshing an instrument panel also serves a couple of important functions: It now has brighter dash lamps and allows a better view of the gauges. We also now have the peace of mind of knowing that the wiring behind our dashboard is sound.***

speedometer needle travels smoothly across the entire face of the speedometer—all the way to the top. Test it multiple times. After all, it's a matter of safety to trust your gauges are accurate, right?

Instrument Restoration

If your muscle car's instruments aren't quite keeping track of engine revs, oil pressure, or fuel tank level the way they should, then it's time to either replace them or send them out for restoration. One upside of sending out your gauges for restoration is that a competent shop should have no problem sourcing all the tiny mechanical and electrical parts

Engine Turning

It's been variously called jewelling, krayling, swirling, sailing, or damascening. Most of the time, however, it's called engine turning, and it lends a snazzy, racy look to many metals, but probably looks most at home on aluminum. No wonder, then, that engine-turned panels have shown up inserted into dashboards on everything from backyard-built racers to Ferraris. In fact, several muscle cars over the years, including the 1964 GTO and Firebirds throughout the 1970s, splashed engine-turned panels around their interiors.

And while it looks expensive–and can be quite expensive if you have a professional machine shop apply the finish to your panels–you can engine-turn a panel yourself at home. All you need are a drill press, a keen attention to detail, and plenty of time. Eastwood, in fact, sells a damascening kit that includes either a 1-inch or 1/2-inch abrasive on a mandrel that will chuck right into your drill press. Or, you can easily make a similar abrasive mandrel by gluing Scotch-Brite or even fine sandpaper to a dowel–or even by using the roughed-up end of a dowel. Different abrasives will result in different patterns, as will the use of a lubricant or polishing compound on your abrasive, so experiment with scrap pieces of aluminum first to decide what patterns you like.

Also figure out just how you'd like the patterns to overlap. Should they overlap in a simple square pattern, or should they alternate in half steps on each row? A good rule of thumb is to allow the swirls to overlap by only about 50 percent, which places the center of one swirl on the circumference of its adjoining swirls. Also keep in mind how the rows should overlap from top to bottom and left to right. Spend some time looking at all the different patterns out there (Google Images is your friend for this step) before deciding on the pattern and size of swirl that you want.

Before beginning, though, you'll want to thoroughly polish the piece of metal you're using. You won't be able to go back and polish it once you've turned the panel.

Setting up your workspace for engine turning is critical. Once you've decided on the pattern you're using, you'll have to figure out the distance between centers of each swirl and set up a system of incremental stops on both the X and Y axes against which your panel will rest for each swirl.

The actual swirling process involves just a light touch of the abrasive against the panel; pressing down too hard will result in bending or punching through the metal. Start with the row and column that you want to eventually end up at the bottom of the stack of swirls, then work your way across the panel from there.

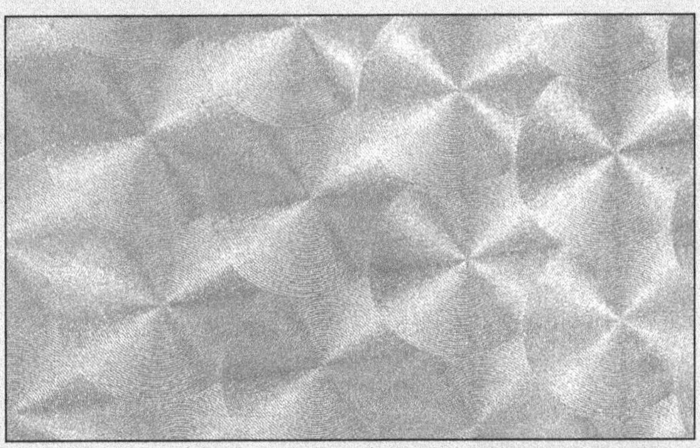

Engine turning was commonly used on automobiles, mostly racing machines, during the 1920s and 1930s, but saw sporadic resurrections during the 1960s and 1970s on muscle cars. Most muscle car applications of engine turning used the treatment on dashboard appliqués, which tend to be available now as reproductions, but it's certainly possible to make your own engine-turned panels.

that are otherwise difficult to find. Also, the shop will have the ability to aesthetically restore your gauges with new dials, and the shop should be able to calibrate your gauges properly.

I visited Instrument Specialties in Oxford, Massachusetts, which had a Rallye instrument cluster from a 1969 Dodge Charger R/T that required a total mechanical and cosmetic restoration. Before any restoration work begins, the crew at Instrument Specialties starts by evaluating the appearance of the gauges and by bench testing all of the gauges to see which ones work and how well they work.

Instrument Restoration

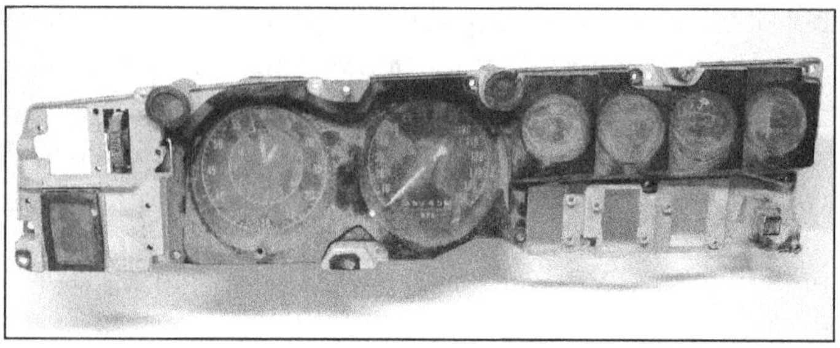

1 ***Though it looks as if it were dragged through a Borneo typhoon, the fact remains that this Rallye instrument cluster from a 1969 Dodge Charger R/T is a much sought-after item. Still, it required a total mechanical and cosmetic restoration.***

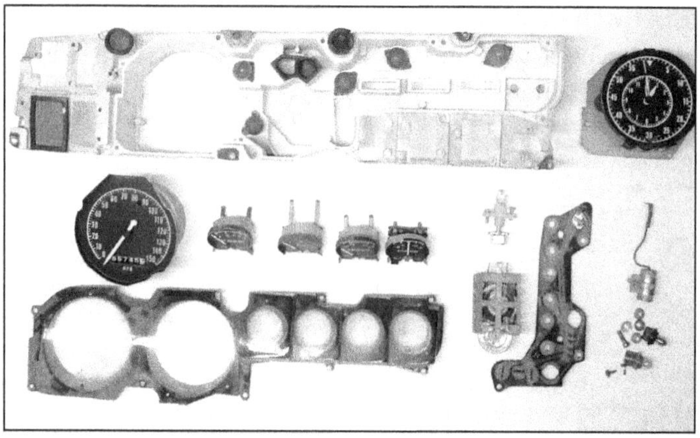

2 ***After evaluating all of the gauges to see which ones work and how well they work, Instrument Specialties completely disassembled the instrument cluster, down to the bare pot metal case.***

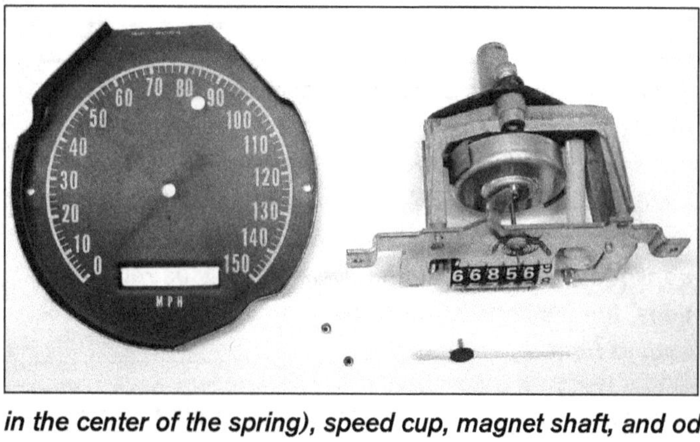

3 ***With the needle and two rivets removed, Instrument Specialties separated the face of the speedometer from its chassis, exposing the hair spring, jewel (the white bit in the center of the spring), speed cup, magnet shaft, and odometer workings.***

This is where the specialty machines come in. For the speedometer, Instrument Specialties uses a specific Kent-Moore speedometer tester; for the tachometer, they use a custom-designed calibrator that incorporates a master tachometer for comparison purposes; for the remainder of the gauges, they place them on a resistance block to verify the correct ohm ranges.

They next strip the instrument cluster down to the bare case. The case of this Charger's cluster is pot metal, but other muscle car cases may be stamped steel, aluminum, or molded plastic. Should they find damage to the case at this point, they can either repair or replace the case using parts from spare instrument clusters in their inventory.

Speedometer & Odometer

Each individual gauge is then restored using slightly different processes. One of the more complex gauges, the speedometer, is further disassembled by removing the needle, then grinding and punching out the rivets that secure the dial face to the frame of the gauge. They then remove the odometer and disassemble it using a Stewart-Warner odometer repair tool from the 1930s that just happens to work on nearly all Stewart-Warner mechanical odometers.

By the way, in the muscle car era as today, car manufacturers relied on suppliers to provide specific parts for their cars. Stewart-Warner was one of the main suppliers of instruments to the manufacturers, along with King-Seeley and Borg, a different division of the same company that built transmissions.

The main problem with odometers is that the white sections on the wheels turn yellow with UV exposure, and often do so unevenly. While some instrument restoration companies use tape decals to replicate the original brightness of the faces, the tape decals can come loose over time and unravel within the speedometer. The proper—and more time-consuming—method of odometer restoration requires individually silk-screening each number on each wheel in the correct font.

Instrument Specialties can then reassemble the odometer either back at zero or at the exact mileage that the customer specifies. Because muscle cars tend to be exempt from odometer regulations, the legality of resetting the odometer to zero is hardly questionable, but you should still check with your state laws to make sure your local DMV won't frown on the practice.

The remainder of the speedometer innards consist of the hairspring, which resides just underneath the dial; the jewel, which is actually a small block of plastic pressed into the speedometer chassis under the hairspring; the speed cup and its shaft, which passes through the jewel; the magnet shaft, which resides behind the speed cup; and the plastic gears for the odometer.

Only two of those pieces tend to require replacement: the jewel and the magnet shaft. The jewel quite simply wears over time where the needle shaft passes through it, thus causing the needle to wobble and return inaccurate readings. The magnet shaft, which takes the input from the speedometer cable and then rotates a pair of magnets around the metal speed cup, often suffers from the lack of lubrication in the speedometer cable, causing the metal in the magnet shaft to wear out.

The remainder of the speedometer components tend to remain in undamaged condition. If any parts do need to be replaced, the crew at Instrument Specialties selects the parts from an inventory of NOS parts they've accumulated over the years. If the instruments have spent any amount of time on a shelf outside of the dashboard, they tend to accumulate dust, dirt, and even metal shavings (thanks to the magnet shaft), so the crew at Instrument Specialties cleans out the speedometer innards before reassembly.

If the dial of the speedometer remains in good condition and the lettering has not faded or yellowed, then Instrument Specialties uses their specially developed solvent cleaning process that will preserve the dial and its lettering. However, while some instrument suppliers

Speedometer & Odometer Restoration

1 ***Compare this odometer, freshly silk-screened and reassembled, with the odometer in the previous picture, which has yellowed from UV exposure. Silk-screening the odometer wheels was done digit-by-digit, wheel-by-wheel.***

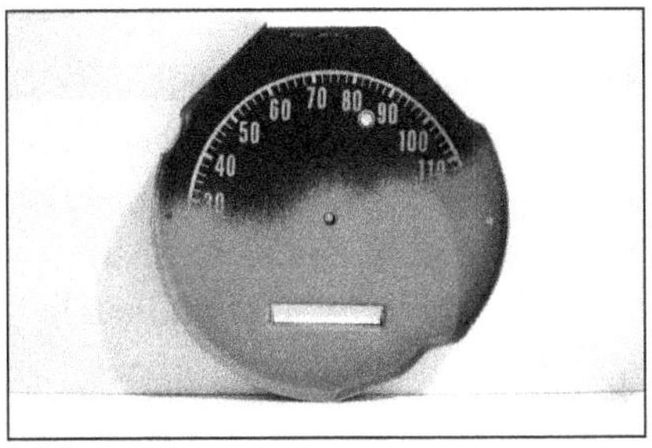

2 ***Refacing the dial of the speedometer started by stripping any rust, old paint, and ink. Instrument Specialties used glass beads. Glass beads impart a softer texture to the metal, important for attaining a smoother paint finish on the dial.***

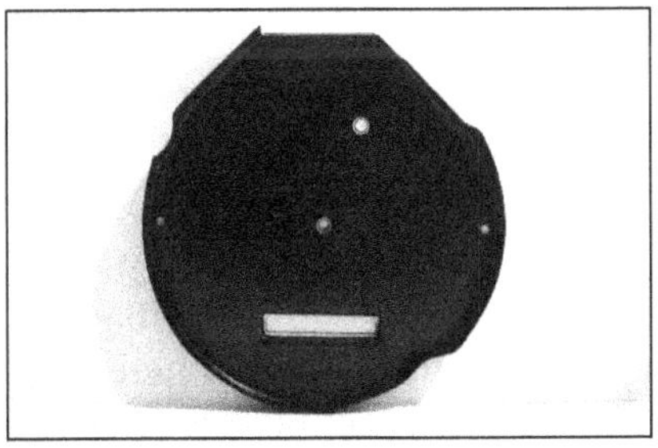

3 ***Though the black didn't fade as much as the white sections of the dial yellowed, Instrument Specialties still used UV-inhibiting black paint for the base of the dial face.***

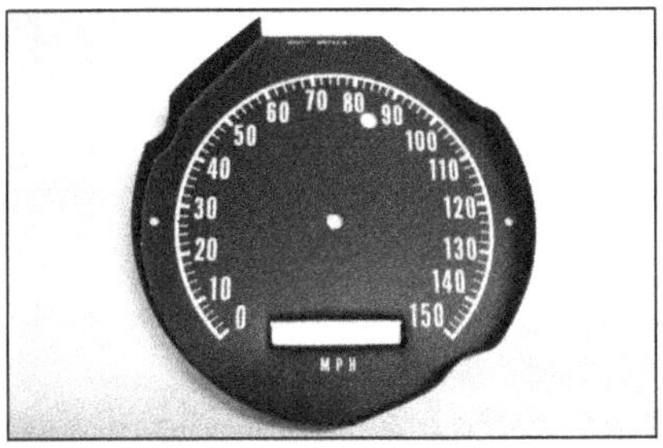

4 ***Perhaps the most important step in restoring gauges, aside from making them work right, comes when replicating the factory markings on the dial. Instrument Specialties uses a factory printing process with the original artwork negatives to apply the white ink to the speedometer face.***

used UV-resistant paints on their dials, others didn't, thus causing the yellowed lettering. In those cases, and in cases where the dial has rusted, Instrument Specialties will strip the paint and/or rust from the dial with glass beads, then lay down a coat of black background paint.

To replicate the lettering and markings, Instrument Specialties uses the same one-step printing process that the suppliers used, but substituting modern UV-resistant ink. The factory printing process actually allows for all sorts of customizing of the dials, using practically any color or font face imaginable. Graphic designers at Instrument Specialties simply create new artwork negatives, which are used in place of the original artwork negatives during the printing process.

This process, which only really works on flat surfaces, is similar to silk-screening, though silk-screening requires multiple steps for multiple colors, while the factory printing process applies multiple colors all in the same step. Instrument Specialties uses normal silk-screening on curved surfaces.

Other instrument restoration companies may use decals to replicate the factory lettering, though those have the potential for peeling and fading. They may also use either hot stamping or pad printing, similar processes that lower an ink pad onto the dial, though those processes have the potential for inconsistency and distortion.

Refinishing the needle tends to require more care than refinishing the dial. From the factory, the needle is perfectly weighted, and any imbalance on the needle, even from excess paint, will cause the speedometer to be difficult, if not impossible, to calibrate properly. Therefore, the crew at Instrument Specialties strips all the old paint from the needle and then airbrushes a new, thin layer of paint on. The lighter airbrushed paint also helps the needle become more responsive and provides more accurate readings.

With the speedometer reassembled, the crew at Instrument Specialties then calibrates the speedometer by either magnetizing or demagnetizing the magnet shaft. The magnet shaft makes no direct physical connection to the speed cup (and thus to the shaft and needle) because it creates eddy currents—a form of electrical current—that influence the movement of the speed cup. By using a magnetizer machine, the strength of the magnet shaft can be altered, thus adjusting the accuracy of the speedometer.

Tachometer

Most tachometers use few moving parts, but rely on electronic signals from an internal circuit board to drive the meter itself, so the faults in a tachometer usually lie either in that circuit board or with the accumulated dirt and metal shavings inside a tachometer. If necessary, the Instrument Specialties crew will replace the circuit board, demagnetize the entire tachometer, and clean out the dirt and metal shavings, then reassemble it with a dial and needle, restored in the same fashion as the speedometer.

Chrysler's Tic-Toc-Tach combines a clock and tachometer into one instrument. The instrument faces are restored via the same printing process as the tachometer, and the clock's movements are converted to quartz.

In the case of this Charger, the owner wanted a Tic-Toc-Tach to replace the original Rallye clock and he wanted the clock movement converted to quartz. Several companies sell quartz movement conversions, which offer greater reliability over the stock mechanical movement.

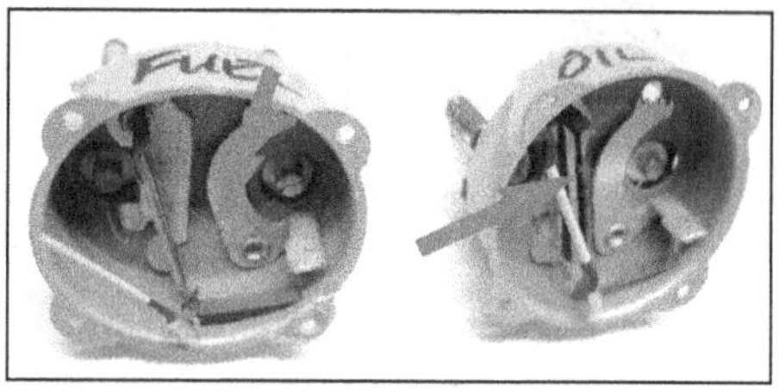

With the faces removed from the resistance-based gauges, you can see the very thin wire wrapped around the bimetallic spring and how the spring is attached to the needle. You can also see the star wheel and how it is used to adjust the needle and calibrate the gauge.

Other Gauges

The smaller gauges—oil pressure, temperature, fuel, and ammeter—are all refaced with a similar factory printing process as the speedometer and the tachometer. All but the amperage gauge (also called the ammeter) are tested on the resistance block. The oil pressure, temperature, and fuel gauges all depend on a resistance range, measured in ohms, to display properly. The current then feeds a bimetallic strip with a thin wire wrapped around it and the needle affixed to it—the higher the resistance, the more heat, so the bimetallic strip warps and the needle moves.

After stripping and painting the case, the instruments were assembled back into the case, along with the lens, the switches, the light bulbs, and the colored gels, which were re-silk-screened wherever they had lettering printed on them.

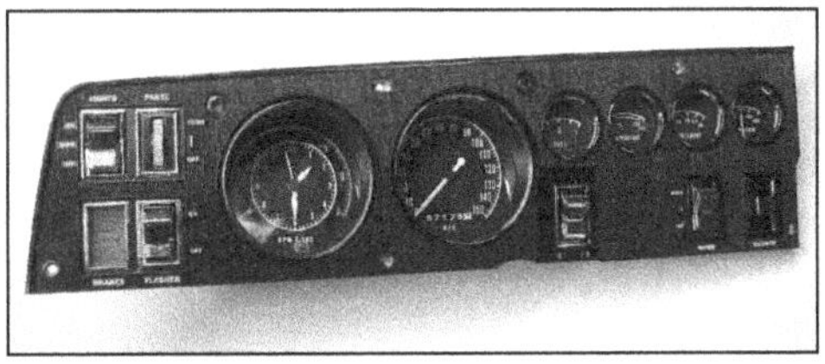

Though having the instrument panel face restored will add several hundred dollars and several weeks to the final bill, you aren't going to want to mount your newly restored gauges behind a face with peeling chrome and faded paint.

In Ford and Chrysler muscle cars, the oil pressure, temperature, and fuel gauges depend on a voltage limiter that reduces the voltage from 12 volts to 5 volts before the electrical current enters the gauge. If that voltage limiter fails, the gauge burns up. That is, the wire that heats up the bimetallic spring heats up too much and physically deteriorates, thus losing its ability to conduct electric current at all and effectively killing the gauge.

If the gauge has burned up, it can be repaired with a new wire around the bimetallic spring. The gauges are then calibrated on the resistance block. Calibration is done by applying the minimum resistance, adjusting the tiny star wheel adjuster on the back of the gauge until the needle points to the appropriate mark on one end, then applying the maximum resistance and adjusting the star wheel adjuster until the needle points to the appropriate mark on the other end.

The ammeter, on the other hand, simply works or doesn't work once it's clean. If it doesn't work, it needs to be replaced with a functioning unit. Some restorers prefer to use voltmeters instead of ammeters for a couple of reasons. An ammeter simply displays whether the vehicle's electrical system is charging or discharging, while a voltmeter (which became common in American vehicles around the mid-1970s) displays the actual voltage of the vehicle's electrical system. Some restorers feel ammeters can possibly cause fires when they fail, while others feel that ammeters tend to be the scapegoat for shoddy wiring elsewhere in the vehicle.

Finishing Touches

With all the instruments restored, the Instruments Specialty crew then cleans (and if necessary, rebuilds or replaces) the original switches, cleans any circuit boards with acid to remove corrosion and tarnish, and replaces all the light bulbs. The plastic lens in front of the gauges is sanded. They progressively sand it with 800- to 1500-grade paper before buffing with a low-rpm air-powered polisher kept below 2,500 rpm to avoid warping or melting the plastic.

The case itself is cleaned and repainted white to aid in reflecting the light behind the gauges from the bulbs. Gels used to color certain lights are cleaned and any lettering applied to the gels is removed and then reapplied via silk-screening. The face of the instrument panel, which usually incorporates the chrome trim around the gauges and switches, is chemically stripped to the bare plastic and wet sanded smooth before the entire face is plastic chromed. The areas to remain chrome are then masked while the rest of the face is wet sanded again before it is painted. Any lettering on the case is carefully applied by hand.

Depending on the amount of repair, calibration, and cosmetic restoration, Instrument Specialties charges about $900 for a simple gauge restoration and about another $300 to restore the instrument panel's face. From start to finish, the entire job takes about 4 to 6 weeks unless the face requires rechroming, in which case, the job extends to 10 to 12 weeks.

Of course, depending on the model and options of your muscle car, you could easily spend that much money and more time hunting for working NOS gauges to replace your busted ones.

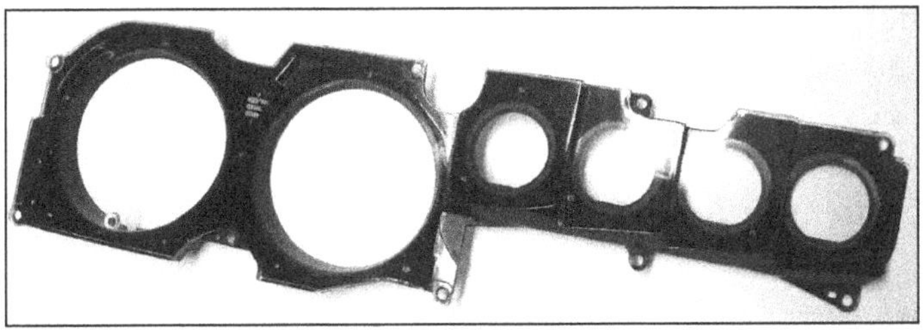

The plastic lens covering the gauges is prone to scratches, especially if left on a bench for any length of time, so scratches arefirst sanded out, then a low-speed buffer polishes the plastic until it looks like glass.

Dashboard Restoration

We've all seen them, especially when on the hunt for a muscle car. They can often be a deal breaker on first sight, even if the rest of the car isn't half bad. And as long as you live somewhere other than underground where you never see the sun, you're going to come across them—dashboard cracks.

The construction of a typical muscle car dashboard, while soft enough to please safety advocates of the day, isn't exactly a design intended to last through the ages, especially when combined with exposure to the sun and varying temperatures. Basically, a muscle car dashboard consists of three layers: the stamped sheetmetal frame that forms the basic shape and structure of the dashboard; a layer of open-cell urethane foam padding (ranging in thickness from as little as 1/8 inch to as much as 1 inch) over most of the surfaces facing the driver and the passenger; and a textured vinyl skin over the foam.

While an extreme example, this GTO's dash shows a sight familiar to any muscle car enthusiast: sun-induced cracks, peeling vinyl, and crumbling foam. It's the result of a combination of UV damage to the vinyl, of extreme heat within the car that causes the vinyl to lose its flexibility, and of drastic temperature cycles that shrink and stretch the vinyl.

Auto manufacturers started to introduce padded dashboards in the mid-1950s, and by 1967, they had not only become standard in American cars, they had become mandatory as part of the first wave of codified automotive safety regulations. Together, the foam padding and the vinyl skin are usually referred to as the dashboard's dashpad or crashpad, if only because that's what will pad your face during a crash.

Vinyl, as we all know, has a tendency to become brittle and less pliable with age and exposure to ultraviolet rays. A 2002 study by the Building and Fire Research Laboratory at the National Institute of Standards and Technology in Gaithersburg, Maryland, showed that vinyl lost as much as two-thirds of its strength in several measurements after just 4,000 hours of UV exposure. Given an average of 12 hours per day of sitting in the sun, that's a little less than a year. Vinyl also loses its flexibility over time as heat—both from direct sunlight and from the greenhouse effect within a car—causes chemical compounds called plasticizers to bake out of the vinyl in a process called outgassing. Not until the mid-1990s did automotive manufacturers begin to engineer plasticizers that didn't outgas until they reached much higher temperatures.

It also didn't help vinyl longevity when automotive manufacturers cut costs for dashboard construction by using the thinnest vinyl possible for dashboard skins—down to around .032 to .035 inch.

Sitting in the sun also leads to wild temperature extremes (only made worse by the use of air conditioning on those really hot days), which in turn leads to the expansion and contraction of the materials in the dashboard. The three basic materials that make up the dashboard all expand and contract at different rates, which leads to a lot of shifting surfaces in the dashboard. Combined with the embrittled and inflexible vinyl skin of the dashboard, a crack is simply inevitable. Thus, more often than not, cracks form in a dashboard, not in the cracks and crevices of the dashboard, where the vinyl skin is under little tension, but in the wide expanses of the dashboard—usually right smack-dab in the center—where the sun-stretched skin has the most tension.

In another cost-cutting measure, manufacturers didn't treat the foam under the dashboard skin with any sort of UV protector, so once the skin cracked, the foam directly underneath quickly deteriorated. This, in turn, led to more cracks in the dashboard skin and more foam deterioration.

So unless your muscle car has rested far away from any windows in a temperature-controlled warehouse for most of its life, you're going to eventually come face-to-face with a nasty crack in your dashpad. Covering the pad with one of those parts-store dash covers is not only cheesy, but is just as ineffective at stopping the spread of cracks as slathering plastic filler over rust is ineffective at stopping the spread of rust.

Repairing the dashboard—first by grinding out the crack, then filling it with a catalyzed urethane compound, such as the Urethane Supply Company's Padded Dash Filler, and applying texture to the filled crack—does nothing to address the embrittled and inflexible vinyl skin on the rest of the dashboard. It also does nothing to prevent more cracks from appearing later on.

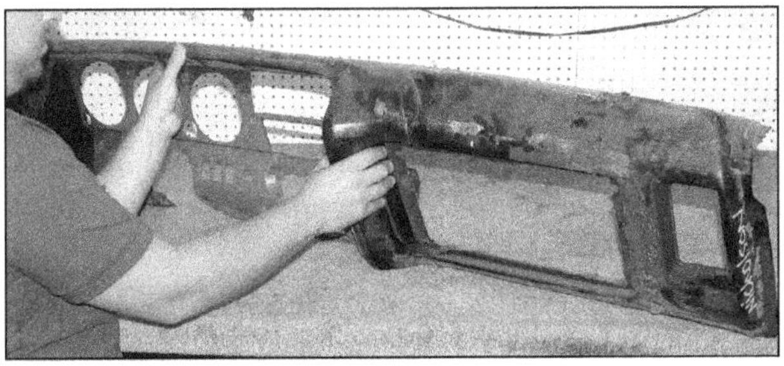

The Just Dashes crew inspected the GTO's dash to determine whether its steel chassis was suitable for restoration. Severe rust can often form due to leaking windshields and the sponge-like ability of open-cell foam padding to absorb water. They also noted the grain of the vinyl skin and the correct (non-sun faded) color of the dash, two important pieces of information for later in the process.

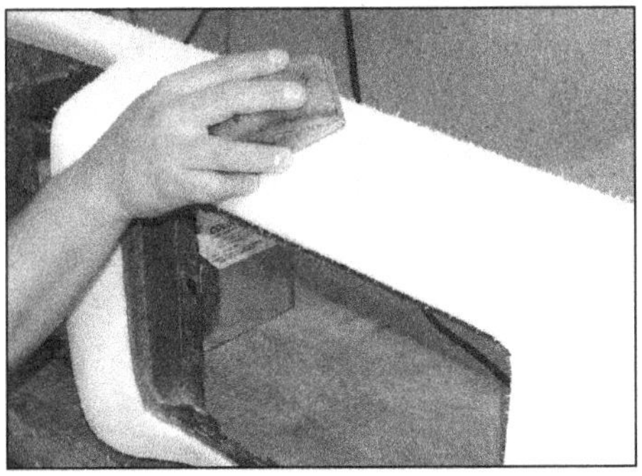

New closed-cell polyethylene foam, designed to expand and contract with the new vinyl skin, was laid over the stripped metal frame in sheets, and glued down. It was then shaped with varying grades of sandpaper to the correct shape and thickness, with more material on the dashboard's eyebrows and less on the flat, top part.

Instead, a proper dashboard restoration requires you to do three things:

- Remove the dashboard from the car (usually accomplished by removing a few bolts on either side of the dashboard, right above the kick panel. Be sure to consult your car's assembly manual).
- Strip off the entire dashpad and apply new foam padding.
- Skin the padding with a new vinyl skin that will conform to all the contours of your dashboard.

It's all doable on simpler dashboards, ones without too many or too complex curves and shapes. You can simply use contact adhesive, closed-cell foam built up and carved to shape, and carefully stretch the new vinyl, applying heat where necessary.

But it's a much tougher process for dashboards with more complex shapes, including many of our favorite muscle cars. To meet the market need in 1992, Just Dashes of Van Nuys, California, began offering a thermo-vacuum forming dashboard restoration process. It is similar to the process the factories used to apply the vinyl skin to the dashboard.

I visited Just Dashes as they were preparing to restore a dashboard for a 1970 Pontiac GTO, and saw first-hand how a nasty old dash can come out looking brand new. After initial inspection of the dashboard, the Just Dashes crew proceeds to strip the dashboard of its vinyl skin and original foam padding. Though normally well protected from the elements by the dashpad, the metal frame of the dashboard can sometimes rust, especially if the car's windshield sprang a leak or if water somehow got underneath the vinyl skin, where the original foam then soaked it up like a

An Ounce of Prevention

You know when you're messing around with something under the hood and you inevitably look over at the heater fan and think about how much of a pain it'd be to change out the heater core? So you usually put that project on the back burner, maybe for when you next have the dashboard out, right?

Well, here's your chance. With the dashboard removed for restoration, you should have easy access to the heater core, one of the few things that can create a huge, ruinous mess in your interior when it goes bad.

For this reason, it's a good idea to schedule the dashboard restoration before replacing the carpet. If you have already replaced the carpet, make sure to protect it with plastic before replacing the heater core. And when actually replacing the heater core, don't forget to replace the hoses, clamps, and foam seals associated with the heater core at the same time. Hose failure, whether due to age embrittlement or clamp biting, can cause an interior coolant flood just as easily as failure of the heater core itself. Also, foam seal failure can potentially lead to carbon monoxide and other noxious fumes in the cabin of your car.

Molding Gauge Pods into the Dashboard

When we were kids and wanted to add gauges to our car in place of the stock idiot lights, we bought a cup to fit the gauge from the speed shop, then drilled a hole in the dash and screwed the cup to those holes. Putting the gauges there made it easy to check RPM without taking our eyes off the guy we were racing against. Eventually, we realized how stupid it was to drill holes in the dashpad, and that it was probably those holes that started the cracks in the dashpad. So we hung the gauges from the bottom of the dash, where we couldn't see the holes, but we couldn't see the gauges either.

Just Dashes has since come up with a solution to that situation. On certain dashes, they can add a trio (or pair, or single) of 2⅟₁₆-inch gauge pods to the leading edge of the dashboard, then cover the pods with the exact same material as the rest of the dashboard to integrate them with the overall dash appearance.

They add the pods after the dashboard has been stripped of its old skin and foam padding. Using a two-part expanding-urethane foam filler, the Just Dashes crew bonds the gauge pods to the dashboard, angling them toward the driver. They then shape and sand the filler to make a smooth transition between the surface of the dashboard and the curves of the gauge pods. An epoxy primer then fills in minor scratches and leaves the surface ready for the application of the foam padding and the thermo-vacuum forming process.

Many other changes to a dashboard can be made at this point in the process, including additional vents for air conditioning or additional holes for dashboard-mounted speakers.

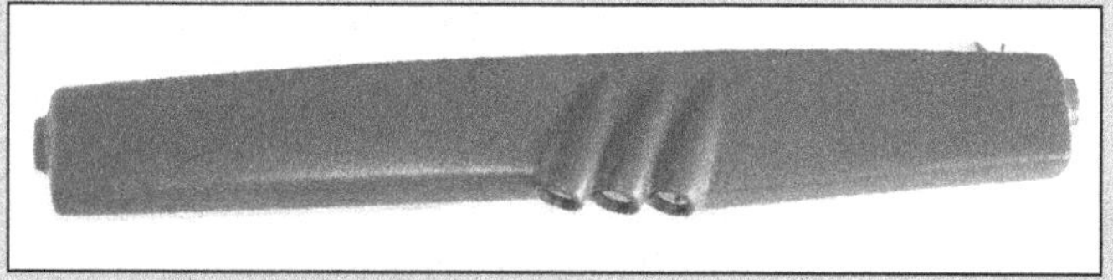

Unlike the tacked-on look of auxiliary gauges in past muscle cars, it's possible to integrate gauge pods into a dashboard during the restoration process. In addition to the clean look, the gauges are also easier for a driver to see without taking his eyes off the road.

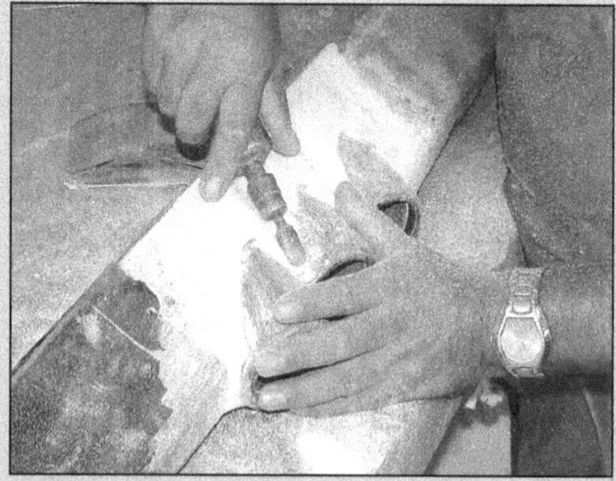

Shaping the filler requires a bit of a sculptor's touch to bring out the right shapes, using either an air grinder, sandpaper, or both. If you mess up, you can apply more foam filler to the area and start over again.

Once the dash was stripped, preformed gauge pods were mated to the surface of the dashboard with a two-part expanding urethane foam filler. The filler acts to both secure the pods to the dashboard chassis and to provide a smooth transition from the dashboard surface to the gauge pod surface after it is shaped.

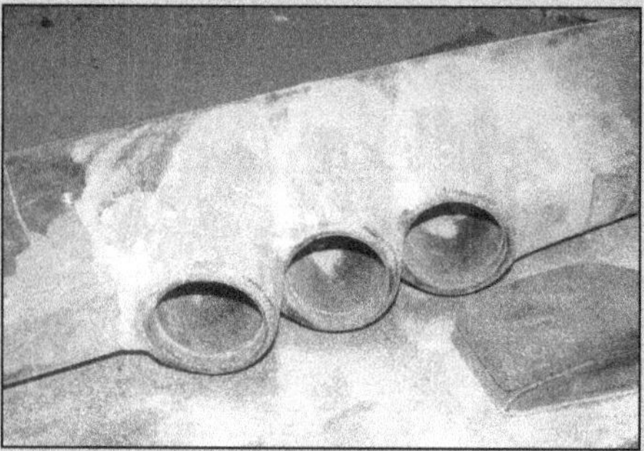

When finished, the pods should have a nice, tapered transition into the dashboard. The foam filler doesn't have to be perfectly smooth; after all, it will be covered with closed-cell foam padding and a vinyl skin. But it should still present a uniform surface without large divots or bumps.

From here on, recovering the dashboard follows much the same process as for a dashboard without added-on gauge pods. Add the closed-cell foam, shape it, then cover it with a vinyl skin. Just be careful not to make the holes in the pods too tight; otherwise, the gauges will not fit properly.

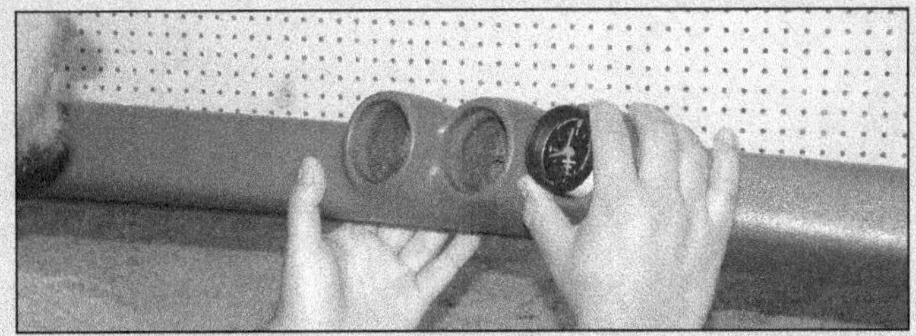

With the dash covered in a new skin of vinyl and painted, the gauges can be fit into the pods. Check now to make sure any wiring or fluid lines for the gauges can be routed to the gauges through the dash without any obstruction or pinching.

The end product looks fully integrated into the dashboard, as though the car came that way from the factory. A similar process can be used for any type of customization, including additional (or subtracted) speaker openings, air conditioning vents, or stereo head unit mounts.

sponge. Any rust-through should be repaired now, before proceeding. Otherwise, the Just Dashes crew lightly goes over the frame with a wire brush to remove any loose foam.

According to Irwin Tessler, owner and founder of Just Dashes, the original foam helped cause many cracks in the vinyl skin because its porous, open-cell composition caused it to expand and contract with temperature changes. The Just Dashes crew replaces the old open-cell foam with new, high-density closed-cell polyethylene foam designed to expand and contract with the vinyl.

After laying out different thicknesses of foam depending on the location—thicker 1-inch foam for the eyebrow of the dash facing the passengers, thinner 1/8-inch or 1/4-inch foam for the top of the dash—they then secure the foam in place with contact adhesive. Using various grades of sandpaper ranging from 40 grit to 320 grit, they then shape the foam by hand, constantly checking the fit of all the pieces that bolt or screw to the dashboard, including the vents, speaker grilles, and instrument panel. The foam cannot have any gouges or pits in it at this point; irregularities in the surface will show through the vinyl skin.

Once the Just Dashes crew has shaped the foam padding, they spray a thin, even layer of adhesive on the foam and place the foam-covered dashboard on a vacuum tray that is sealed to a table and then to a vacuum pump. At the same time, they roll out enough vinyl to completely cover the dashboard and spray a thin, even layer of adhesive on the back of the vinyl. The vinyl that Just Dashes uses has the same grain as the original vinyl skin, but is thicker (about .045 inch), which goes a long way toward resisting damage. Tessler said he has also worked with suppliers to obtain a vinyl that has UV inhibitors molded into it, as well as modern plasticizers that don't outgas at low temperatures. All of these attributes help increase the dashboard's longevity.

The Just Dashes crew then clamps the sheet of vinyl in a frame and heats it in an oven until it becomes pliable, and quickly raises the vacuum tray up into the heated vinyl. The amount of time and the temperature varies for different-size and different-shape dashes. The soft vinyl makes an airtight barrier with the vacuum tray, at which point the technician can activate the vacuum—

Dashboard Restoration

1 *Shaping the foam is essential to achieving the correct appearance even after the vinyl skin is applied. The foam is what gives the dashboard its shape and definition, and any major gouges will show through the vinyl.*

2 *The foam, however, is shaped to exactly the same thickness as the factory-applied foam to allow all the original components—instrument panel, heater vents, glove box—to fit perfectly into the dashboard. For that reason, the Just Dashes crew constantly checked the fit of those components against the bare-foam dashboard during the sanding and shaping process.*

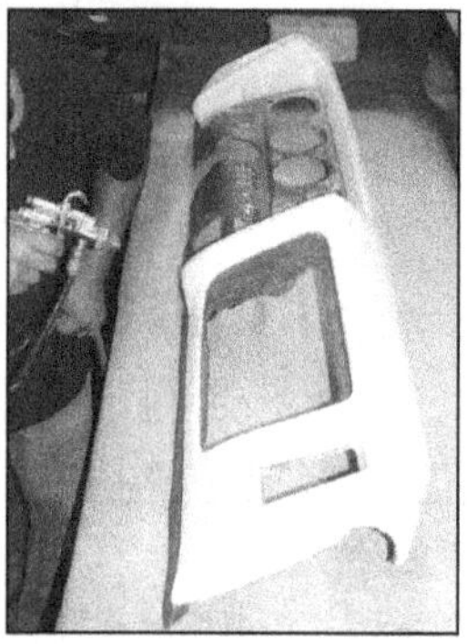

3 *Once the dashboard has been shaped, the Just Dashes crew sprayed a thin, even coat of adhesive to the surface of the dashboard. Again, the adhesive must be as even as possible; otherwise, lumps or voids will show through the vinyl skin.*

4 *Another thin, even coat of adhesive was applied to the back side of the vinyl that will cover the dashboard. The thicker-than-stock vinyl that Just Dashes used comes from a supplier that has reformulated the vinyl to be more durable and UV-resistant over time. Just Dashes has a variety of vinyl grains to choose from, to either match the original, or to provide a custom look for a muscle car.*

5 *Now coated with adhesive, the dashboard was placed on a vacuum table, sufficiently supported to remain stable through the thermo-vacuum forming process. Cloths placed over areas not to be skinned prevented the vinyl from adhering to those areas. The dash must be adequately braced against the table now; otherwise, it may distort under the strong vacuum.*

6 *The vinyl skin was clamped in a metal frame, then heated evenly until it became sufficiently pliable. The amount of heat used varies depending on the size, shape, and complexity of the dashboard.*

7 *The thermo-vacuum forming machine pushed the braced frame and vacuum table up into the heated vinyl skin. Once the skin maked a seal with the vacuum table, the vacuum pump was turned on and sucked the hot vinyl skin to the dashboard. As with the amount of heat applied, the amount of vacuum applied also depends on the size and shape of the dashboard. The operator of the machine checked for air pockets trapped under the vinyl skin or imperfections in the vinyl.*

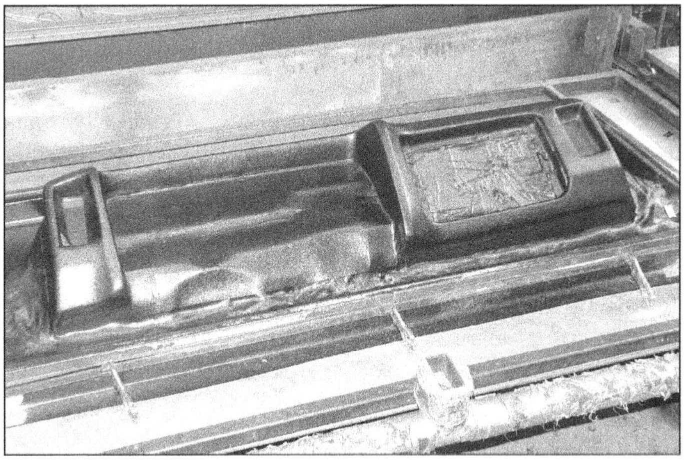

8 *With sufficient vacuum and heat, the vinyl skin conformed perfectly to the shape of the dashboard. Note how it also conformed perfectly to the rags in the opening for the glove box; an observation that hammers home the importance of making the foam padding perfectly smooth and divot-free. A mist of cool water at this point helped the vinyl skin set in shape.*

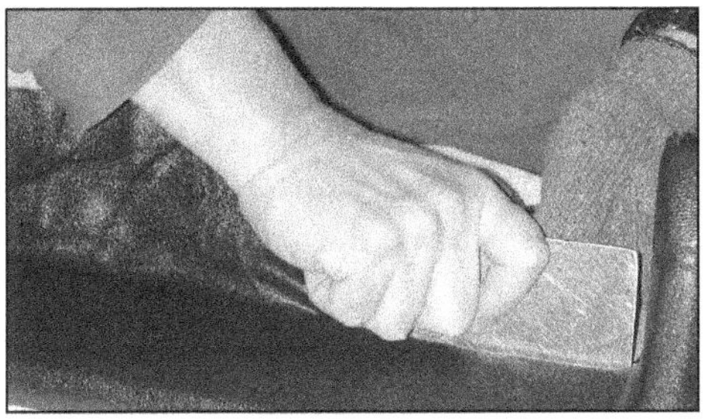

9 *Once thoroughly cooled, the dashboard was cut free from the vacuum table and sent to the finishing department, where finishers trimmed the excess vinyl skin off, down to about 1 inch of excess, and then folded the skin over the sides of the dashboard. Here, a finisher used a tucking tool to help the vinyl skin conform to an edge that the thermo-vacuum forming process couldn't handle.*

10 *Several dashboards cooled on a rack as they awaited their turn with the finishing department. Note how the thermo-vacuum forming process was able to form a variety of dashboard shapes with only minor adjustments in the amount of heat and vacuum applied.*

11 *All the vinyl for the dashboard came off the roll in an uncoated, and thus highly glossy, black. After trimming the skinned dashboard, the Just Dashes finishers painted the dash with a vinyl dye to match the original color. In the vinyl dye, Just Dashes mixed a flattening agent to prevent glare coming off the dashboard and into the driver's eyes.*

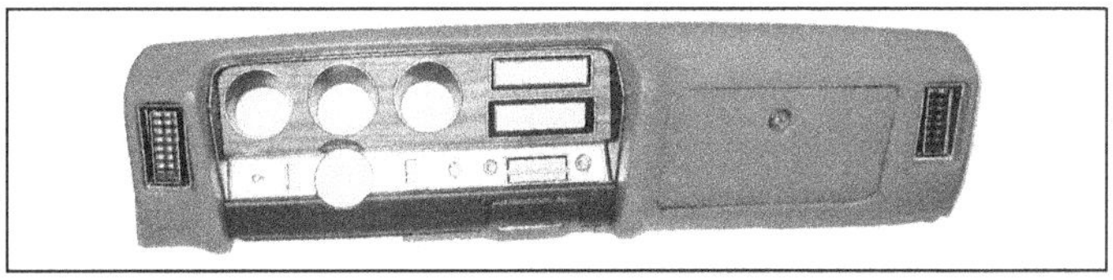

12 *Fitted with the instrument panel, glove box door, and heater vent doors, the dashboard now looked much better than the cracked and crumbling wreck that had entered the Just Dashes shop. With better materials used in its restoration, the new dashboard should also resist cracking and damage much longer than the original dash did.*

again, a varying amount depending on the size and shape of the dashboard—and suck the vinyl down around the dashboard. The use of vacuum forming thus allows the pliable vinyl to stretch around contours and into crevices in much less time than it would take a craftsman working by hand to do the same.

According to Tessler, automotive manufacturers used, essentially, the reverse of the process. They first vacuum-formed the vinyl skin to a negative mold of the face of the dashboard, then back-filled the skin with foam, placed the metal frame of the dashboard into the foam, and then closed the mold around the frame. "Our process loses a bit of definition versus Detroit's process," Tessler said. "But this is the closest anybody can get to how they did it originally without the molds, and you'd really have to set one of our dashes side-by-side with an original dash to see the difference."

To cool the vinyl and help it set in place, a fine spray of water is applied to the vinyl, as the operator visually checks the dashboard to make sure the vinyl formed perfectly to the dashboard and no bubbles appeared under the vinyl skin. Once it has cooled enough, they then cut it free from the vacuum box and the metal frame, leaving between 1/2 and 1 inch of excess around the dashboard.

Over in the finishing department, trimmers remove the vinyl from the openings for the speaker grilles, glove box, vents, and instrument panel. Tuck tools are used to push the vinyl farther into some recesses. At the edges, the finishers dart the vinyl at the corners, then apply even heat to the vinyl, stretch it around the edges, and glue the vinyl flaps to the back side of the dashboard.

All of the vinyl that Just Dashes uses starts out black, so if they are restoring a dashboard of a different color, they can dye it to match using simple lacquer-based vinyl dye, mixed with a flattening agent to cause less reflective glare. Typically, they wait until the end of the process to dye the dashboard, both because the dye would be damaged in the thermo-vacuum process and require touch-ups afterward, and because they don't have to dye the entire sheet of vinyl, only the section they didn't trim away.

Though the thermo-vacuum forming process takes about 1/2 hour, it typically takes Just Dashes about 4 to 6 weeks to complete a dash restoration. A straightforward dash restoration usually costs from $400 to $2,000, depending on the size and shape of the dashboard.

So could you build your own vacuum table large enough to accept an entire dashboard? Sure, plans for those have been floating around on the Internet for years. Using a heat gun, you could probably also heat an entire sheet of vinyl perfectly and evenly to make it pliable enough to stretch over your dashboard, with enough practice. And if you're resourceful enough, you could locate the right vinyl, the right dye, and the right closed-cell foam in varying thicknesses with no problem. According to Tessler, most people who try to recover their own dashboards find themselves in over their heads real quick and make more of a mess than if they had just left the dashboard alone in the first place, but it's certainly possible to nail such a complicated task on the first try.

So let's say you did all of the above to recover your own dash. And let's ignore how much it would cost to buy all those materials and how much time you'd spend researching, designing, building, and testing your own thermo-vacuum contraption versus the money and time spent simply sending your dash out for restoration. Let's say you even did fix it right the first time around. In the end, you went through all that trouble for a setup you'll use once, maybe two or three times for your buddies' dashboards. Was it really worth it?

Just Dashes supplies most, if not all, reproduction dashpads on the aftermarket today, and the removal/installation process for reproduction dashboards is the same for dashboards restored by Just Dashes. They are definitely an option.

Taking Care of your Dash

Of course, if you're going to lay out the kind of money quoted above for a new dashboard, you'll want to take the utmost care of it. The increased durability of the vinyl used in a Just Dashes restoration will go a long way toward preventing future damage, but you should simply keep the dash—and the entire car—out of the sun as well as keep the dash clean of dust and dirt. While Just Dashes does sell a product called Vinyl Life Preserver meant to extend the life of a dash, Tessler said he also recommends using the household cleaner Pledge for its anti-static properties.

Ask a dozen detailers or restorers what to use to keep a dashboard clean and you'll hear a dozen different answers. If you're reselling a car after you've restored it, some simple Armor All or other silicone oil-based product will certainly shine up the dashboard and other plastic surfaces. You can usually spot a silicone oil-based product by warnings on the bottle not to use the product on surfaces where slipperiness would result. Silicone oil-based products also usually suggest multiple applications to build up the product on the dashboard.

Yet applying silicone oil to a dashboard is widely regarded as harmful to its surface over time, and most restorers suggest avoiding such products when choosing a protectant for your dashboard. Much like baby oil—another product claimed to preserve interior vinyls but which actually does more harm than good—silicone oil accelerates heat transfer to the vinyl, which in turn accelerates damage to the vinyl. Think about it in terms of going to the beach in summer: To avoid a sunburn, you wouldn't want to use baby oil or tanning lotion; instead, you'd want to use sunscreen, the higher the SPF the better. Or think about it in terms of frying a turkey: What do you use? Cooking oil.

So what should you use to protect your interior vinyl? Again, most restorers have favorite products. First, they emphasize keeping the dashboard clean, and in most cases, warm soapy water will do the job; ammonia or even hydrogen peroxide diluted with water will take care of mildew or tougher stains. However, avoid using bleach, solvents, or harsh detergents. For a protectant, look for a product that blocks UV rays, such as Waxshop LRV conditioner or the 303 line of products, then follow the product's application directions.

Glove Box Restoration

To model makers and craftspeople, flocking is a fairly well-known process. Most car guys, however, display a look of bewilderment on their faces when you mention flocking to them. "Isn't that what you do to a Christmas tree?" they ask.

In dashboard restoration—and even in a few other places in the interior, such as inside the console and on some window channels and rubguards—flocking is commonly used to provide a soft, non-slip surface, or as a decorative alternative to bare plastic, vinyl, or metal. It's that velvety, suede-like stuff that feels like cloth but doesn't have the padding of a normal cloth surface. It's a lot more common on cars built in the last couple decades, but unless you're going for an all-out concours restoration, there's no reason not to add flocking to your glove box or inside your console. I've even heard of race car builders who use the stuff all over their dashboards to reduce glare. It might look a little tacky, but if it gives them an advantage and prevents them from crashing, I suppose it's worth it.

While the production flocking process involves running an electrical current through the part to be flocked, it's also possible to flock parts at home without any special equipment, just the right supplies and a little time. DonJer, one of the more prominent flocking supply companies in the United States, offers a home flocking kit—available through Eastwood—that represents a good alternative to sending parts away for professional (read: expensive) flocking.

If the part to be flocked already has flocking on it, then the old flocking should be removed with 120- to 180-grit sandpaper or a medium foam-backed sanding pad, such as from 3M. The flocking will eventually cover any sanding marks in the surface of the part, so feel free to be aggressive with the sandpaper to remove all the old flocking. Once all the old flocking is removed—or if the part has no flocking on it—wipe down the surface with acetone or denatured alcohol (available at any hardware store) to remove any dust, dirt, and oils from the surface of the part.

Glove Box Restoration

1 ***Though it wasn't originally flocked, we've chosen to flock the inside of the glove box door on our car. Flocking will add a layer of soft protection for the registration papers and assorted fuses we keep in the glove box. It will also help prevent our drinks from sliding around in those ineffective cup holders, were we ever to actually use them.***

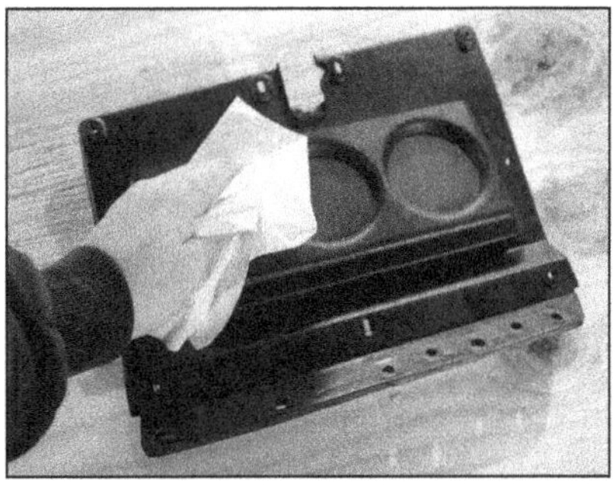

2 ***With flocking, first make sure the surface is totally clean; we wiped the door with denatured alcohol. Any porous surface, such as wood, requires some sort of sealant or shellac to prevent the flocking adhesive from soaking into the base material. It's also a good idea to use a sealant over the glove box door's ABS plastic surface.***

Planning the flocking process is the key to professional-looking results—and the key to not making a huge mess. Decide where exactly you want flocking to appear, and the surfaces where you don't want or need the flocking. Though not required, it's recommended to tape off the areas you don't want to flock (use green painter's tape—it doesn't bleed at the edges as much as blue painter's tape). Plan to flock an entire surface at a time; flocking a surface in multiple sections will create lines between the sections.

The flocking kit instructions strongly recommend you find a box large enough for the part you're flocking and line it with plastic to contain the mess created by the process. A simple clean plastic sheet over your workbench will also suffice. Have a shop-vac handy, but also keep in mind that the flocking fibers can be re-used, so consider a method to recover excess material from the sheet.

The flocking kit contains a unique method for distributing the flocking fibers: a pair of cardboard tubes, each open at one end and designed to slide into one another. One of the cardboard tubes has holes punched in the closed end, like a saltshaker. Fill the other cardboard tube about halfway with the flocking fibers, being careful not to spread the fibers all over the place. If you're not careful, the fibers can act like a small cloud of dust and the slightest breeze can blow them everywhere. Assemble the cardboard tubes and set them aside for a moment.

Next, take the part to be flocked and brush on the adhesive included in the kit. The adhesive looks like a viscous tar, so be sure to spread enough adhesive on the part to even

Glove Box Restoration *CONTINUED*

3 ***The heart of the flocking kit is the small bag of flocking fibers and the applicator tube. The flocking comes in a variety of colors to match your interior. Though the bag seems small, we used more than we thought we needed to and still had plenty left.***

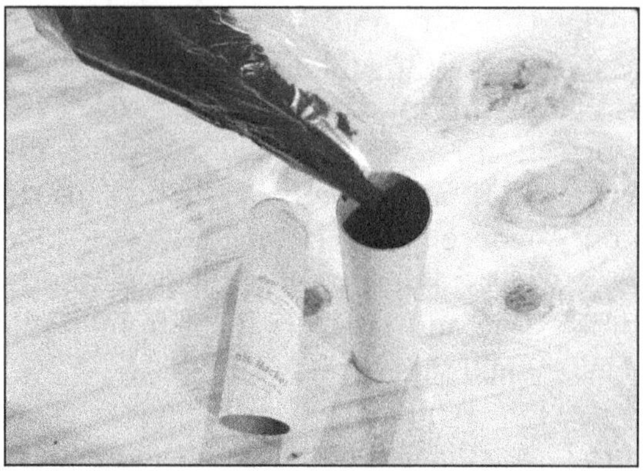

4 ***The applicator tube is actually two tubes. Separate them and fill the smaller of the two about halfway with the flocking fibers. Take care here; the fibers are apt to fly all over the place, so try to keep them contained when pouring them into the tube. Reassemble the tube afterward and set it aside.***

5 ***We set our glove box door on a sheet of plastic to keep from making a mess, and to recycle the excess flocking fibers later on in the process. The adhesive included in the kit should match the color of the flocking fibers. While the adhesive can be thinned and sprayed, we elected to brush it on with the supplied brush.***

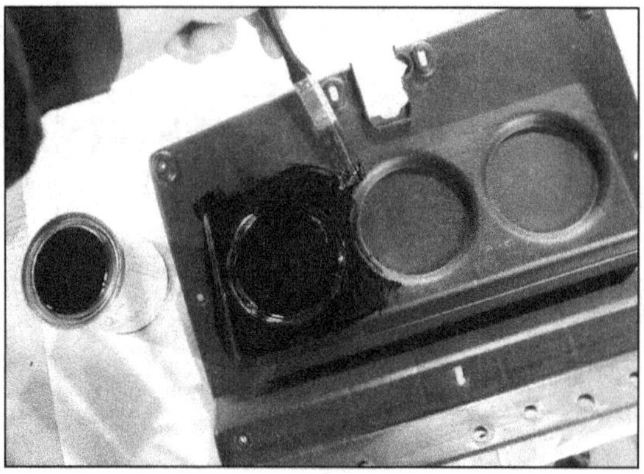

6 ***Brush the adhesive on thickly, but evenly. This is critical; if you miss a spot now, it may be impossible to fill it in later, so keep brushing even after you think the surface is well coated. There is no correct ratio of adhesive to fibers; the fibers will cover whatever amount of adhesive is there.***

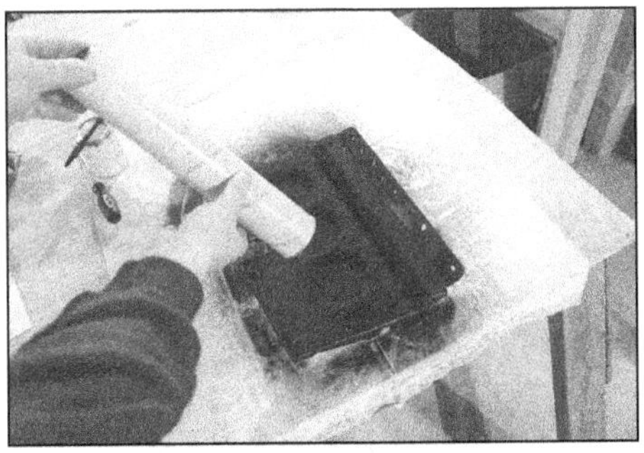

7 *To apply the flocking fibers, invert the partially filled cardboard tube and dust the adhesive-covered surface by pumping the two tubes together to push the fibers out the holes. While pumping the tubes, twist them against each other to stir up the flocking fibers within. Maintain an even distance and angle to the surface.*

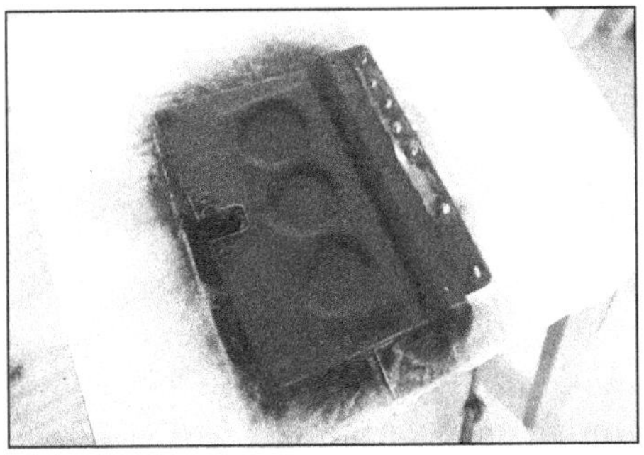

8 *To adequately cover the adhesive, continue applying the flocking fibers long after you think you've sufficiently covered it. Any fibers that don't stick to the adhesive can be recovered by inverting the piece onto the plastic sheet. Don't tap or brush the piece for at least 12 hours, though.*

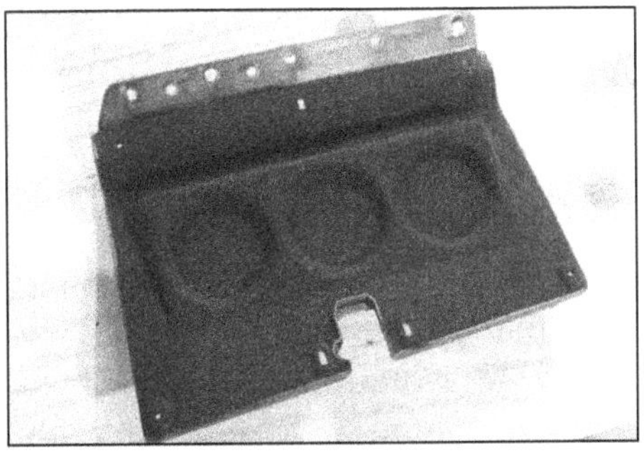

9 *After giving the adhesive up to 7 days to cure, vacuum the excess fibers off the piece, leaving a smooth and evenly flocked surface. Although we flocked this glove box door all at once, it's recommended to flock multiple surfaces (such as those inside a glove box) in stages and to tape off any areas you don't want flocked.*

it out and to cover the entire surface to be flocked. This is a critical step because you won't have a chance to apply more adhesive after you've spread the fibers. Any excess adhesive can be simply wiped off with a paper towel and a little denatured alcohol. A few bubbles may form in the adhesive; pop them with the bristles of the brush before continuing.

One note: The adhesive will soak in to any porous surface. So it's not a big deal if you're flocking steel, but it may pose a problem if you're flocking plastic or vinyl, and will definitely pose a problem if you're flocking wood. The kit instructions recommend shellacking, varnishing, or otherwise sealing the surface you plan to flock before applying the adhesive. If the adhesive is allowed to soak into the surface you're flocking, then less adhesive will be available to get the job done.

The kit gives you a working time of 10 to 15 minutes before applying the fibers, so work quickly, but be thorough with the adhesive application. The kit includes a small brush, which is fine for small to medium parts, but larger parts require larger brushes to evenly coat the part in the working time. The adhesive can be sprayed as long as it is thinned with mineral spirits.

With the adhesive applied, grab the tube of fibers, invert it, and lightly pump the cardboard tubes to blow the fibers over the adhesive-coated part. Hold the tube about 8 to 10 inches from the part and maintain that distance while spreading the fibers. Keep spreading as long as you see any areas that look wet from the glue, and if the part is not perfectly flat, pump the fibers from different angles to evenly coat all sides and shapes of the part. As the kit instructions note, you can't pump too many fibers—only so many will stick to the adhesive. The excess fibers can be reclaimed, so keep at it until you're absolutely sure the fibers cover every molecule of adhesive.

You can turn the part upside down to dump off excess fibers now, but don't tap or brush away the fibers until the adhesive has fully dried. Be prepared to wait. The kit recommends allowing 10 to 15 hours for the adhesive to dry and then another 3 to 7 days for the adhesive to cure completely. To prevent dust from settling on the part during that time, cover the part with something that won't touch the surface of the part—a cardboard box works well.

DonJer claims the nylon fibers (which they offer in a variety of colors) make the flocking water- and UV-resistant, and that the 3-ounce bag of fibers and the small can of adhesive included in the kit are enough to cover 15 square feet of surface. That's more than enough to do the inside of your glove box and the inside of your console. It's also a quick process and shouldn't take more than 1 hour, including cleanup (but, of course, excluding drying time).

Electrical Component, Wiring and Radio Restoration

If you're going to take out your dashboard in this quest for the ultimate interior restoration, you need to address your electrical system—yet another restoration topic that causes most guys to groan. Electrical systems often seem counterintuitive and often frustrate us to no end. As time went on, they became more complex, they added more buzzers and chimes and features, and they became more troublesome to troubleshoot and repair.

But if you leave all that wiring alone and don't at least inspect it now, while you have better access to it, then often down the road—maybe months, maybe years—something in that bundle of wires will go poof. Remember, mice will chew on electrical wires just as soon as they'll chew on anything else; their incisors never stop growing, so they need to chew on something, anything, to keep their incisors in check, and wiring works to that purpose. By chewing through the plastic insulation around the wires, they've then created a big opportunity for a shorted circuit.

Of course, mice aren't the only culprits of electrical trouble. Loose wires, along with wires that chafe and fray on ungrommeted or otherwise unprotected metal surfaces, can short. Corrosion in connectors can cause bad grounds, interrupted circuits, or (most bedeviling) intermittently interrupted circuits. And 40-year-old fusible links give up the ghost every now and then.

The end result of releasing the smoke from the wires could simply cause your muscle car to die by the side of the road, or it could catastrophically send your muscle car up in flames. Do you want to take that chance just because you neglected to check your wiring?

And besides, it could be worse: You could be working on a British car's Lucas electrical system.

Electrical Theory and Components

Entire books have been written exclusively on electrical theory and on wiring automobiles, so to cover those topics in their entirety isn't the aim here. But, much like interiors in general, many gearheads leave all their wiring jobs up to the professionals simply because they refuse to take the time to learn some basics about all those brightly colored wires under their dash.

To understand wiring, you need to understand the basic circuit. And to do that, it often helps to think about electricity in terms of plumbing. Wires are your pipes, and through them, respectively, flow both electricity and water. A battery is similar to a reservoir of water, with the positive terminal at the spigot end and the negative terminal at the fill point; your alternator is similar to a pump that keeps filling the reservoir. Because it'd be pointless to have the water filling and emptying in an ongoing cycle, let's introduce a component: In our plumbing circuit it might be a water wheel, but in our electrical circuit it might be a light bulb. There, now our circuit has a reason for existing.

Two important measurements in an electrical circuit—voltage and amperage—are roughly equivalent to the pressure and flow rate in a plumbed system. An electrical system with higher voltage simply has greater potential or force of electricity, while one rated with higher amperage just has a greater volume of electricity. This is why you can power a 12-volt system with a 6-volt battery—you'll just get a weak result. But you can't power a 6-volt system with a 12-volt battery—twice the push means you'll start overloading components in no time.

Voltage and amperage are obviously interconnected, and the relationship between the two depends on the resistance in the circuit. Ohm's Law expressed that relationship as V=I x R, where V stands for voltage, I stands for current or amperage, and R stands for resistance. You don't have to memorize the formula as you did back in high-school physics class, but for our purposes, it does illustrate how, when the voltage remains the same and resistance increases, current naturally decreases.

By the way, this is all relevant mostly to direct-current (DC) circuits rather than alternating-current (AC) circuits. That's good, because your muscle car uses DC circuits. And, of course, by the beginning of the muscle car era, every manufacturer had switched to a 12-volt system. You're only likely to encounter 6-volt systems in cars older than the mid-1950s, and you're only likely to encounter 24-volt systems in military vehicles.

So in our basic circuit, we have the battery, we have the wires to conduct the flow of electricity, and we have the light bulb. Unlike pipes, however, when wires are left disconnected, they don't just let the electricity spill out. Instead, the flow of electricity stops and nothing happens—you have a dead circuit. The same thing happens when you introduce a switch to the circuit. When turned off, the switch introduces a break in the current and the circuit dies; the light bulb goes off. When turned on, the switch allows the current to flow once again, and the light bulb lights up. The same thing also happens when the grounds in your circuits become too corroded and no longer conduct electricity, except that happens without your control, which is why it's important to check and clean all exposed grounds and other connectors.

Aside from the battery, switches, and light bulbs (or fans, or power window motors, or any other device that uses electricity for a specific purpose), you're likely to encounter a couple other basic components: the relay and the fuse.

The relay is essentially a remote-operated switch. Applying an electrical circuit to a relay (usually with a switch) causes an electromagnet in the relay to close or open a second, separate circuit. This is done for a variety of reasons, usually to provide the shortest physical path possible between two points, because excessive wire in a circuit results in excessive resistance.

The fuse is simply a piece of metal designed to blow when current in that circuit exceeds a predetermined amperage. Fusible links often performed the same task in vehicles from the muscle car era, though they relied on sections of wires in a circuit designed to melt above a certain amperage. The advantage of a fuse over a fusible link is that the former can be easily inspected and replaced, while the latter is hard to locate and can pose a fire hazard if it melts too violently. Fusible links were really used to protect the car's wiring from overloads in case of a violent wreck that pinched the wiring. Consider replacing your fusible links with fuses of the same rating, even if the fusible links have yet to blow.

As long as your muscle car's electrical system has remained untouched, the most common cause for a blown fuse is a short circuit, which happens when the plastic insulation around a wire has been compromised and the wire touches a nearby ground. You'll keep blowing fuses until you've addressed that short circuit. To find the short circuit, you'll likely want to use a multimeter, also called a multitester, which can measure voltage, amperage, and resistance. To use a multitester, simply turn the dial to the scale you want to measure, then use the two probes attached to the multitester to form a temporary circuit.

Once you've located the source of the short circuit (and hopefully addressed the cause of the compromised wiring), it's time to repair the

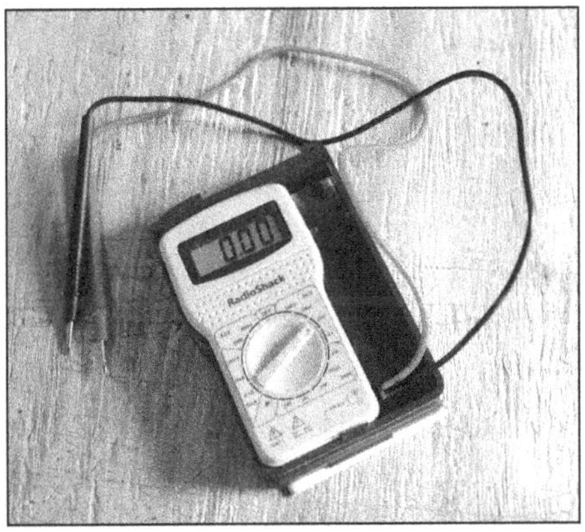

Multitesters are available with either a digital screen or a dial. When troubleshooting your muscle car's electrical system, the two most common functions on the multitester that you'll want to use are the voltage (set your dial to 20V, as we did here) and the resistance (set your dial to one of the ohm ranges, depending on the amount of resistance you expect to find).

wire itself. However, diagnosing and resolving the full range of potential electrical problems is outside the scope of this book. If your particular restoration project requires extensive electrical work, I recommend *Automotive Wiring and Electrical Systems* by Tony Candela.

Wiring Repair

What very few people who work on cars nowadays seem to understand is that wire nuts are not permanent solutions for splicing a wire, at least not in an automobile. In your house, it's fine to twist up a pair of stripped wires and toss a wire nut on them because your house isn't constantly moving and vibrating. Your car, however, does move and vibrate, which is one of many reasons why you shouldn't shop for car supplies at your local home-improvement warehouse.

Wire nuts are a decent temporary solution. If you're on the road without access to a soldering iron and just need to go home, fine. But once you get there, you need to come up with a more permanent fix for your wires, which means you'll want to solder them together.

One quick note to keep in mind before undertaking any electrical work on your car: Disconnect the battery first. If you neglect or otherwise forget to do so, a shock from your car's 12-volt DC electrical system might not be enough to kill you, but it sure could make things a little uncomfortable for you, and the real danger in leaving the battery connected is to your car's components—relays, fuses, bulbs—none of them much appreciate unexpected jolts of electricity. A battery disconnect switch can take the hassle out of repeatedly removing and replacing battery cables from battery posts, but is also useful in preventing battery drain when your muscle car sits out in winter, and in preventing thefts.

The drawback to soldering wires is that the solder makes them stiff at the joint and, thus, more prone to snapping than an uninterrupted piece of wiring. So you'll want to make the joint as strong as possible with as little solder as possible. One of the strongest methods of wire splicing is to strip about 1 to 1½ inches of insulation from the wire on either side of the splice. For thicker-gauge wire, strip more, and for thinner gauge wire, strip less. Only use a quality wire stripper designed for multiple-gauge wires; stripping wire with a knife or with your teeth may nick the strands of wire underneath, causing a mechanical weakness in the wire.

At this point consider the amount of strain that the wire will be under. You don't want to leave the wire shorter after your repair; it will become tighter and more prone to snapping. But you don't want to give

Wiring Repair

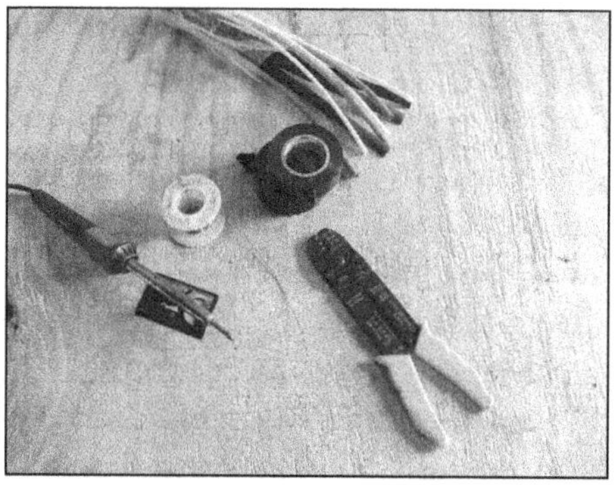

1 ***For wire repair, you need a soldering iron, a roll of solder, a wire stripper (which usually has an integrated wire cutter, though we often prefer to use side cutters to snip wires), and either heat shrink tubing or electrical tape. For simple repairs, don't concern yourself with the many different types of soldering irons out there—they all work well.***

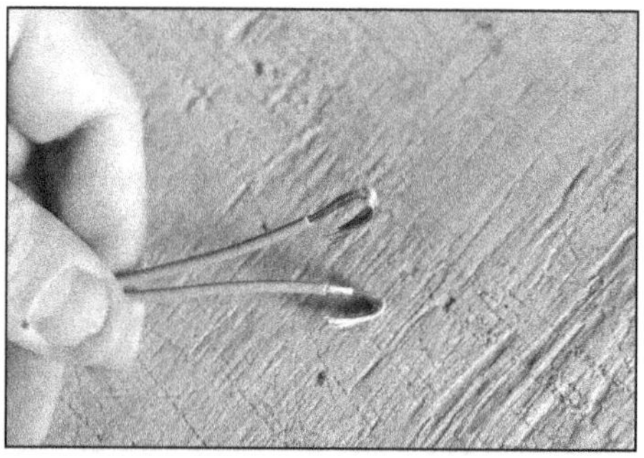

2 ***The strongest wire splicing method we've come across starts with stripping about 1 inch of insulation from the wires, then bending the ends of the wires back on themselves to form a couple of hooks. Note that the copper strands remain shiny and uncorroded; dirty, corroded strands of wire should be replaced.***

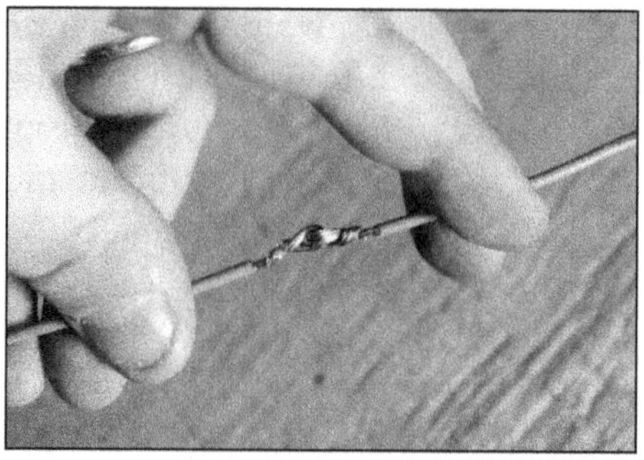

3 ***Next, hook each wire into the other and twist the hooked ends of the wires back over themselves. Though the wires may flop around at this point, they're very difficult to pull apart. Note how little bulk this repair creates.***

it too much slack either, as the wire may come into contact with a heat source or spinning blades, or it may be pinched somewhere else. If you find your wire is too short, cut a scrap piece of wire of the same gauge and splice it into your repair to extend the wire. If you find it is too long, consider incorporating what professional electricians call a service loop elsewhere in the circuit.

Cut an appropriate length of the appropriate gauge of heat shrink tubing and slip it over one of the wires at this point. Then bend the strands of both wires back over themselves in a gentle curve, back no farther than the insulation. You're essentially making two hooks—like two pieces of Velcro—and you're going to hook them together in the same way. After hooking the wires together, twist the strands of the wires back around themselves.

With the strands twisted tightly, try pulling the two wires apart. This joint requires a good yank (more than you'd see in typical automotive use) to separate the two wires now. Add in the benefit of a sleek, less bulky repair, and it's about as good as you're going to find for a joint between two wires. You could actually slip the heat shrink tubing over the joint now and be done, but adding a bit of solder will secure the connection. The soldered area won't have the same level of tensile strength or electrical conductivity as an uninterrupted strand of wire, but using higher quality solder—that is, a solder with greater concentrations of tin over lead and one with fewer impurities—will minimize the losses in strength and conductivity.

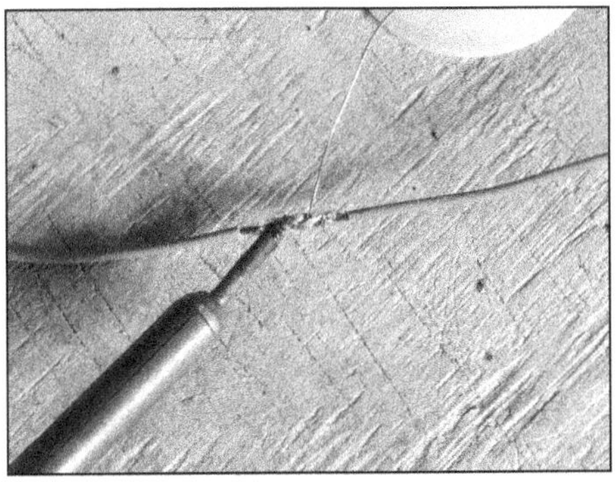

4 ***Here's where you could really use a third hand sometimes. Apply the tip of the soldering iron to the joint between the two wires and, after a minute or so, the wires will be hot enough to allow the solder to wick into the strands.***

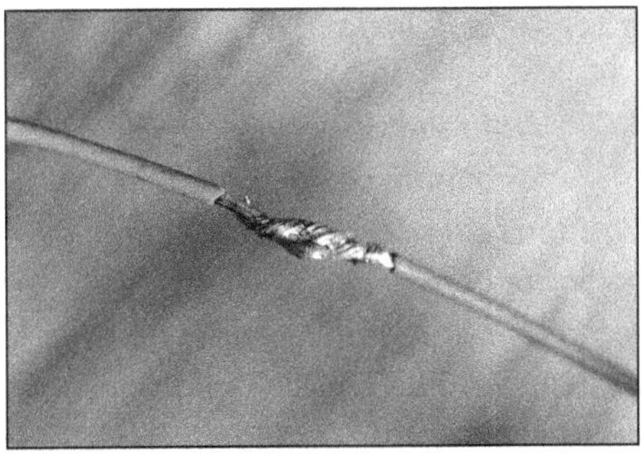

5 ***A good solder joint shouldn't have any big blobs of solder—those come with applying the solder directly to the soldering iron—and should prevent the joint from wiggling, which could lead to an intermittent connection.***

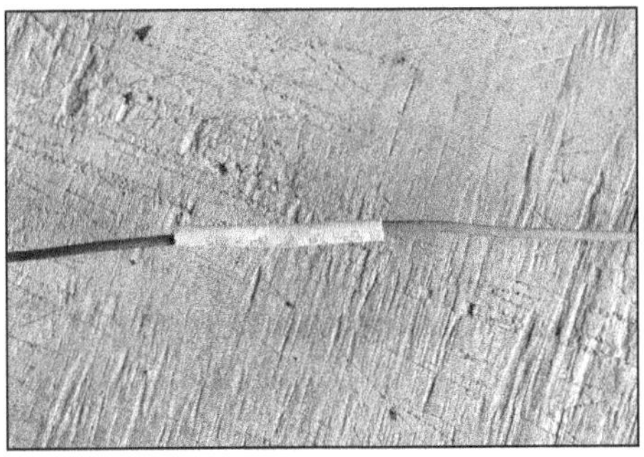

6 ***After letting the solder joint cool, slip the heat shrink over the joint so that it overlaps the insulation on both sides. Logistically, you should slip the heat shrink over one of the wires before making the connection. A bit of directed heat from a butane lighter or from a heat gun will seal the tubing to the connection.***

So, with your soldering iron warmed up, clean off the tip with a damp sponge and apply the heated tip to the wire joint. Give it a second or two to heat up the strands of the wires, then apply the solder to the hot wires—not to the tip of the soldering iron. As long as the wires are hot enough, the solder will flow between the strands by capillary action and it won't be necessary to move the soldering iron. Apply just enough solder to fill the joint; you don't want to see big blobs of excess solder anywhere near the joint.

Remove the soldering iron and let the joint cool before slipping the heat shrink tubing over the joint. Whether you use a lighter or a heat gun, start heating the shrink tubing at the center and work your way out toward the ends; doing so prevents pockets of air from getting trapped. The heat shrink tubing should conform tightly to the wire joint—if it's too loose, you used a piece of tubing that was too large—and its ends should overlap and seal against the wire insulation.

Of course, not all wiring repairs take place in the middle of a wire (where the above method works the best). Many take place at the end of a wire, where a terminal has corroded or gone missing. The first order of business then is to find an appropriate replacement terminal. Your corner auto parts store should have a good selection of automotive-grade terminals. Pick up a large variety pack, even if you only need one terminal out of the pack—it's a pain to have to keep venturing out to the store for one or two small terminals. If the corner auto parts store doesn't have a good selection of terminals, you can find high-quality terminals by browsing the catalogs of industrial supply companies such as Terminal Supply Co. or McMaster-Carr.

Most parts-store terminals, however, have cheap plastic boots on one end, color coded to the gauge range of wire that the connector works best with. They're a good idea for fieldwork, but for a permanent solution, it's best to strip off that boot, exposing the crimp end of the terminal, and use a short section of heat shrink tubing in its place. Follow this procedure:

- Strip a short section of the wire—just enough to fit in the crimp section of the terminal—and insert it in the terminal.
- Place the terminal so the seam of the crimp area will fold in on the wire instead of pucker out away from the wire.
- Using your crimping tool, insert the crimp end of the terminal in the appropriate slot for the gauge of the wire, then crimp the terminal two or three times, depending on the length of the crimp section.
- For an extra-strong connection, solder the crimped area.
- Cover the crimp with heat shrink tubing.
- Coat the terminal with dielectric grease to prevent further corrosion.

What if you don't want to use heat shrink tubing? Well, nothing compares to properly applied heat shrink tubing when it comes to preventing corrosion of the wires exposed in your repair, but it is rather pricey, and if you're making numerous splices, those costs can add up quickly. Garden-variety electrical tape, stretched tight, can seal splices just as well. However, the glue in electrical tape often oozes out under high temperatures and creates a sticky mess, so use electrical tape sparingly. If wrapping an entire wiring harness, instead of electrical tape, use a product such as Eastwood's Tommy Tape or 3M's self-vulcanizing tape, which is not adhesive backed, but instead clings to itself when lightly stretched.

Finally, when using clamps to secure a wiring harness, try to avoid uninsulated metal clamps, not necessarily because they conduct electricity, but because their bare edges can chafe away the insulation from wires over time, allowing the wire to short to ground through the clamp. Instead, use clamps that have a rubber pad that covers the edges of the clamp. For the same reason, make sure every wire that passes through the firewall or other piece of sheetmetal has a grommet to pass

Wiring Repair *CONTINUED*

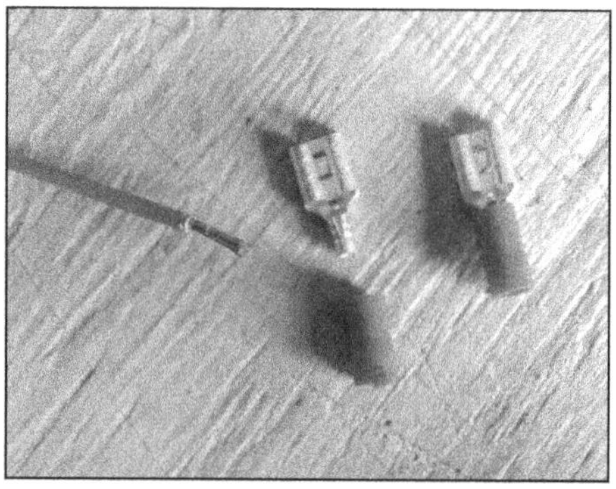

7 ***With just enough of the wire stripped for the terminal, we selected the right gauge of female spade terminal, then removed the plastic boot from the terminal. Plastic boots don't seal against the elements as well as a small section of heat shrink or a small length of electrical tape, so it's best to remove the boots from the terminals.***

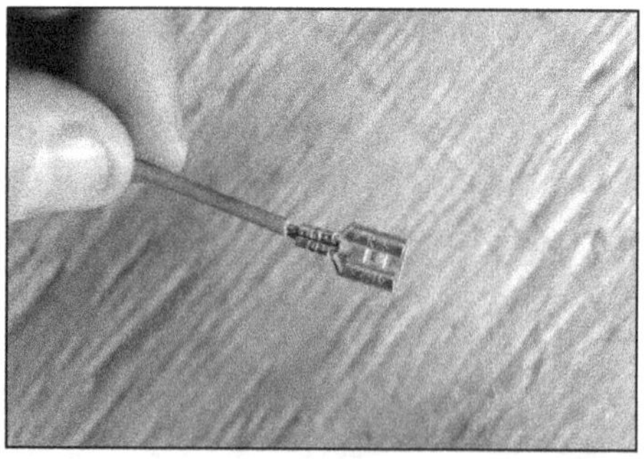

8 ***Note that we crimped the terminal so the seam folds in, and thus grips the wire strands for a stronger connection. Also note the tiny tab at the end of the copper strands of the wire. The tab limits how far you can push the wire into the terminal, to avoid the wire interfering with the terminal's connection.***

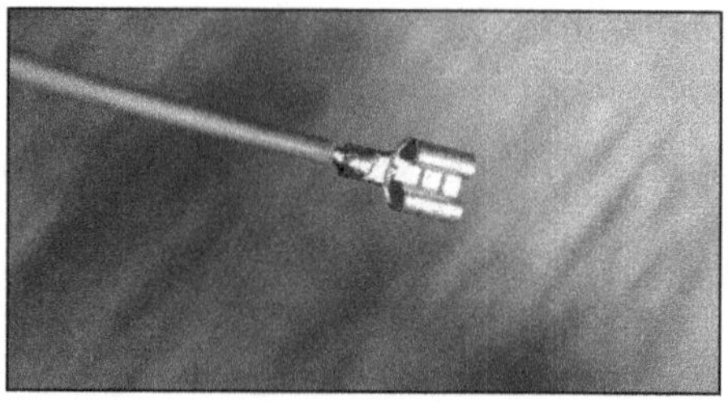

9 ***Next, we secured the crimp with a dab of solder just to be sure that it won't work loose over time. We'll follow the crimp with a short length of heat shrink and a dab of dielectric grease to prevent corrosion of the terminal.***

through, and thus prevent abrasion and unintentional grounding.

If the wiring harness is missing, extensively damaged, or if its repair requires too much effort, several companies offer partial and complete reproduction-wiring harnesses. Thanks to the burgeoning street rod aftermarket, other companies offer complete custom harnesses designed specifically for your muscle car and for its particular electric requirements.

Radio Upgrades

Looking back on the option sheets of most muscle cars from the 1960s and 1970s, one option tended to cost much more than all the other options. Big-block engines? Nah, just a couple hundred dollars here and there for the less exotic ones. Air conditioning? Pricey, but still not a bank breaker. Instead, the top-end stereo options usually topped the lists at around $500 and could include all the latest technology: FM! Balance! Station seeking! Push-button channel selection!

And back then, just as they do today, teenage boys spent as much, if not more, on their tunes as they did on their engines. Maybe they didn't always buy the top-end stereo, however. And they'd certainly freak if they witnessed the audio technology we have today: multichannel, high-wattage sound systems able to play a near-endless stream of music from satellite radio and MP3 players. Internet radio piped through your car stereo has even become a possibility within the last year.

Over the decades, a number of would-be stereophiles have attempted to upgrade the stock sound systems in their muscle cars, and in that process, they probably became one of the main causes of door panel, package tray, and faceplate replacement in muscle cars today. On the plus side, many of those parts are reproduced today, and I cover their replacement in other chapters of this book; I even cover plastic repair in Chapter 6, for those of you with butchered radio faceplates. However, it also means

Here's our traditional before picture of the radio that we're converting to digital. It's a typical mid-1960s Chevrolet AM/FM push-button radio with only a tone dial and no provision for balance or fade control. We'll add the latter two, along with four-channel sound and the ability to play external devices, such as CD or MP3 players.

Playing MP3 Songs on an Original Stereo

So let's say you don't want to go through the expense of converting your muscle car's radio to include all that latest technology. Or your muscle car is all original and you'd like it to remain that way. Or you really don't want to bother with removing your radio from the dashboard. But at the same time, your kids have introduced you to MP3 players and you'd like to take your collection of Jefferson Airplane MP3s on the road with you. (Or is it The Doors? Ozzy Osbourne? What do you crazy kids listen to nowadays?)

Fortunately, there's still a way to play MP3s over your muscle car's radio without making a single modification to the radio itself, as long as your muscle car can pick up FM stations. Most MP3 players can be mated to a device (available at any mall across America) that converts the MP3 player's output into a low-range FM output—essentially turning your MP3 player into an FM station. Just tune your radio to the FM channel over which the device broadcasts.

Of course, this won't work on an AM-only radio. And it won't add four-channel, high-wattage sound like a conversion kit will. But it remains a quick and simple option that your muscle car's original radio is long gone, and you're going to want to find another one.

Fortunately, another advance in technology over the last decade now allows you to stuff all that modern audio wizardry into the simple, little, one-speaker radios and two-speaker stereos that came with your muscle car, all while leaving those radios and stereos looking stock and without any extra controls added. It'll cost a little bit more than a typical stereo restoration back to totally stock innards, but it'll be worth it when you tell your kids they can plug their iPods into your Chevelle.

The downside of the process is that it's difficult to do yourself. Even if you're handy with a soldering iron and surface-mount circuit boards, you'd still have to find a digital conversion kit, which is not sold as a retail item to the general public. Only certified installers can buy the digital conversion kits, so to obtain a conversion, you'll have to send your radio to an installer.

An alternative is to buy one of the many ready-made digital radios out there that fit into your car's dash without cutting the dash apart. You get the same results as a digitally converted radio, but many of these digital radios have digital displays instead of a tuner dial on the face. A digitally converted radio will have the exact same faceplate and dial that the radio came with from the factory.

The digital conversion starts with an inspection and disassembly of the radio. The chassis of the radio, stamped out of sheetmetal, is usually used to ground circuits, so several wires are likely soldered directly to the chassis and will need to be de-soldered or clipped. Also, because the radio provides a flat, hidden, horizontal surface, a common source of damage to a radio comes from mice, which often find the top of a radio a good place to hang out and nest. So while disassembling the radio, wear a dust mask

Radio Upgrades

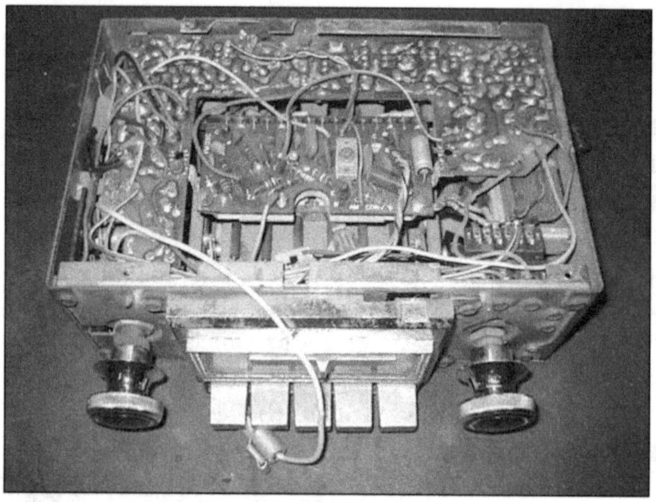

1 ***Disassembly begins with the top plate. The 1960s solid-state electronics were actually rather advanced for their day—no tubes and the ability to pick up both bands of radio. Nearly all of the circuitry, however, will be scrapped for the digital conversion.***

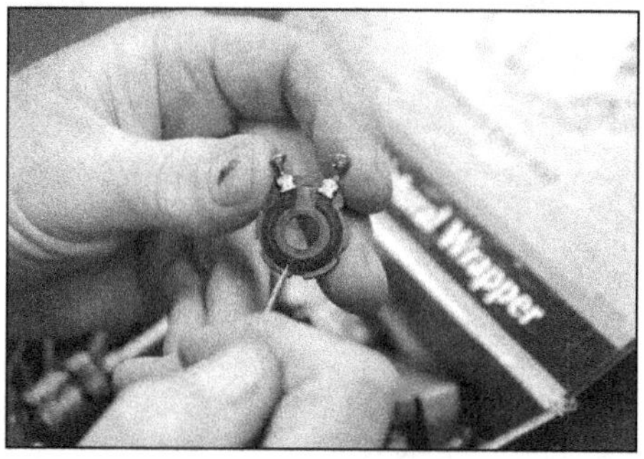

2 ***If you take apart any potentiometer in a volume, tone, balance, or fade knob, you'll find a disc like this one, which is a very simple circuit board with a variable resistor embedded into it. A malfunctioning volume control can, in most cases, be traced to this disc, which is easily replaced.***

3 ***While the radio is apart, the chassis is sandblasted clean, then the individual chassis parts are sprayed with Rust-Oleum's Hammertone paint. Note that we only sprayed the outside of the chassis parts; the insides will remain bare metal to serve as grounding points for the new electronics.***

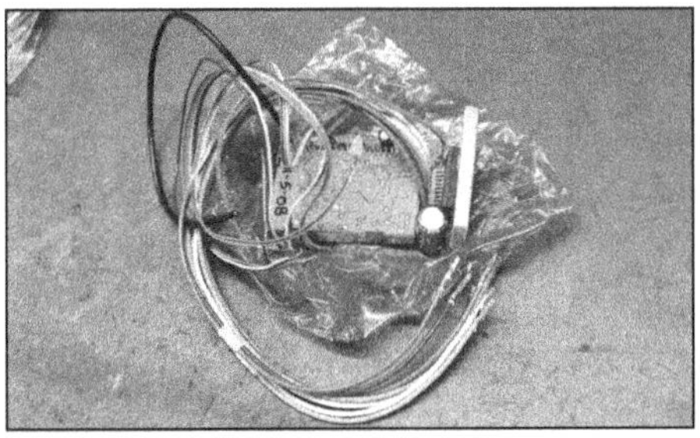

4 The heart of the digital conversion is a much smaller circuit board with attached heat sink, and a spaghetti of wires. The pre-terminated wires go to the speakers, while the rest attaches to the radio's existing controls.

5 The tuning mechanism of the existing radio will remain with the converted radio. All these mechanisms are checked for correct operation and repaired if necessary. The six horizontal cylinders are the actual tuner that figures out what frequency you're listening to, based on the physical position of the smaller rods inside the cylinders. An AM tuner, with just three cylinders, is on the left for comparison.

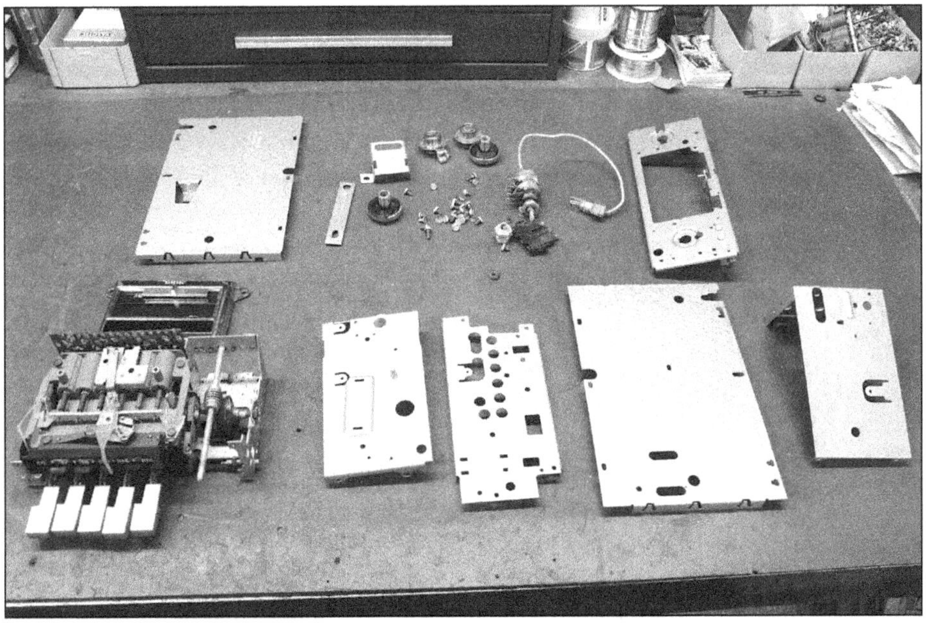

6 All of the radio's original components to be reused are laid out, including the cleaned and polished faceplate and the original volume/tone knob. They will be inspected, and if necessary, repaired.

until the dust and debris inside the radio has been removed.

Because the digital conversion kit uses the existing mechanical workings of the radio, but replaces most of the electronics, check all of the mechanisms, including the knobs, the push buttons, and any selector switches, to make sure they work properly. If they don't, the mechanisms will need to be repaired or replaced. For example, radios are often damaged during shipping—or even while in the car—when the knobs are struck from the front and the force of the impact shatters the switches and potentiometers behind the knobs.

However, in most cases, any damage to a radio is in the electronics and is done over time as the components, such as the capacitors and transistors, either decay from use or fail from voltage spikes. Returning to our example of the knobs, if you were to take apart the potentiometer that the knob turns, you'll usually find a thin, round circuit board with a copper trace embedded into it. With repeated use over the decades, the copper trace starts to break apart, forming a poor connection, and can only be realistically repaired by replacing that little component. If the entire potentiometer can be replaced, it's often quicker and easier to do just that.

Fortunately, most of the electronics inside a stock 1960s radio are removed for the digital conversion. All that really needs to remain are the contacts on the switches and potentiometers behind the tuning and volume knobs, and the tuner itself, which looks like a row of either three or six conjoined cylinders—three for AM and six (actually two banks of three) for FM. In most muscle cars,

Radio Upgrades *CONTINUED*

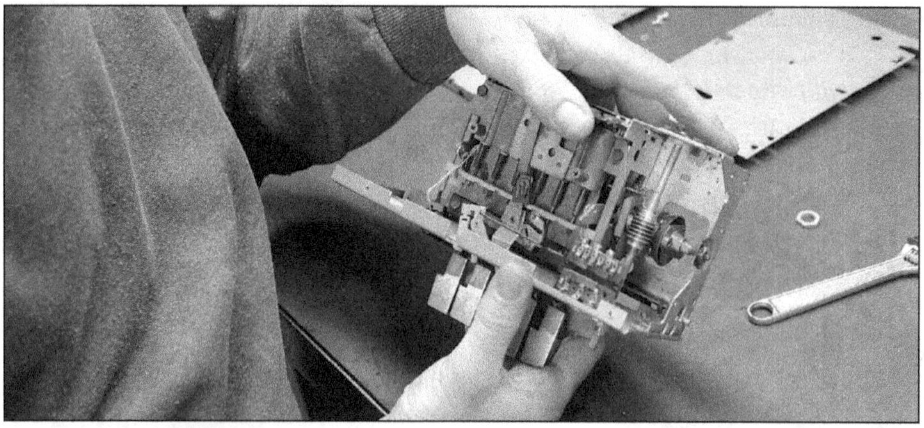

7 *Reassembly begins by mounting the tuning mechanism to the chassis and the faceplate. The device attached to the spiral gear on the right side of the tuner mechanism adjusts the operation of the push buttons and can be tricky to repair.*

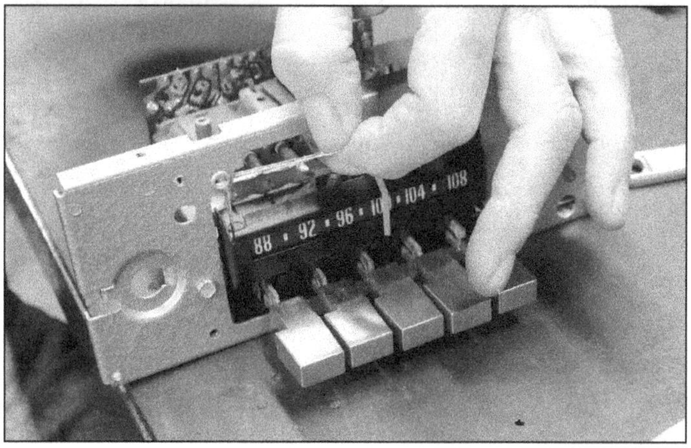

8 *It may seem rather simplistic, but this string, when attached to the slider on the faceplate, pulls the FM dial into view when the FM band is selected. A separate switch, connected to the slider by a short rod, electronically chooses the band and will be connected to the digital conversion kit.*

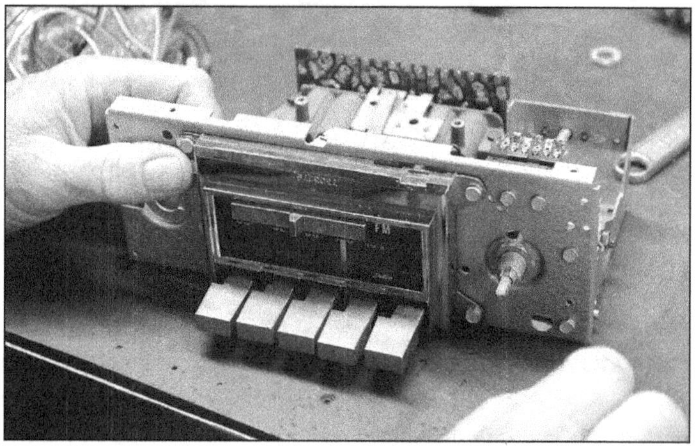

9 *The pull string is attached to the slider and the polished faceplate is screwed to the chassis. Note the stalk of the tuner control on the right and how its nut is tightened against the chassis. These nuts are meant to remain tightened against the chassis, while a second set of nuts is used for the actual installation of the radio in the car.*

10 *The top and bottom plates of the chassis are left off for now, to install the digital conversion kit. The knobs will go back on the tuner and volume controls to ensure that those operate smoothly. The circuit board above the tuner knob is the AM/FM switch that will connect to the digital conversion kit.*

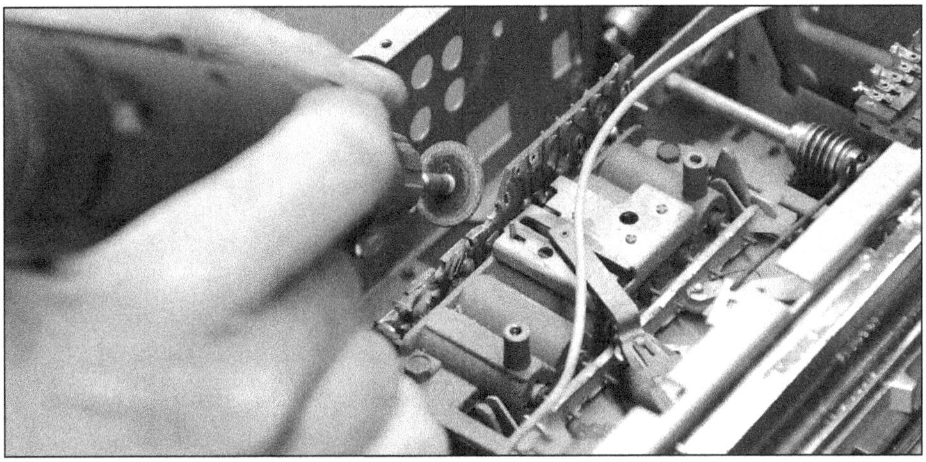

11 *The circuit board behind the tuner cylinders will eventually connect to the digital conversion kit as well, but most of it is no longer necessary and will interfere with the chosen mounting location of the conversion kit. Because of that, we took a rotary tool and carved out the interfering section of the circuit board.*

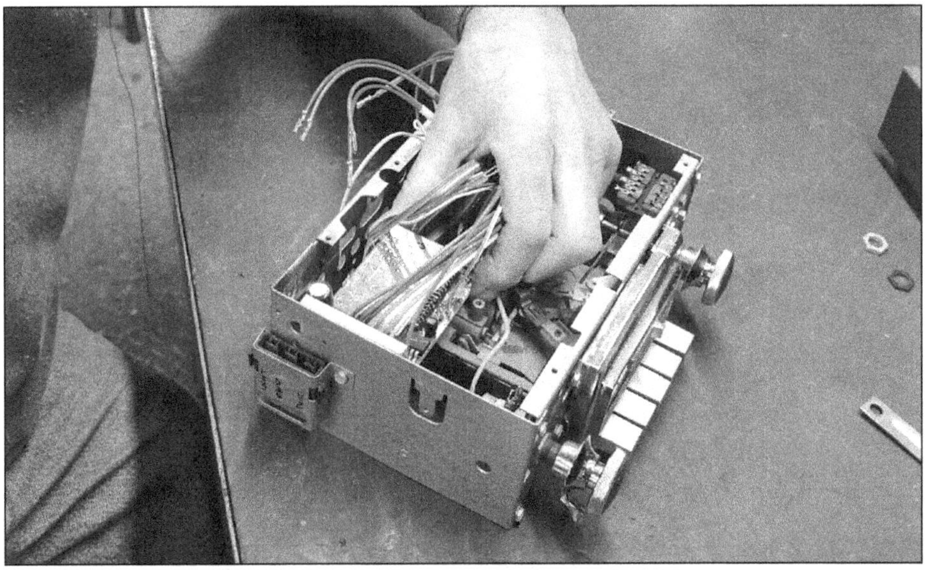

12 *Though some radios of the 1960s and 1970s offer limited space for the digital conversion kit and require more-creative mounting methods, this one fit rather well after trimming. The heat sink will mount directly to the chassis using holes already drilled and threaded in the heat sink.*

13 *We used a second matching heat sink to locate the holes we needed to drill in the chassis. This method of locating the holes takes all the guesswork out of the process. It can be done with a paper template, just as easily.*

14 *With the locations for the holes marked with a center punch, they can be drilled out. Though we had plenty of room inside the chassis, we still drilled cautiously and slowly to avoid unintentional damage.*

Radio Upgrades *CONTINUED*

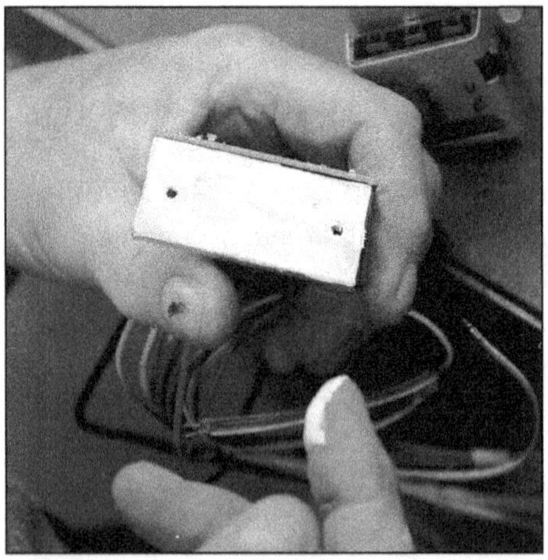

15 *Thermal grease applied to the side of the heat sink facing the radio chassis helps transfer heat away from sensitive electronics and to the chassis. Though heat isn't much of a worry at normal volumes, heading toward the maximum 45-watt output of each channel will generate enough heat to warrant heat dissipation measures.*

16 *The heat sink is aluminum and thus doesn't act as a ground, so all the grounding for the digital conversion kit goes through one wire to the radio's original ground. Not believing that one wire was a sufficient ground, we soldered a short length of wire from the conversion kit's circuit board straight to the chassis.*

17 *The connections can now be made, starting with the blue and white wires, which provide the signal from the tuner to the conversion kit. Also note the bare wire soldered from the conversion kit to the tuning mechanism. Besides providing another ground for the conversion kit, it also acts as a brace at the normally unsupported end of the conversion kit's circuit board.*

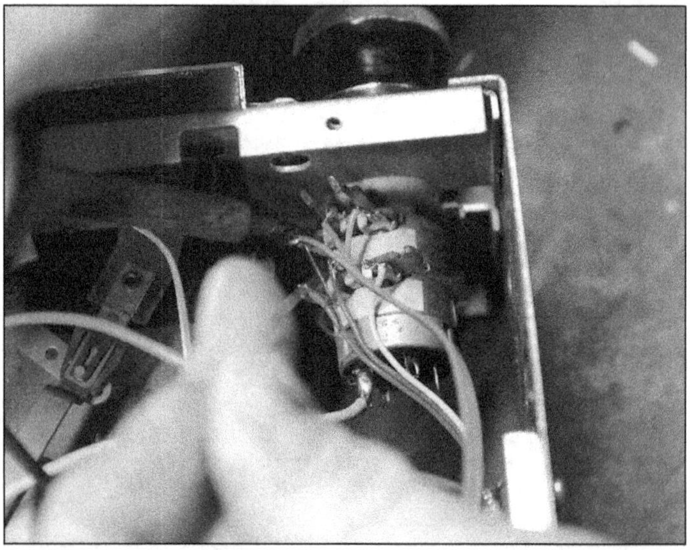

18 *We then made connections from the digital conversion kit to the radio's original volume and tone knob. We were careful to get the polarity correct on the volume knob in particular. This particular knob also functions as the power switch, so reversing the polarity will cause the radio to jump to full volume instead of low volume immediately after switching it on.*

19 ***A short length of coaxial cable connects the digital conversion kit to the radio's original antenna connector. The car's original antenna remains the same and doesn't need to be changed.***

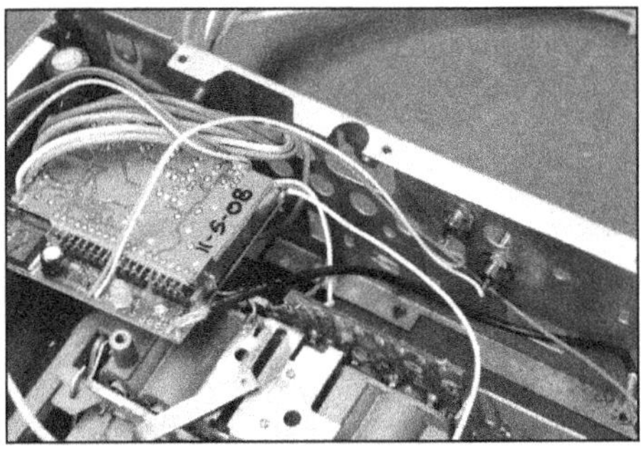

20 ***A pair of RCA jacks, available at any electronics store and used to hook up external music devices, were mounted to the back of the chassis. Fortunately, this chassis had several holes of the right diameter for the RCA jacks. The gray and white wires connect the RCA jacks to the digital conversion board.***

21 ***Remaining connections include those for the AM/FM switch and for the 12-volt power, the latter of which is done using the radio's original power feed. The light bulb that illuminates the dial mounts to the top plate of this particular radio, so it's left dangling for now.***

technically the tuner is called a variable inductance transducer, and what it does is take the mechanical input (from your fingers turning the tuner knob) and convert it into an electrical output signal. If you leave the tuner mechanism hooked up, you can watch a series of pistons slide in and out of the cylinders as you turn the tuner knob to go up and down the dial. Combined with the antenna, the signal that the transducer outputs then becomes translated into something that your ears recognize by all the electronic guts of the radio that are about to be replaced.

With the radio disassembled, the easiest part of the restoration comes next. All the sheetmetal parts of the chassis are sandblasted to remove any rust or debris, then painted in Rust-Oleum's Hammertone finish. Only the outer surfaces are painted, however; the inner surfaces are left bare to allow the chassis to continue to be used as a grounding path.

The faceplate should now be cleaned and polished with any commonly available plastic polish (see Chapter 2), as should any chrome trim that is visible when the radio is installed in the dashboard. Knobs should be cleaned or replaced with reproductions, if available. As long as the mechanisms inside the radio are still functional, they don't necessarily need to be taken apart to be cleaned; a few blasts of compressed air, followed by an acid-based wheel cleaner, quickly rinsed away with water and dried with another few blasts of compressed air, should clean out the mechanisms.

Those mechanisms, along with the tuner, faceplate, and knobs, can now be reassembled to the chassis, leaving off the top and bottom plates of the chassis for now.

Next the actual digital conversion kit—a compact circuit board with a large aluminum heat sink and a number of wires coming off it—can be placed in the chassis. Where it goes in the chassis depends on the space available inside each different radio. If not enough space is available, the tuner's circuit board can be partially trimmed away with a rotary tool—just be careful to leave at least the area on the circuit board with the

Radio Upgrades *CONTINUED*

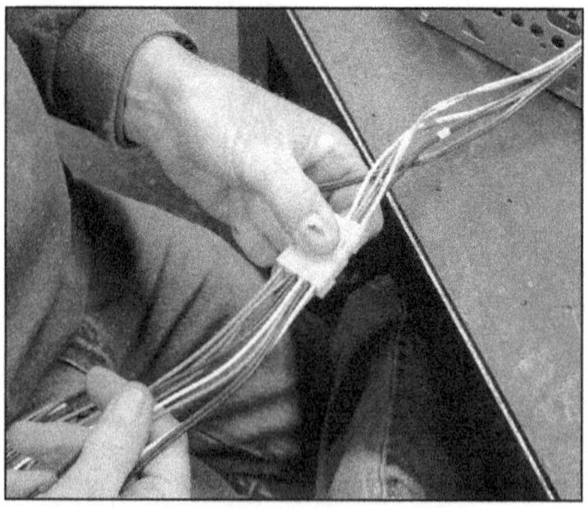

22 ***We pulled the speaker wires through the back of the chassis and connected them to the harness supplied with the digital conversion kit. In lieu of a grommet to prevent chafing on the hole in the chassis, we wrapped the wires in electrical tape at that point and used a plastic clamp to secure them to the outside of the chassis.***

23 ***Before reassembling the converted radio, we tested it to ensure that we made all the right connections and then programmed it to learn both AM and FM bands. (The kits come unprogrammed in case somebody installs one in a Europe-bound car.)***

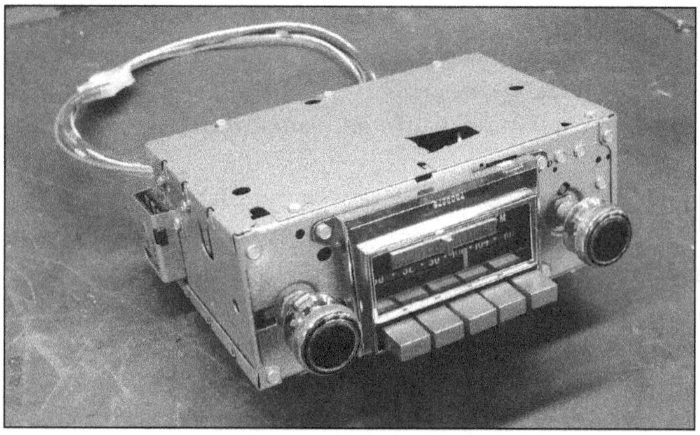

24 ***Once the conversion checks out, we finished the reassembly by hooking the light bulb to the top plate and screwing on the top and bottom plates. From the outside, it simply looks like a restored radio, with absolutely no indication that it'll now play music from any audio device you can conceive, in top quality sound.***

contacts to which the digital conversion kit will connect. If trimming won't create enough room for the kit's circuit board, then as long as space permits outside the chassis itself (but still behind the dash), it may be necessary to fabricate a small sheetmetal box just large enough to house the circuit board, and then secure the box to the radio chassis. Wherever the circuit board is placed, it should not interfere with the mounting location of the stock illuminating lamp. And if you're going all out, consider an LED bulb for the lamp; this is one bulb you'd hate to replace when it burns out.

The heat sink, which dissipates the heat created when the four channels (at 45 watts each) are cranked up to full volume, is also threaded for a couple screws, so the circuit board should ideally be mounted with the heat sink up against the radio chassis, which will help dissipate the heat away from the heat sink. To take the guesswork out of drilling holes for the two mounting screws on the chassis, make a paper template of the side of the heat sink that will mount up against the chassis and mark the mounting holes on the template. Hold the heat sink up against the chassis and place the paper template on the other side of the chassis, but in the same location as the heat sink. It's now possible to mark the holes with a scratch awl and then center punch and drill them out. File the holes so the heat sink will sit flush against the chassis, then blow away any shavings or filings. Before actually mounting the heat sink and circuit board, apply a thin layer of thermal grease, available in any hobby or computer store, to the mating surface of the heat sink.

Now comes the tough part that requires the training. A couple specific wires already soldered to the circuit board are soldered at the other end to the tuner, to catch the AM or FM signal. A couple short lengths of wire provide additional grounds from the circuit board to the inside of the chassis. More wires connect the circuit board to the AM/FM switch, to the volume potentiometer, to the tone potentiometer, to the balance potentiometer (if included), and to the antenna connector. Yet another pair of wires connects the circuit board to a pair of RCA jacks, holes for which are drilled in the back of the chassis.

Another wire connects the circuit board to the power source and the power switch. In some radios, the plug for the power and ground wires outside of the radio is separate from the plug for the speakers, and in those cases, the speaker plug can be discarded, but the power plug can remain in place. The ground wire for the power plug is soldered directly to the case, and a capacitor can be used on the power wire to reduce electrical noise.

An optional LED can be connected to the circuit board and hot glued to an unobstructed location behind the faceplate. The LED has three colors: green when the power is on, yellow when the converter picks up an FM stereo station, and red when it picks up an AM station.

Finally, the bundle of wires for the speakers, already connected to the circuit board, is threaded through one of the holes in the back of the chassis. The wires come preterminated and can be snapped into a connector plug; the other half of the plug is supplied with its own matching wires, which can then be spliced into the existing speaker wiring. Make sure the colors of the wires all correspond on either side of the plug. One additional wire in the bundle provides 12-volt power to an external device, such as a CD player or satellite radio receiver.

If you want to keep your muscle car in a state where it can be returned to exact showroom condition, or if you're otherwise queasy about snipping the perfectly good wires in the factory speaker harness in your car, then it's a good idea to create an adapter harness to go between the factory speaker harness and the new speaker plug that is supplied in the digital conversion kit. To create an adapter harness, simply locate the radio half of the factory speaker plug (which should have still been attached to your original stereo when you removed it from the dashboard) and cut it from the radio's original electronics. Splice the wires into the appropriate wires from the speaker side of the conversion kit's plug. Or, to make matters simpler, use your car's original speaker plug in place of the digital conversion kit's speaker plug.

With the speaker wiring taken care of, the digital conversion kit is then programmed to learn the entire FM and AM frequency ranges (it can also be programmed to learn European frequency ranges) and tested. If any of the connections between the circuit board and the radio mechanisms are made backward, the radio could potentially not work, or it could not work as intended. For example, one pair of connections on the volume potentiometer, when made backward, isn't a big deal unless the power switch is combined with the volume knob, in which case, the radio goes to full volume immediately after it's switched on.

Here comes the ingenious part of the whole deal. If the radio was originally an AM-only radio, it now receives both AM and FM. To switch between the two bands, turn the radio off, wait five seconds, then turn it back on.

If the radio originally came without balance or fade controls, those are now controlled by the tone knob. To adjust the balance, first tune the radio to a station and adjust the tone, then quickly tune the radio to the bottom of the dial; when the station last playing starts playing again, the tone knob can be used to control the balance. Similarly, to adjust the fade, tune the radio to a station, then quickly tune the radio to the top of the dial; when the station last playing starts playing again, the tone knob can be used to control the fade.

The other genius aspect of the digital conversion is that it doesn't require a special switch for an external music device. Using the RCA jacks, any such device—from a CD player to a satellite radio receiver to an MP3 player—can be connected to your stereo. (You could theoretically also connect an 8-track or even a record player to your car stereo this way; the latter is not recommended for obvious vibration reasons, while the former is not recommended unless you plan on growing a 1970s moustache and letting your chest hair hang out while wearing bellbottoms and heading to a disco.) The circuit board will automatically recognize a signal coming in through the RCA jacks and switch away from the radio to that input. When the circuit board no longer senses a signal coming from the RCA jacks, it automatically switches back to the radio.

When everything works to satisfaction, the top and bottom plates of the chassis go back on, and the reassembled radio can go back in the dashboard. If you're planning on using an MP3 player or any other device that you don't want permanently installed in your muscle car, consider running a cable with RCA jacks on one end and a mini stereo jack on the other end up to your glove box, or any other more easily reached location than the back of the radio. For more permanent external audio devices, consider installing them in the trunk or glove box and run the cable connecting the external device to the radio under the carpet. If you're planning on using both a permanently installed external audio device and a non-permanent device, an RCA Y-jack can allow two inputs to plug into the stereo at once (just don't play them both at the same time). Peruse the audio cable aisle at your favorite electronics store to get a feel for how to set up your input devices.

Though it could theoretically feed its output to a line-level amplifier, the converted stereo has enough power to make an amplifier unnecessary. With the stereo in the dashboard, hook up your speakers (most anything with 4 ohms of impedance that can handle at least 45 watts will work; usually, the more you spend on speakers, the better your stereo will sound), connect it to a 12-volt power source, and rock out with your bad self.

Just don't hold me responsible for any disturbing-the-peace tickets you might receive.

Speaker Installation

With a new, thumpin' stereo, you want to take full advantage of it and upgrade from the one speaker mounted in the center of your dash to a full four-speaker setup. I don't blame you. But please, don't go hacking away at door panels and package trays to install the speakers. Kids and their boom boxes on wheels take that simplified approach, which has no place in a muscle car's interior. You'll want to conceal those additional speakers to maintain the original aesthetic of your muscle car's interior.

If at all possible, find door panels, kick panels, and package trays designed to accept speakers for a multi-speaker system. If your car had a multi-speaker system as an option, you only need to figure out what size speakers the system used and then assemble the correct door panels, kick panels, and/or package tray.

If a multi-speaker system wasn't an option for your car or if those panels aren't available, choose locations for the speakers that will not interfere with any window mechanisms, trunk hinges, or fresh air vents. At the same time, consider how water is channeled through your doors and behind your kick panels–you wouldn't want your new speakers to become wet or even damp.

Mount your speakers–usually using a simple sheet-metal bracket when necessary–to the metal body structure underneath the door panel, kick panel, or package tray. Try to make the speakers mount flush to or behind the panels to preserve your interior space. But you'll need a hole through which the speaker will project. Cut the hole to the same size and shape as the speaker. If cutting through the door panels, use a razor blade to cut only the cardboard backing to that size and shape, and leave enough vinyl to dart and wrap around the perimeter of the hole. Kick panels and package trays tend to be made from ABS plastic (except for the package trays in most GM muscle cars, which used a pressed cardboard similar to the cardboard that backs door panels), so use a rotary tool with a wood-cutting or plastic-cutting bit to cut the holes.

Now consider what sort of speaker grille would most closely match your interior–plastic grate, wire mesh, or perforated fabric weave. Some car audio shops sell already-built grilles in varying sizes, shapes, and textures, but you may want to build custom grilles. Browse the aisles at craft stores, hardware stores, and home improvement warehouses to find the right material. With it cut to size, hot glue or plastic weld the mesh to the back of the panel. Finish by installing some sort of trim around the opening; thick-gauge fence wire can easily be bent, polished, and painted to trim most openings, and most big-box parts stores carry strips of universal chrome trim that can be cut to fit.

STEERING WHEEL AND COLUMN, AND PEDAL RESTORATION

Look around your interior long enough, and you'll come to the conclusion that just about everything in it is there for the sole purpose of the driver's and passengers' comfort and pleasure. The seats are there for the comfort of your hind end; the trim is there to make the interior more aesthetically pleasing; the carpet and padding are there, partially, to keep heat and noise from entering the cabin; the radio is there for your listening pleasure.

And while you may gain pleasure from cranking the steering wheel on your favorite twisty mountain road or from stomping the loud pedal and initiating a big smoky burnout, the main purpose of those input devices is not to comfort or please the driver; they exist to control the car. Think about any stripped-down race car, and the interior will always contain at least a steering wheel and pedals (even the seat is nonessential as long as you have an empty milk crate laying around). For that reason, they're going to be the most mechanical aspects of your interior restoration.

And that is not to say the steering wheel and pedals need to look mechanical as well. Your muscle car left the assembly plant with a definite purposeful aesthetic, but also with a touch of comfort, and the mechanical control inputs such as the steering wheel and pedals were no exception.

Steering Wheel Removal

Almost everything else in an interior can blend into the background, but the steering wheel has no other option than to stand out. It's a role that's often overlooked until somebody has replaced the stock steering wheel with a gaudy aftermarket wheel or until cracks develop in the rim of the steering wheel. The former problem can be solved by a straightforward replacement with a reproduction steering wheel, but the latter is a little trickier to solve, so all too often you see those parts-store steering wheel wraps used to cover up the signs of age and abuse.

In either case, you should start by removing the steering wheel currently on your car. Practically every factory steering wheel you come across attaches to the steering column

Our 1972 Buick Skylark convertible is more of a driver than a show car, and a few areas show it, including the steering wheel. We knew it had a couple cracks, but we kept a wrap on it, so we'd forgotten how bad the cracks really were (at three, nine, and twelve o'clock, and extensively on the back side). Fortunately, they're easily repaired.

Steering Wheel Removal

1 ***The first step in removing the steering wheel consists of pulling off the horn pad. In the case of our Buick, we had two screws to loosen in the back side of the wheel, then we withdrew the horn contact wires from where they entered through the wheel itself, right by the nut at the center of the wheel.***

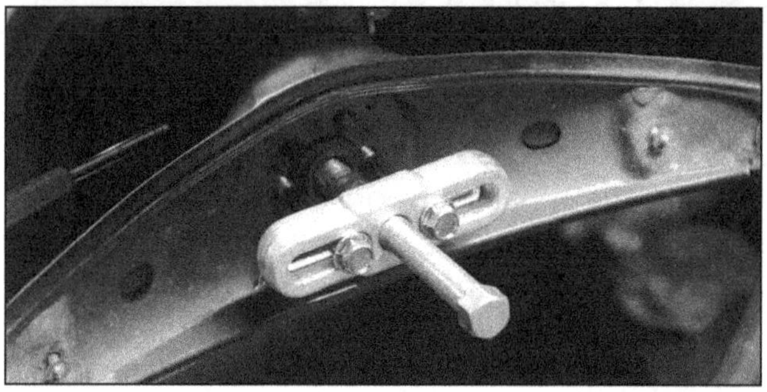

2 ***After removing the nut, we placed the steering wheel puller on the steering shaft, then inserted two bolts into the threaded holes on either side of the shaft. The steering wheel puller works by turning the center bolt, which pushes against the steering column shaft and, in turn, pulls the steering wheel off the splines farther down on the shaft.***

3 ***We put the nut back on the threads, so we wouldn't lose it while repairing the steering wheel. Now would be a good time to go in and replace the turn signal cam and resolve any issues with the ignition lock.***

by use of a splined shaft in the column, a mating hub in the steering wheel, and a big nut holding the wheel to the column. The nut is really only there for safety reasons; the splined coupling between the wheel and the column is usually so tight that it's nearly impossible to separate the two by hand. In an accident, however, you want to be sure that the two don't separate, thus the presence of the nut.

The whole coupling is concealed by the horn pad. Usually only two or three screws hold the horn pad to the steering wheel, and those screws are usually found on the back side of the steering wheel. Carefully remove the horn pad to access the horn button and wires and remove them, taking care not to lose the small spring for the horn button.

After removing the nut on the splined shaft, you can try yanking the steering wheel off the column to prove your Herculean strength, but you also run a risk of damaging the steering wheel rim or your face by doing so. Instead, and for those of us without Herculean strength, use a steering wheel puller, available at any decent auto parts store. If you've ever used a harmonic balancer puller, then you'll see that a steering wheel puller works on the same principle: A threaded rod passes through a cast chunk of metal called a hub, with a pair of (or sometimes three) slotted ears on either side of the threaded rod. Through the ears, a couple long bolts attach to the steering wheel itself. It's so simple, you could probably make one yourself as long as you have a thick enough chunk of metal, a large enough tap, and a good-sized length of threaded rod.

To use the puller, you back the threaded rod nearly all the way out of the cast hub of the puller, then rest the tip of the threaded rod against the splined shaft. Some steering column shafts may require a special foot adapter to go between the threaded rod and the splined shaft to prevent damage to the shaft. Many mechanics recommend leaving the nut on the steering column to give the steering wheel puller something to push against and to prevent damage to the splined shaft. Most steering wheel pullers come in a kit with an assortment of bolts that pass through the slots in the puller hub and thread into a corresponding pair of holes in the steering wheel. If you need bolts with a different thread, find a pair of Grade 8 bolts of the same length as the bolts in the steering wheel puller kit.

Make sure those two pass-through bolts are threaded an equal amount into the steering wheel, then use a socket wrench to start turning the threaded rod. As you crank on the threaded rod, the puller hub will first contact the heads of the bolts threaded into the steering wheel, then gradually start pulling the steering wheel off its splines. Once the steering wheel has separated from the column, remove the puller by unthreading the pass-through bolts.

At this point, you have access to the guts of the steering column, including the turn signal cam, ignition switch, hazards switch, column shifter (but really, what self-respecting muscle car owner shifts on the column?), and any other gizmos the factory loaded onto the steering column.

Steering Wheel Restoration

1 *The heart of the steering wheel repair kit is the PC-7 two-part epoxy, very similar to (if not exactly the same as) J-B Weld. It seems to take just a little longer than J-B Weld to set up, however, which gives you ample time to work with the epoxy.*

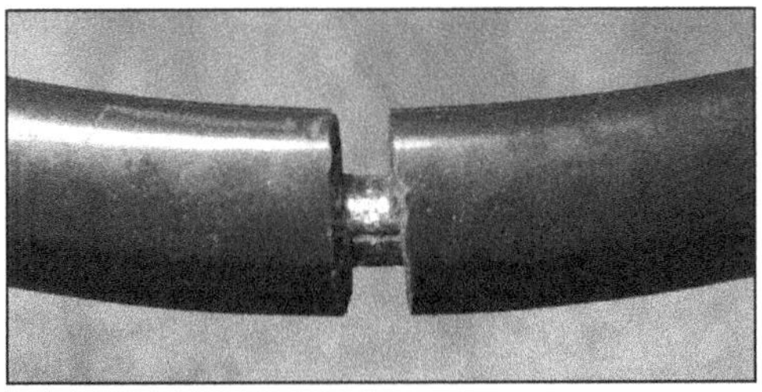

2 *Repairing the steering wheel itself starts with grinding out the crack to have a decent working surface. Technically, you're supposed to grind the crack in a V-shape, but this crack was so wide, we just made sure the sides of the canyon were at least parallel. We also cleaned out as much rust as we could from the steel ring at the core of the steering wheel.*

3 *Once again, preparation is the key. After grinding out the crack, we wanted to remove any grease or dirt or loose particles in the areas, so we wiped the crack down with Eastwood's PRE Painting Prep. Denatured alcohol or acetone works just as well.*

4 *Dig out equal amounts of both parts of the epoxy and thoroughly knead them together. If you see streaks of either part (black or light gray), the epoxy is not yet thoroughly mixed. Note that we used an old cookie tin as a work surface; this stuff gets messy and we didn't want our workbench spattered with epoxy.*

Your factory service manual should contain instructions for repairing and replacing those items.

Also at this point, you need to decide whether you really want that chain-link steering wheel or if you want to restore your stock steering wheel. I'm going to assume you're taking the restoration path.

Steering Wheel Repair and Restoration

As you'll recall from the discussion on vinyl-covered dashboards in Chapter 2, UV exposure cooks plastics, and combined with age, makes plastics extremely brittle. And because windshields do nothing but let UV rays straight into your interior, both dashboards and steering wheels soak up way more UV exposure than the rest of the interior. Hairline cracks thus expand quickly as the plastic shrinks, forming huge gaps that expose the metal core of the steering wheel.

So what should you do with the gaps that inevitably show up on a plastic-rimmed steering wheel? Fortunately, a backyard mechanic with no special tools or fixtures can fix cracks on steering wheels with just a little patience. Several companies, including Eastwood, offer steering wheel restoration kits that any average home restorer can use. The upside to these kits is that they leave the steering wheel stronger in the repaired areas; the downside is that the remaining areas of the steering wheel are still at risk for cracks down the road, and only a labor-intensive total meltdown and remolding of the steering wheel will solve that issue.

Unfortunately, these restoration kits work only on the plastic-rimmed

Steering Wheel Restoration *CONTINUED*

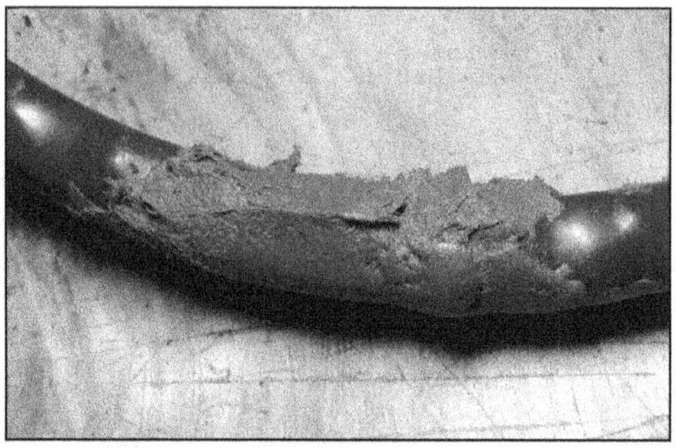

5 ***Force as much epoxy into the crack as possible. You want the crack thoroughly packed with the epoxy because any air pockets will weaken the bond. We used way more epoxy than necessary, but we also had several other cracks to fill, so what we didn't use in this crack, we used in the next.***

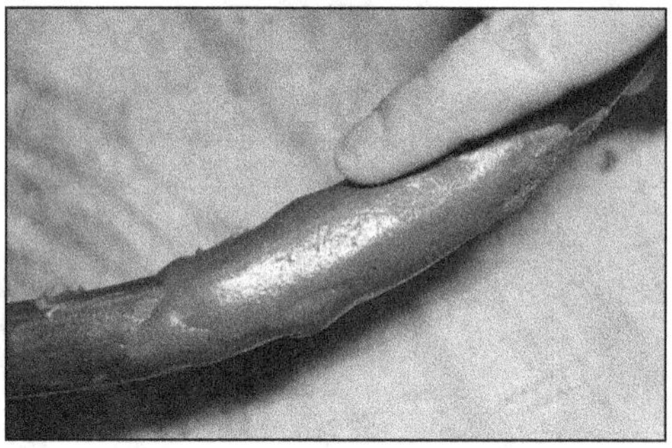

6 ***Once we scraped away the excess epoxy, we thinned and smoothed the remaining epoxy by wetting a finger with denatured alcohol. Some people prefer to use water for wetting the epoxy, but we found the alcohol is a little more aggressive at thinning the epoxy and dries off quicker than water.***

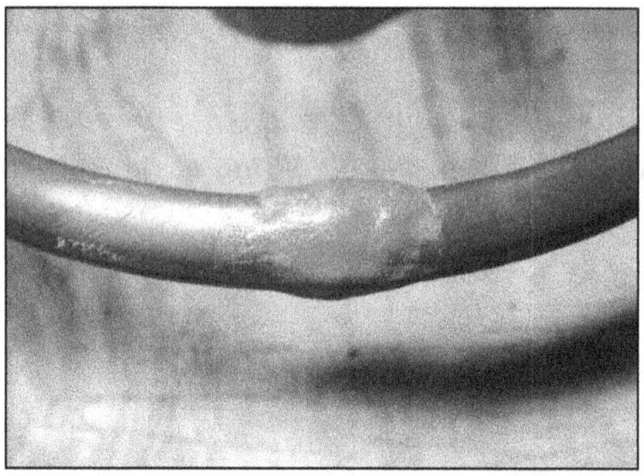

7 ***The more we thinned the epoxy away from the crack, the more of it we could scrape away. In the end, we wanted a nice mound of epoxy above the crack, with the excess epoxy extending only 1/4 to 1/2 inch on either side of the crack. The less excess we have now, the less we'll have to sand away once the epoxy cures.***

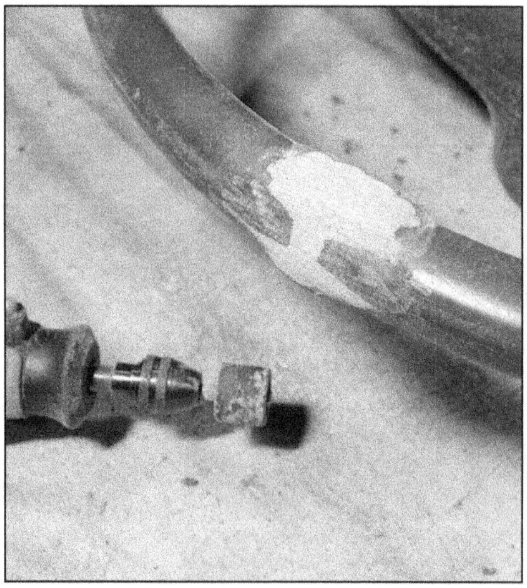

8 ***After letting the epoxy set up at least overnight (we gave it two nights because the crack was very wide), we busted out the rotary tool with the sanding drum attachment and started sanding away the epoxy. We found that the sanding drum was capable of grinding away too much material and biting into the existing steering wheel plastic, but with careful sanding on the medium-to-high setting and by constantly moving the sanding drum, we were able to evenly grind away the epoxy.***

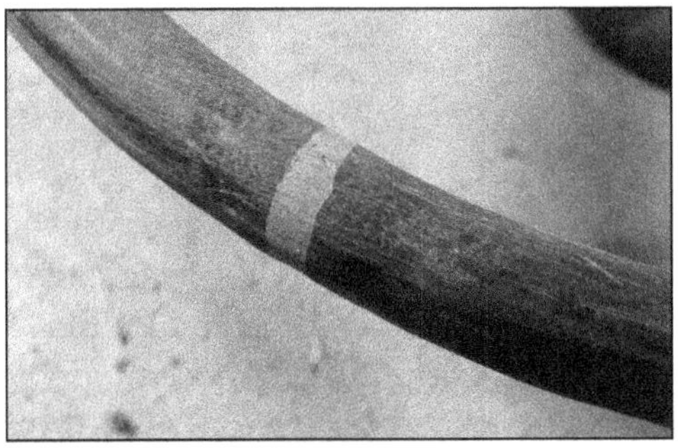

9 ***With the excess epoxy sanded away, the remaining epoxy should take the form of the crack. Note the few pockets on the surface left from small air bubbles. That shows us we should have kneaded and smoothed the epoxy a little more than we did.***

10 ***Grinding the front side is rather simple: Go side to side and don't create any low spots. Grinding the back side with the finger grips is a little tougher and requires some patience and care to replicate the grips' compound curves. The same goes for the cracks at the spokes: Just look to the surrounding contours as guides for the appropriate shapes.***

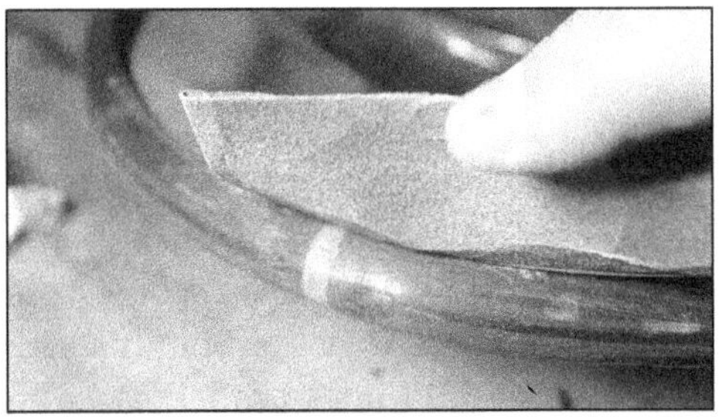

11 ***A second, thinner coat of epoxy might be necessary to fill in air pockets and deep grinding marks. By hitting the area with a succession of sandpaper grits, you should be able to smooth out any rough patches without removing too much material. Before painting the steering wheel, apply some adhesion promoter (included in the kit) to allow your paint to fully bond with the steering wheel surface.***

steering wheels that were fairly ubiquitous through the end of the traditional muscle car era. Wood-rimmed steering wheels, an option for a few muscle cars, can be repaired with a different process.

So after removing the steering wheel from the car and identifying all the areas that require repair, use a rotary tool to notch out the crack in a V-shape, cutting all the way down to the metal core of the steering wheel. A silicon carbide grinding wheel in the rotary tool at a bit more than half speed will make quick work of the V-notch without melting the surrounding plastic.

If the metal core of the steering wheel shows any surface rust, clean that off now with a narrow strip of sandpaper or sandblasting. If it shows any significant structural rust, stop right now and toss your steering wheel into the trash. The metal core should be solid enough to withstand the impact of a crash, and proper repair of significant structural rust is often not worth the time, effort, and money compared to simply replacing the steering wheel with a reproduction or NOS steering wheel.

But as long as your steering wheel is structurally sound, continue by thoroughly cleaning the repair area with denatured alcohol or Eastwood's PRE Painting Prep. The next step involves mixing up a small batch of two-part epoxy such as PC-7, which is included in the Eastwood kit, or even the more common J-B Weld. Only a little is necessary, and you can always make more later if you didn't mix enough the first time.

With the epoxy mixed, you have about 1 hour to work with it before it sets, so take your time packing the epoxy into the crack. Build it up a little beyond the surface of the rim and over the sides of the crack. If you applied too much epoxy to the crack, carve away the excess with a hobby knife or scraper tool while the epoxy remains pliable. The more excess epoxy you leave around the repair area now, the more you'll have to grind away after it hardens, so take care to make the repair as neat as possible. To smooth the surface of the epoxy, wet your finger with denatured alcohol or water and rub your finger over the repair, creating a nice mound over the filled-in crack.

After the epoxy has hardened for at least 24 hours, it can be shaped. The silicon carbide bit used earlier in the rotary tool won't touch the epoxy, but a sanding drum at about the same speed will quickly and effectively remove the hardened epoxy. It's a good idea to wear at least a dust mask and shop glasses while shaping the epoxy.

Be careful not to be too aggressive with the sanding drum, however; it'll easily remove hard plastic from either side of the repaired crack. Instead of running the sanding drum constantly back and forth over the hardened epoxy, thus creating wear spots in the hard plastic where you reverse direction, try swirling the sanding drum to remove the bulk of the material, then follow up with a couple light passes back and forth. You'll likely find your own sanding techniques, but the important part is to only press lightly on the rotary tool and let the action of the sanding drum be its own pressure against the epoxy. The real artistry then comes on the back side, where the finger grips form a less-than-regular surface.

If you do mess up and cut too deep, never fear—you can always add more epoxy and try again. If the repair is acceptably smooth and blends well with the rest of the steering wheel (by touch, that is; it doesn't visibly blend just yet), then the next step is to rough up the surrounding rim of the steering wheel with sandpaper. About 450 grit is the finest you'll want to use. Follow with a couple light coats of a self-etching primer; some plastics may require a coat of adhesion promoter before the primer, so test the primer on an inconspicuous surface of the steering wheel first. Follow that with a vinyl dye in your choice of colors. And make sure the primer and vinyl dye are both compatible with whatever UV-blocking interior protector you decide to use. Even though the unrepaired areas of the steering wheel are still prone to cracking, you'll want to do your best to prevent that from happening by keeping the steering wheel clean and by keeping the UV rays off it.

Installing the steering wheel after restoring it is actually much simpler than removing it. If the steering wheel has a dead spline or some other method of correctly aligning the steering wheel hub onto the steering column, use that to center the wheel to the column. Otherwise, use your best judgment and try to have the steering wheel and the front wheels pointing straight forward together. Push the steering wheel hub down on the steering column splines far enough to start the nut, then tighten the nut to finish pushing the wheel down onto the column. Replace your horn pad and bask in the thought of the money you just saved by not sending the steering wheel out to a specialty shop.

Wood-Grained Steering Wheels

Somewhere between plain ol' steering wheels and actual wood-rimmed steering wheels lies the wood-grained steering wheel, a wheel with a hard plastic rim painted to look like wood. Sure, a wood-grained steering wheel still feels like plastic, still shrinks and cracks under UV exposure like plastic, but hey, it looks like a more expensive steering wheel, right?

Except that over time, it doesn't. Constant rubbing from your hands, and the oils and dirt left behind, erase the black ink from the steering wheel surface, leaving a dull brown, unmarked finish. The worst part is that the black wears away only where you repeatedly put your hands (at the ten and two o'clock positions, if you paid attention to your driving instructor), but remains on the rest of the steering wheel surface, advertising to the world that your car's restoration still isn't complete.

Woodgraining is a fairly simple process with the right tools, and all those woodgrainers whose services you see advertised in the back of your favorite magazines use much the same process. They evenly spread ink over a metal or vinyl plate with a specific pattern etched into it, with different patterns to represent different types of wood. Using hard rubber rollers of varying sizes, they pick up the ink in that pattern, then roll the ink onto the piece to be grained, carefully matching the end points to repeat the grain pattern. If you don't like the way it turned out, wipe it off and start again.

However, a certain amount of artistry and patience is required to blend the grain patterns, and an extra heavy dose of dexterity and expertise is required to apply the patterns to a complex surface like a steering wheel. It's certainly possible to replicate your steering wheel's wood grain, and companies such as Grain-It Technologies in Winter Haven, Florida, offer the tools and supplies necessary to do woodgraining at home. But, as with replacing your dashboard in Chapter 2, why go through all that trouble and expense perfecting a technique you'll use once or twice in your life? Instead, you may find that it's much easier to save your pennies and either purchase a reproduction steering wheel or let a woodgraining service take care of your existing wheel.

Wood-Rim Steering Wheels

Typically, within the domain of Italian exotics and sports cars is the actual wood-rimmed steering wheel, though a couple muscle cars, including the Shelby GT 350 (rather exotic and sporty itself, actually), do sport real wood on the tillers. What you gain with those wooden steering wheels besides bragging rights is questionable, though: They still crack, deteriorate, and lose their finish over time, just like their plebeian plastic counterparts. The splits in the wood usually follow the grain of the wood rather than crack against it, however, and a proper repair takes that into account.

They can be repaired by stripping off the varnish and sealer, applying wood filler or wood glue in the cracks, and then clamping the split shut while the wood glue dries and sets. Some woodworkers like to use string wrapped tightly around the wheel as an improvised clamp. The wheel can then be carefully sanded smooth before being re-varnished and sealed.

If it were me, though, I'd just take it to a local cabinet maker.

Steering Column and Pedals

Boil down the function and the physics of the steering wheel and you'll soon come to the conclusion that it's simply a big round lever—just try to turn the splined shaft that the steering wheel mates to without the steering wheel itself. Boil down the steering column and you'll find that it's just a long shaft that transmits the steering wheel's leverage. What complicates a steering column are the accessories that the manufacturers have hung off the columns: turn signal stalks, horn buttons, ignition switches, and column-mounted shifters, for much of the era with which we're concerned.

Almost any problem with the operation of a turn signal stalk boils down to the plastic turn signal cam inside the column. That cam tends to be the first thing you see in the steering column after removing the wheel and the horn switch. It's a plastic ring with a couple tabs protruding from it, a couple springs associated with it, and a whole mess of wires heading down the column from it. Either the springs, or more likely the cam, tend to crack over time—it seems each different cam design has its own foible that manifests over the decades—causing the switches in the cam not to remain in place or not to self-cancel. Most new turn signal cams, which are often available at corner parts stores under the Help! section, will include not only the plastic ring, but also the springs and the wiring.

Note that the actual flashing of the turn signals is accomplished not by any mechanism in the steering column, but by the aluminum-cased thermal flasher units usually plugged into the fuse block. The turn signal stalk only activates the switch that causes the resistive wire in the flasher to bend a small piece of metal, making the contact that activates the turn signal bulbs. So as long as the wiring from the turn signal stalk to the flasher checks out, any problems in the turn signal circuit can usually be traced to a bad flasher, bad grounds, or a burned-out bulb. If the flasher is bad, consider replacing the thermal unit with a full electronic flasher. Electronic versions, while more expensive, are not as susceptible to varying loads (say, from a burned-out bulb) as the thermal versions.

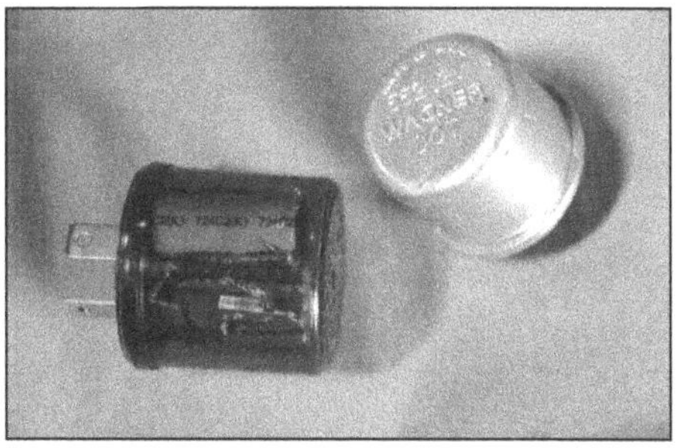

On the right is a typical thermal flasher unit for your turn signals and on the left is an electronic turn signal flasher unit. The electronic unit plugs in to the same fixture as the thermal unit. It comes at a higher price, but blinks at the same rate, even under varying loads.

Similarly, the horn button in the steering column is a simple switch that activates another device away from the steering column. Though in this case, the other device is a relay, usually located in the engine compartment, close to the horns themselves.

The column-mounted ignition switch sometimes uses a two-part design. Up toward the steering wheel is the lock cylinder, into which you insert and turn the ignition key. In the two-part design, rather than directly activating a switch up high in the steering column, turning the lock cylinder instead pushes or pulls a rod that runs the length of the column. At the other end of the rod is the ignition switch itself, along with the associated wiring, mounted to the outside of the column. The disadvantage of such a design means that you have twice the number of parts, but the advantage comes in being able to isolate electrical problems to the switch down low on the column, and mechanical problems to the lock cylinder up high on the column.

As for pedals, which also work on the leverage principal, new bushings (usually available at your corner parts store), go a long way toward smoothing the operation of the pedals. Should you find the pivot holes egg-shaped or otherwise misshapen from repeated use, oversize bushings are available and only require drilling out the pivot hole by a small amount. New rubber pads should be available from restoration supply companies and installed simply by expanding around the face of the pedal.

CARPET AND HEADLINER RESTORATION

It may be necessary to add a bit of contact adhesive under the carpet to keep it from sliding around. The kick panels secure the corners of the carpet, the console secures the center, and the front of the bucket seat brackets secures the trailing edge.

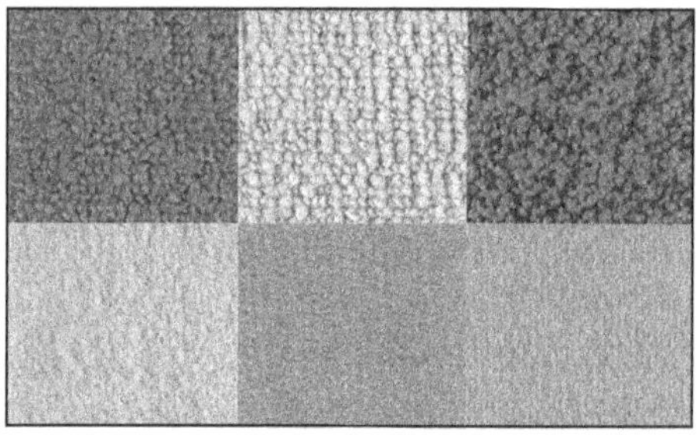

Before replacing your carpet, you need to know what type of carpet originally came in your muscle car and whether you want to stick with that type or replace it with something more modern. Clockwise, from top left: 80/20 loop, nylon, tuxedo, TruVette, Essex, cutpile.

In many ways, carpets and headliners perform many of the same functions. On the surface, it would seem their primary function is one of aesthetics—preventing cabin occupants from seeing the sheetmetal and structure of the ceiling or floor. But the manufacturers also intended them for a couple other purposes. They prevent damage to the sheetmetal above and underneath, which in many muscle cars was left unpainted or simply primed for cost savings. They also act as insulators against noise and heat and thus contribute to the comfort of a muscle car, which in turn contributes heavily to your appreciation of the driving experience of your muscle car.

But the installation procedures for carpets and headliners differ greatly, as do the abuses each suffers. A carpet is designed to incur some sort of crushing, while a headliner simply isn't; but a headliner is made of less durable materials, has to block the heat from the roof, and constantly fights gravity.

The good news, however, is that a home restorer can easily replace both using simple tools. Also, you can easily upgrade them to provide a more comfortable driving experience without sacrificing the original aesthetics of your muscle car.

Carpet Types and Ordering

Actually installing the carpet is more a matter of preparation than anything. The carpet is basically held down by seat brackets, console (if so equipped), sill plates, and interior panels, so removing those components should come first. For that reason, you want to figure out an ideal point during your muscle car's restoration to replace the carpet. If you're planning on also re-covering your seats and replacing

This is a typical carpet tack in a muscle-era car. Though most manufacturers stopped using tacks by the start of the muscle car era, some continued, so you may come across them from time to time. They're easily removed with pliers, but make sure to repair and seal the holes left behind.

your door panels, consider replacing your carpet right around that time as well, just to save yourself the hassle and labor of removing the seats multiple times.

If your old carpet does not lift straight up and out after removing those interior components, it may have some adhesive or a few tacks holding it down around the edges, or at specific recesses and humps. The tacks should easily pull out with pliers, some twisting, and a little coercion. Feel free to plug the holes left behind—carpet adhesive or regular contact adhesive performs the same function and doesn't create the potential for rust by perforating the sheetmetal.

If your carpet has survived the years in relatively decent condition and needs only a cleaning, it's possible to do so with a non-chlorine-based carpet cleaning solution. If dirt has somehow become embedded deep in the carpet, but the carpet itself remains physically intact, try spraying the carpet with a pressure washer (once you've removed it from your muscle car, of course) and then letting it dry for a few days.

Even if your carpet has to go, don't chuck it just yet. Try to remove it without shredding it to pieces, because you may have to use it later on as reference for the location of seat belt holes, for the shapes and dimensions of certain pieces of carpet, and for the actual carpet material. I've also found scrap carpet to make an excellent floor mat for lying on the cold concrete garage floor.

When ordering your replacement carpet, consider the type of carpet your muscle car originally came with and the type you want to use now. First off, take note that your muscle car's floor isn't completely flat, so you'll need a carpet kit that will compensate for that. Before the mid-1950s, cars used a cut-and-sew method to shape the carpet to the contours of the floor. But by the muscle car era, Detroit had figured out how to mold carpet to the shapes of the floor, and several aftermarket companies, including Auto Custom Carpets, offer reproduction molded carpets nowadays.

So you'll want a molded carpet, of course, and there are several carpet materials to choose from: 80/20 loop, cutpile, Essex, shag... Okay, maybe not shag. If you browse Auto Custom Carpets' website, you'll see about nine different types of carpet to choose from, most of which can be molded to the shape of your floor, so what's the difference between them?

Well, if you're restoring your muscle car to its original appearance, you're rather fortunate and really only have one choice: the 80/20 loop. "About 98 percent of the 1960s muscle cars used 80/20," said Roger Niehaus, the vice president of sales for ACC. "And it lasted until about 1975, when the catalytic converters became standard."

He noted that 80/20 loop was a fairly inexpensive product for Detroit to produce. The 80 part of the equation was rayon, classified as a semi-synthetic fiber, but essentially wood pulp. The 20 part of the equation was nylon, still a fairly new petroleum-based synthetic that was used as a color stabilizer for the petroleum-based dyes. In the early 1970s, though, Detroit started to switch to a 100 percent nylon, which appeared slightly different from the 80/20 loop.

"The 80/20 had an indiscriminate twisted look, a real random look to it," Niehaus said. "The pure nylon was more a set of rows—we call them cornrows."

Nylon carpet also held its color better than 80/20, which often faded. Those of you going for complete accuracy in material selection are out of luck, however: ACC's suppliers no longer produce rayon, so ACC has switched to 100 percent nylon for all of its loop-type carpets, which still look and feel the same as 80/20.

Starting in the mid-1970s, Detroit switched from loop-style carpet to cutpile, which essentially remains the choice of auto manufacturers today. Niehaus said it's a popular upgrade from loop-style carpets because it doesn't wear out as fast as loop-style carpets. "Every time you run your heel over all those loops, it catches on the loops and frays them just a little bit," Niehaus said. "You obviously don't have that problem with cutpile." Essex, a version of cutpile carpet, uses a taller pile height for a plusher look and feel.

Along with those four types of carpet, ACC also offers tuxedo, a two-tone variant of 80/20 commonly used on full-size and luxury

The gray mat attached to the back side of the carpet is called jute padding. It offers a measure of sound and heat insulation and is inexpensive on the production line, but is notorious for soaking up water and trapping moisture against floors. The construction of the carpet doesn't help much either, because it doesn't allow for moisture to evaporate, further trapping it.

cars, and TruVette, a shorter version of cutpile used on Corvettes since the early 1990s.

In addition to all the carpet types, you have the choice of ordering your carpet with or without jute padding. Jute, which is really just shredded rags, is often blamed for rusting out floorboards because it soaks up water like a sponge should it ever become wet. But Niehaus argued that what really keeps the water in the jute is the fact that all molded carpet is, essentially, a watertight plastic sheet that does not allow for evaporation, and so it traps water in the jute and, thus, against the floorboards.

Some restorers recommend ordering carpet without jute padding for another reason: At 1/2 inch thick, it can bulk up the carpet, making it look overstuffed and not shaped to the floorboards. Ordering carpet sans padding allows it to fit better into the recesses of your floor and add definition to your carpet.

Of course, the factories didn't install jute padding underneath the carpet for no reason at all. It helped soften the carpet and reduce road noise. Fortunately, a number of modern-day noise and heat barriers exist that perform the same functions without the bulk or water-absorbing properties of jute padding.

Noise and Heat Barriers

By far, the most popular noise and heat barrier in the aftermarket today is Dynamat, one of several products that look and feel kind of like a thick, stiff tar paper, similar to the asphalt-based roof insulation you see at your local hardware store. Yet Dynamat, along with its competitors, has been fine-tuned for automotive applications, and specifically started with car audio enthusiasts looking to reduce the rattling in their trunks caused by big, thumping woofers. Soon after, the rest of the automotive world realized the potential of these foil-backed insulators in not only improving their sound systems, but also in reducing road noise—leading to less fatigue while driving, along with a more modern driving experience—and in reducing heat coming into the car's cabin, a benefit probably of more importance to muscle car drivers, whose engines pump out way more BTUs than your garden-variety collector car's engine.

Dynamat—or more accurately, Dynamat Xtreme—is rather thin, at a bit more than 1/16 inch thick (.067 inch, to be precise), which is good, because unless you're putting it on the floor of a Corvair, you're going to have a lot of contours that the Dynamat will have to mold around, and the thinner it is, the easier it molds to those shapes. Its major drawback, however, is that it's expensive, at about $300 per Bulk Pack of nine sheets, which in total cover 36 square feet. Many competitors, including Insulshield, B-Quiet, Cascade Audio Engineering, Elemental Designs, Lizard Skin, FatMat, RAAMaudio, and Secondskin Damplifier, among others, have emerged in recent years to

There are many competitors out there in the undercarpet insulation field that advertise similar performance, but few have the name recognition of Dynamat. For our AMX, we'll be using the 18-by-32-inch sheets of foil-backed Dynamat Xtreme, followed by a few different thicknesses of Dynaliner. Both are paperbacked for ease of installation.

offer alternative sound deadeners and insulators. ACC even offers what they call mass backing, which is a heavy rubber backing molded directly to the carpet that acts as a sound deadener. The installation process for the different mat-style barriers is much the same no matter what brand you choose, so I went with Dynamat for this project muscle car.

As with many other procedures, preparation is the key to getting the Dynamat, which is self-adhesive, to stick to your floors. After all, you want it to stick to your floorboards and not to any detritus on your floorboards. First, remove the Dynamat from its box and lay it out flat to

Noise and Heat Barriers

1 *After removing the seats and ratty carpet from this late 1970s AMX, we found a layer of jute and cotton padding. Underneath that, we found a factory sound deadener and heat insulation that had become cracked and torn. Fortunately, underneath it all, the floors remained solid. Were we to do this again, we'd seriously consider taking the dashboard out of the car to give us more room near the firewall. The fact that our AMX is a hatchback means we have better access to some of the floor sections, but it also means that the area is larger than in a typical sedan.*

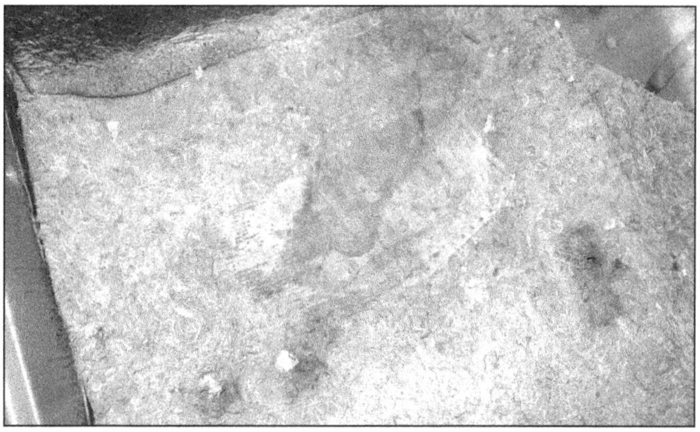

2 *When ripping up your old carpet, take care and don't toss it all immediately in the trash. Assembly-line workers often left your muscle car's build sheet under the carpet, which is where we found ours. A build sheet is one of the most valuable pieces of documentation for your car, especially if you're restoring it to showroom stock condition. You wouldn't want to accidentally throw it in the trash.*

3 *On the wheel wells we encountered some jute padding that just wouldn't rip away from the metal. Most factories tend not to glue down padding or carpet on horizontal surfaces because it's not really needed; but on vertical surfaces, something had to hold up the padding. The plan worked; the jute was next to impossible to remove by hand.*

4 *The first step in removing the remaining jute was to use a stiff wire brush to break up the bulk of the padding. Jute isn't like normal fabric in that it separates and crumbles quite easily, so the wire brush was able to remove all but the jute directly glued to the metal. The wire brush loads up with jute quickly, but a flat-bladed screwdriver easily removes the jute crumbles from the brush's wires.*

Noise and Heat Barriers *CONTINUED*

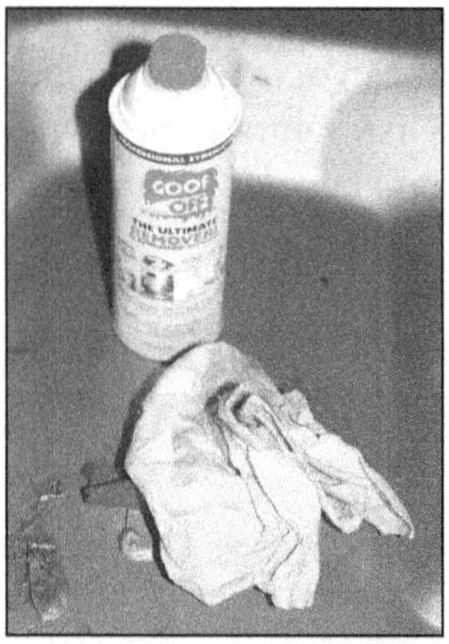

5 *With the majority of the jute removed, we used some Goof-Off adhesive remover to lift the old glue. This stuff also liquefies seam sealer and makes a sticky mess, so it's best to apply the Goof-Off to a rag or paper towel instead of directly to the metal, where it can drip into your seams.*

6 *It takes some elbow grease and patience to rub off the old glue with the Goof-Off, but it does steadily come off, as evidenced by the bare spot on the wheel well. The Goof-Off leaves a residue, which is easily wiped off with denatured alcohol.*

7 *Even if you're not laying down Dynamat or a similar product, you'll still want to thoroughly vacuum the floorboards to remove years of accumulated spider droppings, loose change, gum wrappers, and so on. Invest in a name-brand wet/dry shop-vac instead of using your household vacuum cleaner.*

8 *After vacuuming and before laying the Dynamat into place, we wiped down the metal with denatured alcohol just to be certain that no dirt, grease, or other residues remained on the metal. A similar product is Eastwood's PRE Painting Prep.*

remove the fold marks from shipping. Putting some heat on it—either from the sun or from a good, hot lamp—will speed up the process. Then, turning to the car itself, once you've removed the old carpet and jute padding, thoroughly vacuum the floorboards and remove any loose seam sealer. Now is the time to attack any rust on your floorboards, including surface rust; it won't be accessible once you've laid down the insulation.

If the factory happened to have glued down the jute padding to make it stick to vertical or nearly vertical surfaces, then you're likely going to have a mess to clean up

9 *We thoroughly vacuumed the sheetmetal after removing all traces of the old padding and carpet, and found a few blooms of surface rust that could flower into full-blown problems down the road. So we took the opportunity to spot blast the rust and paint over it before laying down the Dynamat.*

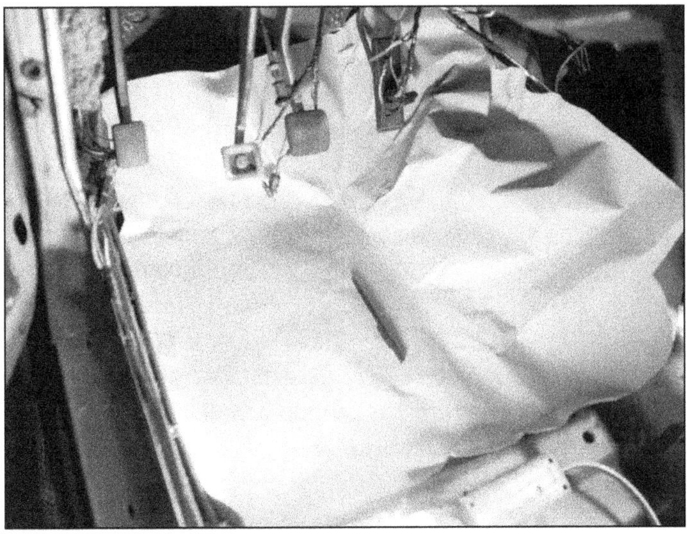

10 *To maximize our usage of the Dynamat we first created, from craft paper, templates of the general shapes of the floorboards. To create a template, we laid out a section of craft paper, then marked all but the most gradual of shapes with a pen and cut the templates based on those markings.*

11 *To keep our templates properly oriented as we removed them from the car, we marked the location and direction of the templates on the side facing up. It could be a costly mistake if we were to get these backward when transferring the templates to the Dynamat.*

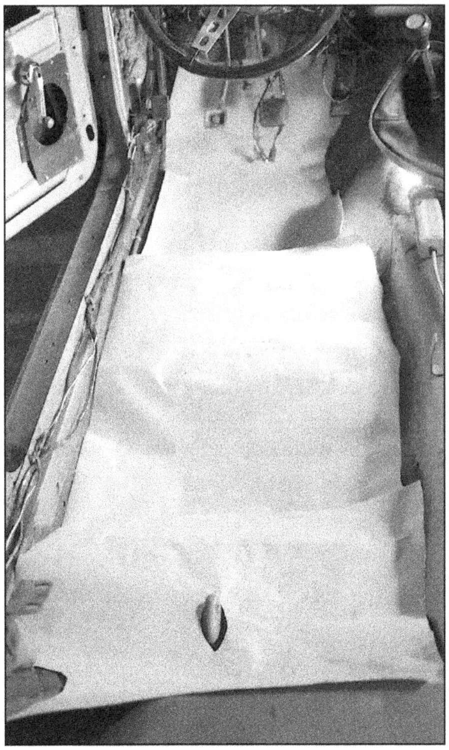

12 *We double-checked our templates after cutting them and laid out templates for entire sections of the floorboards all at once, to visualize how multiple pieces of Dynamat would fit together. As we progressed, we also made notes directly on the templates regarding obstructions and tight radii.*

after you've ripped out as much of the jute padding as possible by hand. To remove the rest, start by rubbing a stiff wire brush over the padding. The bristles break up the bulk of the jute rather effectively, leaving just the old adhesive. Some time spent with Goof-Off or any other adhesive remover will then leave you with fresh sheetmetal. Just be careful not to apply too much adhesive remover on the seam sealer; doing so will create a sticky mess.

Did I mention *how* clean you need to have the floorboards? You should vacuum the interior again, then wipe down the floorboards with denatured alcohol. Even if the floorboards look clean, the dirt and grease still there will prevent full adhesion of the Dynamat to the sheetmetal, and the denatured alcohol will remove that dirt and grease. Denatured alcohol also does not leave behind a film like some other cleaning agents, nor does it attack the seam sealer.

The urge to just start cutting up sheets of Dynamat is strong at this point, but you'll want to hold off for just a bit. Remember that this stuff is kinda expensive. That means you'll want to make the most of each sheet and at the same time have as little overlap between sheets as possible. For many of the more-popular cars, Dynamat offers pre-cut kits that take the guesswork out of laying it down.

If you don't have pre-cut kits to choose from, however, you'll want to create patterns from a less expensive, more disposable material (if not from the car's original carpet and padding) and then transfer those patterns to the Dynamat.

Noise and Heat Barriers *CONTINUED*

13 *When transferring the template's shape to the pieces of Dynamat, use a Sharpie or other dark-colored felt-tip marker. Leave the backing paper on while cutting the Dynamat with a razor or a sharp pair of scissors.*

14 *Be sure to save all your scraps from trimming the sheets of Dynamat. The scraps will come in handy later when filling small gaps between the sheets of Dynamat. The scraps can also be combined to cover irregularly contoured areas that a whole sheet wouldn't easily cover.*

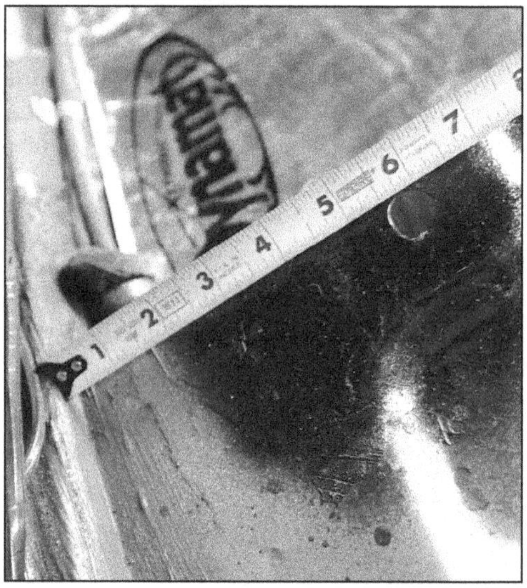

15 *Test fitting the sheets also allowed us to measure and mark the seat belt and seat-mounting post holes on the sheets beforehand, rather than fumble around afterward trying to locate the holes.*

16 *We like having our foot to the floor, and even the thickness of the Dynamat can make a difference in how far the butterflies open, so we elected to leave the floor uninsulated directly under the throttle pedal. It probably won't make a difference in the long run, but it's easier to leave that section out now than to cut it out later.*

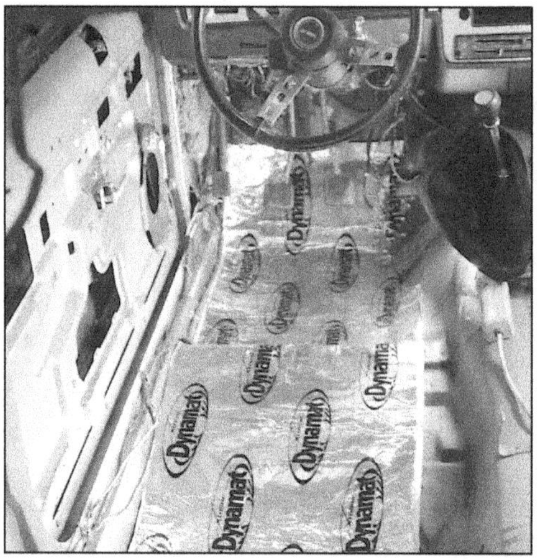

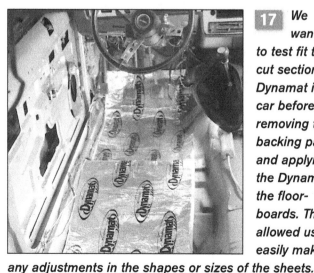

17 *We wanted to test fit the cut sections of Dynamat in the car before removing the backing paper and applying the Dynamat to the floorboards. This allowed us to easily make any adjustments in the shapes or sizes of the sheets.*

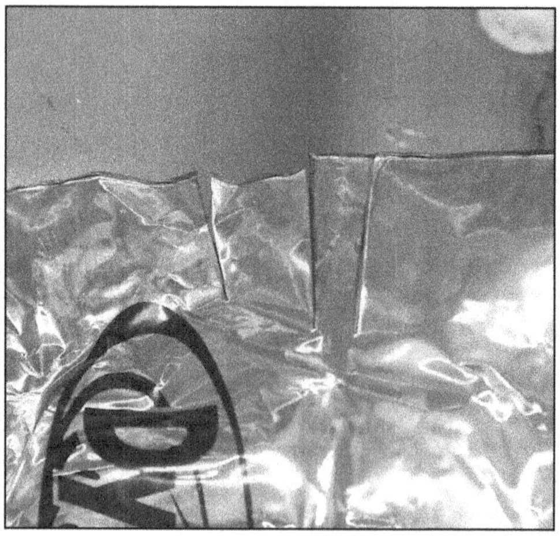

18 *It may be necessary to cut relief darts in the Dynamat before rolling it out. For example, this section has concave and convex shapes in close succession, and the relief darts help the Dynamat expand and bunch up over those shapes.*

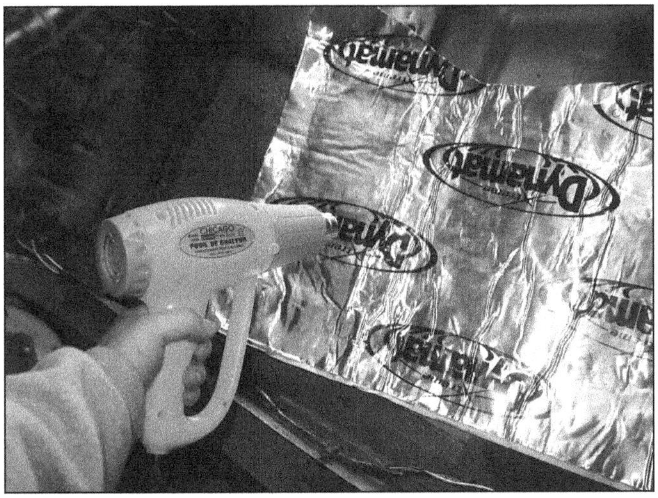

19 *With the sheet test fitted and trimmed, apply some heat to the sheet immediately before removing the backing paper. Applying heat makes the sheet more flexible and able to fit to the contours of the floorboards.It also helps the adhesive bond to the metal.*

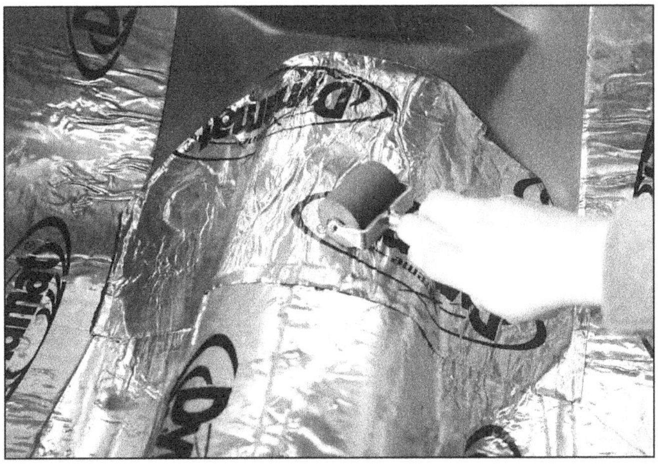

20 *After applying the heat and removing the backing paper, we laid down the section of Dynamat, careful not to overlap the edges with nearby sections. While the sheet remained hot, we used the Dynamat-supplied roller to press the Dynamat to the floorboards, starting from the middle of the sheet and working our way out toward the edges of the sheet.*

21 *If you hear a crinkling in the Dynamat while rolling it smooth, you've probably trapped an air pocket between the sheet and the floorboard. If you're unable to roll it out, slice the Dynamat with a razor in an X pattern and roll toward the slices to eliminate the air pocket.*

Fortunately, craft paper is perfect for pattern making, and it's available at just about any craft store or office supply store across the country. If possible, buy a roll of craft paper close in width to the 32-inch width of each sheet of Dynamat (doing so will save you a lot of cutting down the road, trust me).

Creating the patterns is then a matter of choosing the most logical shapes that encompass the flattest areas of your floorboards with the minimum number of bends. You're essentially creating a big jigsaw puzzle, with pieces that fit into each other, but of dimensions and shapes of your choosing.

Start with the forward-most floorboards, those under the driver's and front passenger's feet on either side of the driveshaft tunnel. These are relatively flat, with one simple bend where the floor meets the firewall. Cut a piece of craft paper roughly the width of the floorboards here and mark the transition from the flat floorboard to the curve of the driveshaft tunnel. On most muscle cars, that transition is rather well defined and should be easy to mark. Don't worry about smaller humps or contours in the floorboards; the Dynamat can easily conform to lesser shapes.

With the pattern in the car, you can make notes for where to extend the Dynamat beyond the borders of the craft paper or where the Dynamat should be notched or cut with relief darts for particularly tricky corners. If you're planning to reuse the templates later on (or if you might loan them to friends with the same car), make notes indicating which side is up, the location of the pattern in the car, and the direction of the firewall or other reference points.

On your workbench, lay out a sheet of Dynamat, foil side up. Lay the cut pattern over it and transfer the pattern with a pen or felt-tip marker, then trim the Dynamat to that shape. Don't remove the backing just yet, though; you'll want to confirm the shape, so set it in its place in the car and trim if necessary.

Once you're happy with the shape, wipe down the area again with denatured alcohol. While waiting for any excess alcohol to evaporate, apply some heat directly to the sheet of Dynamat with a heat gun to make it pliable. The more heat you apply, the more pliable the Dynamat will become, but at the same time, though, the more heat you apply, the more heat it will retain, so use gloves if you're applying a lot of heat. If the area has a very irregular surface, or some sort of undercoating that you don't want to remove, crank up the heat.

Peel off the backing paper and set the sheet of Dynamat into place. It's a good idea to set down one edge of the sheet first, to make sure it's properly located, then gradually roll the rest of the sheet onto the floorboard. This approach also helps reduce air pockets underneath the Dynamat, another huge deterrent to the Dynamat adhering to the floorboards.

If you made a mistake in dropping the sheet onto the wrong spot, it's still possible to lift it and try again.

Now comes the fun part. Using a small, hard, rubber roller (sold by Dynamic Control, the company that markets Dynamat, should you not be able to find a roller at the hardware store), start rolling the sheet from the center out, trying to work out any air pockets trapped between the sheet and the floorboard. Remember

Noise and Heat Barriers *CONTINUED*

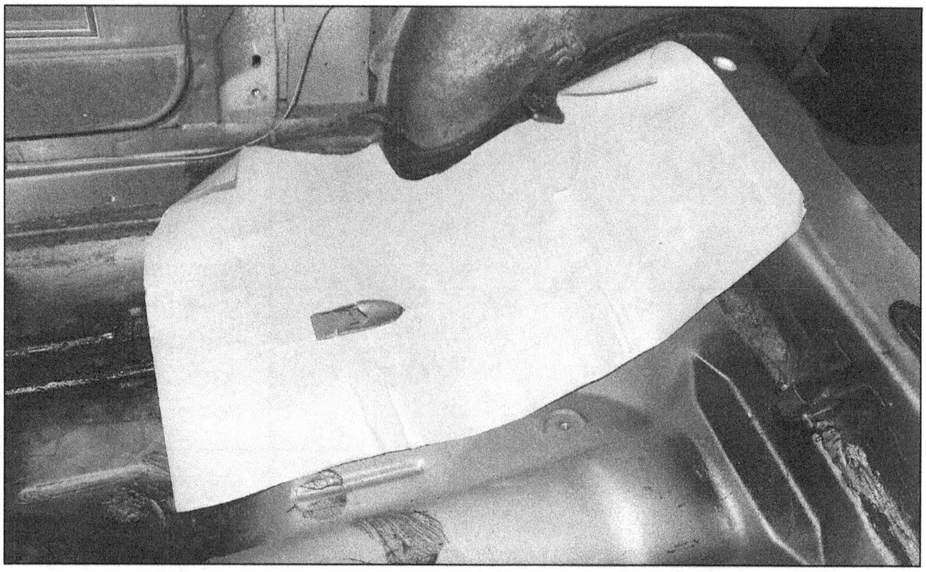

22 ***When you remove the backing paper, don't throw it away. After all that trimming, the piece of backing paper is the exact shape you needed. By flipping it over, it becomes a reverse pattern and eliminates the need to make a second craft-paper pattern for the opposite side, thus saving you time and effort.***

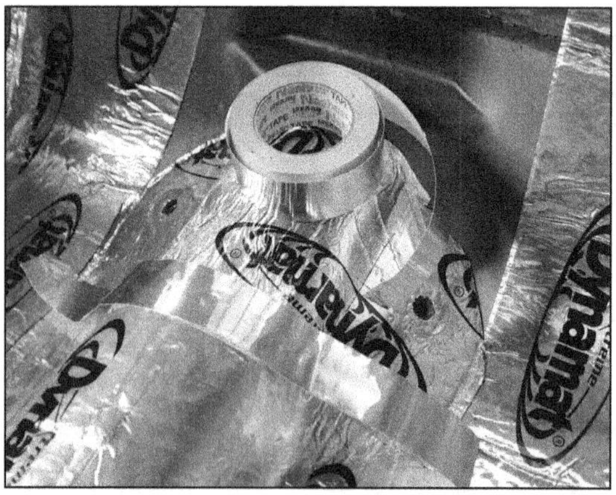

23 ***Lay a section of aluminum tape at the seams between sheets of Dynamat and over sliced air pockets and relief darts. Any adhesive that pokes through the seams can make a sticky mess, so the aluminum tape not only contains the adhesive, but also aids in sealing the Dynamat against heat and noise.***

24 ***Note how the Dynamat clings tightly to the shapes of the floorboards, especially around the raised areas surrounding the seat mounting holes. The tighter the Dynamat conforms to these shapes, the better it will perform.***

that the hotter the Dynamat is, the more pliable it becomes, so work the Dynamat around the contours in the floorboard with the roller while it's still warm. The purpose of the roller is to push the Dynamat into those contours, where it'll be the most effective at blocking noise and heat. If you find that you need more heat, keep applying it with a heat gun while rolling out the air pockets and around the irregular areas.

When you're done, the Dynamat sheet should look less like a blanket tossed over the floors and more like a sprayed-on insulation, through which you can pick out the floor's shapes. Heck, you should be able to pick out the holes for the seat brackets and plunge a razor through them to open them up.

Should you create an air pocket under the sheet (and you'll hear it while rolling if you do), you should be able to close it with additional heat. If you can't eliminate it that way, simply slice the pocket down its length with a razor blade, then add short relief slices perpendicular to the main slice. Roll the sheet toward the slice to flatten out the air pocket.

Installing Dynamat is a time-consuming task, especially when creating templates for each sheet. The symmetry of your car should alleviate some of your pattern making, however, especially beyond the front footwells; in that case, the backing paper from one side, which has already been perfectly trimmed to your car, can be used as the template for the opposite side—just make sure to flip the template to avoid creating a duplicate of the piece you just laid down. In areas with a bracket or some other protrusion from the floorboard, cut the template to fit over that protrusion, then use the

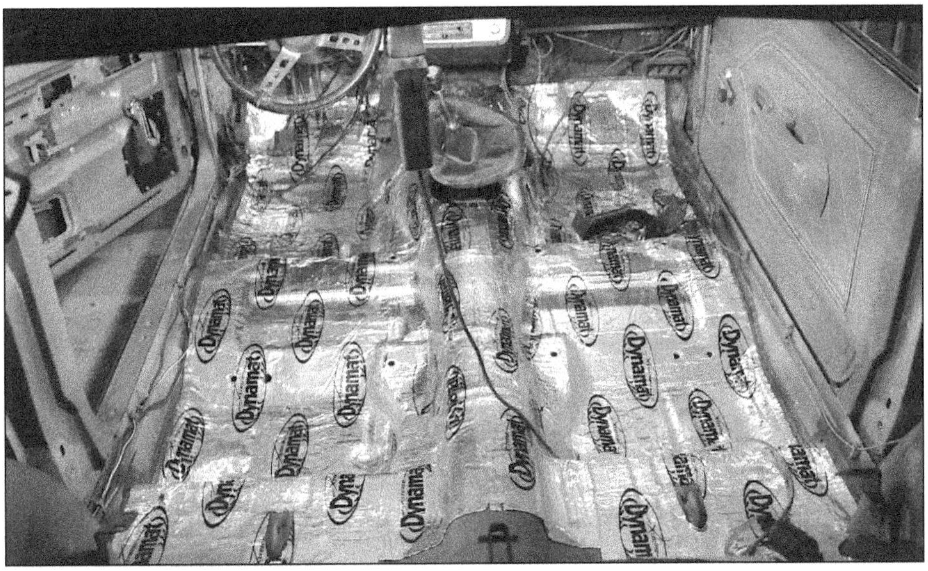

25 ***With both sides of the floorboards covered in Dynamat, it looks as if we just finished building a satellite for NASA. And hey, we even managed to get the Dynamat logos facing the same direction on each side of the trans tunnel.***

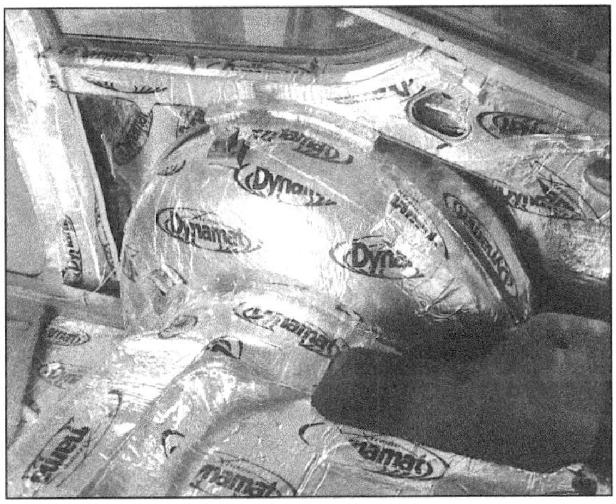

26 ***Quite a bit of wind noise comes from the wind beating against your body panels like a big drum as you drive down the road. Adding the Dynamat against the back side of the body panels helps reduce that noise. Here it's critical to heat the sheets of Dynamat to make them properly stick against the vertical surfaces.***

WHAT SIZE DYNALINER DO I NEED?

	Floor	Roof	Under Hood	Under Trim (Doors)	Fiberglass Enclosures
1/8" 3.2mm				✓	✓
1/4" 6.4mm	✓	✓	✓	✓	✓
1/2" 12.7mm	✓	✓	✓	✓	✓

Be sure to choose the thickness that best suits your application.
✓ Indicates a thickness that is not optimal for that particular application.

27 ***Dynaliner comes in three thicknesses with varying degrees of applicability, as this chart from Dynamic Controls shows. We used the thicker, 1/2-inch Dynaliner for the front half of the car, for a plusher feel where the driver's and passengers' feet rest. The 1/4-inch Dynaliner was used for the hatch area.***

protrusion as a reference point for cutting the sheet of Dynamat.

Remember, you want little-to-no overlap between the sheets of Dynamat; besides wasting the material, overlapping creates unnecessary bulges. Should you find gaps between the sheets, or should you create gaps by cutting reliefs in a sheet, use your trimmings from the sheets to fill in those gaps. Much like how a container can't easily hold water with gaps in it, the Dynamat loses effectiveness with gaps between or among its sheets. Finally, apply strips of aluminum tape over every seam and every slice, including the slices made to remove air pockets.This not only reinforces the insulating properties along those seams and slices, but it covers the sticky and sometimes sharp edges of the Dynamat that are exposed at those seams.

You'll find that once you've finished covering your floors with Dynamat you'll be left with extra material. Instead of chucking the excess or the trimmings, consider covering your roof pillars, kick panels, inner door skins, rear bulkhead, and trunk with the stuff. The more exposed metal surfaces you cover, the more solid your muscle car will sound and feel.

Dynamic Control also offers Dynaliner, a lighter, more foam-like material that comes in several thicknesses: 1/2, 1/4, and 1/8 inch. It is recommended, but not necessary, as an additional sound and heat barrier atop the Dynamat on the floor, which is probably not a bad idea if you've ordered your carpet sans jute padding.

Like the Dynamat, the Dynaliner is self-adhesive, so trim it to shape before removing the backing paper. Unlike the Dynamat, however, the thicker 1/2-inch Dynaliner, recommended for floors, does not easily conform to irregular shapes, nor does it easily roll out, when laying it down. You need to be very intentional and push it hard into those irregular shapes while working from one end to the other. The thinner 1/8-inch Dynaliner more easily conforms to irregular shapes, but is only really recommended for roofs and behind door panels. The 1/4-inch Dynaliner is recommended for use in the same places as 1/2-inch Dynaliner.

Before laying down the carpet or installing the headliner, consider how best to route any wiring that will connect to devices (lamps, speakers, switches, etc.) in the center of the car. Wiring should be easily accessed for repairs, so lay it above the Dynamat and Dynaliner and secure it with short sections of aluminum tape.

Noise and Heat Barriers CONTINUED

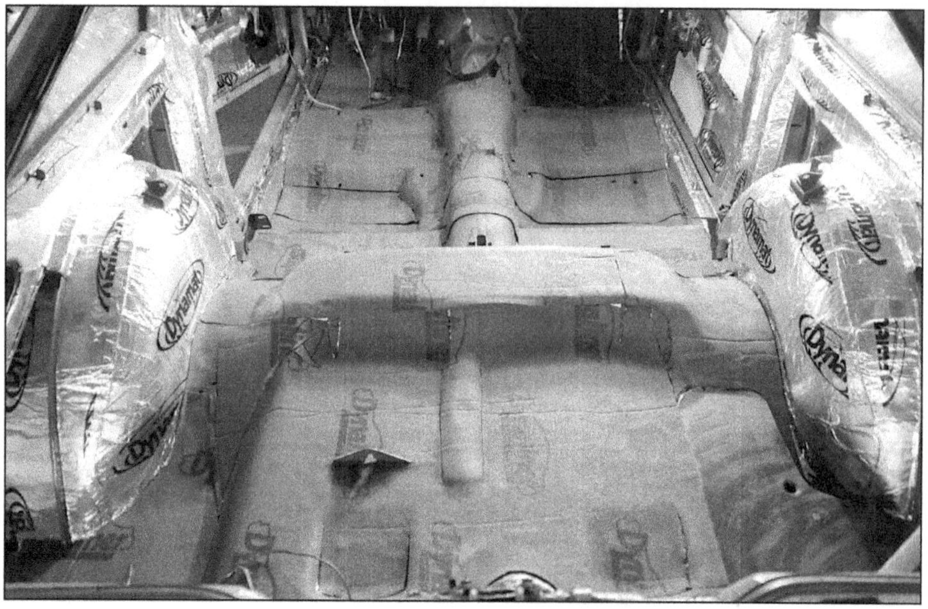

27 ***The Dynaliner adds a second layer of noise insulation to your car. Using templates again helps maximize your investment. The Dynaliner, especially the thicker versions, does not roll as easily as the Dynamat, however, so it's often easier to cut the Dynaliner into smaller sections to get it to conform to the shapes of the floorboards.***

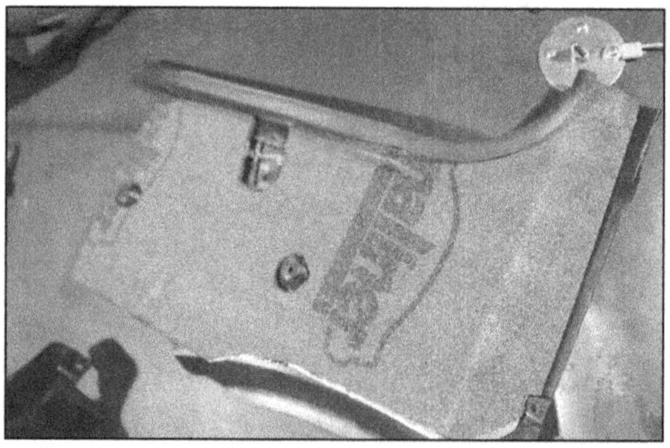

28 ***For the areas in the car we couldn't easily cover with Dynamat, such as behind the kick panels, it was simpler to just cover the back sides of the kick panels with Dynamat and Dynaliner. It will serve the same purpose when the kick panel is attached to the sheetmetal on final reassembly.***

Carpet Installation

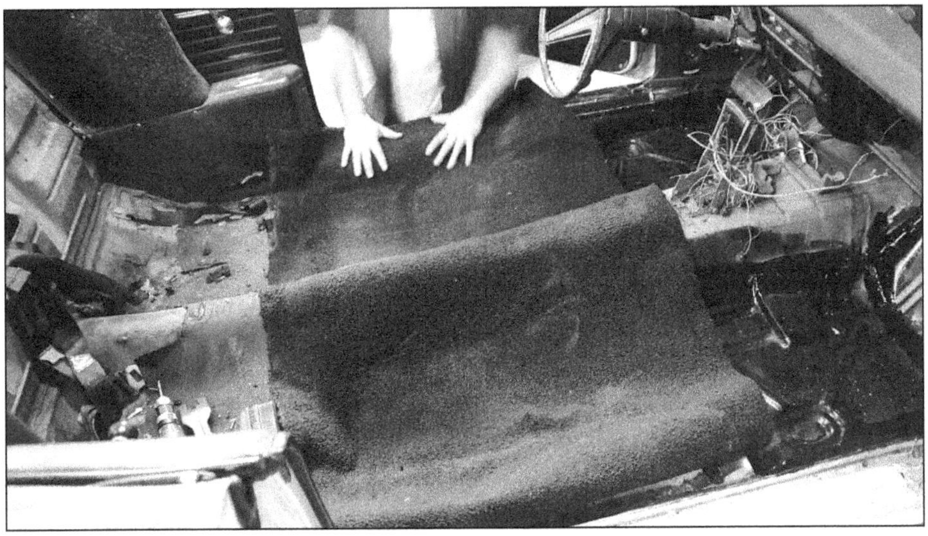

1 Carpet installation starts by centering the rearmost carpet segment in the car. Preferably, you should let the carpet sit out in the sun for a little while after unpackaging it, to remove any creases or folds. Note that the carpet section in this first-generation Camaro ends just behind the leading edge of the rear seat. The rear seat will cover the floor behind that point.

2 We notched the trailing edge of the rearmost carpet segment to clear the mounting latch for the rear seat. A sharp, new razor blade makes quicker work of carpet notching than an older, duller blade.

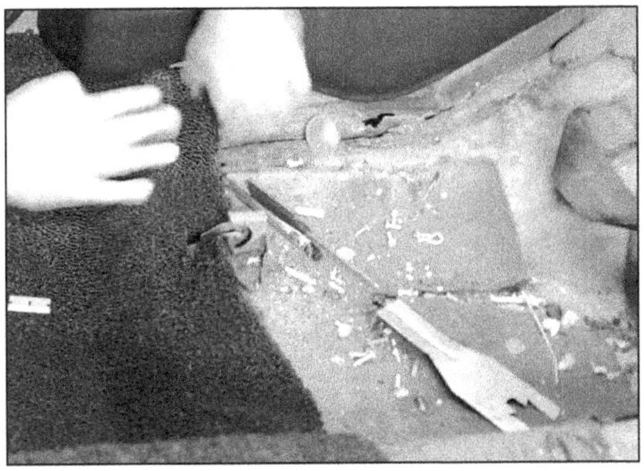

3 On this Camaro, the carpet is held down at the rear corners by the interior panels, so we tucked it in. Other cars may use contact adhesive or tiny pins that are hammered through the floor to secure the carpet.

Carpet Installation

With the Dynamat installed, roll out the carpet to smooth out the folds and creases from its time spent in its package. You may want to lay it out in the sun for 1/2 hour or so to help it lay flat.

For the restoration of our 1968 Camaro project car, I ordered a loop-style reproduction carpet kit from Classic Industries. The kit came in two pieces: One section lays across the width of the car and extends from just behind the leading edge of the rear seat cushion to just behind the leading edge of the front seat cushions. The second section, which also lays across the width of the car, overlaps the other strip and extends to the firewall.

We began with the rearmost section, first centering the carpet, then sliding it forward as far as possible while leaving the rear edge of the carpet underneath the rear seat cushion so it won't show with the seat installed. We had to notch the rear edge of the carpet with a razor blade (a carpet knife will work just as well) so it would clear the brackets for the seat cushion. And on this Camaro, the interior panels held down the rear corners of the carpet strip.

Moving forward, we located the four mounting holes for the bucket seat brackets. Around the forward holes, we could simply notch the carpet again, but around the rearward holes, we cut flaps in the shape of three sides of a square to allow the seat brackets to slip under the carpet and become somewhat hidden. You may want to mount the seat brackets on top of the carpet; in that case, rather than cutting flaps, you'll want to cut smaller holes through the carpet.

When installing loop carpet, however, do not drill through or even near the carpet. A spinning drill bit can easily catch a loop of the carpet and yank out an entire strand, tuft by tuft, causing more damage in just a few seconds than you'd think possible. Instead, poke a hole through the carpet with an awl, use a razor blade to cut an X pattern over the mounting hole. Or you could even use an old soldering iron to melt away the carpet fibers from the mounting hole and effectively cauterize the hole, preventing the loops from catching on the screws. Another slick trick is to install all the screws that go through the carpet before actually laying down the carpet. Then, once the carpet is in position, feel out those screws and cut the carpet around the heads of the screws.

With the rear section of carpet laid, we then centered the forward section of carpet, temporarily draping it over the shifter assembly, still installed in the car. Knowing that a console will mount over the shifter assembly, we conservatively cut away the carpet around the shifter assembly. While it would seem to be simpler to just cut the forward section of carpet in half and fit each side of the carpet individually, the carpet would then become loose and shift around. Instead, we left the carpet section intact forward of the shifter assembly.

We made sure the molded section of the carpet fell to place in the driver's footwell under the pedals. With the stomp switch for the brights still in place, we cut out a hole just large enough for the switch and installed the switch grommet, included with the carpet kit. On either side, the kick panels held

Carpet Installation *CONTINUED*

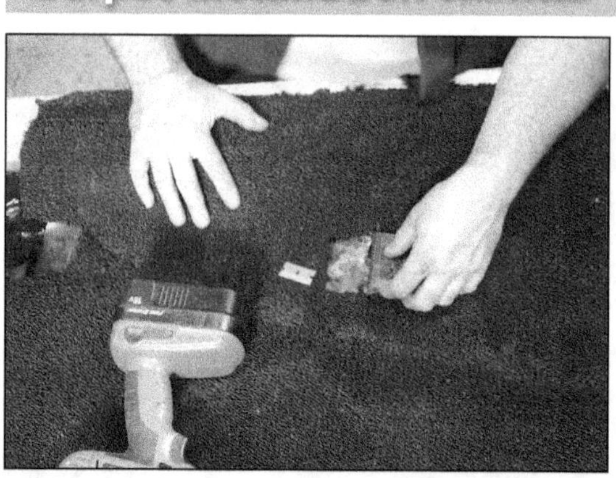

4 ***For the bucket seat's rear bracket mounts, we cut three-sided flaps, about 1-1/2 inches to a side, under which the mounts will slide, thus hiding them from view when installed. You may also consider slicing holes through the carpet directly above the mounting holes if you don't mind leaving the seat brackets exposed.***

5 ***Placing the forward section of carpet is a bit trickier, due to the floor-mounted shifter and the tight spaces near the firewall. Again, it should be centered first, then adjusted fore or aft.***

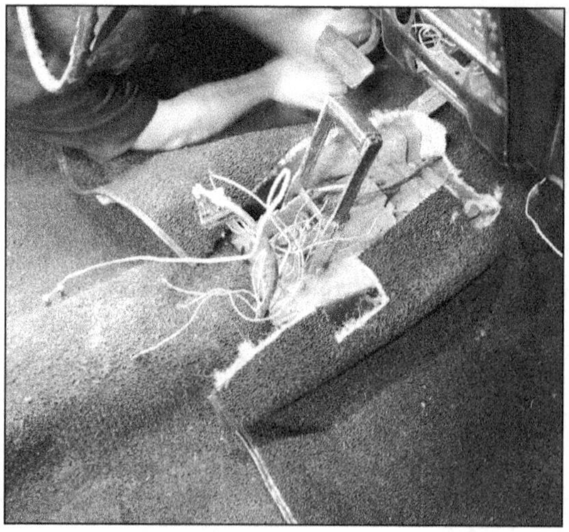

6 ***Once the forward section of carpet has been properly located, it can be trimmed up the center for the floor-mounted shifter. We didn't entirely split it in half, however, and left the section uncut forward of the shifter.***

7 *Nearly every carpet set of the muscle car era had the heel section molded in a tough-wearing plastic to reduce wear on the carpet in that area. Any good reproduction carpet set should have this section molded in as well.*

8 *The hole for the stomp switch for the high beams doesn't come cut from the factory, so once we located the carpet section, we cut the hole, then trimmed it with the rubber grommet-like piece included in the carpet set.*

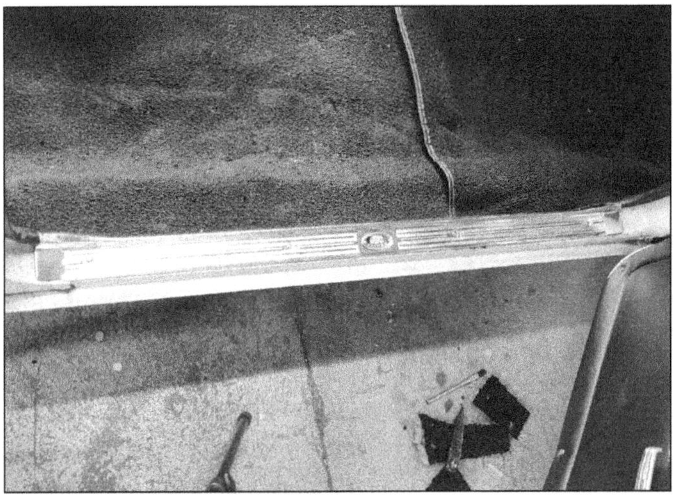

9 *Finally, the reproduction sill plate covers the sides of both front and rear carpet sections. Misaligned doors, stray seat belts, and carelessness combine to beat up the thin aluminum sill plates on almost every muscle car. Fortunately for restorers, they're widely available and easy to replace.*

down the corners of the carpet strip. At the trailing edge of the strip, as long as the strip had been positioned correctly, we didn't need to notch the edge or cut any flaps; the seat brackets slipped under the strip just far enough to reach their mounting holes.

If any excess carpet exists on either side at the door sills, it should be in equal amounts. We trimmed the excess at this point, then installed the sill plates, supplied with the kit from Original Equipment Restoration (OER). We were again careful to punch any holes in the carpet for the screws with an awl so the screws didn't catch a thread in the carpet.

Note that we did not use any adhesive or tacks to secure the carpet, mainly because the Camaro didn't require anything more than the interior panels, seats, and console to secure the carpet. If you want additional methods of securing the carpet, I recommend adhesive. To glue your carpet to the floor, follow the above installation directions: center the carpet sections, then adjust the sections forward or backward, trimming for shifters, brackets, or other obstructions, Once you've placed the carpet exactly where you want it, fold it over on itself, spray both the underside of the carpet and the floor that the carpet will lay over with adhesive, then fold that section of carpet back into position and start to smooth it out, working from the center outward. Repeat the process for the other half, then trim as necessary. You should only have to glue the flat floor sections, which then keep the carpet in position and prevent it from sliding around; it's not necessary to glue the carpet to the transmission tunnel.

If possible, order a set of floor mats to match the style and color of the carpet. Floor mats will obviously take the brunt of the damage inflicted by foot traffic and are much easier to replace than an entire carpet. If your carpet supplier cannot make a matching set of floor mats, order a couple yards of extra carpet material and have a local seamstress or upholsterer trim and bind the floor mats for you.

One last tip on carpet: Consider ordering enough extra material to cover your trunk floor. You don't have to permanently install it; you can have it trimmed and bound like the floor mats for a removable alternative to a bare steel trunk floor.

Bow-Type Headliner

If you've cruised the product aisles at your local big-box-type auto parts store, you've no doubt seen the magic aerosol sprays that claim to fix all droopy headliners. Don't buy them expecting to follow the directions and magically restore your headliner back to new. Spray adhesive is really only a Band-Aid fix and should be considered neither a permanent nor a proper solution.

My 1971 Plymouth 'Cuda required a new black headliner to match its new black carpet. Mice had chewed holes through the liner and made a few nests between it and the roof skin, so I had no choice but to remove the headliner, sail panels, sun visors, and trim, and start nearly from scratch. The trim pieces and sun visors thatcould be saved were thoroughly cleaned and set aside. The old sail panels and headliner were carefully removed and kept for reference during reinstallation. As I removed each bow from the headliner, I

Headliner Installation

1 ***Mold, mice, and general lack of care can individually or all together destroy a headliner. Unfortunately, replacing a headliner is often viewed as a complicated and laborious process. However, now that the restoration aftermarket offers reproduction headliners, with a little bit of instruction and a few hours, it's possible to replace your headliner yourself in your own garage.***

2 ***After removing the headliner from the car—hopefully intact and as a complete assembly—mark the position of the bows from front to back using a small piece of masking tape. The bows differ slightly in size and shape depending on their position and, for that reason, should not be mixed up. Remove the marked bows from the headliner and set them aside.***

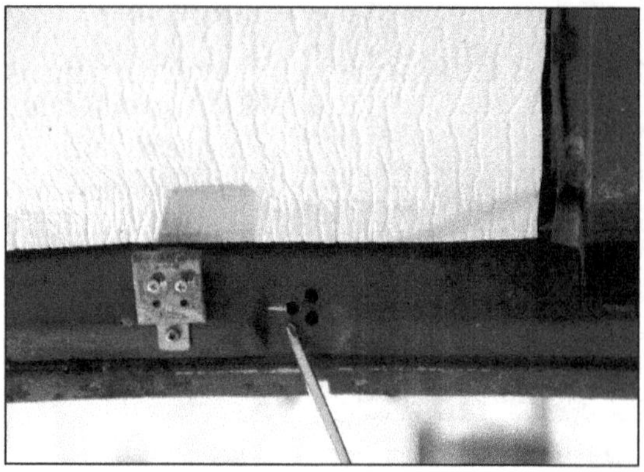

3 ***When removing the headliner from the car, use a piece of chalk to mark the exact hole that each bow fit into. The factory may drill a few holes in the general area for a variety of purposes, including adjustment of the headliner's slack and optional equipment that may affect the headliner's fitment.***

4 *On our 'Cuda, as with many Chrysler products from the 1960s and early 1970s, a hook protruding from the rear roof structure anchors the headliner to the rear of the car. Other cars may use teeth attached to the center roof structure to anchor the headliner. Pay attention to exactly how your car's headliner is mounted when removing the headliner from the car.*

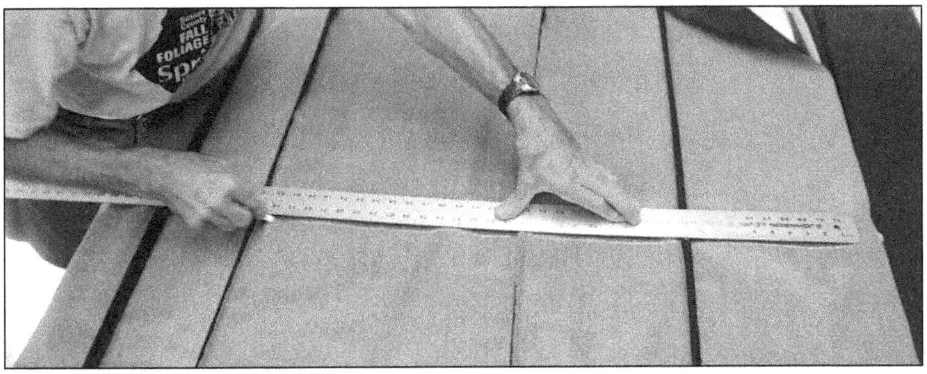

5 *Turning our attention to the new headliner, we marked the headliner's centerline with a piece of chalk and a straightedge. Note that the new headliner is a simple rectangular shape; it will be trimmed to fit the 'Cuda later in the installation process.*

marked its order, front to rear, with a small piece of masking tape and a marker. I also noted the bow's position in one of three mounting holes in the body as the bow came out of that hole.

Approximately from the 1930s through the 1970s, American car manufacturers used a couple variations on the same bow-type headliner. A series of four, five, or more bows inserted through loops in the top of the headliner and then hooked into holes or pockets in the body's substructure to keep the headliner up against the roof skin. Teeth built into the body substructure around the perimeter of the roof skin then gripped the edges of the headliner, assisted by an adhesive that bonds the fabric to the sheetmetal.

The main difference between Ford, Chrysler, and GM bow-type headliners was the method of anchoring the headliner, which provided the starting process for the actual headliner installation. Some muscle cars used teeth at the midpoint of the roof structure—crossing the car from right to left—to anchor the headliner. While that method works well for the first couple headliner installations, the teeth tended to break off from the car's substructure after repeated bending from multiple headliner installations, forcing an alternative or custom headliner installation method.

Almost every Chrysler product, however—including this 'Cuda—used hooks on the end of rods attached to the back of the body substructure to anchor the headliner. After attaching the headliner to the hooks, the installation of the headliner consists of pulling the headliner forward until each bow hooks into its proper place.

Sufficient preparation work at this point made the rest of the headliner installation proceed smoothly. The windshield and back window were removed from this 'Cuda shortly before this headliner installation, for another aspect of the car's restoration. This is not necessary to do for a typical headliner installation, though it certainly helped us position our hands around the edges of the headliner. We did, however, remove the trim around the windows, both interior and exterior, to provide clear access to the sheetmetal where the edges of the headliner would be glued. We also removed the seats, then laid down heavy blankets over the carpet and package tray to act both as cushions, and to prevent glue overspray on the already finished parts of the interior.

If necessary, any teeth that grip the headliner should be straightened and pointing in the same direction. Loose or broken teeth should be fixed, and dull teeth should be sharpened.

I like to use a little trick now that saves an incredible amount of time and energy in the long run. Rather than set all the screws aside in a container when removing trim, sun visors, and dome lamps, I thread the screws back in their mounting holes. Not only does this prevent misplaced fasteners, this also helps positively locate the screw holes during the headliner installation.

Insulating the Headliner

Many products on the market are designed to insulate the cabin of your muscle car and lay behind or under firewall pads or carpeting, including Dynamat.Insulshield, on the other hand, claims its line of insulators is specifically designed to line the roof above the headliner.

Unlike the installation of insulators under the carpet or behind the firewall pad, the roof insulator has to fit in the spaces of exposed sheetmetal between the roof braces, similar to how some insulation pads mount under the hood of a car.

Insulating the roof above the headliner not only reduces heat transfer from the roof into your muscle car, but also reduces noise. Start by making templates of the area you wish to insulate with craft paper. Note how our template covers only the flat expanses of the roof's underside, not the roof braces.

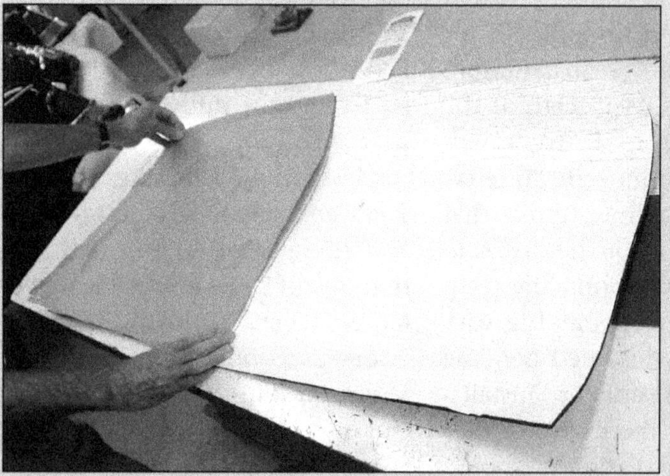

As with the Dynamat, we first made a craft paper pattern or template of the area in which we intended to install the Insulshield. However, we only made a pattern of half of the roof, based on the chalk centerline we already drew for the headliner installation. We then cut the pattern from the craft paper and transferred the pattern onto the Insulshield.

The underside of the roof skin should be thoroughly clean before the Insulshield is applied; acetone or denatured alcohol sufficiently cleans sheetmetal roof skins.

We then removed the backing paper from the Insulshield and began to position the Insulshield in the car. We intentionally cut the pattern leaving a little extra on the edges, which we then tucked under the roof braces with a tucking tool. With the Insulshield properly tucked, we then smoothed the expanses of Insulshield with a roller tool to make sure it all adhered to the roof skin.

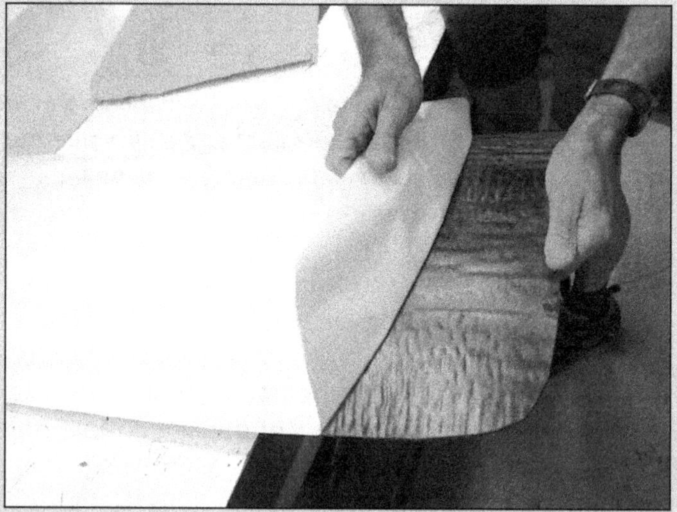

Most insulating material is adhesive backed, so simply pulling the paper backing from the adhesive is the final step in preparing the insulating material. The adhesive is pressure activated, so try not to press anything up against it before it's in position.

Making a template of only half of the roof saved time and effort, and by flipping the template over, we generated a perfectly symmetrical outline of the area to be insulated. We then transferred the pattern to the insulating material and trimmed the material to size.

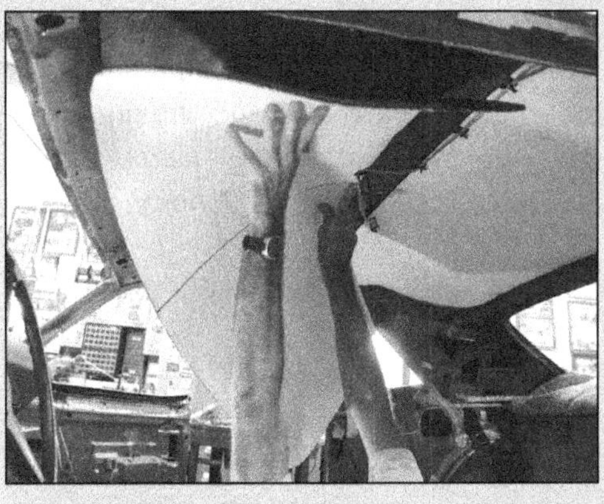

The centerline marked on the insulating material when transferring the pattern should line up with the centerline already marked on the roof. With the centerlines matched, start pressing the insulating material up into the roof skin. Note the notch cut for the dome lamp wiring.

We intentionally cut the insulating material slightly larger than the flat expanse of roof skin so we could tuck the edges of the insulating material under the roof braces. To tuck the edges under, we used a special tucking tool, though any flat, dull, somewhat stiff tool, such as a body filler spreader, will work just as well.

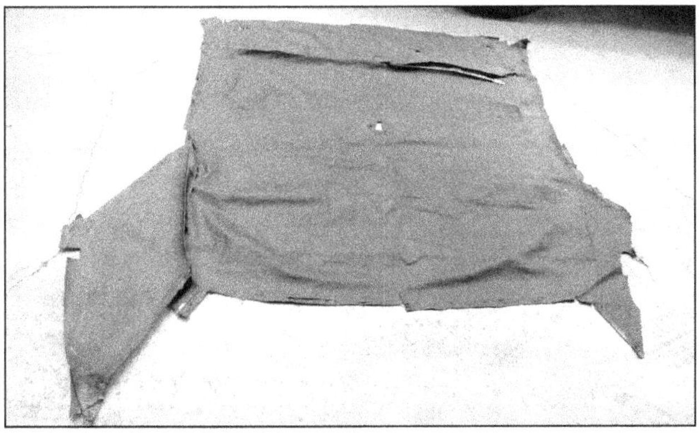

Do not toss out the old headliner just yet. In fact, find a spot in your shop where you can spread it out and where it won't be disturbed. That way you can quickly refer to it for measurements, fastener locations, and general guidance as you install the new headliner. Only when you've completed the new headliner installation should you throw away the old headliner.

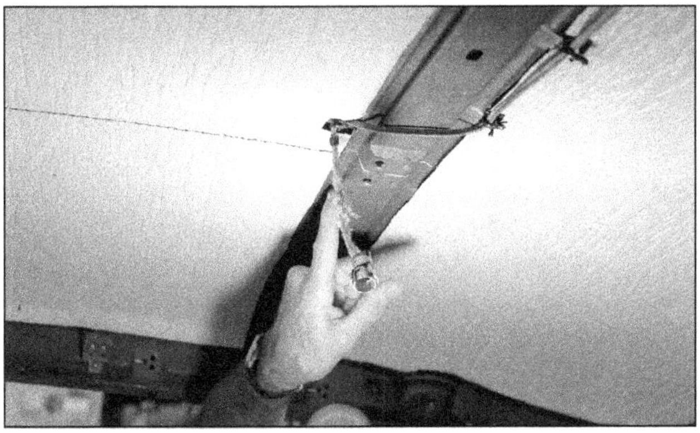

Now's your chance to clean up the underside of the roof; you won't have access to that sheetmetal once the headliner is installed. For headliners anchored by teeth, prepare the roof by straightening any bent teeth and repairing any broken teeth. To save time and effort later in the installation process, insert the screws for the trim, dome lamp, and sun visors now.

Were this a car with little aftermarket support, we would have had to sew a custom headliner, using the old headliner as a pattern. Were we to do that, we'd have to cut the headliner down the middle, using one half for the pattern and the other half for reference for the number of stitches, placement of features, and directionality of the fabric. But in the case of this 'Cuda, we were able to order a replacement headliner, already stitched together with the loops for the bows, from Legendary Interiors.

Most resto shops tell you that not all reproduction headliners are made to the exact specifications of the originals. and that some headliners, especially on a concours car, may not fit as desired. With this in mind, we closely compared the reproduction with the original to make sure it would fit properly. In this case, it would, so we saw no need to rework the 'Cuda's headliner.

Unfortunately, shipping reproduction headliners often results in folds and wrinkles in the headliner material. As with the carpet set, we usually unfold the headliner when we first receive it and then put it in the sun to let it warm up. After enough time in the sun, the wrinkles and fold marks naturally dissipate.

We next measured the center of the headliner and marked it on the underside (or the topside, if you consider it as it will be installed in the car) of the headliner, then drew a chalk line through the marks with the aid of a straightedge. We drew a corresponding chalk line along the centerline of the underside of the roof. The chalk can later come off with a damp paper towel.

We also noted with the chalk which end of the headliner went toward the rear of the car. This allowed us to insert the bows in the order in which we numbered them as we removed them from the old headliner. As the headliner came from Legendary, though, the loops for the bows extended too far out toward the edges, which didn't allow enough room to maneuver the bows into their positions and didn't allow the headliner to hang properly. So after we inserted the bows, we measured and marked 4 inches in from the end of each loop, then cut away that portion of the loop.

At this point, we were able to put the headliner assembly—complete with all the bows—into the 'Cuda. With the headliner oriented according to our chalk marks, we first attached the rearmost bow to its mounting holes, then hooked the anchors (which sprout from the structural brace over the rear window) to the rearmost bow. We then pulled the second bow forward, placed it in its mounting holes, and repeated the procedure for the third

Headliner Installation *CONTINUED*

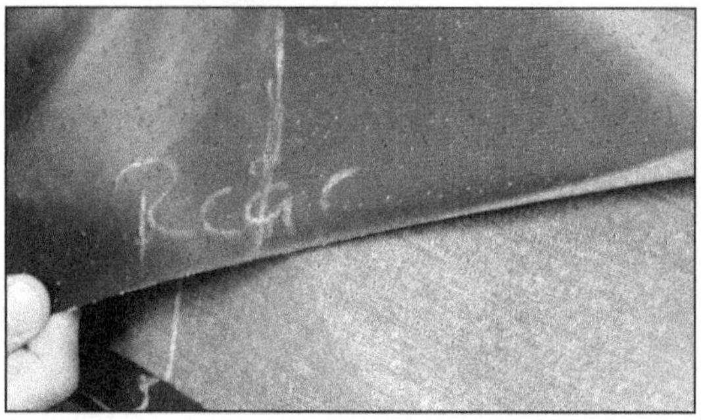

6 *We also marked the rear of the headliner to avoid confusion later. This is necessary because of slight differences in bow spacing and in the seams of the headliner material. Those differences help the headliner to conform to the compound curves of the roof.*

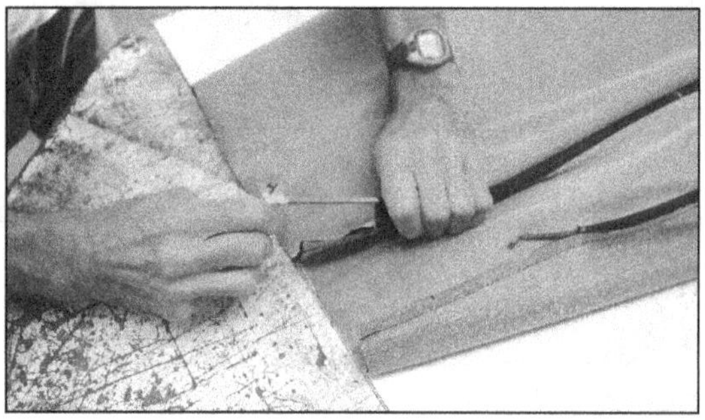

7 *Next, we inserted the bows in their proper order through the loops already stitched into the seams of the headliner material. Removing the rust from the bows before this step helped the bows slide easier through their loops.*

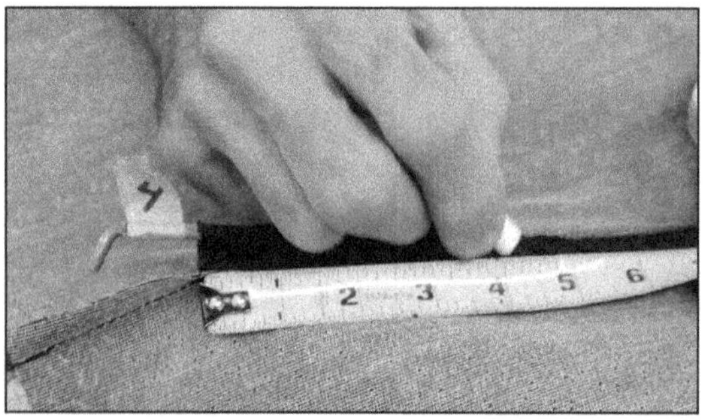

8 *Because the bows tend to bow, their loops require relief cuts at either end. We figured 4 inches is enough; any less and the headliner material won't easily slide over the curvature of the bows; any more and the headliner material will droop excessively.*

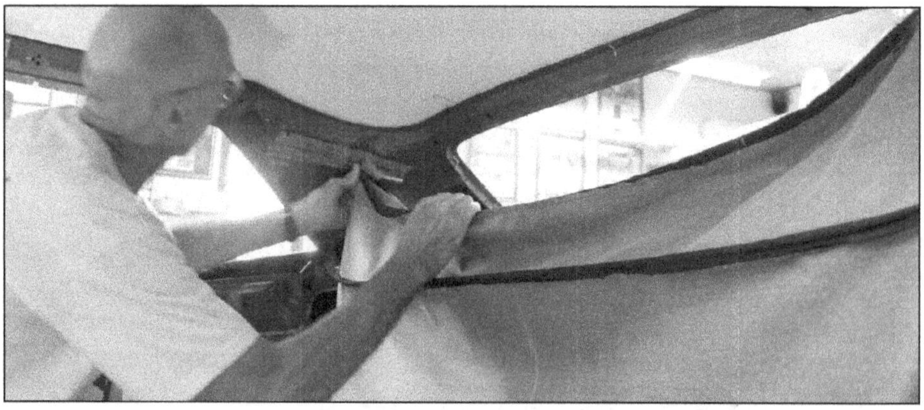

9 *After preparing the headliner material, we took it into the 'Cuda and hooked the rearmost bow into the holes we'd previously marked on either side of the roof structure. By rotating the rearmost bow in its holes, we can then hook the bow with the anchoring hooks, which slip over the bow through tiny slits cut into the loops.*

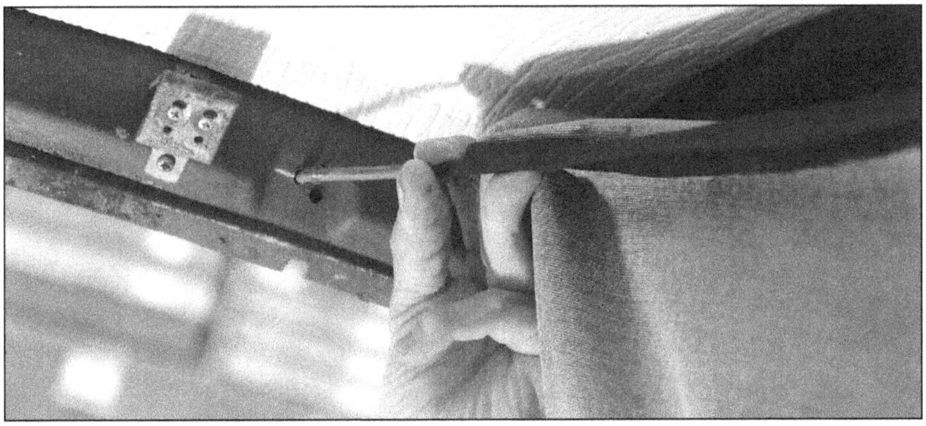

10 *Next, we hooked each bow into its marked holes to check the fitment. Placing the bows in different holes can adjust the headliner's slackness to a certain extent.*

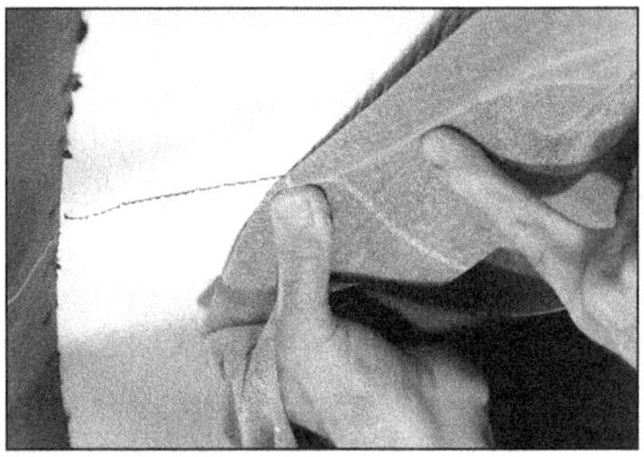

11 *As we hooked each bow, we checked to make sure the centerlines we marked earlier continued to match up. Keeping the centerlines matched now will prevent headaches down the road when we stretch the headliner side to side.*

12 *The bows only secure the headliner to the roof structure through the middle of the headliner. The edges, on the other hand, are secured to the roof structure with adhesive—simple contact cement, really—and we first sprayed a film of adhesive on the header.*

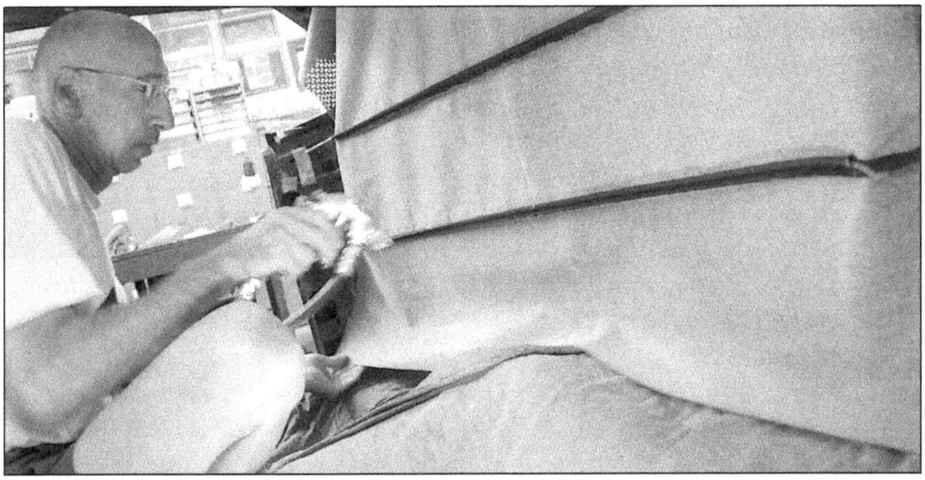

13 *The mating surfaces of the headliner material also received a film of adhesive. We sprayed the metal surfaces before the cloth surfaces, only because the adhesive takes slightly longer to set up on the metal surfaces.*

and fourth bows. After each bow placement we checked to make sure our chalk centerline matched up to the centerline on the underside of the roof. We also checked to make sure the new headliner didn't stretch or sag too much between each bow.

Satisfied that the headliner fit alright so far, we sprayed both the forward brace of the underside of the roof (also called the header) and the mating surface of the headliner with a liberal and even layer of contact cement, starting with the metal surfaces, only because the cement takes longer to dry on metal than it does on fabric.

After giving the contact cement a couple minutes to set up, we double-checked the alignment of our chalk centerlines, then began to pull the center of the headliner—gently, but firmly—forward, grasping the material at the leading edge of the headliner. Once we felt the headliner was taut enough, we brought the leading edge of the headliner around the header, then pierced it on the teeth at the forward edge of the panel.

Headliner Installation *CONTINUED*

14 *Once the adhesive set up, we stretched the headliner material forward to mate against the header. We pulled the material tight, but not taut; the opportunity to pull the material tighter will come momentarily.*

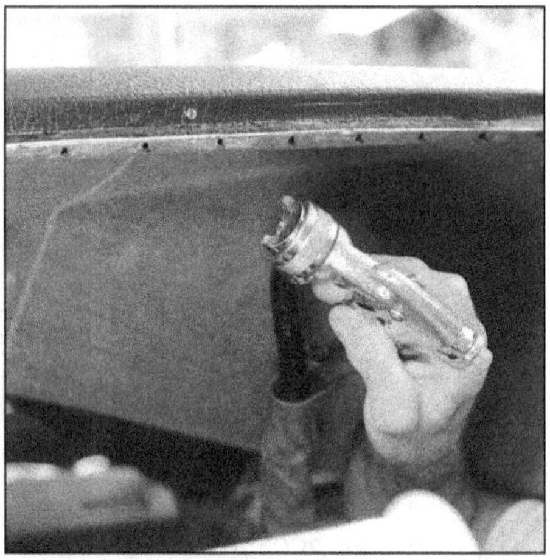

15 *The rearmost roof brace, behind the anchor hooks and just above the rear window, also got a shot of adhesive. The spikes along the edge of that brace, along with similar spikes along the edge of the header, only serve to hold the headliner material in place while the adhesive cures; the adhesive is what actually secures the headliner to the roof braces.*

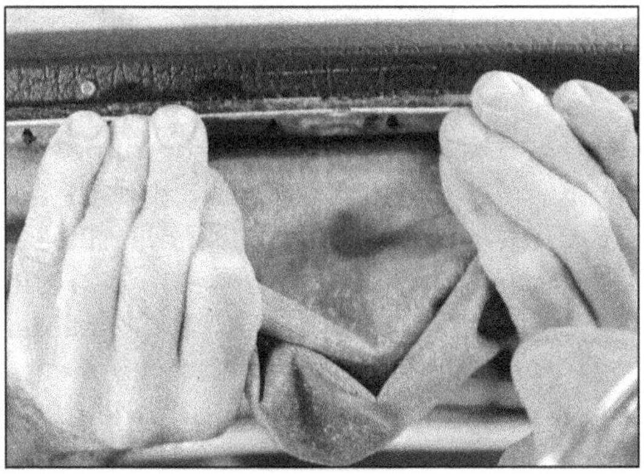

16 *Stretching the headliner material takes patience and multiple passes over the material. It also takes a gentle, but firm touch. Stretching the material too far will either damage it or cause it to droop. At the same time, not stretching it enough won't rid the material of wrinkles, and can cause it to hang unevenly.*

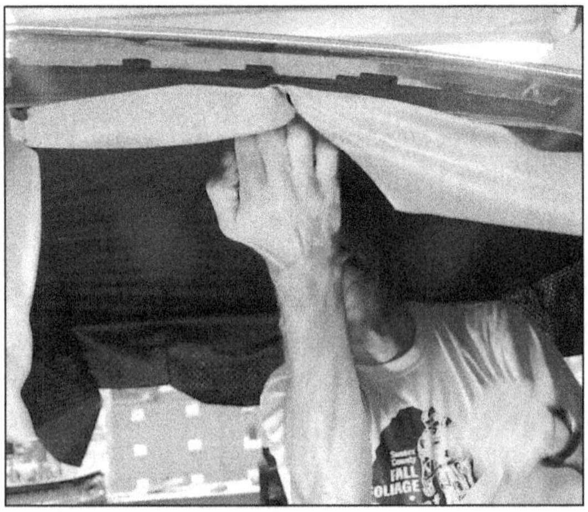

17 *With the front and rear edges secured, we glued the sides around the sheet-metal lip at the top of the door opening. The door opening trim will hide the edge of the material.*

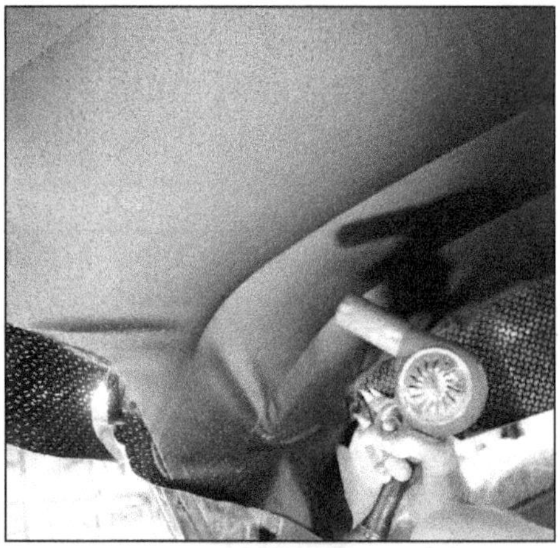

18 *We used a two-stage stretching process to eliminate wrinkles from the headliner and to get it to hang smoothly and evenly. First, we stretched the headliner in a plus-sign pattern: toward the front and rear and toward the sides. We used heat from a heat gun to make the headliner material more pliable for stretching.*

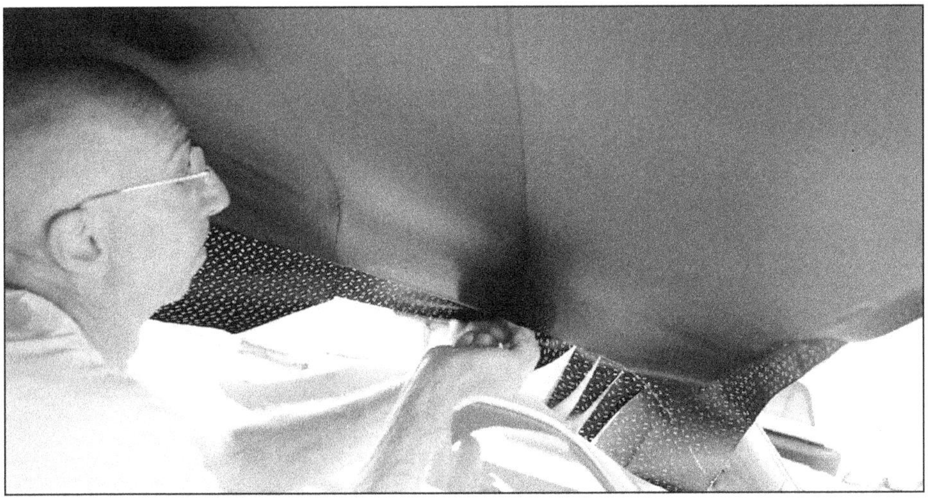

19 *The second part of our stretching process pulls the headliner in a multiplication-sign pattern: toward the corners. While stretching, we took care not to pull the headliner fabric too far to one side or another, checking opposite corners for signs that the headliner fabric had shifted too far to one side.*

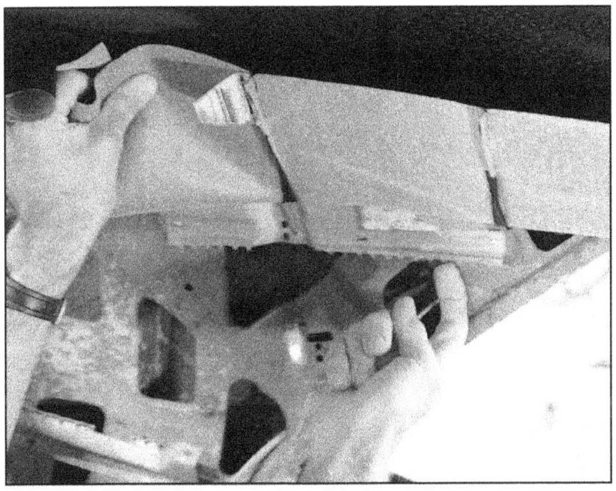

20 *This 'Cuda uses a toothed panel riveted to the inside of the C-pillars to grab the headliner at the rear corners. Without the toothed panel, the headliner would have no anchor point in those corners and would thus have to be glued arbitrarily to the inside of the C-pillar.*

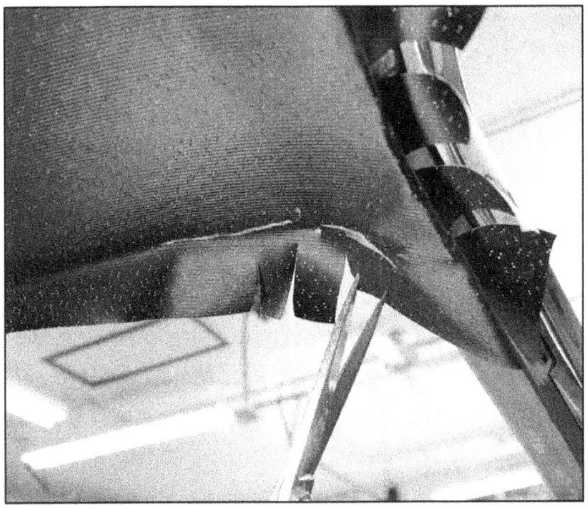

21 *At anything more than a gradual bend, we cut darts that allowed the headliner material to conform to the curves of the body. This way, the headliner material doesn't bunch up or stretch too much when folded over the sheet-metal lips that anchor the headliner in certain places.*

We only brought the center front section of the headliner forward, however. To attach the edges of the headliner, we used a two-stage approach: First, we secured the center of the front edge, center of the rear edge, and the center of each side in a cross or addition-sign pattern. Then, we secured the corners in an X or multiplication-sign pattern. This approach essentially divided the headliner into quadrants, each of which we could stretch and smooth out relatively independent of the other quadrants.

Although the header panel and its counterpart at the rear of the roof have teeth to secure the headliner while the contact cement dries, most of the sides do not. The headliner material thus glues directly to the body of the car at the door opening. Chrysler did, however, provide a strip of teeth on the inside of the sail panel to anchor the rear two quadrants of the headliner. Using a tuck tool will help the material wrap around those teeth.

Stretching the headliner should only be done along the seams, where the material is the strongest and least likely to droop later on. Stretching between the seams runs the risk of overstretching the material, causing droop or damage. For this step, you don't need to start yanking like a madman and overpulling the headliner; instead, you need finesse, and you pull the headliner only enough to smooth it out.

The application of heat from a heat gun while stretching the headliner speeds up the process by loosening the headliner material. We continued to stretch the material until all the wrinkles smoothed out and the headliner appeared fairly even, side to side and front to back.

While stretching, we constantly checked the alignment of the headliner side to side to make sure it hadn't shifted off center from the stretching process. If it had, we simply shifted the headliner back toward the center.

As we stretched the material to the sides, we encountered a few curves around which the material wouldn't fold neatly—especially around the radiused corners of the doors. In these areas, we cut relief darts from the edge of the material to the corner of the curve. These darts allowed us to fold the material over the edges of those corners without the material stretching (which can then lead to damage of the surrounding headliner material) or bunching up (which could cause both poor adhesion of the headliner to the metal and poor fit of the trim later on).

Unlike the original headliner, which was cut to a certain shape at the factory, Legendary's reproduction headliner came in a rectangular shape, not trimmed to the same shape as the original headliner. Thus, when we secured the headliner to the edges of the roof, a lot of excess material hung loose beyond the edges. Satisfied with the installation of the headliner so far, we cut away that excess material with a razor blade or with shears, using the edge of the roof as a guide for where to cut and exercising caution not to trim too far in from the edge of the roof.

Recall that we left the screws for the trim installed on the car before we covered them with the headliner. With the original headliner laid out nearby, we looked for the original screw holes in the headliner to gauge where we could find the screws underneath the headliner. After feeling for the installed screws with our

Headliner Installation *CONTINUED*

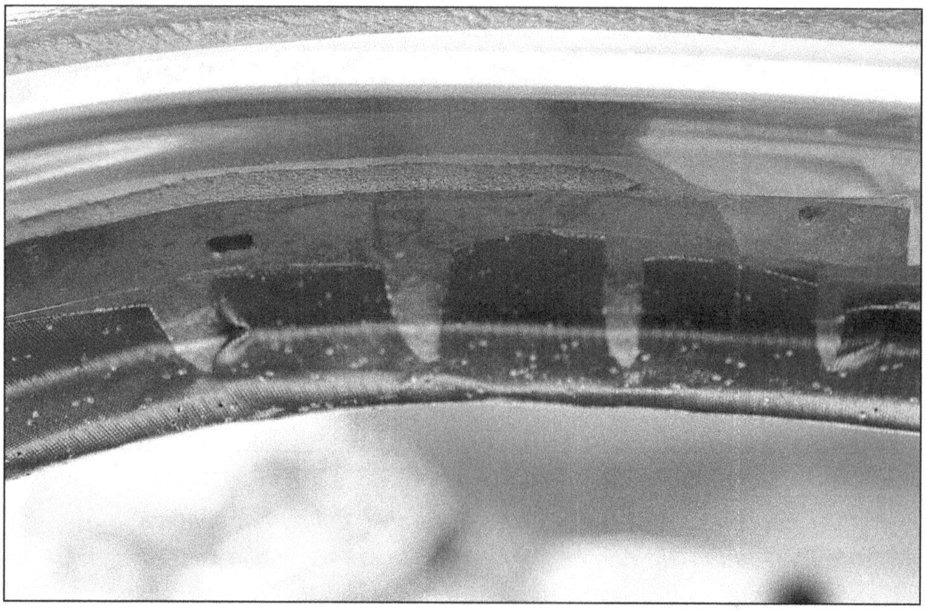

22 ***Note that the darts don't cut all the way to the point where the material folds over the lip, only most of the way. Cutting too far would reveal the snip outside of the trim that will later conceal the darts. With the darted material folded over the lip, you can see how easily it conforms to the curve. Darting, of course, is not necessary on straight edges.***

23 ***With the headliner glued into place and stretched to utter smoothness, we trimmed the excess headliner material from the edges of the headliner. Always make sure to use a fresh razor blade; razor blades that have been used even just a handful of times can become dull and start to tear at the fabric rather than cut it.***

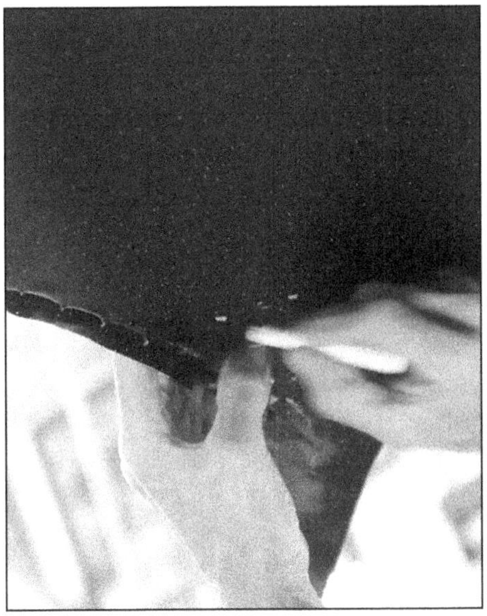

24 *Keep in mind that we left the screws for the dome lamp, sun visors, and trim in their holes, now covered by the headliner. We meant to do that. By feeling around through the headliner, we were able to mark the screw heads with a piece of chalk.*

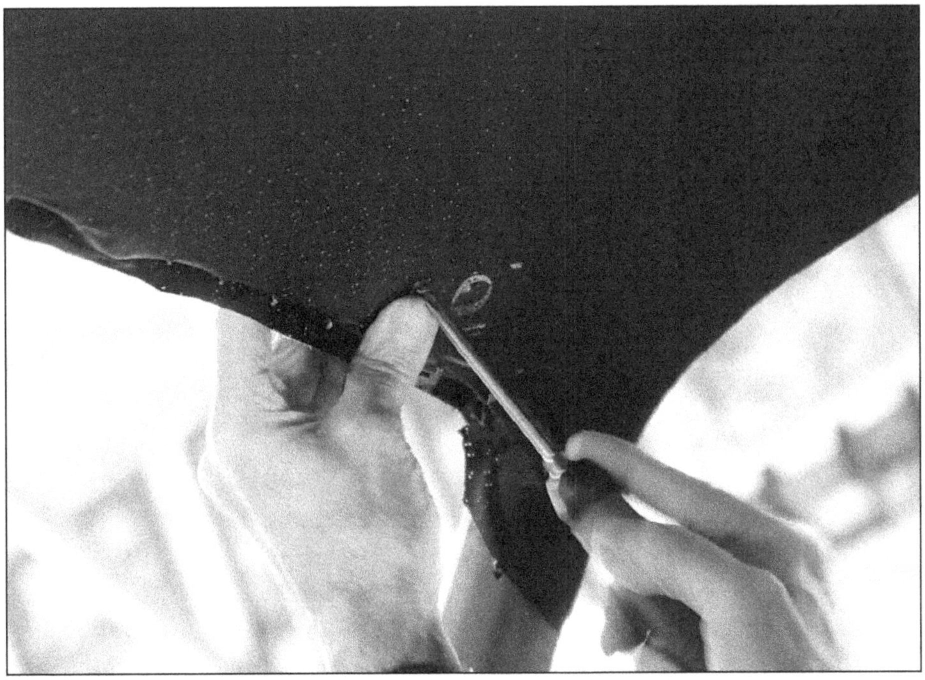

25 *Through the headliner material we used a Phillips-head screwdriver to back the screws out of their holes. Once we backed them out far enough, we pushed the headliner down around the screw heads, creating a perfectly sized hole for the screws.*

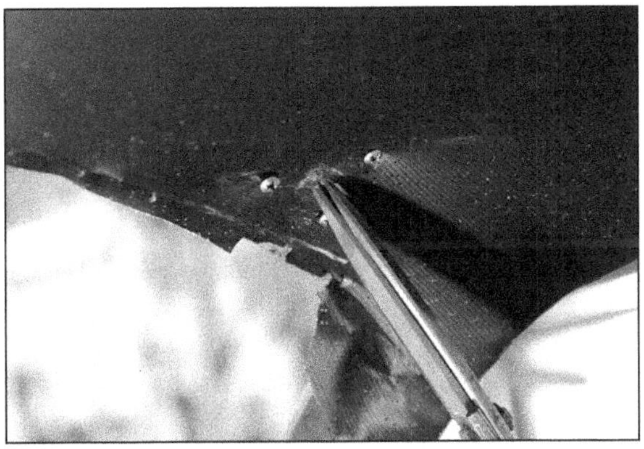

26 *Unfortunately, the method doesn't work well for large bolt heads or for holes that simply need to remain open, such as the holes at the center of the sun visor mounts. For those holes, we use a standard pair of shears or a razor blade.*

hands, we poked a screwdriver through the headliner to start backing the screw out of its hole. With the screw partway backed out, we then pushed the headliner material down around the screw head, creating a neat little screw hole in the headliner.

We repeated the process for the rest of the screws and installed the trim, sun visors, and dome lamp. Any screws that happen to fall behind the headliner can easily be retrieved with a magnet and brought back up to the hole for that screw.

The upper seat belt mount, however, used a bolt of significantly larger diameter than simple screws, so we had to leave it out when installing the headliner. Pushing the headliner material around the bolt head would have caused too much damage to the headliner material. Instead, we used the original headliner as a guide once more, felt for the bolt hole under the headliner, and used a razor to cut a small X in the headliner material above the bolt hole. We then threaded the bolt into the hole without damaging the headliner.

Shell-Type Headliner

So what do you do if you have a post-1970s muscle car, or one of the few types of muscle cars—mostly AMC products—that used shell-type headliners? These headliners insulate the noise and heat from the roof with a somewhat different method. They eliminated the complex bows and integrated some insulation in their construction, thus making a

Headliner Installation *CONTINUED*

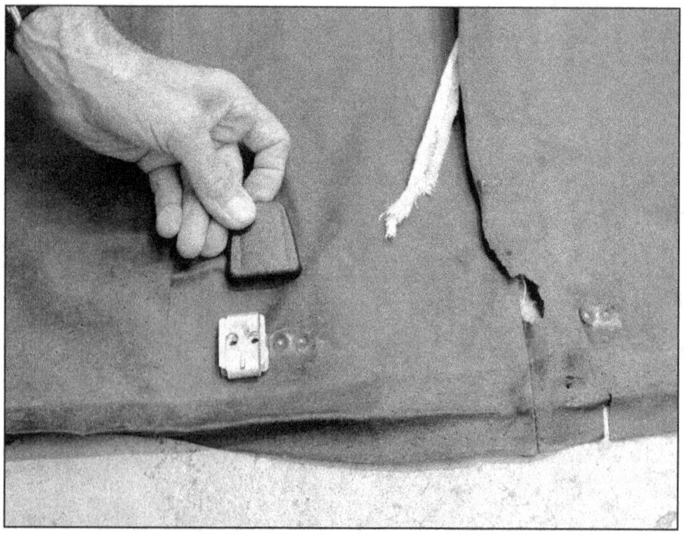

27 *Keeping the old headliner material on hand makes finding mounting pads for certain pieces of trim and accessories simple. Just find the right holes in the old headliner material, measure their distances from the edges, and use those measurements as a general guide to find the existing holes under the headliner material.*

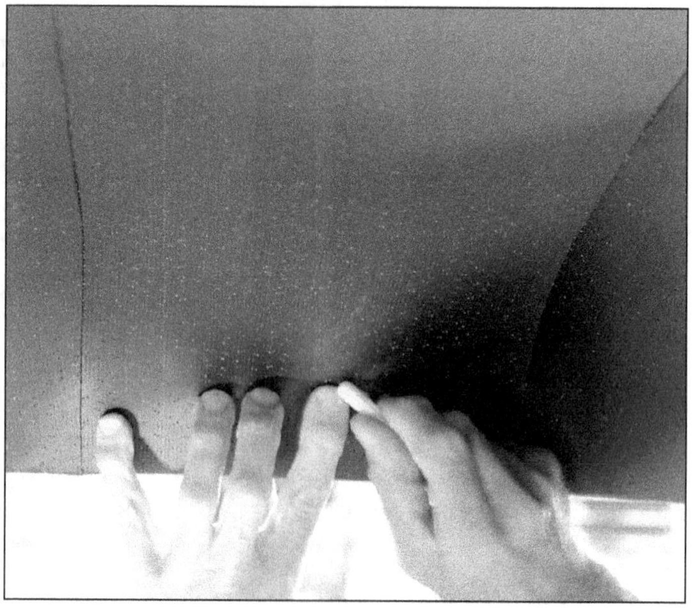

28 *Rather than jump right in to cutting open the holes for the trim, we instead marked the holes with chalk first and checked to make sure the trim would line up with the holes. Chalk marks can easily be cleaned up afterward.*

Fastener Etiquette

You're going to encounter a lot of screws through the course of your interior restoration–perhaps more than anywhere else in or on your car. And through the course of disassembly, test fitting, and re-assembly, you're going to encounter a lot of opportunities to cross-thread screws, which can lead to frustration, or worse, the added cost of repairing those threads.

First, to avoid cross-threading, especially when installing trim and using an awl, the way to save a lot of headaches is to properly locate the hole. Simply stick the awl through one of the trim piece's screw holes to positively locate the piece of trim while threading the other screws for that piece of trim.

Second, when starting a screw in a hole, first back it out while gently pushing it in. Only when you hear the click of the threads engaging each other do you know for sure that you can start threading the screw into the hole without fear of any damage.

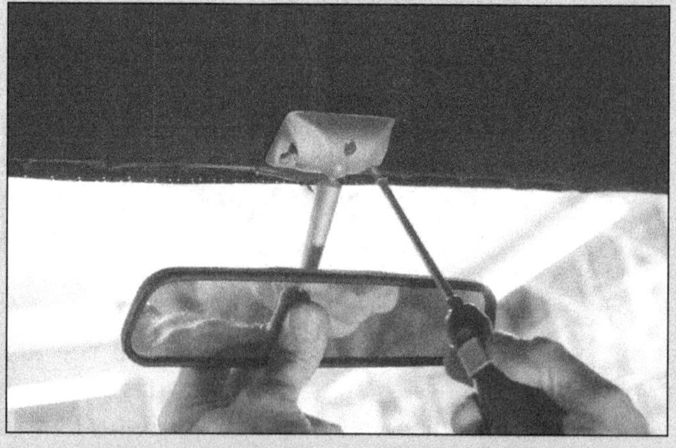

Any trim or accessory items that screw in through the headliner can be first aligned to the proper screw holes with an awl through one set of screw holes while screws are threaded into the other holes. To avoid damage to the threads during installation, first turn the screw counter-clockwise before cinching it down.

shell-type headliner simpler to install and more comfortable than a bow-type headliner.

A shell-type headliner consists of two basic parts: the molded fiber backing board, called the shell, and the headliner material, which glues to the shell and incorporates an insulating foam layer. Is it as simple as that? Yes and no. It's much simpler than a bow-type headliner in that the shell-type headliner doesn't require as much pulling and stretching. Also, a shell-type headliner's restoration can be done outside the car on a bench, without crawling around the interior of the car. However, a shell-type headliner requires a great deal more preparation.

First, make sure you remove the shell in one piece, without cracking it or folding it over on itself. It must retain its basic shape throughout this process, otherwise the headliner material may not adhere properly to the shell. Double-check to make sure that all the interior trim holding the headliner in place has been removed, and try not to rip the existing headliner material from the shell just yet; doing so may inadvertently damage the shell.

With the shell extracted from the car, flip it over and set it on a workbench. Note whether the headliner material wraps over the edges of the shell or if it's trimmed flush with the edges of the shell. Also note the alignment of the fabric on the headliner shell.

Very carefully, start removing the headliner material and foam backing, peeling away everything but the molded shell. Pay particular attention to the edges and the mounting holes for the sun visors—constant pressure over the decades makes those areas particularly difficult to remove without tearing or cracking the shell underneath. You'll notice a fine dust lifting off the headliner material and shell. This is what's left of the foam layer originally bonded to the headliner material; time and heat disintegrated it, eventually causing the headliner material to sag.

The most important part of the process now involves removing all trace of old adhesive and old foam from the shell. Using some sort of light abrasive—perhaps a whitewall tire brush, a Scotch-Brite pad, or fine-grade sandpaper—go over the entire shell until you reach the actual shell surface. Similar to how you need to strip sheetmetal down to bare metal to repaint it properly, you need to strip a shell down to the bare surface to restore it properly. Make sure, however, not to

Shell-Type Headliner Installation

1 ***Perhaps the most important step in restoring a shell-type headliner comes right at the beginning, when removing it from the vehicle, and when the potential for damage is high. Here, our headliner material has already come loose from the backing shell, leaving behind a crumbly foam residue.***

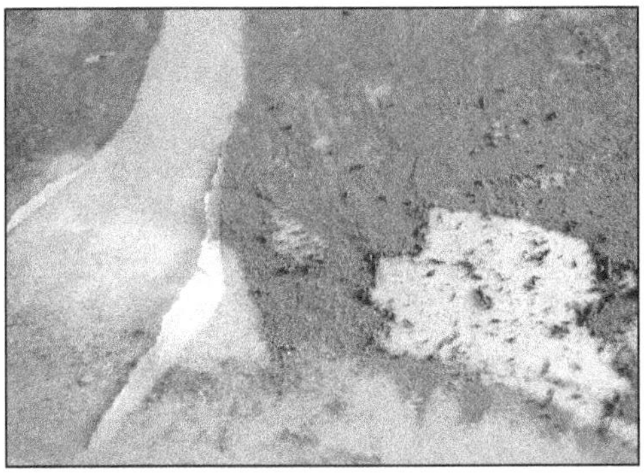

2 ***The foam residue will easily rub off under our fingers and will need to be entirely removed for the new headliner material to adhere to the backing shell. Note also that a thin layer of old adhesive under the foam residue is already starting to peel from the shell; this also needs to be removed.***

remove any material from the shell itself—you'll want to perform this step by hand rather than with any power tools.

Examine the shell for any minor tears, cracks, or gouges. Surface imperfections may cause the new headliner fabric to detach from the shell and prematurely sag. Fortunately, minor surface imperfections are easily repaired with fabric tape or duct tape.

New headliner material should be available at most upholstery supply stores, or even at the fabric stores your wife visits. I ordered this material from Hancock Fabrics, which described it as Alpine style.

Once you've finished preparing the shell, spread the material out over the shell in the correct orientation and with the foam backing down, against the shell. Fold the material in half, back over itself, exposing half of the shell and half of the foam backing. Next liberally spray both the shell and the foam backing with trim adhesive or contact cement. For this step, we used 3M's Super Trim Adhesive.

After letting the adhesive set up, slowly fold the headliner material back over on to the shell, starting from the center and working your way toward the edges, constantly and evenly applying pressure to the material. Working your way outward prevents bubbles from forming between the shell and the foam backing. No tools are necessary for this step, and probably aren't even desired; using your hands will allow you to press the material into all of the shell's contours better than any tool.

At the edges of the shell, pay particular attention to any reliefs for the trim and try to make the

Shell-Type Headliner Installation *CONTINUED*

3 ***We weren't as careful as we should have been when removing the shell from the car and we ended up with this crack going in from the edge of the shell. Survey the shell now for any similar damage. This crack is easily repairable, but shells with extensive damage should be replaced.***

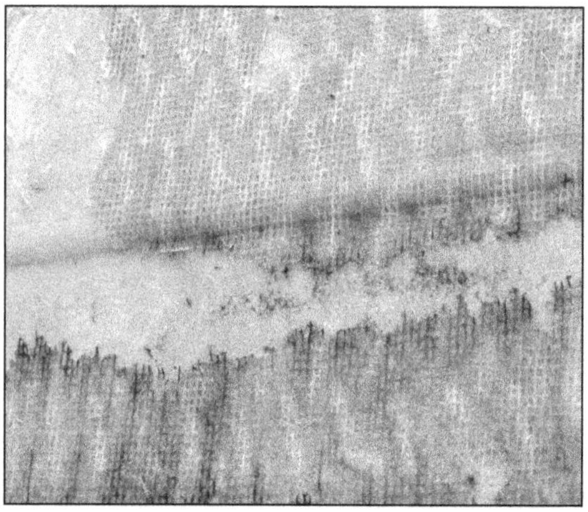

4 ***On the top side of the shell, a thin woven material had been bonded to the shell, but had started to peel off. We removed the loose pieces of it. Note how excessive heat radiating from the roof had scorched parts of the woven material. Insulating the roof should prevent this in the future.***

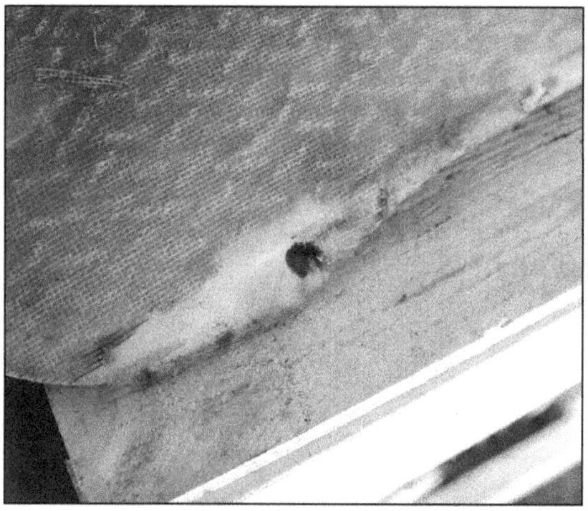

5 ***While inspecting the edges of the shell, take note of holes stamped in the shell that allow access to mounting points behind the shell. For instance, this hole permits access to the screw hole for a piece of trim.***

6 *Fortunately, the thin layer of old adhesive peeled straight off the shell, taking the foam residue with it. To avoid damage when peeling adhesives or tapes, and to get as much of the adhesive or tape as possible in one swipe, always hold it 90 degrees to the surface from which you're peeling it, and pull evenly and without stopping.*

7 *Removing the old adhesive exposes the bare shell. Only the areas around the edges did not easily peel away from the shell, likely due to a combination of heavy amounts of adhesives applied at the factory and constant pressure from the trim that held the headliner in place for decades.*

material conform to those reliefs. Keep smoothing the headliner material until the material both conforms to and remains conformed to the shapes of the shell. If necessary, put your other hand behind the shell to hold it steady as you press from the front.

Once the first half is adequately smoothed, repeat the process for the other half, folding it back over on itself, gluing it, then smoothing it, from the center outward. When both sides have been glued and smoothed and the glue has fully dried, you can start to trim the edges. If the original headliner material folded over the edges, trim the material on the new headliner down to about 1 inch from the shell's edges, and cut darts at every corner to allow the material to fold over evenly.

At this point you can flip the shell. If folding over the edges, spray both the perimeter of the shell and the headliner material with adhesive, then proceed with folding over. You'll notice that the material has covered the pre-punched holes in the shell for the dome light, the sun visors, and other accessories, so now you'll have to cut holes in the headliner material from the back side to once again mount those accessories.

Use a sharp razor blade; most of those holes only require a few small radial slits to permit the mounting screws for the accessories to pass through the headliner material. Larger holes—such as for the dome lamp—may require you to cut out sections of headliner material. Just don't cut away too much.

By the time you've trimmed the headliner, it should be ready to go back in to your car. If you take care with your mounting screws, you

Shell-Type Headliner Installation *CONTINUED*

8 *For those areas that did not peel away, we had to scrub them off the shell with a Scotch-Brite pad. A tire brush or coarse sandpaper also works here, just make sure not to scrub any harder than necessary to avoid damaging the shell underneath.*

9 *Everywhere that we earlier identified some damage around the edges, we used simple tape to reinforce the structural integrity of the shell. We used blue masking tape, but a tape with a stronger adhesive element, such as duct tape, cloth tape, or aluminum-backed tape, would have worked better. The tape in the middle of the shell covers slight gouges that may show through the headliner material.*

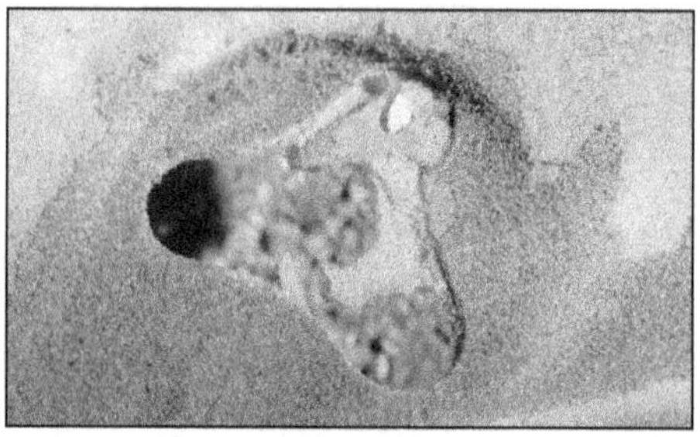

10 *The shell underneath one of the sun visors had taken a beating over the years, and a section of it likely ripped off when a previous owner removed the sun visors. We could have left it as it was, but we weren't sure how the headliner material would fill in the divot left behind.*

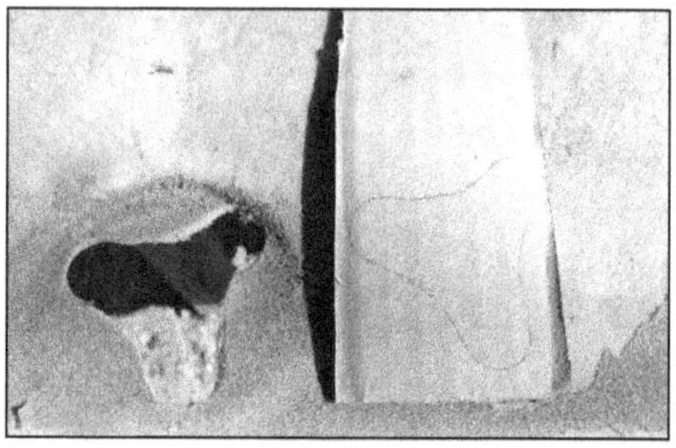

11 *To thicken the divot area before we applied the headliner, we cut a piece of corrugated cardboard to fit. We cut out the remaining part of the shell, and traced the hole onto the cardboard.*

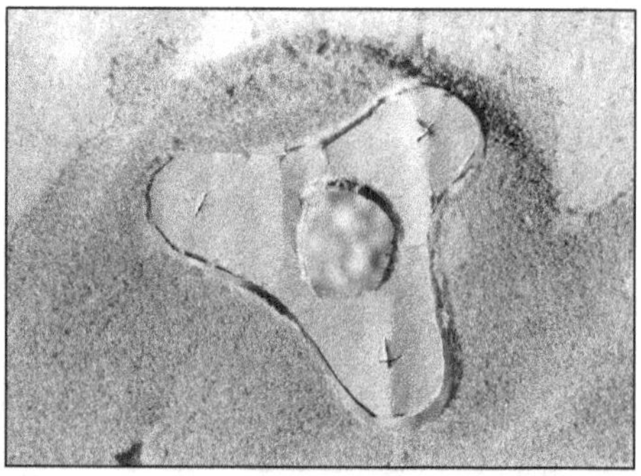

12 *With a hole for the center of the sun visor cut, along with Xs cut for the screws, we taped it into place. Sure, it looks a bit rough here, but it'll all be covered up momentarily.*

13 *The headliner material has about the same fabric as the original headliner material, backed with about 1/4 inch of foam. It is this foam that degrades over time and causes the headliner material to droop away from the backing shell, so order the highest-quality headliner material possible. For most muscle cars 2 yards should be enough.*

14 *We unrolled the headliner material and draped it over the underside of the shell (the side that we'll see with the headliner in the car). We made sure the headliner material was oriented square to the shell, then folded it in half, back over itself to expose the shell and the foam side of the headliner material.*

15 *Using 3M's Super Trim Adhesive, we evenly coated both the exposed side of the shell and the exposed foam side of the material. Following the directions on the can (a 19-ounce aerosol can was just enough for this headliner), we sprayed the adhesive back and forth horizontally, then back and forth vertically, before letting it set up for a couple minutes.*

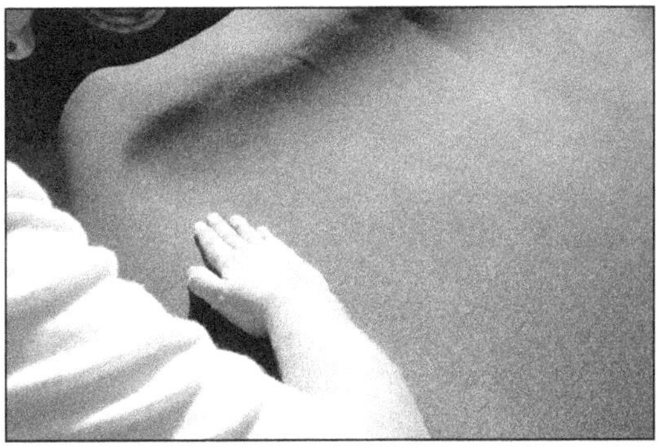

16 *After the adhesive set up, we flipped the material onto the shell, careful to maintain the correct orientation of the material to the shell. We then began pressing the material firmly to the shell with our hands, starting from the center and working our way outward. At the edges, we made sure that the material followed all the contours of the shell.*

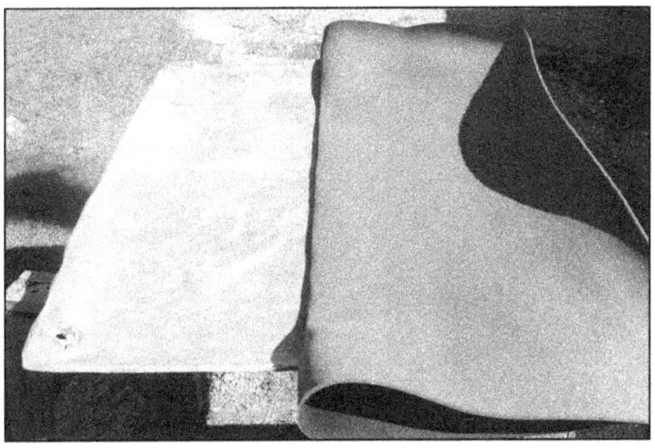

17 *With the first half glued down, flip over the other, unglued half of the material and repeat the process. Take care not to crease the centerline on which you're folding the material; otherwise, the crease will appear in the material and will need to be smoothed out.*

Shell-Type Headliner Installation *CONTINUED*

18 *Spend some extra time going around the edges to ensure the headliner flows into the contours and takes on the defined shape of the shell. If necessary, peel back any edges that aren't as well defined, apply some extra adhesive, and go over those edges again.*

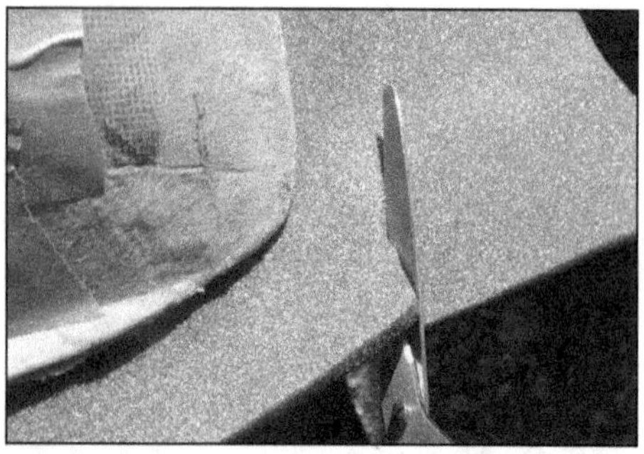

19 *The method by which the factory secured the headliner to the roof determines exactly how you trim the excess material from the headliner. If the edges of the headliner still show when the headliner is installed in the car, leave about 1 inch of material around the edges. If interior trim pieces cover all edges of the headliner, you can trim the material flush with the edges of the shell.*

20 *If you leave material around the edges of the shell, make sure to dart the corners so the material can fold over the edges of the shell.*

21 *Any openings in the headliner, such as the dome lamp opening shown here, should be cut out from the topside of the shell to make sure you don't cut away too much material. Use a sharp razor blade for clean cuts.*

shouldn't spot a difference from how the headliner looked when the car was new.

All told, restoring this shell-type headliner (minus the time spent removing and reinstalling it) took about 4 hours, not a bad task for one Saturday afternoon.

Some muscle car guys decide to switch from a bow-type headliner to a shell-type headliner. Doing so certainly offers several advantages—as long as you're not worried about authenticity, of course—but it also requires a bit of custom work. You first have to come up with a shell, which is the hardest part of the switch. If you can find a modern junkyard shell that can be trimmed to fit in your muscle car, then simply follow the directions above to re-skin the shell in a fabric matching your existing interior and somehow figure out how to secure it to the roof (don't rely on just the dome lamp

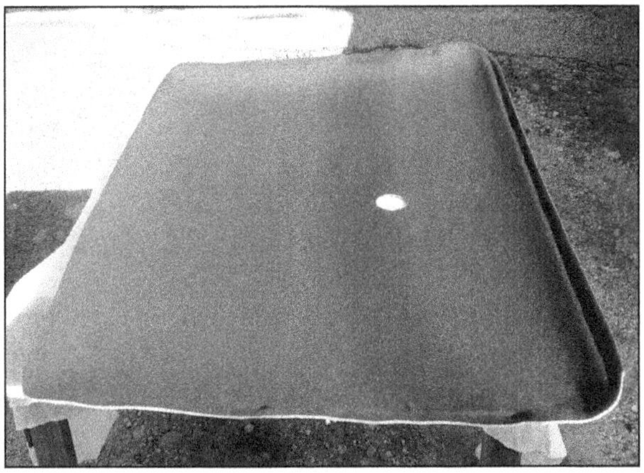

22 ***We ultimately trimmed our material flush with the shell and the dome lamp opening. In the end, the cost of materials totaled no more than $30, and we were able to take this headliner from ugly shell to ready-to-install in about 4 hours. It sure beats pushpins holding up the material, doesn't it?***

23 ***We popped in our finished headliner, which was simply a matter of tucking it into the metal hooks on either side above the door. The dome lamp assists in anchoring the headliner to the roof, as does the trim. The trim also hides the bare edges of the headliner and completes the professional appearance of our newly restored headliner.***

and the sun visors to hold it up—try to have your trim involved too).

If you can't find a suitable junkyard shell, you may just have to create a shell of your own out of fiberglass, taking a mold off the roof skin and adjusting its dimensions to fit inside the car. Flatter, less contoured shells could be made out of simple 1/8-inch luaun. But with a shell-type headliner, you'll find it easier to add an overhead console, sunroof, or custom designs to your interior.

Sail Panels

Most muscle cars are like our 1971 'Cuda and will have sail panels that cover the inner structure of the C-pillar. The headliner would normally serve this function, except to do so would require the headliner to make several compound curves. Instead, a separate piece is used. Some cars may use molded plastic panels, and for those restorations, see Chapter 2. The rest, however, use thin, molded backing boards covered in the same material used for the headliner. Sound familiar? It should; the process of restoring sail panels is very similar to the process of restoring a shell-type headliner. The same company that provided the headliner material for the 'Cuda, Legendary Interiors, also provided the sail panel material.

The old sail panel material should easily pull away from the backing boards, and all of it should be removed. If the boards are damaged, find a replacement or reproduction board. We removed all traces of the old adhesive from the backing boards with light sanding and cut enough headliner material to overlap the edges of the backing boards by several inches.

We then laid the material on the side of the board that faces the interior, aligned the material so the pattern faced the right direction, then folded it in half to expose half of the backing board and half of the back side of the material. As with the edges of the headliner, we sprayed a liberal amount of contact cement on the board and the material, then gave it about a minute to set up.

Once the contact cement set up, we flipped the headliner material back onto the backing board and began to gently press the material against the board, starting from the center and working toward the edges, smoothing any wrinkles or bubbles in the material. Once we removed all the wrinkles, we went over the glued area with a small roller. Once that half was dry, we pulled back the unglued half and repeated the process.

With both sides glued and smoothed, we flipped the sail panel over, trimmed the excess material down to a couple inches, and sprayed both the edges of the backing board and the excess material with more contact cement. While letting the contact cement set up, we cut darts into the loose material around the corners, then folded the loose material over the top and bottom edges of the backing board,

Snail Panel Installation

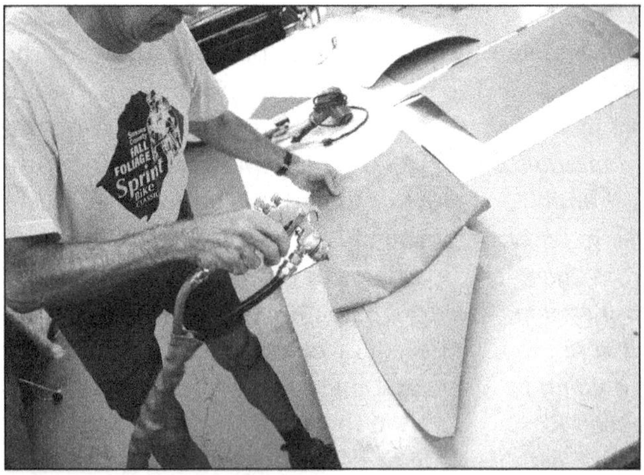

1 ***Sail panel restoration is a lot like the shell-type headliner process. We laid reproduction sail panel material out on the 'Cuda's original sail panel backing boards, folded half of the material over, and sprayed down both sides with adhesive.***

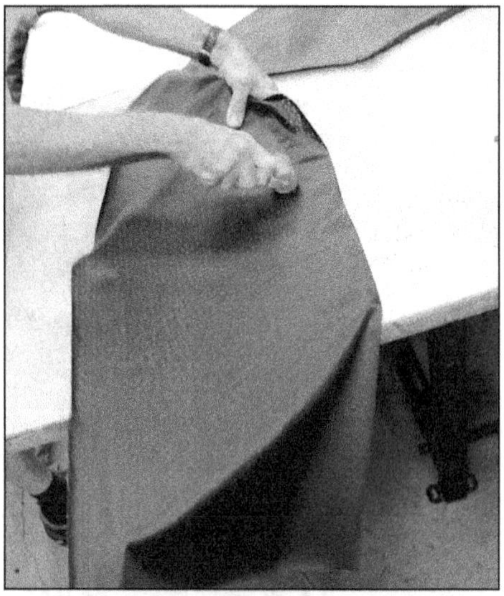

2 ***With one half glued, we flipped it over and glued the second half. To ensure that the material lays smooth on the backing board, we went over the sail panels again with a roller tool.***

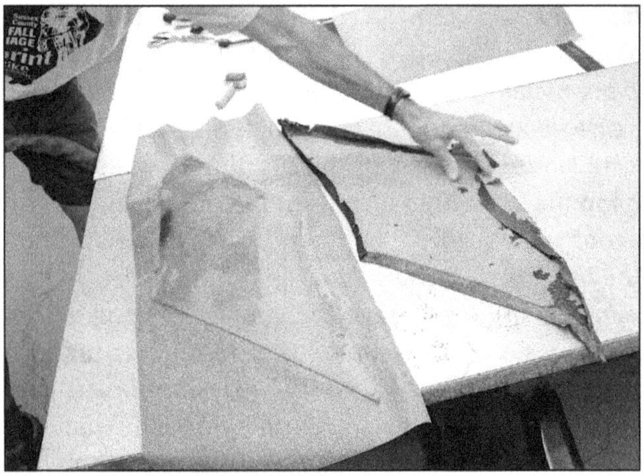

3 ***We flipped over the sail panel to check it against the other panel and noticed the notch on one edge, which we took into consideration when trimming the panel. As with the original panel, we trimmed the new panel with about 1 inch of overhanging material.***

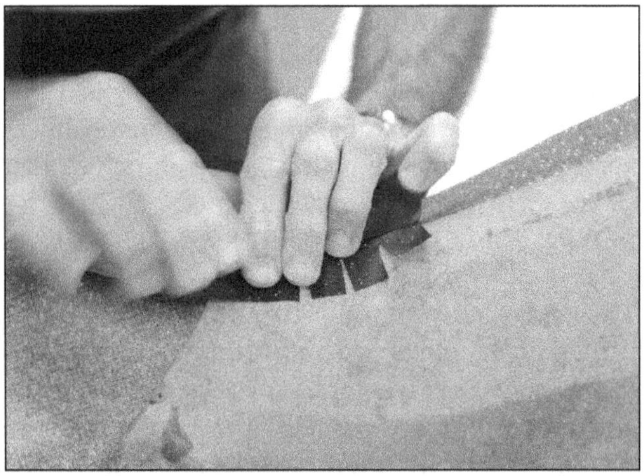

4 ***At any curve or corner, we made sure to cut darts. We then sprayed the edges of the back side of the panels with adhesive and folded over the edges. However, we didn't fold over the leading and trailing edges of the material just yet.***

leaving loose material hanging over the the front and rear edges.

Once the contact cement had all dried, we were then able to pop the sail panel into place, where it bridged the gap between the 'Cuda's headliner and the rear side panel. The overhanging material at the front and rear edges of the sail panel were hit with a spray of glue, then darted and folded over the edges of the quarter-window and rear window openings.

You'll notice a world of difference in your interior after addressing your carpet, headliner, and sail panels. Sure, they're ambitious projects, particularly the bow-type headliner, so don't expect to do them all in one day, especially on your first attempt.

If you find yourself handing the whole job over to a professional, they do advise that you can save them time and thus yourself money by at least prepping the interior: removing and cleaning the trim, ordering the correct headliner, and cleaning out mouse nests and other debris. But unlike recalibrating gauges or building a thermo-vacuum chamber, these tasks can be accomplished by any home restorer with a bit of time and effort.

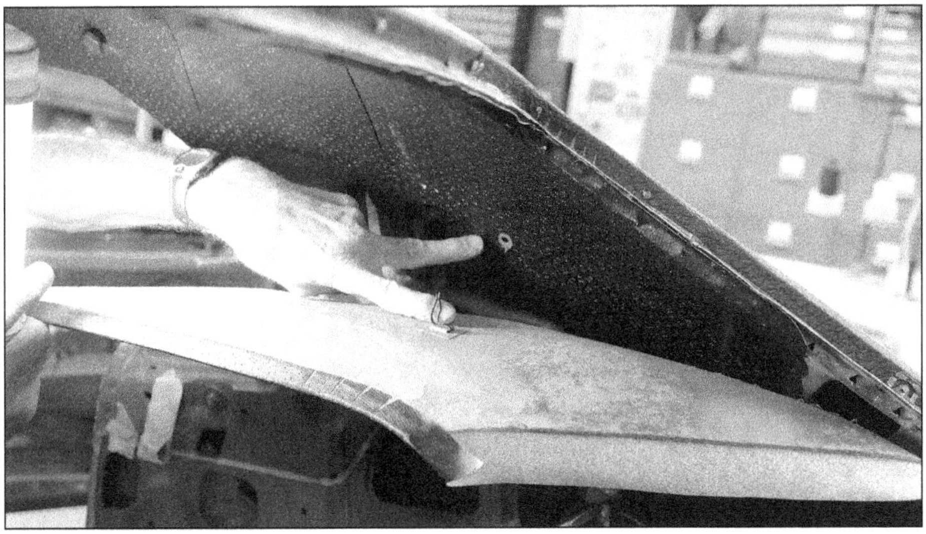

5 *Using the sail panel's clip as a reference, we located the hole that the clip fits into, then removed the headliner material from around that hole. If the clip or the clip holder in the sail panel is damaged, the sail panel should not be used.*

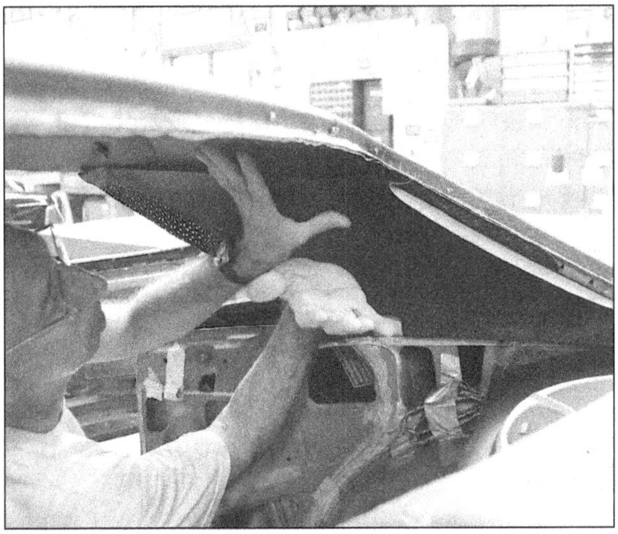

6 *After lining up the clip with its hole, we popped it in with a quick slap from the heel of the palm. Note the body structure component that necessitated the notch we had to cut earlier.*

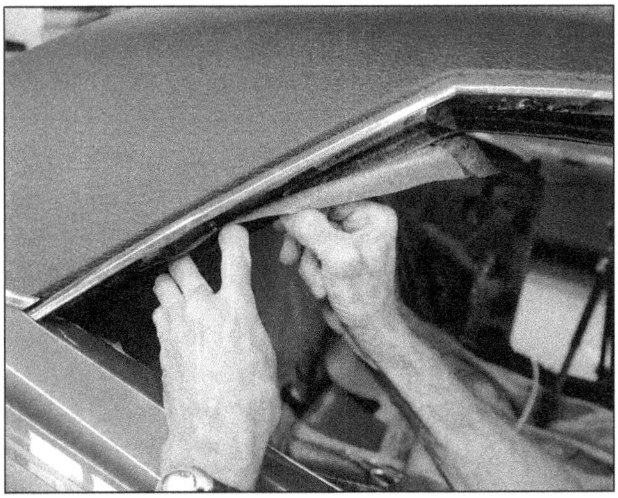

7 *Earlier, we left the leading and trailing edges of the sail panels unglued—for a reason. The panels need more than just that one clip to hold them to the body, so the leading and trailing edges of the material wrap around the quarter-window and rear window channels, respectively.*

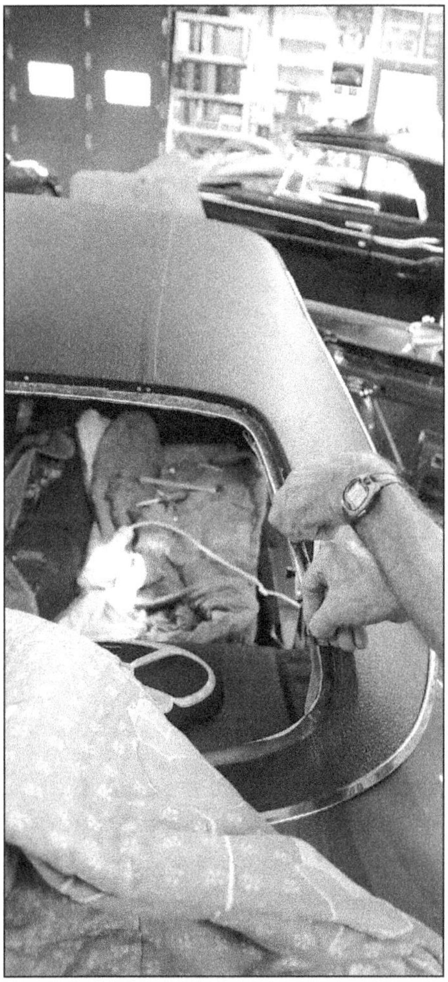

8 *With those edges glued down, we trimmed any excess material from the window channels.*

DOOR PANEL AND GLASS RESTORATION OR REPLACEMENT

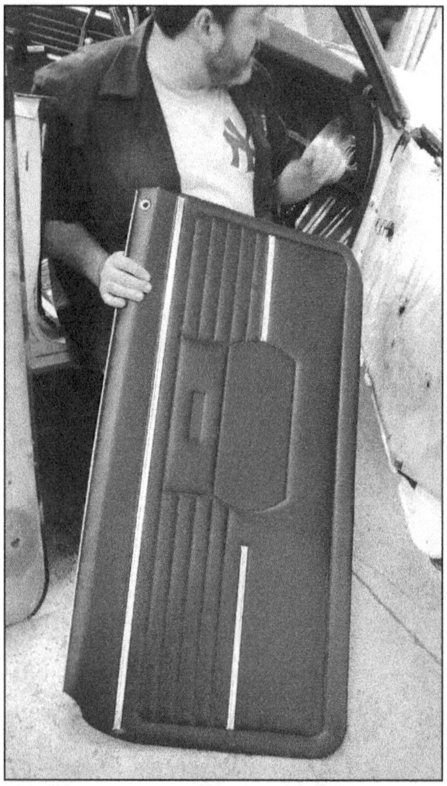

Though door panels are built to withstand abuse and wear, water damage or the occasional tear can warrant replacing them. Many times they simply come up missing in a project car. Fortunately, the aftermarket has a wide range of reproduction door panels with the correct dielectrically stamped patterns.

One method of addressing door panel restoration is, of course, to chuck the door panels altogether—saves weight, sure does, and it's worth another tenth in the quarter—and to use a pair of Vise-Grips in lieu of actual window crank handles. But we really should use those Vise-Grips for something a little more productive than rolling up windows.

Perhaps that's a little extreme. But in the great scheme of things, door panels—and the stuff they hide inside your doors—tend to be ignored until and unless something goes wrong with them: The window doesn't roll up smoothly, or your key snaps off in the door lock.

Granted, door panels tend not to suffer as much abuse or wear and tear as seat covers and carpet. They occupy a low-touch, low-function position. Yet they still gather dust, they still fade in the sun, and they do suffer whenever you happen to forget to roll up your windows before a thunderstorm passes through.

Fortunately, door panels are some of the simplest parts of your interior to replace, as long as the aftermarket has smiled kindly on your chosen make and model of muscle car (or as long as you've found NOS replacements). Unless you're double-jointed and have arms as thin as a little girl, however, all the mechanisms and the glass behind the door panels, are a little trickier, but not impossible, to restore and maintain. So I'm going to give you a look inside those panels and provide instructions on how to address some common door and glass maladies.

Door Panel Replacement

Our 1968 Camaro from Chapter 5 had door panels that remained in rather decent condition, save for the mildew all over the door and interior panels. While we could have cleaned the mildew away, we discovered that the door panels had some water damage, hidden from normal view, so we opted to find some reproduction panels sans living organisms.

As with every remove-and-replace procedure, we first checked that the reproductions, ordered from Classic Industries, matched the originals in every detail. While street rod upholsterers create custom door

Door Panel Replacement

1 *On our 1968 Camaro, the door panels looked as if they could use just a simple cleaning. However, we suspected the real damage lay beneath the surface, so we ordered reproduction panels and began removing the old, moldy panels. Removal starts by unscrewing the armrest.*

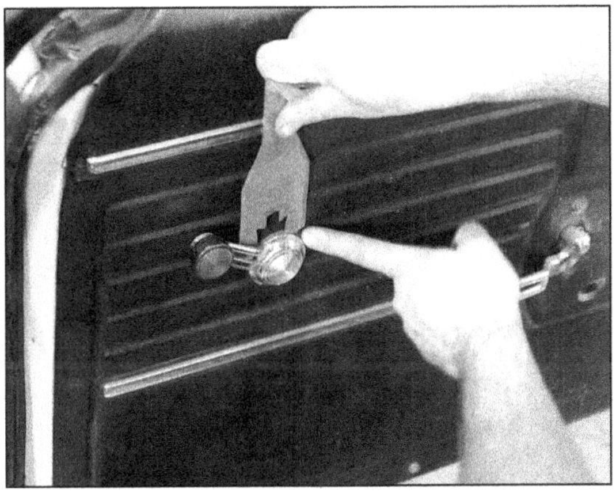

2 *Using this special tool, we were able to get behind the window crank's base to remove the clip that secures the crank to its post. Note the protective plastic disc; you'll need to slide the tool between the disc and the base of the crank to access the clip.*

3 *Here you can see the back side of the window crank handle's base and the spring clip that keeps the handle in place. You can also see how the tool pushes the clip away from the window crank post, allowing the handle to be removed from the post. Try to keep the clip with the window crank handle.*

panels all the time, often from scratch, it's difficult to match the exact detail of original muscle car door panels without a process called dielectric stamping, which bonds dissimilar materials together under vacuum and with a high amount of detail.

New door panels usually come in one of two levels of finish: assembled or unassembled. Despite the implication in their name, unassembled door panels usually come mostly complete, lacking only some trim items that can easily be transferred and the metal top section of the panel.

Every now and then, depending on the car, a reproduction door panel skin will come separate from its backing board. In that case, it is simple enough to line up the new panel with the new backing board, glue the two together with spray adhesive, and then trim to fit. For most guys who work on projects in their home garages, the preferred option is the assembled panel. But even assembled panels don't include everything, as we'll see momentarily.

We started the replacement process by removing the armrest, which is screwed to the door through the door panel. We next removed the door latch handle and the window crank handle, for which we used a special tool available in just about any auto parts store in the country, even those big-box chain stores. We've found that the clip holding in the crank handle is always between the handle itself and the trim ring, and that it's usually inserted from the back of the car at the factory (the easiest, and thus most efficient installation procedure), so we approached the clip from the front of the car to back it out. Rather than shooting the clip across the shop, we carefully left the clip in position on the window crank to make reassembly simpler. We then slid the crank off its splines and removed the door lock knobs.

After removing a couple screws from the bottom of the door panel—your muscle car's door panel may have as few as none or as many as six screws—we then slipped a pry tool behind the door panel and slowly worked it around the perimeter of the panel to remove the metal clips holding the panel on. We removed these clips one by one, taking care not to tear them away from the cardboard-like backing panel, which usually becomes weak over time and with exposure to moisture. Fortunately, metal clips of some sort, which are reusable in new door panels, were employed through the 1980s, until the factories started to replace them with one-time-use plastic clips.

At this point, we unhooked the door panel from the inside window channel at the top of the door and set the panel aside. If your car has power windows or locks, it may be necessary to unplug the wiring harness from the switch panels after separating the panel from the door, but before totally removing the panel. Behind the panel is what is called the vapor barrier—essentially a piece of tar paper that covers the openings stamped into the inner door. The vapor barrier is held on with dum-dum, which usually remains pliable and sticky enough after all these years. Finally, behind that and around the window crank post, is a coil spring used to keep tension on the window crank handle.

With the door panels off, it is a good time to check the insides of the doors for rust or anything that might cause rust. This may be the only time in your ownership of the

Door Panel Replacement *CONTINUED*

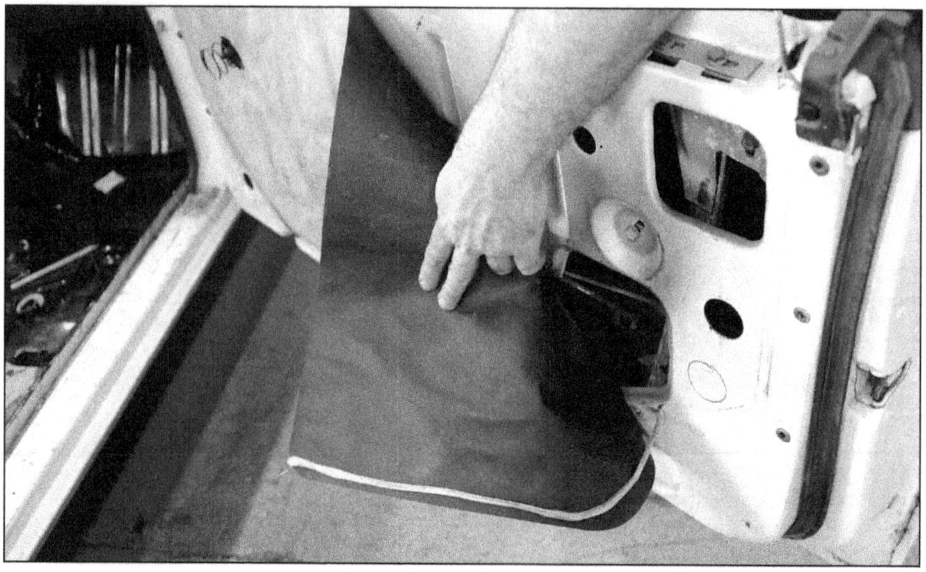

4 ***Under the door panel is the vapor barrier, which the factory affixed to the inner door structure with dum-dum. If your vapor barrier is missing or damaged, you can replace it with tar paper or house wrap. Our Camaro's vapor barrier remained in good condition, so we decided to reuse it.***

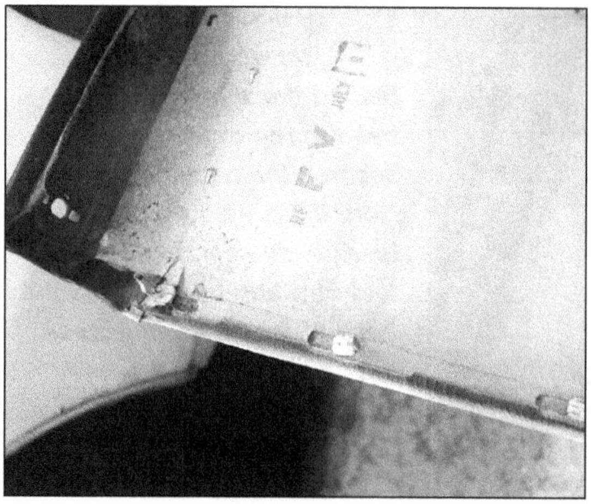

5 ***The spring clips are usually inserted into the pressboard backing of the door panel, which is one reason you don't want to yank the clips away from the door, especially if you're planning on reusing the door panel. Note the pressboard has started to tear around the top spring clip, illustrating how easy it is to damage the pressboard.***

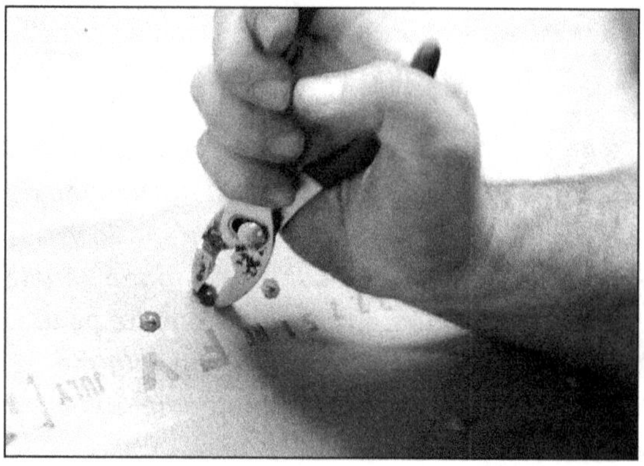

6 ***Our new door panel did not come with the Camaro nameplate pre-installed, so we had to transfer it over from the old panel. We gently pried the clips from the nameplate's three studs. Because the nameplates were usually cast from pot metal, the tiny studs can be very brittle and easy to snap off.***

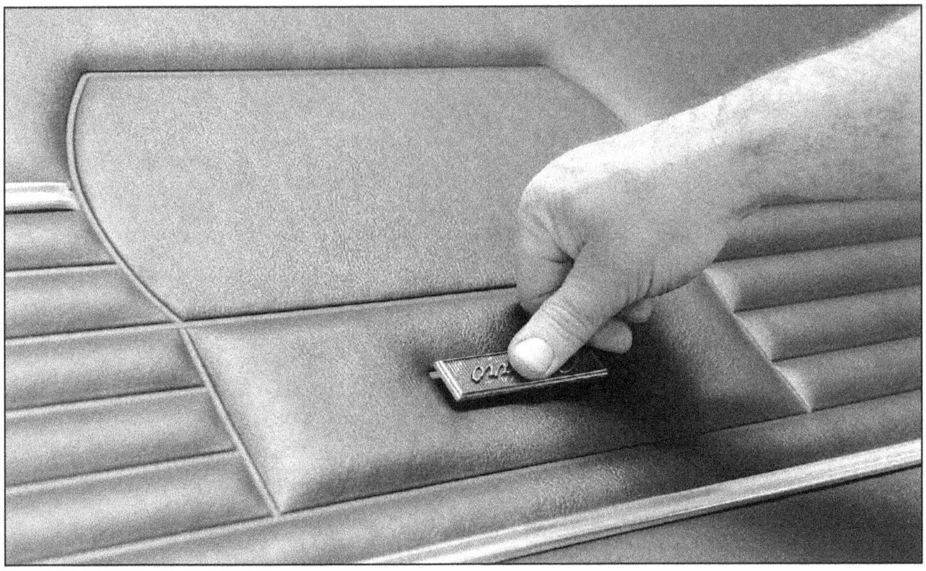

7 With the nameplate removed from the old panel, we centered it in its location on the new panel and firmly pressed down to allow the three studs to create three indentations in the exact locations where we needed to punch holes for the studs.

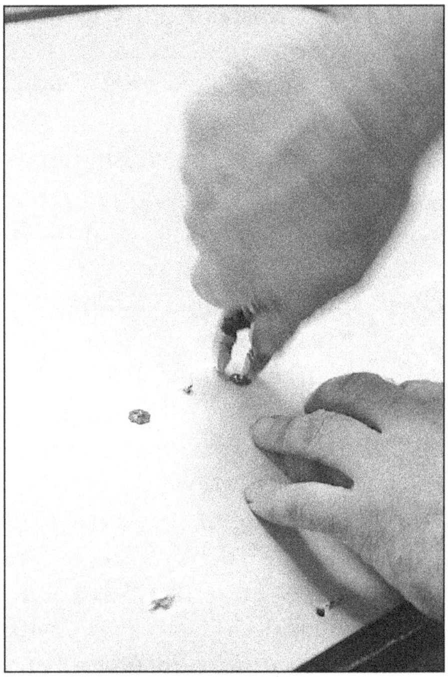

10 Next, we affixed the nameplate to the door panel and carefully pressed the nuts back onto the studs. Note the center stud, which only protrudes from the pressboard by a couple centimeters.

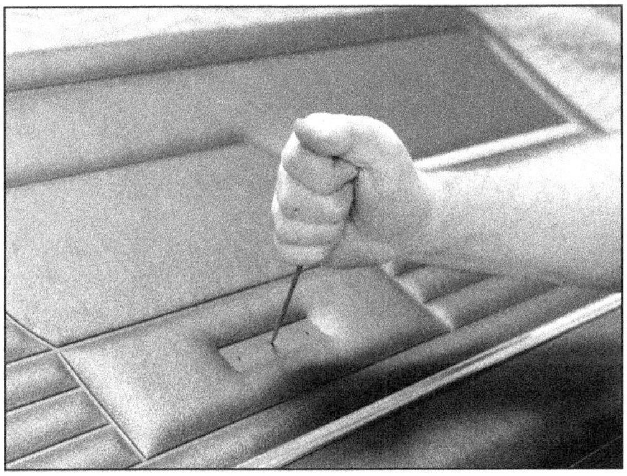

8 Using a sharp awl, we punched out the three holes. We pressed down only until we felt the awl punch through the pressboard backing of the door panel.

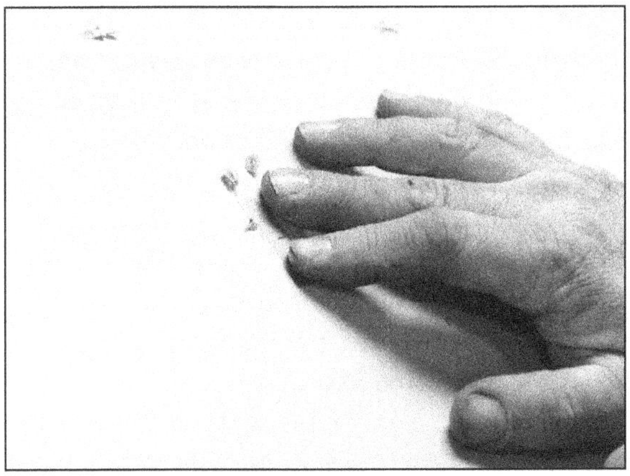

9 Because the nameplate studs were rather short, the back side of the door panel (where we punched the holes) needed to be perfectly smooth. Even the small amount of material punched through would not leave enough stud length for the clips, so we trimmed the pressboard flush with a razor blade.

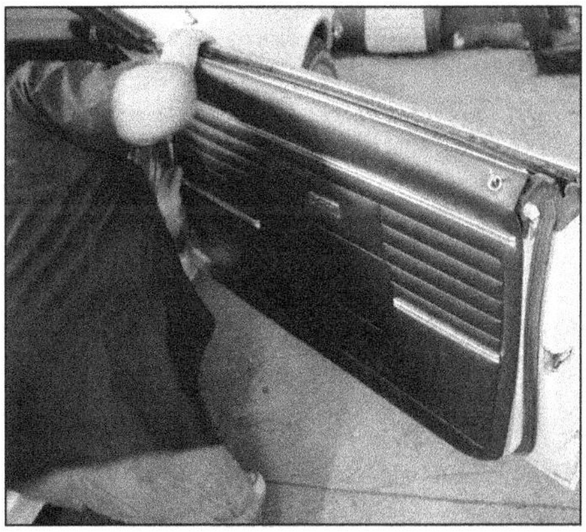

11 We also transferred the spring clips from their pockets in the old door panel to the pre-punched pockets in the new one, noting their correct alignment. Reinstallation of the door panel starts by hooking the window fuzzy strip over the window channel, then pushing in the spring clips from top to bottom.

car—or even in your car's lifetime—that the door panels come off and afford you the opportunity for such an inspection. You'll be amazed at what can accumulate there, especially if your window sweeps are broken or missing. Dirt, dust, mouse nests, and other debris are prime examples, so poke your shop-vac in there and suck out all you can. Also check your drain plugs and/or weep holes. The people who designed your car figured out methods to evacuate the water that inevitably enters your doors, and without those methods, you're sure to see rust in the bottoms of your doors. Some of the debris may have become caked on to the interior surfaces of your doors, so reach in with a wire brush or a paint scraper and knock off the caked-on debris.

Also while rooting around inside your doors, take a moment to grease everything that moves, including door lock mechanisms, latch mechanisms, and window mechanisms. Removing the interior panels—we'll discuss that in a moment—allows similar opportunities for inspection, cleaning, and lubing. With both apart, now would be a good time to inspect and, if necessary, replace your side windows (which you can read more about later in this chapter).

The new door panel came assembled, but did not include the rectangular Camaro emblem situated above the armrest. Reproduction emblems are available, but the original emblem on the old door panel remained in decent shape, so we decided to transfer the emblem from the old door panel to the new one.

The most difficult part of transferring the emblem was removing the tiny clips from the tinier pot metal posts that secured the emblem to the door panel. With a pair of pliers, we gently wiggled the clips back and forth until they separated from the posts. We then positioned the emblem over the new door panel and pushed down to make three indentations in the panel exactly where we wanted the posts to poke through the panel. Next, we used an awl to open up those holes, then used a razor blade to shave off the material punched through the holes

Door Panel Replacement *CONTINUED*

12 ***The posts for the window crank and the latch handle are usually not punched on reproduction panels. As you push the spring clips into the door, the posts will push out against the vinyl skin of the door panel, showing you where you need to cut with a razor blade to allow the posts to poke through.***

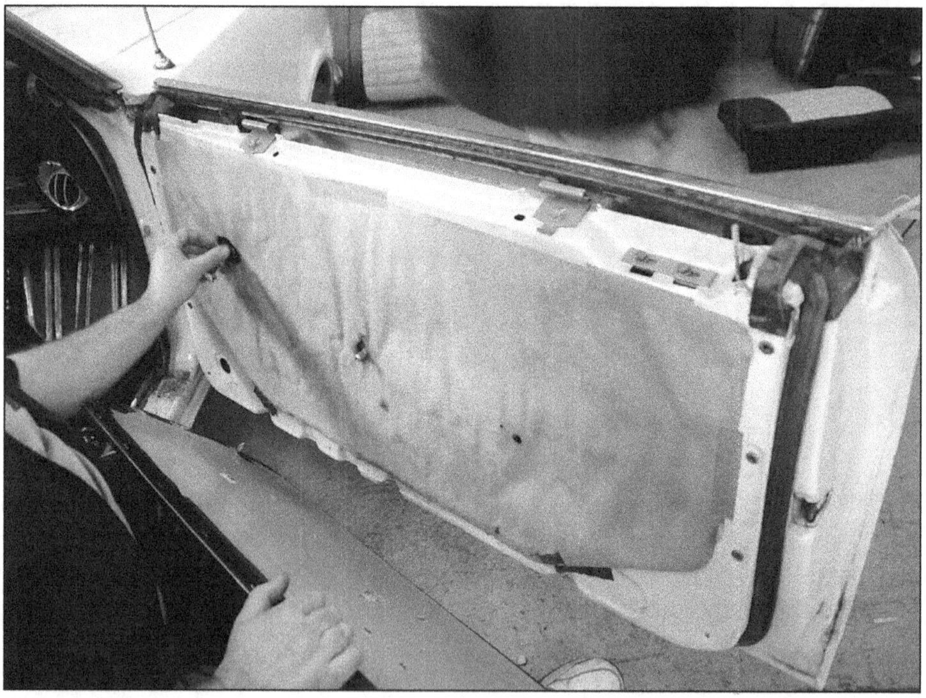

13 ***With our posts located and those holes punched, we removed the new panel, taped down the vapor barrier, and popped on the spring that holds tension on the window crank handle. Now would be a good time to replace any cracked or damaged weather stripping.***

14 ***With the vapor barrier in place, we installed the door panel once again, affixed the latch handle, and screwed the armrest back on. To reinstall the window crank handle, we placed the spring clip on the handle itself. Once we slid the protective plastic disc and the crank handle back over the crank post, we were able to push the clip into place.***

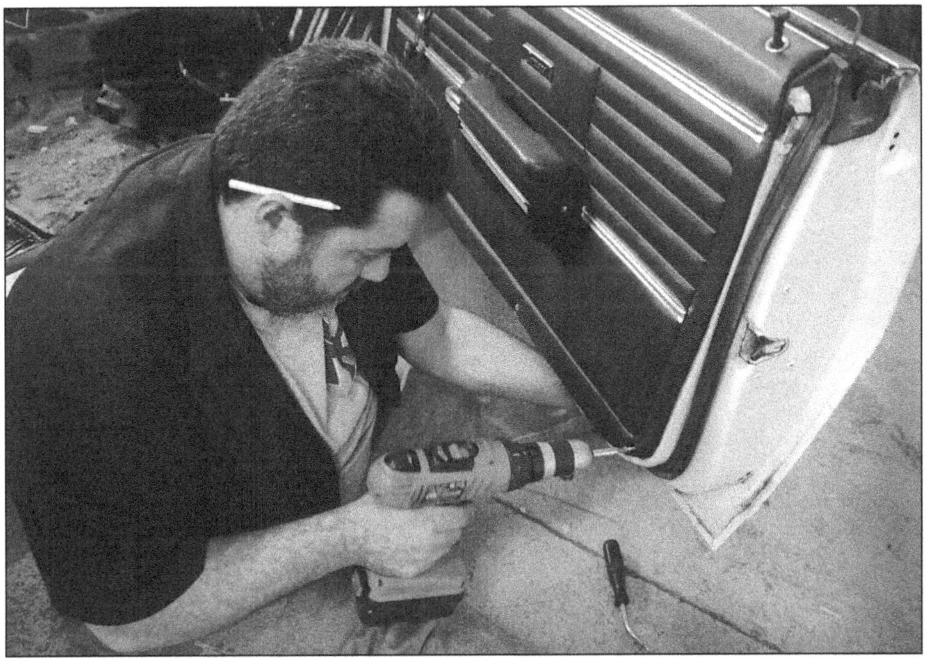

15 ***Finally, a line of screws secures the bottom edge of the new door panel, and a new lock knob on top finishes off the installation. If you have all of your supplies ready and don't shoot any clips across the garage, prompting a three-hour search for one tiny piece of metal, you should be able to complete both door panel replacements in about 1 hour.***

by the awl. The excess material that's punched through sometimes makes the cardboard too thick for the clips to attach to the posts of the emblem. Reinstalling the clips on the posts also requires a gentle touch to avoid snapping the posts from the emblem.

- In the case of a car equipped with power windows or power locks, the reproduction door panel should have punchouts in the pressed cardboard backing for the switches in their proper locations. Go ahead and punch those out, then cut an X in the vinyl from the back side. With a bit of spray adhesive, you can fold the resulting flaps back over the cardboard backing and then transfer the switches and bezels from the old door panel to the new door panel.

The new door panel also did not come with the metal clips that hold the sides of the panel to the door, so we had to transfer those before popping the new panel to the door. Before removing the clips from the old panel, however, we noted their orientation—clipped up or clipped down. If we were to orient the clips improperly, then the clips would not line up with the door.

Installation, as is often the case, is the reverse of disassembly. If you are replacing the vapor barrier, do it now, making sure to keep the spring on the window crank post. Hang the top of the panel over the rod for the door lock, then make sure all the clips are aligned with their holes in the door. If the new panel doesn't include holes for the window crank and door latch handle posts, make sure the panel is aligned perfectly with the door before using a razor blade to cut out the holes for the posts—by pressing the blade of the razor against the posts (through

Behind Closed Door (Panels)

Recall from the Chapter 5 that Dynamat and other noise and heat barriers were originally marketed to car audio enthusiasts, and they quickly found noise control to be essential not just on the floors, but also behind the interior panels and behind the door panels. Putting a mass damper on the insides of quarter panels and door skins helps relieve wind and road noise, and has the added benefit of providing a more solid *thunk* when your car door closes.

With the door panel off, now is the perfect time to consider adding a noise and heat barrier to your doors, both on the back side of the door skin and on the structural part of the door. Installation is largely the same as discussed in Chapter 5, though you'll want to add much more heat to guarantee that the pieces stick.

Depending on the size of the access holes stamped into your door structure, it may be necessary to cut the barrier into smaller strips to fit them behind the door structure. When adding the barrier to the door structure, keep in mind how the door latches and window cranks work, and place the barrier where it won't interfere with the operation of those mechanisms.

Also, when adding the barrier to the door, do not cover all the holes punched into the door structure. Some of those holes–especially the larger ones–were designed to allow access to the mechanisms inside the door. You'd hate to have to remove the Dynamat the next time you need to lubricate your door latch.

However, you do need to keep a vapor barrier up between the interior door panel and the bulk of the door.

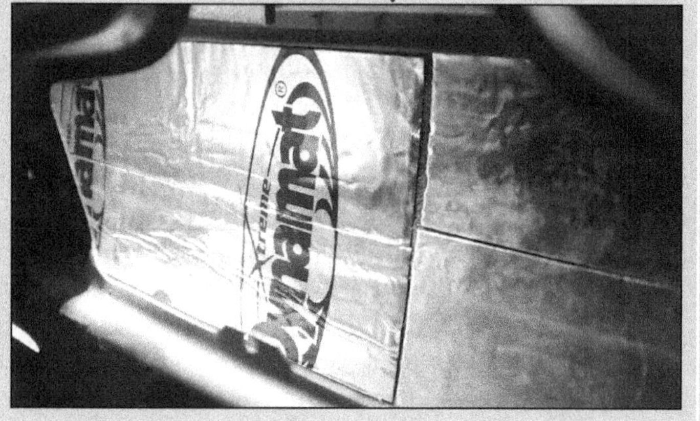

Many of the same methods for installing Dynamat outlined in Chapter 5 apply when installing it in and on doors. However, making paper templates is much tougher, especially for the back sides of the door skins, so we simply measured the lengths we needed. We also found it simpler to cut the Dynamat into strips to negotiate the material through the narrow openings in the inner door structure.

We wanted to retain access to the door mechanisms, so rather than cover all of the holes in the inner door structure with the Dynamat, we cut those holes out. We used plenty of heat on these vertical panels to ensure that they adhered to the metal.

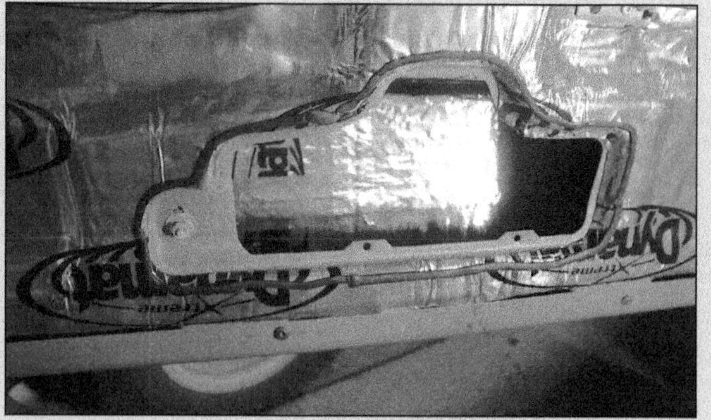

In lieu of dum-dum, we used 3M's Strip Caulk, a seam sealer-like substance that comes in strips and is normally used to seal off irregular areas. It sticks well to solid surfaces, but is easily removed for repositioning.

A vapor barrier functions to keep the water that flows down your windows directed toward the bottom of the doors and toward the drain holes built into the doors. Without one–or with one that has become torn or detached–water flowing down your windows can easily become misdirected toward your door panels and then inside your car. So if your door panels are moldy or display other water damage, it's usually due to a faulty vapor barrier.

A vapor barrier in a muscle car is usually some form of tar paper stuck to the door structure with dum-dum. If reproductions aren't available for your car, it's simple enough to make a new vapor barrier with Tyvek or a plastic drop cloth, using the old vapor barrier as a pattern. The factory-applied dum-dum has by now long outlived its usefulness, so remove it and attach your new vapor barrier with tape (the stronger the adhesive on the tape, the better) or with a dum-dum-like material, such as 3M's Strip Caulk. Whatever attachment method is used, make sure it seals the entire perimeter of the vapor barrier. Also, do not block the holes punched into the bottom of the doors–those are designed to channel any water that might've made it past the vapor barrier back away from your car's interior.

We found that the backing paper from the Dynamat we applied on the doors–along with the Dynamat itself–actually made a decent vapor barrier, so we cut the backing paper into the shapes of the access holes that we weren't able to cover with the Dynamat, then attached those pieces of backing paper with Strip Caulk. Should we ever need to repair or adjust the door mechanisms, we can now easily remove the pieces of backing paper for access.

One quick note about adding Dynamat or other noise and heat barriers to your doors: The weight of the barrier can prove to be detrimental to your door's hinges over time, especially if your hinges are already notoriously weak, so make sure the hinges are up to handling the additional weight, replace the hinges if they're worn, and add no more Dynamat than what you think necessary.

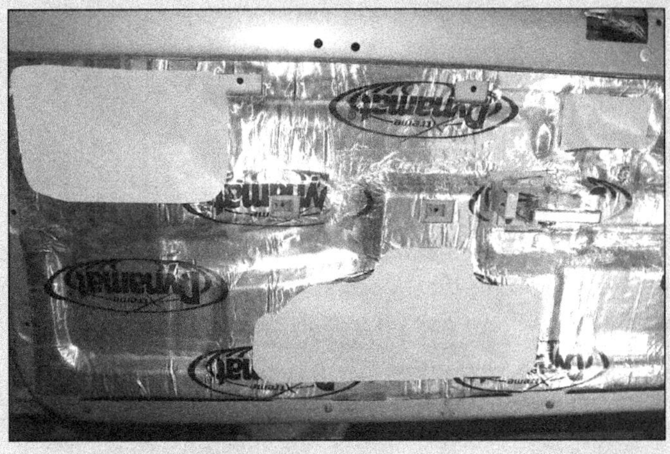

Instead of tar paper, we used the waxy-coated Dynamat backing paper in small sections as vapor barriers over the access holes. In conjunction with the Strip Caulk, these sections are easily removed for door mechanism repair work, but still keep moisture from the door panel.

the panel) in an X pattern. The holes for the armrest's screws may also need to be cut, so hold the armrest up to the panel to judge where the holes need to go and use either an awl or a razor blade to punch those holes.

Give the clips around the perimeter of the panel a good pop, and screw down the bottom of the panel. The window crank handle, still with its clip loaded, can now slip over the splines of its post. Either the clip removal tool or a good whack on the handle will seat the clip into its locked position. With the door latch handle and the armrest reinstalled, the installation of the new door panel is complete.

Interior Panel Reskinning

Most reproduction door panels come in a kit that includes the materials to refresh the interior panels also, those panels to either side of the rear seat. You wouldn't want to have those sticking out like a sore thumb against a fresh, new door panel. And if your interior panels are held in with clips, as the door panels are, then you should be good to go—just repeat the door panel installation process.

This Camaro uses stamped sheetmetal to form the interior panels. It also uses a vinyl skin—similar to the door panel's skin—to cover the sheetmetal with a thin layer of cotton or foam between for padding in certain places, most notably the

Interior Panel Reskinning

1 *Moving to the rear interior panels, this Camaro convertible used three different pieces to make up the entire interior panel section. Reproduction skins for two of the pieces and a new dielectrically stamped panel for the third piece mean we don't have to bother de-fungus-ifying the panels.*

2 *After removing the screws that secure the lower two pieces, we were able to set them aside and access the convertible top's springs and hydraulics. We removed the rear window crank handle using the same exact process as we used for the front window crank handle.*

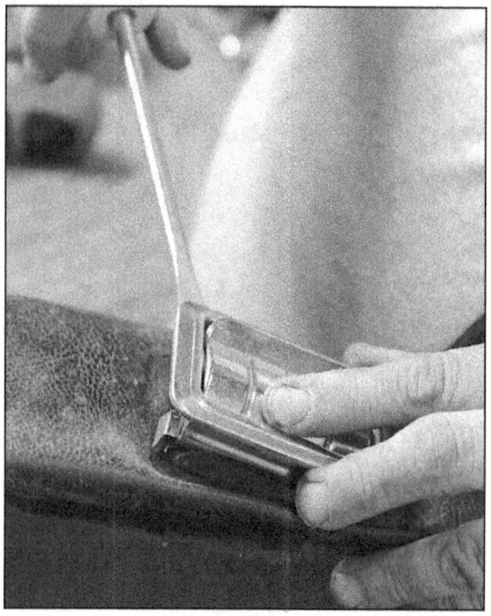

3 *We were able to simply lift the ashtrays out of their holes in the armrests. Most ashtrays are designed to be lifted out so their contents can be swiftly emptied. A bit of chrome polish will clean up the ashtrays and have them looking like new.*

4 *With the lower two pieces out of the car, we can strip off the old vinyl skins. The pieces are quite simply constructed of a stamped section of sheetmetal with the skins glued to them, and with the occasional piece of cotton or jute padding on the armrest surfaces.*

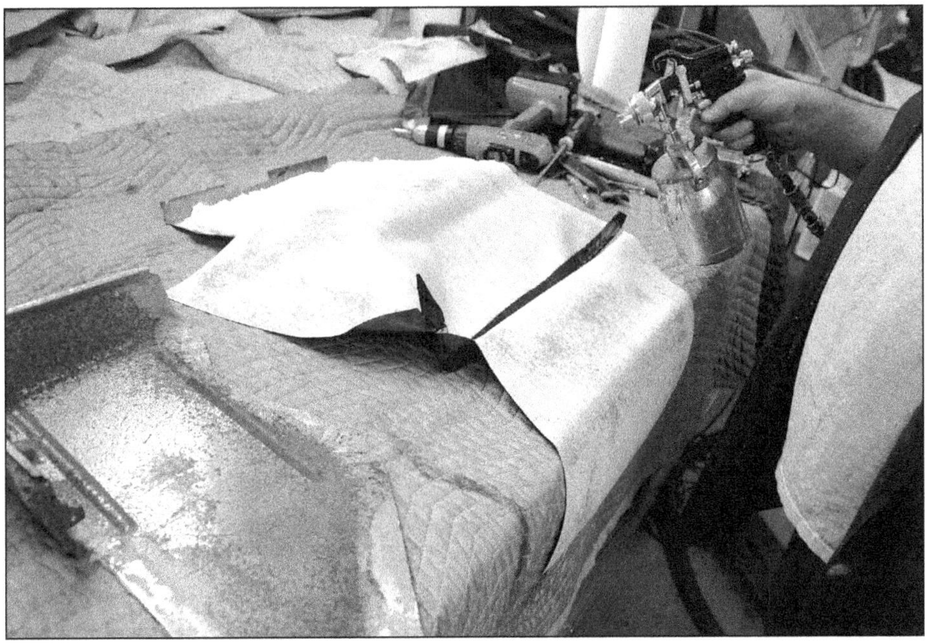

5 *Once we've stripped the old vinyl skins from their sheetmetal cores, we can lay out the new skins and spray both the back side of the skins and the cores with contact adhesive.*

6 *Using the seams of the skins as a guide and starting point, we stretched the vinyl over the sheetmetal cores, working our way outward toward the edges in incremental steps. Once we reached the edges, we sprayed the overlaps with contact adhesive, then folded them over to the back sides of the cores.*

7 *The upper stamped panel hooks over the window channel as did the door panel, and is trimmed for the window crank post the same way. The two lower pieces screw into their respective locations.*

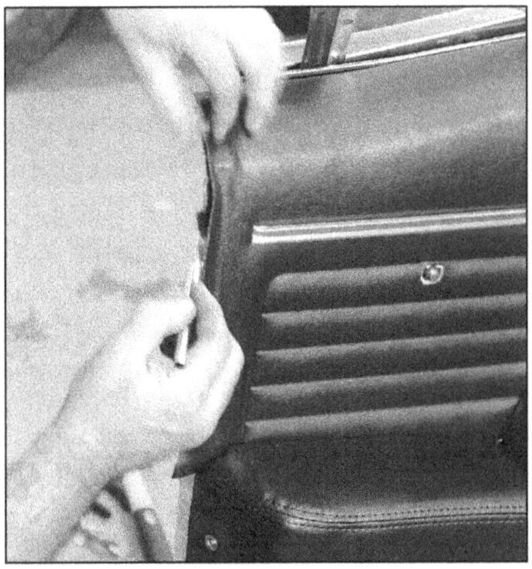

8 *The sides of the stamped panel, however, are not held in with clips. Instead, they are left loose and wrap around the sheetmetal stampings of the door opening. To keep from smearing contact adhesive all over the place, we brushed it into this area rather than spraying it.*

integrated armrest. Removing the panels from the car is as simple as removing a handful of screws, normally hidden by the rear seat.

With the panels on the workbench, and after removing the ashtrays or other trim, the old vinyl can easily be stripped from the sheetmetal by pulling at a loose edge. While removing the vinyl from the sheetmetal, note how they fit to one another. On this Camaro, for example, a stitched seam between two pieces of vinyl marked the edge of the armrest section of the panel.

Also note where the panel was originally glued. It's usually not necessary to bond the back of the vinyl skin to the thin cotton layer, so you should spray adhesive only on the sections where the vinyl meets the bare metal. With both the vinyl and the metal sprayed with adhesive, it's then just a matter of stretching the vinyl over the metal and folding the edges over, darting where necessary. Start stretching by matching the centers of the vinyl skin and the metal frame, or by matching a hard reference point like a stitched seam, then work toward the edges of the metal frame, using clamps where necessary. The new skin likely will not have holes for the ashtrays or other trim cut out, so do that now, cutting any necessary holes from the back side of the panel.

Plastic Welding

1 ***Some simple storage rash turned into actual damage on this plastic console from our AMX. A section of the top edge had cracked right off. We were afraid we'd have to locate another console, which could prove costly and time-consuming, so we thought we'd try to plastic weld the piece back onto the console.***

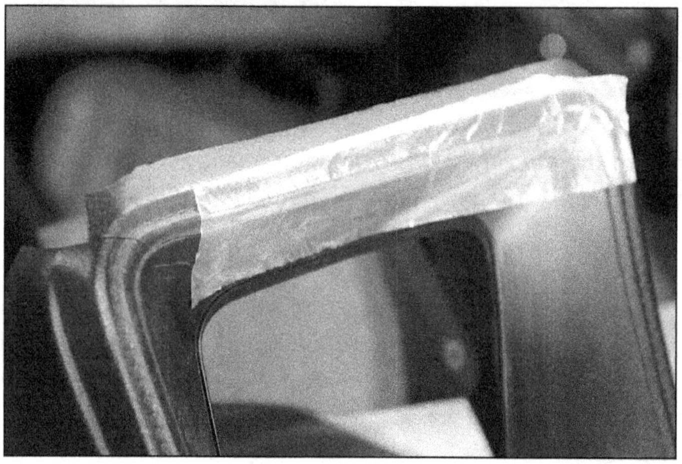

2 ***We only have so many hands, so the first thing we did was use some aluminum tape to hold the broken piece to the console. Aluminum tape works perfectly here because it holds well, leaves no residue when removed, and the aluminum acts as a slight heat sink to keep the heat from the plastic welder from building up and damaging the surrounding plastic.***

Hard Plastics Restoration

But the above discussion doesn't address the use of the hard plastics that became increasingly common in muscle car interiors right around 1970, especially in Mopars. You know the type—molded ABS with a shallow grainy texture, prone to cracking and not as easily reproduced as dielectric soft vinyl panels.

If you go back to the discussion of vinyls used in dashboards in Chapter 2, you'll see how UV exposure, along with the steady progression of time, degrades the hard plastics used in trim, consoles, package trays, and even in entire door panels, causing them to become brittle. They weren't very strong to begin with, so a careless move here or a bit of storage rash there can easily snap a hard plastic piece in two or cause a significant crack. I've even occasionally seen hard plastic pieces that were placed too close to light bulbs melt from the heat given off by the bulbs.

Most people turn to replacement first, which is understandable as long as you can locate an intact NOS, used, or reproduction piece. If that's not the case, or if you would rather save a few bucks, it has become rather simple to repair the piece yourself. And depending on the specifics of the piece, you can choose from a couple different methods of repair: plastic welding or Plastex's plastic repair kit.

Plastic Welding

The first method is plastic welding. Though it sounds daunting, it is actually rather quick and easy in its

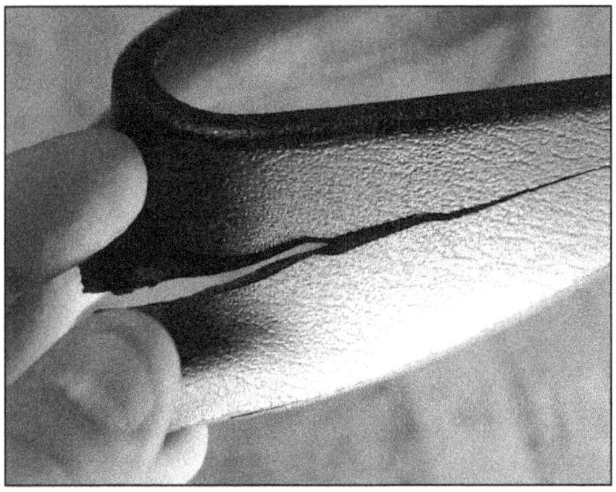

3 ***To be certain that this plastic weld would work on this type of ABS plastic, we found a scrap piece of cracked plastic trim that matched our console to use as a test piece. We taped it up with aluminum tape just as we did the console.***

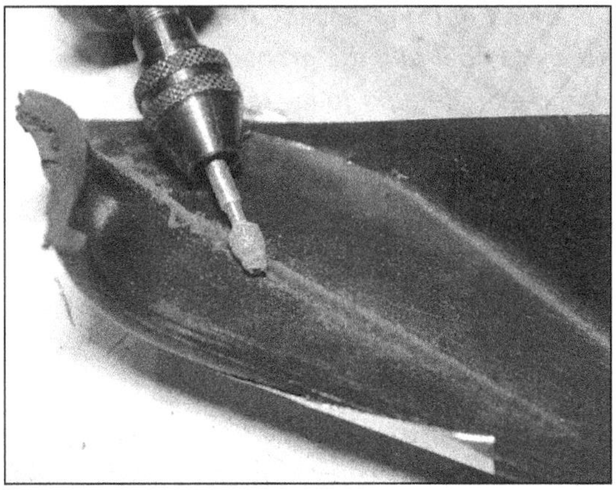

4 ***On the back side of the trim piece, we cut a V-shaped groove along the length of the crack with our rotary tool. We found that a green silicon carbide bit is not too aggressive on the plastic, but still shaves away enough material and remains easy to control.***

most basic form. While plastic welding can be rather complex, with advanced adjustable temperature airless welders and almost automatic filler feeds, the mostly decorative and totally nonstructural trim we want to repair can easily be fixed with the plastic welding kit shown in Chapter 1 and sold through Eastwood as a basic plastic welding kit.

For those familiar with metalworking, this kit is more akin to brazing than actual welding, in that it doesn't actually penetrate and melt the base material as it lays down the filler material. Instead, the filler material included in the kit, the FiberFlex rods, are designed to bond to most basic types of plastic and essentially bridge the crack or the gap between two broken pieces. The other part of the kit is essentially a soldering iron with a flat, round tip that's used to heat the FiberFlex rod until it melts.

Start by plugging in the iron to warm it up, then set the iron to the side. Identify the crack or, if reattaching two pieces, loosely fit them back together like a jigsaw puzzle. Use a piece of aluminum tape to hold the pieces in place, applied to the side of the trim opposite the side you'll be welding. Note here that most plastic interior trim has a grain on what is called the front side, and as long as you want to preserve that grain, you won't be welding on that side. Instead, you'll be welding on the back side of the trim, so it's important to line up the separate pieces so as to minimize the appearance of the crack on the front side of the trim.

Using a Dremel or any other rotary tool and a pointed grinding bit, cut a groove along the length of the crack on the back side of the trim. Make sure to set the rotary tool to a low speed to avoid melting the plastic from the heat generated by higher speeds. Low speeds also give more control over the rotary tool, and in a situation like this, you can hold the rotary tool almost like a pencil as you trace the crack with the tip of the grinding bit.

Blow or brush away the grinding dust and double-check the alignment of the separate pieces again—now is your last chance to make sure they will go together correctly. The iron should be hot now, so begin by placing one side of one end of the FiberFlex rod against the iron's tip. Once it starts to melt, place the partially melted end of the rod on the groove you just created in the piece of trim and apply the tip of the iron to the end of the filler rod, moving the tip of the iron back and forth, across both sides of the groove, as the filler rod melts.

Through this process, you hardly need to move the filler rod, so you should start melting the rod at one end of the groove in the trim. The other end of the rod, the end you're holding with one hand, should be aimed toward the other end of the groove in the trim. Your other hand will be holding the iron, and the iron tip should work its way along the length of the groove, melting the filler rod as it goes. At a minimum, you should use enough material not just to fill the groove, but also to effectively bind both sides of the crack.

Plastic Welding *CONTINUED*

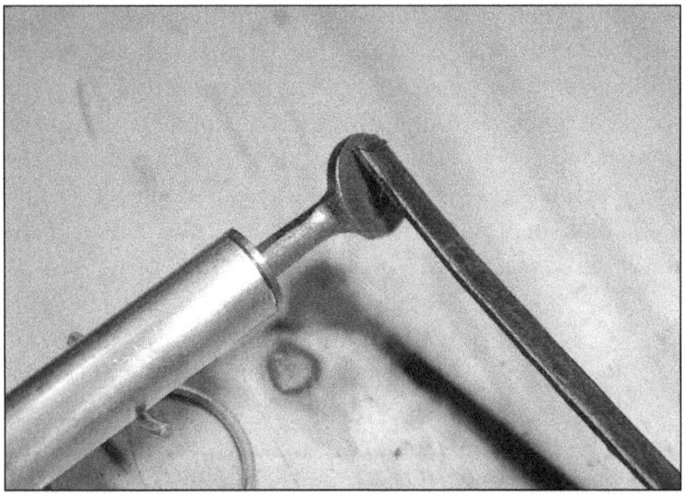

5 *The plastic welding process starts by heating up the iron with the special flat tip. Immediately before beginning the welding itself, take a piece of the FiberFlex rod and warm it on the flat tip to just shy of melting. You don't want it to melt until the rod is actually on the plastic.*

6 *Start at one end of the grooved crack and begin melting the rod so it fills the groove and bridges either side of the crack. It helps to lay the rod along the length of the groove, holding it by the end opposite the iron, and approach with the iron, slowly melting and spreading the rod's material.*

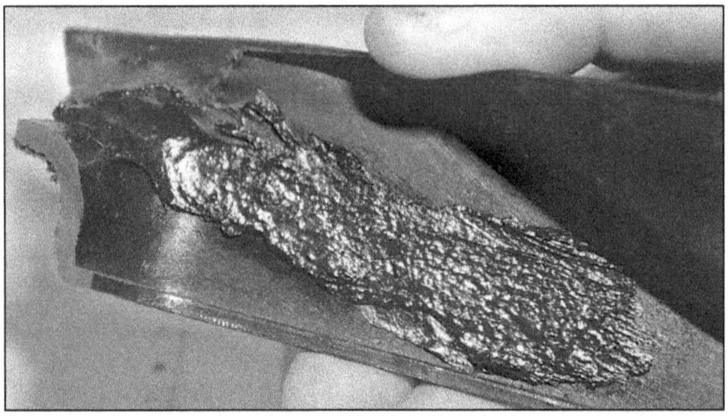

7 *The melted rod solidifies within seconds after removing heat. By welding just one side of the crack, the test piece now has nearly all of its former strength back. For full strength, it's recommended you weld both sides of the crack, though that means eliminating any texture that may be on the front side of the piece.*

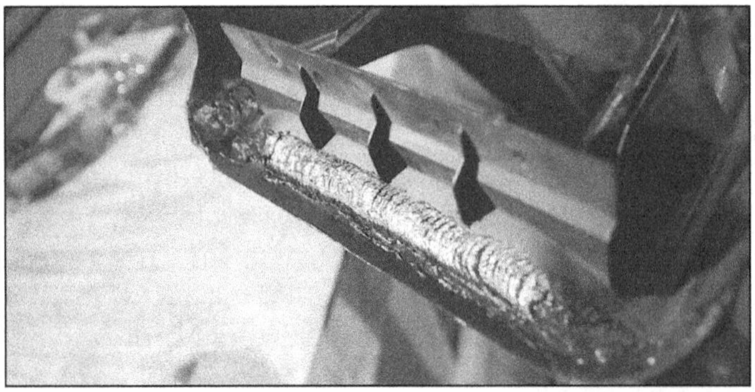

8 *Assured that the welding process would work on our console, we went ahead and welded the piece back on. This time, we were a little less slapdash with our welding technique and ended up creating something similar to the stack-of-dimes look that most metal welders strive for.*

The filler material cools quickly, so apply some pressure on the joint as it cools to keep it in place and to minimize the appearance of the crack on the front side of the trim. Once the material cools entirely, check the joint for strength by gently flexing the piece of trim. If the joint appears weak, repeat the process. If not, remove the aluminum tape. Should the piece of trim not have any grain and, instead, have a smooth face, a stronger joint can be made by welding the opposite side of the crack using the same process. To return the smooth face of the trim piece, chuck a sanding bit into your rotary tool or sand the excess filler material away by hand.

Plastex's Plastic Repair Kit

The second method of repairing hard plastics is a bit tedious, but doesn't require heat and can be used for finely detailed repairs. Plastex's plastic repair kit centers around a

9 ***We admit that the weld on the back side didn't look pretty, but it's functional, and who's going to see the back side anyway? We wanted to see what it'd look like if we dressed the weld on the front side of the test piece, so we put a sanding drum into our rotary tool. You can no longer see any evidence of the crack, but the drum did indeed remove the texture from the front side.***

10 ***On our console, we decided to weld only the back side to preserve the grain on the front side. The section we welded isn't in a high-stress area, so we felt that most of its original strength was good enough. You'd have to look closely to see the cracks, even with the console out of the car.***

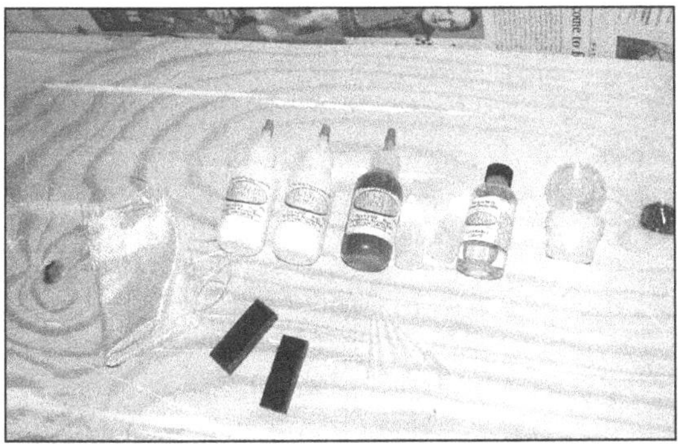

11 ***The Plastex kit included the basics: liquid catalyst, powder, pipettes, and small containers for mixing the powder and catalyst. The kit also included a pair of molding bars, used to replicate shapes and textures, and a fiberglass sheet, used to back larger repair areas.***

plastic resin which, when combined with a liquid catalyst, essentially cold welds most hard plastics and fiberglass. The kit includes three types of powdered resin—black, white, and clear—in small bottles, along with a bottle of the liquid catalyst, applicators, mixing dishes, and a molding bar.

Preparing the broken plastic piece is much the same as the plastic welding method: Clean it, use aluminum tape to hold the broken pieces together, then grind a groove along the cracks and seams. Then choose the appropriate resin. Black resin has graphite mixed in, which gives it additional strength and heat resistance. White and clear resins are suggested for better adhesion. (We found that the black resin adheres just as well as the white and clear resins, however.)

Pour some of the resin into a mixing dish, then with the applicator, pick up a few drops of the catalyst. Add one drop of the catalyst into the resin powder, then quickly pick up the ball of wet resin that results with the tip of the applicator. Apply the wet resin to the crack or seam in the plastic trim, squeezing out another drop or two of the catalyst to make the wet resin flow into the crack.

Plastex designed the catalyst and the resin to seek out their own mixture ratios. Any excess catalyst will evaporate off the repair area, so the more catalyst you use, the better the resin will mix and penetrate the crack. If you use too little catalyst, any unmixed resin will simply blow away and not adhere to the repair area.

It takes a bit of practice and a steady hand to apply the drops of wet resin without making a mess. The tediousness of repeating the process of picking up the resin, applying it to the crack, picking up the resin, applying it to the crack, over and over and over, provides that practice, but leads you to think of other, speedier methods. Pouring the powder directly into the repair area and wetting it with the catalyst there certainly does the job, but can waste resin and make a mess. Also, take care to avoid clogging the tip of the applicator with resin, which will quickly solidify and render the applicator useless.

One thing the Plastex method offers that plastic welding doesn't is the ability to replicate shapes or textures with the molding bar in the kit. The molding bar first needs to be heated to 130 degrees F, either in hot water or wrapped in foil above a hot plate, then applied to the shape or texture to be duplicated while still hot. As the molding bar cools, it creates a negative mold of that shape or texture. Because the Plastex does not adhere to the molding bar, it can take the shape or texture to be duplicated.

Once the repair is finished, the resin, which dries within a couple of minutes, can be sanded, drilled, or dyed just as easily as the base material in the plastic trim. According to Plastex, the resin actually forms a chemical, rather than mechanical, bond with the surrounding plastic. For that reason, it works well on ABS, polycarbonate acrylic, and PVC, but not so well on plastics that don't create chemical bonds, such as polypropylene or polyethylene.

These techniques can be used for most types of plastic repair. Fixing cracks is obviously a fairly straightforward process, as is reattaching separated pieces. For mangled or melted areas on a piece of plastic trim that is otherwise salvageable, you may have to cut out that area and find another piece of plastic trim with an undamaged area that you can splice in to your otherwise good piece of trim.

To fill in large areas of missing plastic, it's also possible to use the screen included in most plastic repair kits (or widely available at any hardware store) as a framework for the plastic repair method to build upon. And for the plastics that don't easily form chemical bonds, using the plastic welder to soften the plastic

Plastex's Plastic Repair Kit

1 ***Our ABS dashboard had an integrated speaker grille that had suffered damage by its previous owner. We weren't in much of a mood to replace the entire dashboard because of this one damaged area, so we thought we'd use the Plastex kit to repair it.***

2 ***The simplest repair method seemed to be to use a section from a good speaker grille in a spare dashboard that was damaged in other areas. So using our rotary tool and a plastic-cutting bit, we cut out the section of damaged grille from the good dashboard and cut out a corresponding section of good grille from the damaged dashboard.***

3 ***Aluminum tape wouldn't easily work here, so we decided to hold the section of grille in place with a pair of clamps and work from the center of the dashboard out toward the edge. We notched into the more solid section of the dashboard to provide more area to hold the repair than just the thin speaker grille slats.***

4 *After grooving the mating lines between the two pieces, we mixed the drops of catalyst into the powder, one at a time, and applied the powder-laden drops to the grooves with the pipette before the catalyst evaporated. It was laborious, time-intensive, and messy, but we did achieve a finer degree of control over the repair area than with a plastic welder.*

5 *We tried to speed up the process by applying the powder to the mating lines and then dropping the catalyst onto the powder, thus bypassing the one-drop-at-a-time approach. Unfortunately, that trade-off came in a bigger mess and sloppier application. The powder-catalyst mixture also appeared not to seep into the grooved crack as well with this method, which seemed to lead to a weaker bond.*

6 *Once dried, the catalyst/powder mix becomes as strong as the surrounding plastic and can be sanded and shaped just as easily as the surrounding plastic. The catalyst takes only minutes to fully evaporate, but we let the repair area sit overnight to be certain that it fully cured.*

enough to sink the mesh screen into the plastic can form a rather strong mechanical bond.

Dyes vs. Paints

Whatever plastic repair method you do use, you'll inevitably come across a mismatch in the colors of your plastics. The Plastex repair kit mentioned above allows you the option of repairing your plastic trim in a few bright colors, but most other colored plastics require additional steps.

Vinyl dyes, such as Duplicolor's Vinyl and Fabric Dye or Plastikote's Ultra Vinyl Color, are often available in rattle cans at your corner parts store, and come in a wide variety of colors to match your plastic trim. Just Dashes, which provides restoration products for more than just dashes, now has a plastic and vinyl recoloring kit called Fade Away. And in the last few years a number of paints specifically formulated for plastics—which means they have had special compounds called flex agents added—have become widely available, including Krylon's Fusion and SEM's Color Coat.

The difference between a vinyl dye and a plastic paint comes down to the fact that vinyl dyes penetrate into the base material to recolor it; plastic paints simply lay on the surface of the base material and can later wear away. Most interior specialists recommend using vinyl dyes to recolor plastic trim—dyes are less likely to lift off when cleaning your dash, they leave a more natural (less glossy) finish to the trim, and they don't obscure the texture of the trim surface.

Test your chosen vinyl dye or plastic paint on an inconspicuous section of plastic trim, such as the back side of the trim or leftover pieces of donor trim, to make sure it looks right and matches your original trim. As with any rattle-can endeavor, thoroughly clean the surface beforehand and spray in a well-ventilated area.

Finally, what holds true for protecting your dashboard (see Chapter 2) holds true for protecting hard plastic trim. Choose a UV blocker without silicone oils. Also, if you've recolored your plastic trim, test the protector against your chosen vinyl dye or plastic paint; some protectors have been known to lift dyes or paints. Again, test the protector on an inconspicuous section of the trim first.

By now you've probably come across chrome-plated sections of your interior trim—likely on the dashboard or the door panels. If the plating remains in decent condition, that is, it hasn't been scratched or worn off, you'll want to mask it before dyeing or painting the piece of trim. Use a good, low-bleed masking tape available at your local hardware store, such as Painter's Mate Green or Frog Tape. If the plating has been damaged, you'll have to send the trim piece to a plastic chroming shop, just as you'd have to send your chrome-plated bumper or rocker arm covers to a regular chroming shop.

Plastex's Plastic Repair Kit CONTINUED

7 ***With some black vinyl dye, the repair doesn't completely disappear, but it definitely looks less obvious than a big hole punched in the speaker grille. A little more time spent dressing the repair area, sanding it down, and applying texture with the molding bar likely would have produced a seamless repair.***

8 ***Once the molding bar is heated, it softens and becomes malleable for a short period of time, allowing it to create negatives of any texture or shape. We wanted to replicate the grain on our piece of plastic trim and saw no other way to do it.***

9 ***The molding bar did indeed pick up the grain, which we could then use to impress on the powder-catalyst mixture as it dried. The molding bar doesn't seem to stick to any surface, but a light spray with a release agent might not be a bad idea. The molding bar can then be reheated and reshaped an unlimited number of times.***

Glass Restoration

Returning to the doors, you may notice that the glass in the windows has seen better days. It's a bit scratched, a bit hazy, maybe it even has some paint overspray on it from when your muscle car was assembled 40 years ago. You will have to disassemble the door to take the glass out, so why not take a look at it now, with the door panels already off?

If the glass is scratched, though, it's your first piece of bad news. Since the late 1950s (specifically, 1957 for Chrysler products and 1959 for GM and Ford products), Detroit used tempered side glass instead of laminated glass in all of their cars. Laminated glass continued (and continues today) to be used for windshields for one big safety reason: It prevents occupants from exiting a vehicle during a crash. Using laminated glass would make sense in side windows for the same reason, except for the need of emergency responders to quickly break into a

Glass Restoration

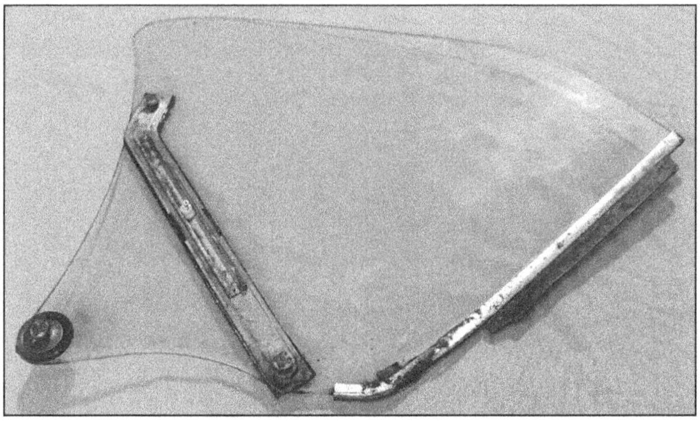

***1** With a quarter-window out of the car, we can see that glass restoration is about more than just cleaning or replacing the glass itself. A number of guides, channels, rollers, and other mechanisms contribute to the proper alignment of glass and prevention of scratches. Also, trim often adorns the glass.*

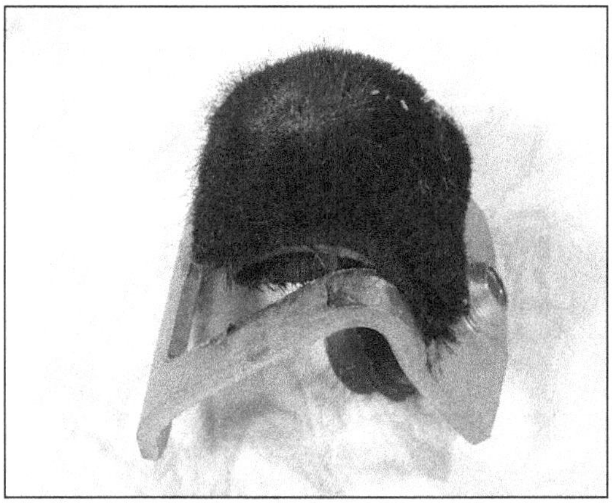

***2** We removed this window guide from inside a door to show its fuzzy surface and to show how little separates the glass in your car's windows from bare metal surfaces that can easily scratch the glass. These should be replaced or recovered while you have your door panels off and can access them.*

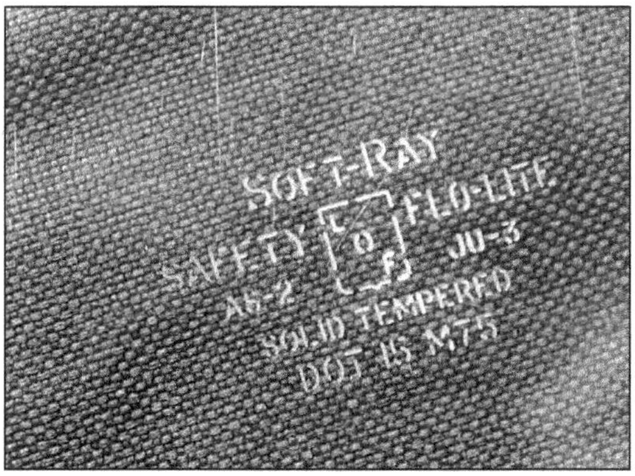

***3** Here is a typical GM LOF window etching. The Soft-Ray terminology indicates this window was tinted from the factory, and the date code resides on the second line to the right of the LOF logo. The first letter indicates the month, the second letter indicates the year, and the digit after the dash indicates the day of the month.*

car and pull a crash victim out. Thus the use of tempered glass in side windows, which breaks apart into those pebble-like chunks of glass.

As the name implies, tempered glass has been hardened to achieve that result. For that reason, it's often more difficult to scratch than the softer, laminated glass used in windshields, but it's also nearly impossible to polish out a scratch from side glass. Glass shops do polish out scratches from windshields all the time. Using a polishing compound to keep the glass lubricated and cool, the polishing process actually removes material from the windshield surface until the material in which the scratch resides has been removed, which often results in distorted glass. Unfortunately, on tempered side glass, the only recourse for a scratched piece of glass is to replace it.

Of course, you'll want to track down the source of the scratch and correct it before installing new glass. Scratch sources vary from car to car and can include guides with the felt padding worn off, wayward screw points, dirt or dust trapped against the glass, worn plastic alignment guides, or even cracked or missing window sweeps. With the glass out of the door, check for all of these, and replace and lubricate as necessary.

When ordering replacement glass, make sure the date codes correspond with the build date of your car. Each manufacturer used different date codes and different glass suppliers (for example, GM used LOF glass, while Ford used Carlite glass), and the coding on the glass often tells whether it's tinted or not, so check with your particular car club for glass date-coding references. Reproduction glass can even be ordered with the correct date code acid-etched into the glass.

If using older glass or if reusing your car's original glass (in which case, it's still a good idea to remove it from the door for cleaning), a brand-new razor blade, in conjunction with lacquer thinner, can make quick work of any paint or undercoating oversprayed onto the glass, or rust stains from metal trim attached to the glass. When using a razor blade, experts suggest keeping it lubricated

Glass Restoration *CONTINUED*

4 *On a typical Chrysler window etching, the date code is the two-digit number on the right on the last line of the etching. The first digit indicates the month; the second digit indicates the year. The first digit may also be a letter.*

5 *This is a typical Ford window etching. The date code is the two-digit alphanumeric combination on the left on the next-to-last line. The number indicates the year, while the letter indicates the month.*

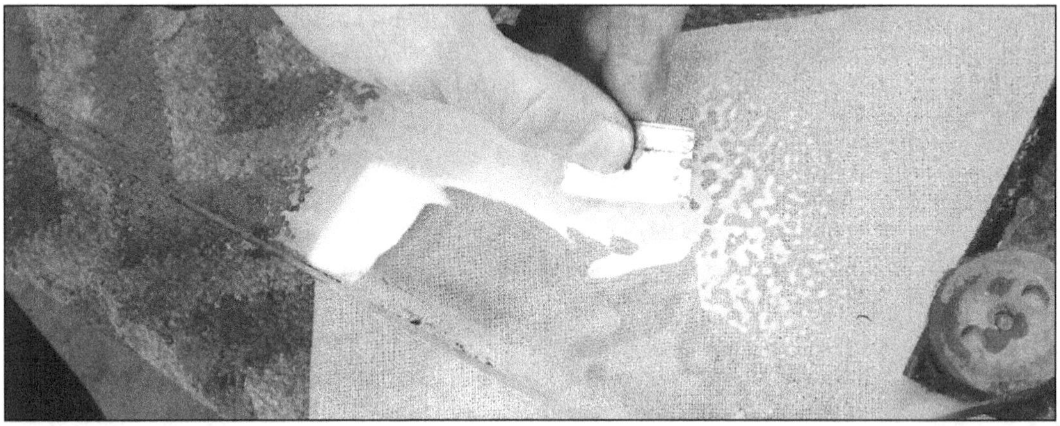

6 *Fresh, sharp razor blades can be useful in removing rust stains, paint overspray, and dirt buildup from glass surfaces, and should be kept well lubricated with glass cleaner or lacquer thinner. If any nicks develop in the blade, the blade should be exchanged for a fresh one.*

Window Sweeps

Technically, window sweeps are called window weather strips, and they've also been called by other names, including window fuzzies and cat whiskers. They're the soft, brush-like bristles on the inside of door windows, and the stiff rubber strips on the outsides of the windows. When they're not doing their job, they can often lead to scratches in the glass.

One would believe their main purpose is to prevent water, dirt, and dust from filtering into the door cavities, but according to Fritz Wurgler of First Place Auto Products, their main purpose is actually to hold the door glass in place (preventing it from contacting the metal inside the door) so it doesn't rattle. "When you can hear the glass rattling, you're actually hearing it scratching," he said.

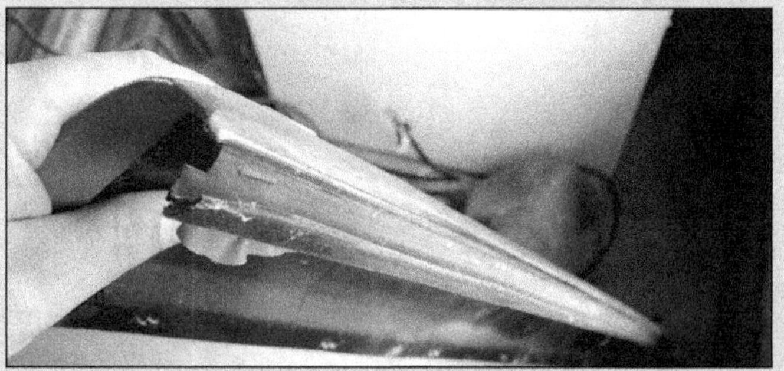

The window sweeps on this particular door panel are stapled into place. They feature a stiff rubber channel, along with a felted strip against which the window glass rubs. The felted strip not only cushions the glass, but is important in removing dust and dirt as the window is rolled up and down.

7 *To clean the glass, always start with glass cleaner. Glass shops seem less picky about the brand and type of glass cleaner than they do about the towels used to apply and wipe away the glass cleaner; the towels should be lint-free paper towels or old newspapers. Continually change the towels to avoid picking up dirt that can scratch the glass.*

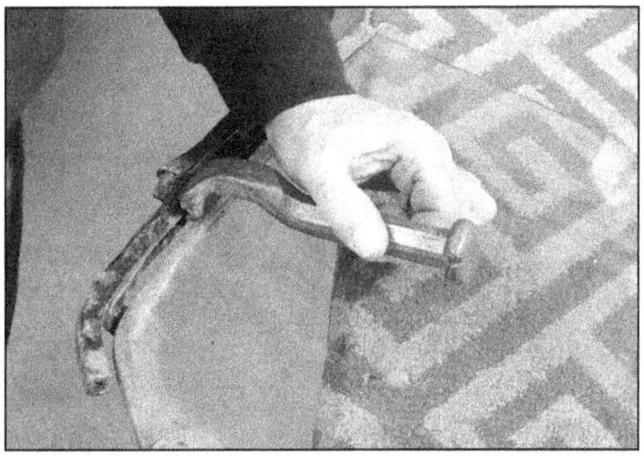

8 *Most glass shops have this special tool, used to remove trim from glass for a thorough cleaning of the surface and for replacement or restoration of the trim. The tool simply hooks onto the lip of the trim and with a couple blows of a hammer, pushes the trim away from the glass.*

9 *When faced with no other option but to store glass for any period of time, you should wrap it in cardboard and stack it on end, preferably in a place where you won't accidentally kick it or toss a wrench toward it.*

with glass cleaner to avoid nicking the edge of the blade; nicks in the blade can cause scratches in the glass. General-purpose glass cleaner, applied with lint-free paper towels or old newspapers, will remove any remaining dust or dirt.

Some muscle car windows, especially those in convertibles and hardtops, used thin chrome trim around the edges of the glass and a putty or caulk-like material that cemented the trim to the glass. To clean the glass fully, it's often necessary to remove the trim, which is difficult to do without damaging it. Most glass shops have a special tool that looks like a deformed railroad tie that safely punches off the trim. For most of us without access to that tool, leaving the window to soak in a tub of soapy water will soften the putty or caulk, though sometimes it's necessary to slide a razor between the glass and the trim to slice through the putty or caulk. When prying the trim away from the glass, use a wooden or plastic spatula handle to avoid chipping the glass.

Inside the doors, remove any dust or dirt from the felt padding in the window channels. If it's necessary to replace the felt padding, new felt can be found at a local hobby or craft store. Be sure to buy new felt of the same general thickness as the old felt (some restorers recommend scrap speaker-cabinet felt, which is usually a bit thicker and heavier than garden-variety craft store felt). With the old felt removed and the window channel cleaned, spray the back of the felt with contact cement and work it into the window channel with a tuck tool or other blunt object, then trim the felt even with the window channel edges. The window may seem tight in the channel at first, but by manually raising and lowering the glass in the channel several times, it'll loosen up. You may find rub strips or rub blocks that require flocking instead of felt padding. In that case, refer to the flocking procedure in Chapter 2.

Relubricate all the window mechanisms with white grease, moly wheel grease, or Lubriplate—preferably brushed on rather than sprayed on in order to contain the mess. If for some reason it's necessary to store pieces of glass, fold a large, flat piece of cardboard around the glass and stand it on end. When reinstalling the glass, especially on older hardtops and convertibles without much of a window frame to keep the glass in alignment, closely follow the window glass alignment instructions in your assembly manual.

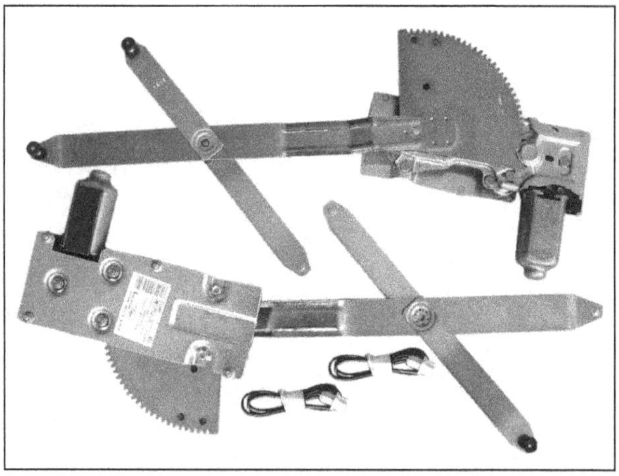

Adding power windows can be as simple as finding the correct power window parts from another, better-optioned version of your muscle car, or it can require ordering a power window kit. The burgeoning street rod aftermarket has made universal power window kits widely available and easy to install.

Adding Power Windows and Power Door Locks

Muscle cars didn't just exist in the realm of low-price, low-option sedans; consider the Chrysler 300H or the 4-4-2 or the Cougar—all performance cars with a touch of luxury added. And normally, that touch of luxury included power windows and power door locks. And it's alright to admit that you always wanted the comfort and convenience of those options in your Charger or Mustang.

The easiest way to add those options, is to find a car like yours with those options and start swapping parts. For power windows you'll need the motor, regulator, and switch plates. For power locks you'll want to grab the solenoid and switch plate, plus the wiring harness and the sleeve for the wiring harness as it passes through the door jamb.

If you can't find a factory-equipped power window and lock setup, a number of companies focused on street rods, including Autoloc and Electric Life, have developed near-universal power window and power door lock conversion kits that fit in confined spaces. One of the more intriguing innovations to come out of those kits is Autoloc's power window switch, which mounts behind the door panel hole for your stock window crank. The window crank then fits over the switch's splined shaft and acts as the handle for the switch; a little nudge in one direction and the window goes up, a little nudge in the other direction and the window goes down. It's perfect for when you want to add the option of power windows but don't want to replace your door panels, or want to maintain your car's stock appearance. Just make sure the splines of the switch match the splines of your stock window crank. Oh, and remember to inform your passengers exactly how the power window switches work before they start cranking on them and damage the switches.

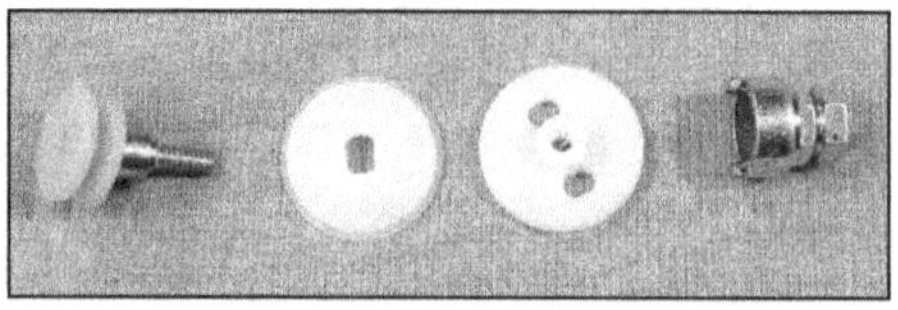

Here is a close-up of the roller guides out of the car. The two white plastic plates, which can sometimes be stamped sheetmetal, sandwich holes drilled in the window glass by the manufacturer. The special socket on the right, available from MAC Tools, has the correct notch spacing for the plate next to it.

Troubleshooting Power Windows

Most trouble with power windows come from a couple sources. The first one is the roller guides, which serve the same function as in non-power windows, but can see a lot more stress and wear in a power window setup. A power window motor can't feel when a roller has become worn, deteriorated, or is sticking; it just just keeps cranking and exerting the same amount of torque. When your hand on a manual window crank detects such a situation, it adjusts how much effort to put into rolling the window up or down. New rollers are usually available at your corner parts store or from a restoration parts company that specializes in your car.

The second source of trouble in power window setups is the power window motor itself. The motors that can't be replaced can usually be rebuilt, but before going to that much expense and bother, check the wiring, relays, fuses, and switches in the power window circuit.

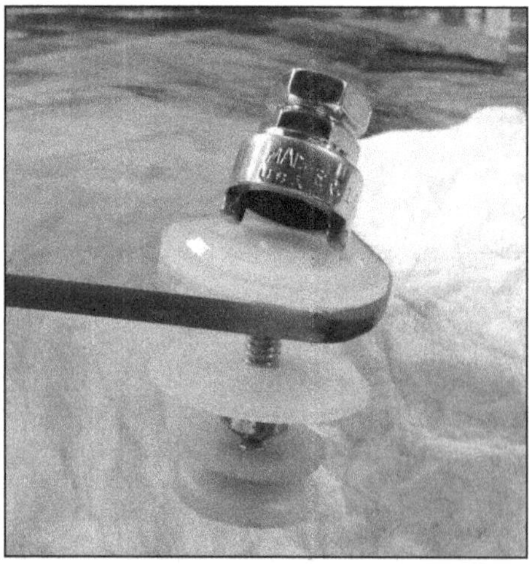

This is how the roller guides stack together around the glass inside the door. You can see that they're simply made of nylon and soft plastic. They can easily be damaged if they're not lubricated and rolling properly.

CHAPTER 7

Convertible Top Restoration and Replacement

If one of the main functions of an interior is to make your muscle car more comfortable to drive, then you cannot ignore the convertible muscle car and its top mechanism. After all, a muscle car with a convertible top that lets in rain, wind, and noise when in the up position doesn't exactly rate high for comfort.

But face it, if you're lucky enough to own a convertible muscle car, you rarely look up to check out how it's put together. Likely the most attention you pay to it comes when you make sure it folded correctly and without bunching when putting it down; otherwise, until it becomes ragged or torn, you don't give it a second thought.

This is probably why most convertible muscle car owners have absolutely no clue what goes into replacing a top when it does become ragged or torn. They think of a complicated mess of framework and cables, when in fact most muscle cars are far simpler than expected.

To find out how simple, we replaced the convertible top on a 1967 Firebird. The old white top, while not trashed, certainly did not complement the new paint and interior planned for the Firebird.

Some people feel a bit intimidated when it comes to replacing their convertible top, what with all the cables and braces and mechanisms. Take, for instance, this 1967 Firebird. After 40 years, the vinyl top material had become wrinkled and dingy, and the plastic rear window had become yellowed and hazy.

We'll replace the vinyl top and plastic rear window with a new Haartz cloth top and actual glass rear window. Both the Haartz cloth and the glass window will hold up better to wind, sun, and rain than the original materials, though the installation process is the same for whatever materials you use.

The owner decided to replace the stock pinpoint vinyl top—fitted with a hazy plastic window—with a new, black Haartz cloth top with a glass window.

Haartz cloth is found mostly on newer, more expensive convertibles. It actually holds up better to rain and sun than pinpoint vinyl, though it is somewhat harder to keep clean, especially in white, and can't be dyed as easily as pinpoint vinyl. Glass rear windows are often hinged like the one in this top to fit in the car's original well when folded. Glass offers the advantage of a clearer window that won't yellow over time. Obviously, neither a Haartz top nor a glass window are considered correct for most muscle cars, and both represent more costly restoration options, but both will add to the resale value of a customized or otherwise non-original muscle car.

The installation process remains the same, regardless of the top material or type of back window.

Disassembly

As discussed in Chapter 1, it's important to decide when in the restoration time line to perform certain tasks. Ideally, convertible top replacement should take place before the installation of the seats and carpet, to permit total access to the convertible top frame. But it should happen after the car has been painted, sanded, and buffed, so sanding dust does not blow onto the top, particularly important for a Haartz cloth top.

Before starting the top disassembly, determine whether the bows or the motors for the power top system require any restoration or refinishing. It's important to have a functioning power top system for the top replacement process, so the system must be in good working order. This particular Firebird already had a perfectly functioning top and perfectly shaped bows that didn't require restoration, so the framework and actuators all remained, as did the battery (hooked up to a battery charger) to put the top up and down as required.

We laid out the new replacement top, ordered from ARO 2000 in Walden, New York, on a clean surface to make sure it included all the necessary pieces. A lot of people make the mistake of ordering just the top, even though the entire convertible top assembly consists of more than just the top material. If you're replacing the top material, you should replace everything associated with the entire assembly, including the pads, the well liner, and, if necessary, the tack strips.

Another mistake most people make is to just start ripping the top from the frame when, in fact, it should be removed a little more methodically. In this case, the sides of the top material around the window openings are covered by pieces of weather stripping, which need to be unscrewed from the convertible top frame. Another piece of weather

Getting It Up (and Down)

An acquaintance of mine, who once designed convertibles for one of the Big Three, told me that the greatest failing of any American automaker in the realm of convertibles was that nobody could figure out how to design and produce a manual top that wasn't too cumbersome for one person to put up and down, the way foreign automakers could. Thus, more often than not, you'll see power convertible tops in domestic convertibles.

For most muscle cars, any issues with the power top mechanisms can be traced to just a few potential problems. The first is the top frame itself. Any damage can cause unnecessary strain on the rest of the power mechanism, so you should inspect the frame for wear or bends, and make sure to lubricate the pivot points.

The second potential problem is in the hydraulic rams and pumps. Any leakage in the rams, pumps, or lines between them will cause the power top not to operate correctly, and will also likely cause a mess. Leakage in these components usually requires the replacement or rebuild of that component and full bleeding of the lines. It's not uncommon to see missing hydraulic components because a previous owner didn't want to bother repairing a leak.

Third, if the top frame and the hydraulics are good, the culprit may be something as simple as the electrical circuit that activates the hydraulics. Check for blown fuses and bad grounds as you would any other electrical circuit (see Chapter 3 for more on electrical circuits).

Disassembly

1 Disassembly begins by removing the screwed-in metal brace under the first bow behind the header. Plan to install your convertible top before your seats and carpet so you can have total access to the top, as we did here. Also, if it's a power top, leave the power mechanisms in place to make it easier to raise and lower the top while working on it.

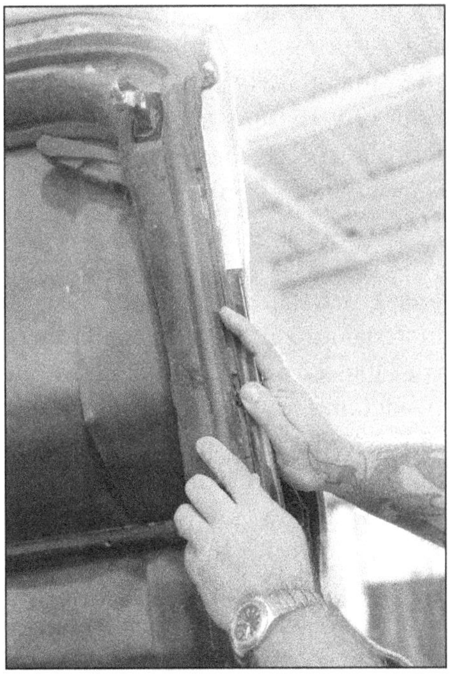

2 Disassembly next moves to the pieces of weather stripping on the sides of the top, held in by screws. Here we're about to remove a piece from the driver's side. Most restoration companies specific to your car should have reproductions available.

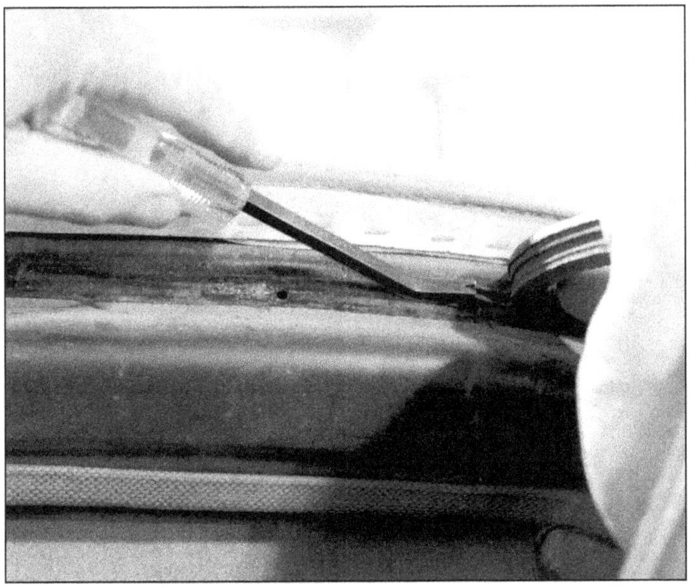

3 Next, the weather stripping at the leading edge of the header was pried away from the header carefully, so as not to damage the push-in clips that kept it in place.

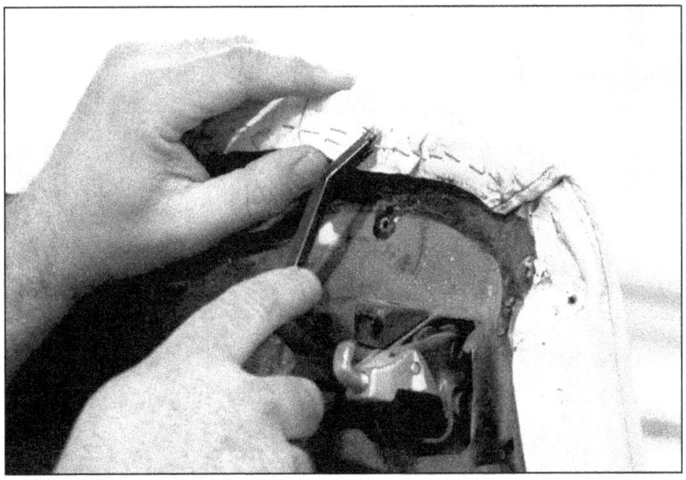

4 Using a staple remover, we carefully removed each individual staple holding the leading edge of the top to the header. Don't just yank the top material from the header—doing so may damage the tack strip and may leave behind fragments of the staples, which will still need to be removed before the installation of the new top material.

stripping that covers the leading edge of the top material should also be removed, exposing a row of staples securing the leading edge of the top material to the header. We removed these staples one-by-one with a special upholsterer's staple remover; any staples that broke—as 40-year-old staples are wont to do—were removed with a pair of side cutters. These staples go through the top material into a tack strip—a plastic or cork-like compound fitted into the header and top bows—so ripping the top material from the header or top bows can possibly damage the tack strip, which we intend to reuse. We also didn't want any staples left in the tack strip to eventually cause headaches when we staple the new top material to the old tack strip.

One removable bow, which fits into a pocket in the underside of the top and aids in preventing the top from billowing, must also be removed at this point.

Next, we removed the cosmetic strip from the rearmost bow—the one just above the rear window—which was also held down with staples. At this point, we were ready to unbolt the rear rail, to which the top, the well liner, and the rear window section were stapled. In turn, the rear rail is bolted to the body structure of the Firebird and keeps the entire top assembly anchored.

With the rear rail unbolted, we then removed the staples—again, one-by-one—and separated the rear rail from the top material and from the rear window section. We didn't entirely remove the well liner material from the rear rail, however. Three pieces made up this particular rear rail, and to keep the three pieces in their original alignment, we left a strip of the well liner stapled to the rail pieces.

Disassembly *CONTINUED*

5 ***We started to separate the top material from the top frame, noting as we did where the top material was secured by staples and where it was secured by other means.***

6 ***This photo shows the tack strip in the header, into which the staples were shot, thus securing the top material. Not all of the staples came out whole with the staple remover—40 years can cause a staple to become rather weak—so we removed the remnants of the broken staples with side cutters or pliers.***

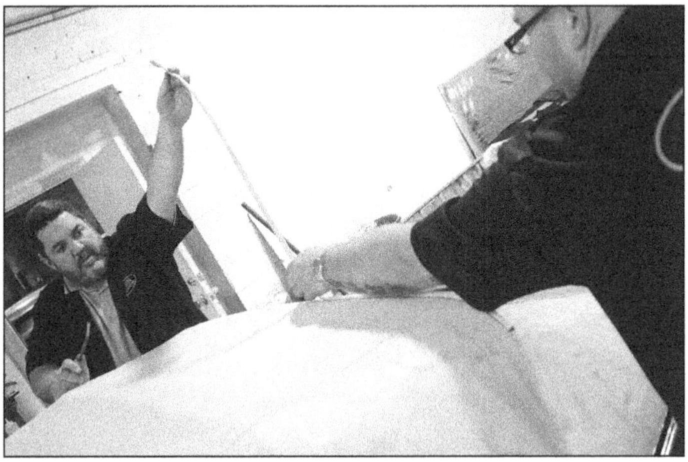

7 The wire-on comes off next. Its ends are held down by small metal trim pieces, which are easily unscrewed. The wire-on itself is held to the rear bow by staples.

8 Next, we unbolted the rear rail from the body. Several pieces of the top were stapled to this rear rail and could not be removed from the rail without first removing the rail from the body.

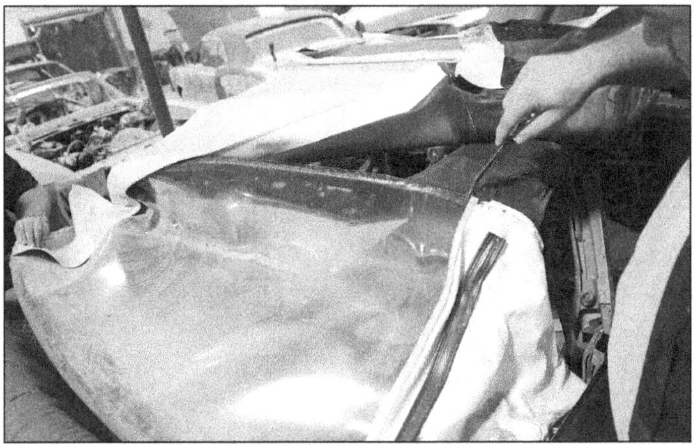

9 The pieces that were stapled to the rail were also stapled to the rearmost bow underneath the top material. If you are replacing the convertible top material and rear window with exact reproductions of the original materials, take note of how the pieces fit together.

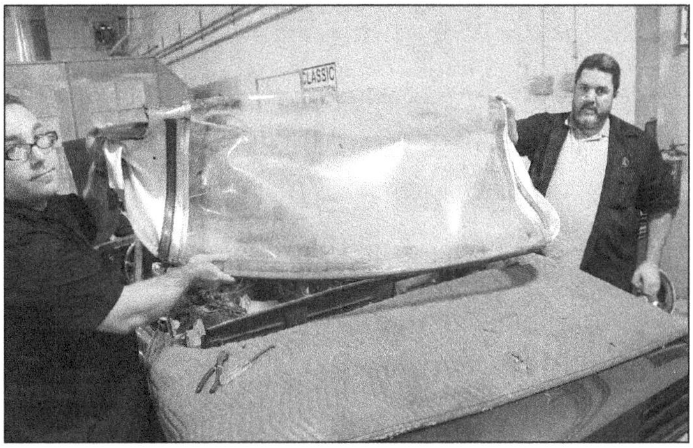

10 Here are the rear rail and all the pieces that attach it to the rear window, the side pieces (similar to the sail panels on a hardtop), and the well liner. It would be easier to separate the rear rail from those pieces off the car, so we moved the assembly to a bench.

11 The pads that are sandwiched between the top frame and the top material are all that's left of the top now. At this point, you should probably determine whether you intend to restore the top frame or leave it as is. The owner of this Firebird was fine with leaving it as is.

The well liner, by the way, loosely hangs between the rear bulkhead—what the rear seat leans back against—and the body structure under the leading edge of the trunk lid. The well liner's basic job is to protect the top when it's folded down.

Other than any staples we might have missed, the only thing left to remove were the side cables, which keep tension on the sides of the top and prevent air from blowing under the top and billowing it out. These pass through pockets stitched into the underside of the top and attach to the folding frame with bolts or screws. Over time, the cables can become kinked where they fold with the top and can then damage the top and the pad. So if the new convertible top came with new cables, make sure to replace them at this time.

With the cables removed, we then lifted the old top, rear window, and well liner off the top frame, leaving only the two pads still stapled to the bows.

Fitting New Pads

Though they appear to be a part of the top from the underside, the pads are actually two separate pieces that run nearly the length of the top, from the header to the rearmost bow, but not down to the rail where the top and well are stapled. Their main function is to keep the top from bunching in the hinges and rubbing on the bows, but they also help properly locate the rearmost bow.

Before removing the pads, we measured the height of the rear bow to make sure it sat the correct distance from the panel to which the rear rail bolts, and compared that measurement with what we knew the height should be for a 1967

Fitting New Pads

1 *With the old pads still in place and the top fully raised, we made sure the rear bow was the correct distance from the body. If it were off at all, the reproduction top, which was designed and stitched around that measurement, would not fit right.*

2 *As long as the top was the correct distance from the body, we proceeded with the removal of the pads, which were stapled or screwed to the bows. Note the speaker enclosure toward the bottom of the photo. Now would be a good time to address any issues with that speaker or to add a second speaker.*

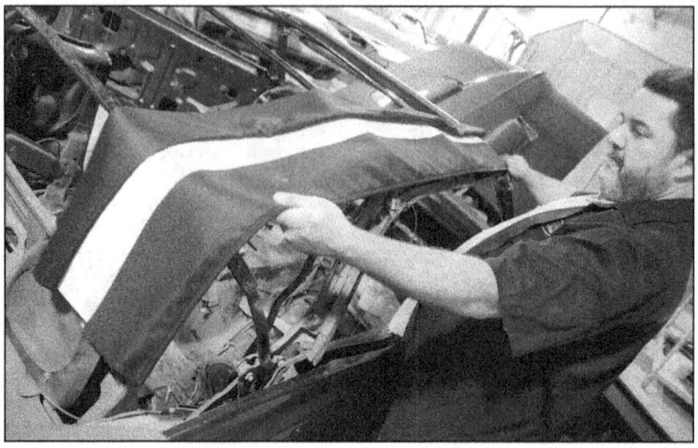

3 *The new pads have two slightly overlapping flaps, and we laid them out with the flaps facing upward. We held the rear bow at about the correct height just to make sure we had plenty of material to work with.*

4 *Leaving a bit of excess forward of the header, we started stapling the bows—flaps open—to the header. We made sure not to staple them right at the ends of the top bows: too far over and the pads would show from the outside; too far inside and they wouldn't sufficiently protect the underside of the top material from the top frame.*

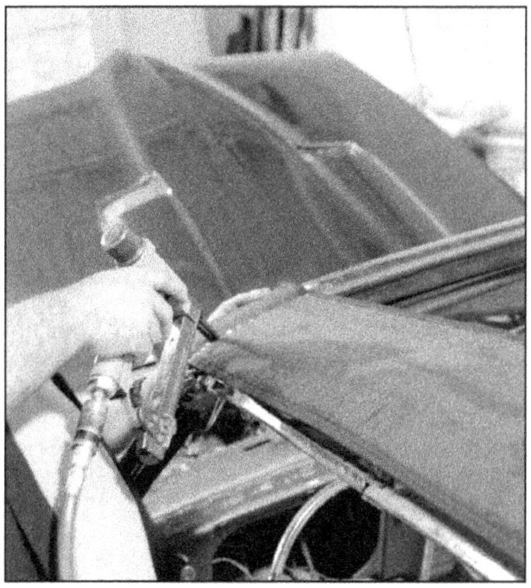

6 *Next, we glued the flaps closed over the top of the jute, and added a few staples to make double-sure everything stayed put every time the Firebird's top went up and down.*

5 *With the pads anchored at the header, we held the rear bow at exactly that correct height again, then stapled the pads to the rear bow. Once we set the correct height for the rear bow we stapled the pads to the middle bows.*

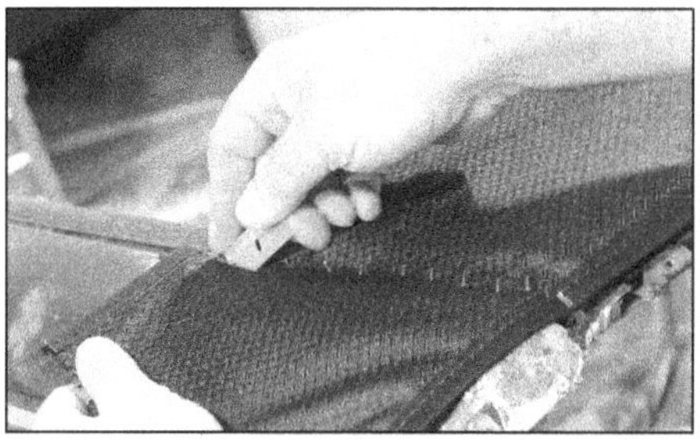

7 *The final step for the pads was to trim them to length just before the header and just after the rear bow. We made sure to hold the loose end taut when trimming.*

Firebird—about 22½ inches. It's important to make sure the rear bow remains that distance from the body; otherwise, the top and the rear window will not fit properly.

We then proceeded to remove the staples holding the pads to the bows, noting that one bow used screws to hold down the pads. With the old pads removed, and with the top fully raised and latched, we then laid the new pads across the bows. (One side of the pads should have a pair of flaps that expose the foam backing; this side should face up.) The pads came with more material than needed and we trimmed them to length after we'd secured them to the top bows. We laid the pads with extra material at both the header and the rear bow, then opened the flaps.

Using a staple gun with No. 7 staples, we anchored the pads to the header, making sure they ran parallel to each other and perpendicular to the bows. At the rear bow, we held the bow at the exact height that we measured earlier, then stapled the pads to that bow. Sure that the rear bow was located at the proper height, we then filled in the staples and screws on the middle bows, locating the screw holes with a small awl.

We then took two strips of thin jute padding the width of the pads' foam backing, and cut them just short of the header and the rear bow. If the jute pads were to go over the header or rear bow, they would make those areas look lumpy, with the top material installed over them. Using contact cement, we glued the jute padding to the pads' foam backing, glued the pads' flaps to the topside of the jute padding, and stapled through the entire pad-jute combination at each bow for good measure.

Finally, using a sharp razor blade, we trimmed the excess pad material from forward of the header and aft of the rear bow.

Well Liner and Rear Window Replacement

We cleared off a workbench and laid out the well liner, then marked the liner's centerline at the rear of the liner. While some liners already come with a marked centerline, either with a notch or a chalk line, it's always a good idea to double-check that centerline.

We then spread the liner over the rear rail, matched the liner's centerline with the centerline of the rear rail, and stapled the liner to the rail. As we stapled, we felt for the bolt holes in the rail, put a thumb over the hole, and stapled on either side of it. Placing a thumb elsewhere not only invites the risk of shooting a staple into a hole, but also of shooting a staple through the hole and into the thumb or a finger on the opposite side. And that hurts.

As long as the liner was stitched to fit loose, matching centerlines was all that was necessary to align the liner to the rail. Aligning the rear window section to the rail required a bit more care, however, to make sure the rear window was not cocked or incorrectly positioned when compared to

Well Liner and Rear Window Replacement

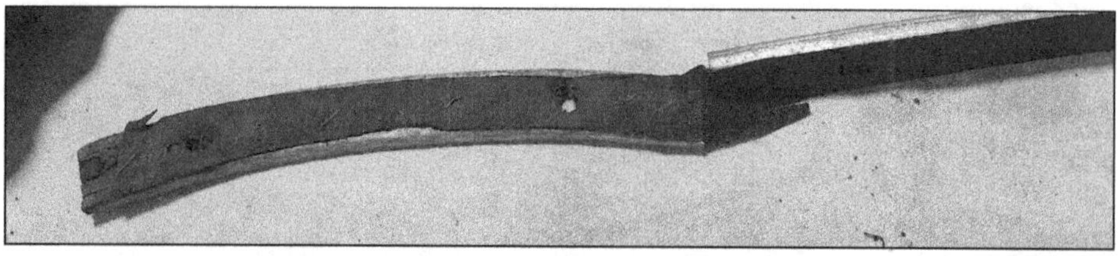

1 *Returning to the rear rail, we removed the rear window and the side pieces entirely from the rail, but left a strip of the well liner still attached, cutting away the rest of the liner. Because the rail is made up of three pieces that need to stay in their same relative positions throughout this process, we used that strip of the well liner to keep those three pieces aligned.*

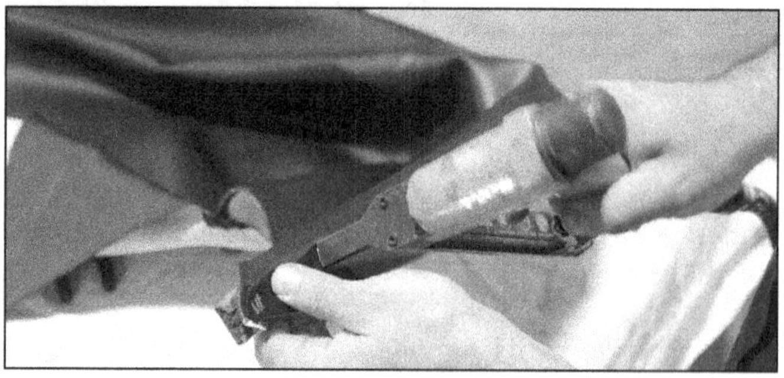

2 *We stapled the new well liner to the rear rail, making sure to line up the centerline marks for each. Staples every 3 or 4 inches were enough to secure the two.*

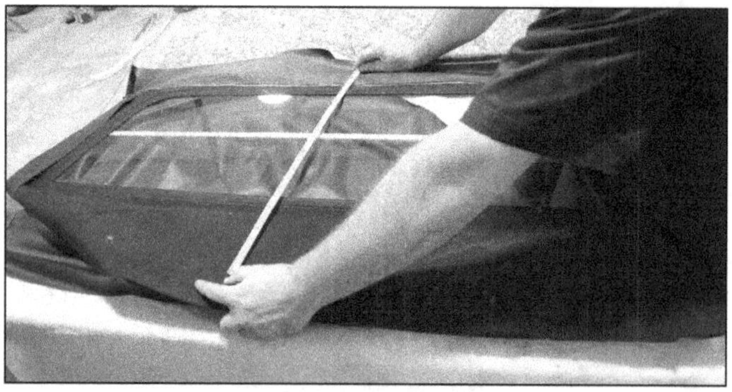

3 *Before stapling the new rear window section to the rail, we not only aligned the centerline marks of each, but also measured the height of the rear window to make sure either the window or the zipper did not go above the rear bow, and also to make sure the Firebird's driver would be able to see out of the rear window.*

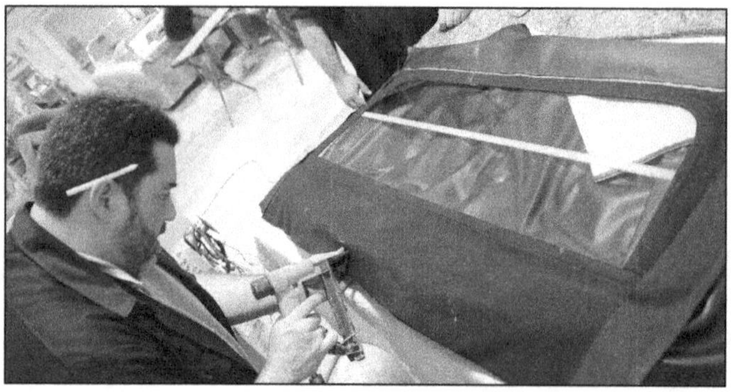

4 *Confident that the rear window was at the right height, we made a chalk mark at the bow to mark that height, and stapled just the center of the rear window piece to the rail, avoiding sending a staple through the bolt holes in the rail.*

the car. In addition, it had to be at the right height. If the window was too low, the driver wouldn't be able to see through it, and if it was too high, the glass would be too close to the rear bow.

The Firebird's stock plastic window did not have this height problem. From the factory, the window extended from the bolt-in rail up to the rear bow and the opening was defined by the edges of the convertible top itself.

Unfortunately, when changing a rear window from plastic to glass, there aren't any reference points to go by, so you're left to your best judgment.

We started the next phase of restoration by measuring the rear window piece, then comparing that to the 22½ inches we knew we had to work with. We then laid the rear window piece over the rail, with the top of the window piece approximately 22½ inches from the rail. We matched the centerlines and stapled the center of the window piece to the rail, then checked the distance of the lower corners of the window to the rail on each side, to make sure they matched up. Once they did, we stapled each side of the window piece to the rail. We popped a few more staples along the length of the rail, but only enough to hold it, perhaps one staple every 2 to 3 inches.

We then placed the entire assembly of the rail, well liner, and rear window onto the Firebird. Before we began to secure the assembly to the car for a trial fit, we unlatched and slightly raised the top frame to give us some slack. We bolted in the rail, then stapled the

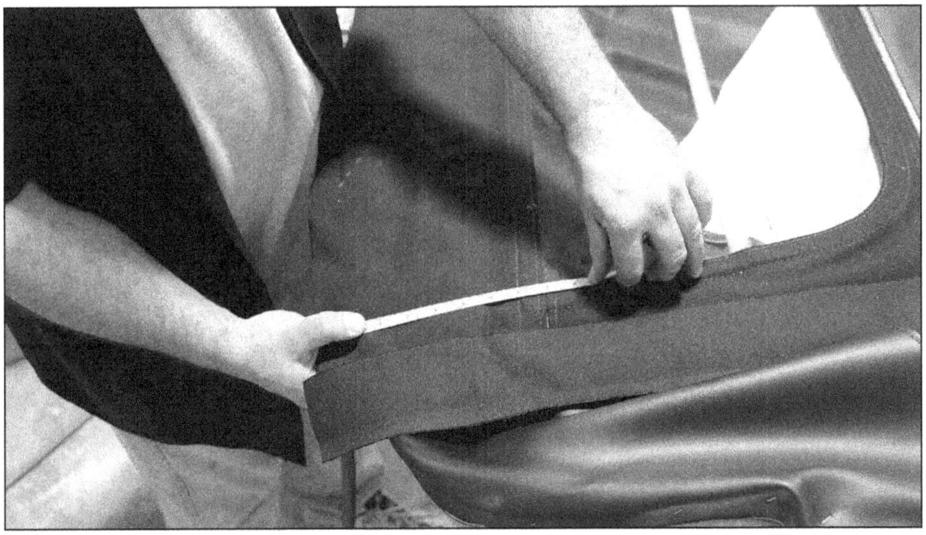

5 *We measured the height of each lower corner from the rail to make sure they were even, side to side. As long as they were, we put a couple staples into the rear window piece directly below each corner. We then stapled the rear window piece in a couple more places between where we'd already stapled it.*

6 *We didn't want to staple the entire length of the rear window piece to the rail because we first wanted to install the rail, liner, and rear window for a trial fit. We bolted the rail to the body, aligned the rear window piece to the rearmost bow, and marked the rear window piece exactly where we wanted it to meet the rear bow.*

7 *Following our chalk marks, we stapled the rear window piece to the rearmost bow, starting in the center, evening out the upper corners of the window, then filling in the unstapled areas in between. These staples will be permanent, so we inserted the normal number of staples instead of a reduced number.*

top of the window piece to the rear bow, making sure to leave the appropriate slack in the window piece. At the same time we made sure to space the top of the window a couple inches away from the rear bow. Confident that the top of the window was an acceptable distance from the rear bow, we trimmed the excess material from the window piece forward of the bow.

After removing the slack from the frame and latching it, we noted a bit of looseness in the window piece. To correct it, we first made a chalk mark all along the width of the window piece where it ducked under the leading edge of the trunk lid. We then pulled the rear window piece tight by pulling it down toward the trunk lid. When we had it pulled tight, we made another chalk mark, again where the material ducked under the trunk lid edge. The second chalk mark thus ended up about 1/2 inch or so above the reference line we initially drew, which told us exactly how far we needed to reposition the window piece on the bolt-in rail.

Repositioning, of course, required unbolting the rail and pulling out the staples we just shot in half an hour before. Most convertible top installations require one or two repositionings, and it's always a good idea to start with material on the looser side in case it's necessary to pull it tighter in another repositioning.

We then bolted in the rail to check that we tightened the window piece enough with our adjustments. Confident that we did, we unbolted the rail again to trim the excess material from under the rail and to shoot additional staples into the rail to permanently secure the window piece to the rail.

Well Liner and Rear Window Replacement *CONTINUED*

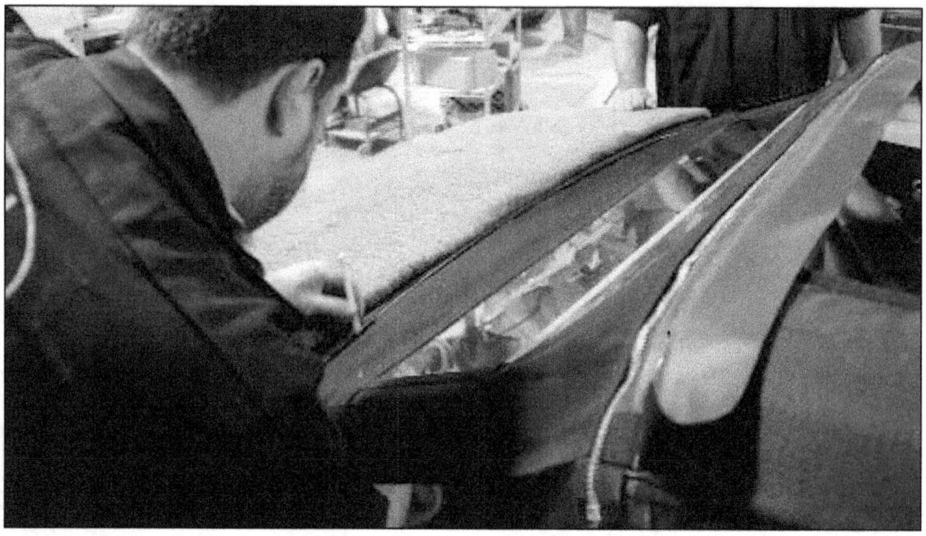

8 ***We raised the top and latched it to see if there was any slack at all in the rear window piece. There was, so we pulled down the rear window piece to remove the slack, then marked the body line against the cloth. We then pulled the rear window piece up and marked that body line.***

9 ***With the rail unbolted and free of the body, you can see those two lines. The difference between those two lines is the amount we need to relocate the rail on the rear window piece. This is why we inserted a reduced number of staples earlier, to minimize the number of staples we'd have to remove to adjust the rail height.***

10 ***After making sure we took out enough slack and that everything lined up, we secured the window piece to the rail with a full complement of staples.***

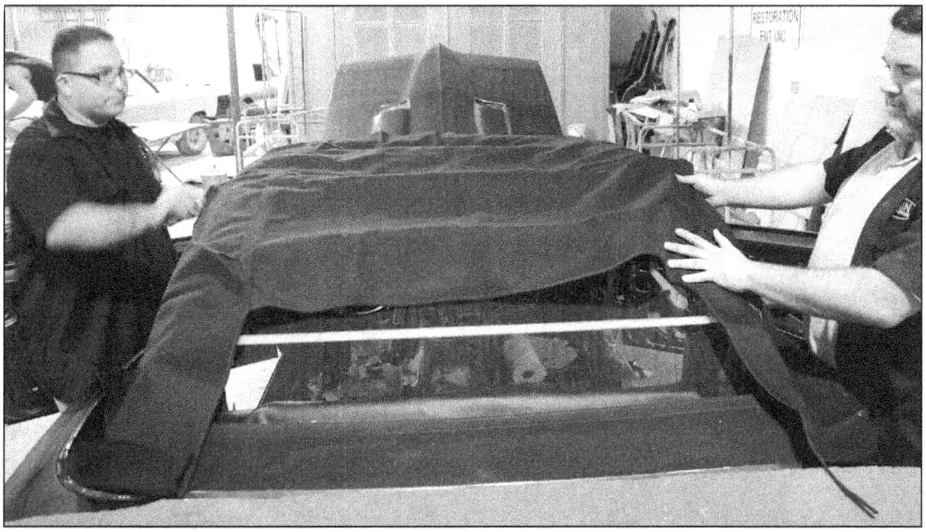

11 *Ideally, the new top material should be removed from the packaging well before installation to remove any creases. We quickly tossed it over the frame to check that it would fit properly.*

12 *Here we have the old, kinked side cable beside the new side cable, already bolted down at the back. A complete convertible top kit should include new side cables, which help prevent wind from getting under the edges of the top.*

13 *Using a long, coat-hanger-like tool, we pulled the side cable through the pocket for it on the underside of the top. Each end of the cable bolts or screws to a specific place on the top frame.*

Fitting the New Top

As long as everything to this point has aligned well, actually fitting the top should be a breeze. We start by laying the top over the top frame, making sure to unlatch the top and lift it slightly to introduce some slack.

Inserting the new side cables through their respective pockets in the sides of the top was the next order of business. We did so using a special tool that resembled a straightened coat hanger with a screwdriver handle on one end and a small rigid hook on the other end. By inserting the tool through the pocket from front to back, we could then attach the leading edge of the side cables to the hook on the end of the tool, pull the cable forward, and then attach the ends of the cable to the convertible top frame.

We also slid the removable bow into the pocket on the underside of the new convertible top and screwed that rail to the convertible top frame. Attaching these loose pieces at this point helped keep the top material in alignment and gave us some slack that we wouldn't have later on in the installation process.

Unlike the pads under the top material, the convertible top itself anchors at the rear and then pulls forward, so aligning the top to the bolt-in rail and to the rear window is critical. We saw some faint alignment marks applied by ARO 2000, but wanted to double-check them, so we bolted in the rear rail once again, then centered and aligned the convertible top material over the rear window piece, and marked the inner edge of the convertible top's window opening on the rear window piece. At the same time, we made sure two

Fitting the New Top

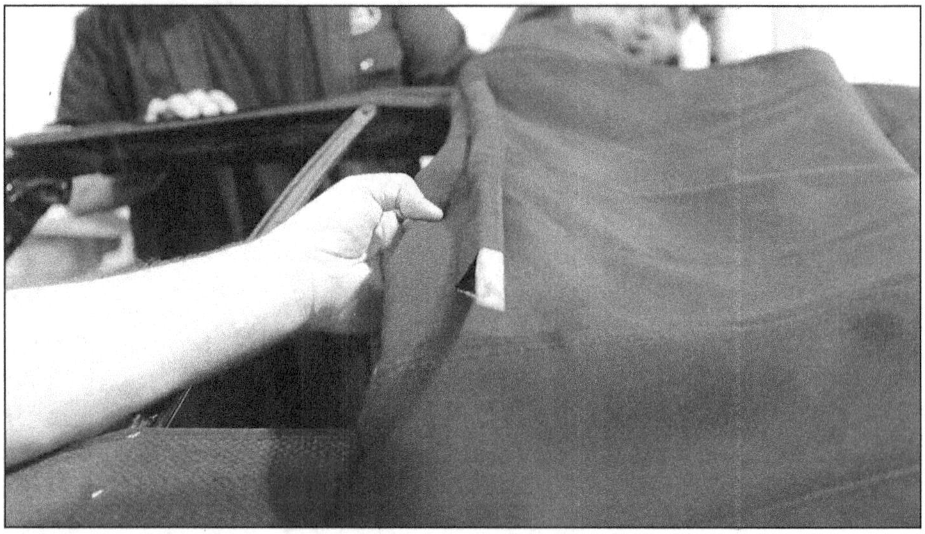

1 ***Another pocket on the underside of the top material houses the rail that we earlier unbolted from the first bow. This rail prevents the top from billowing up should any wind get underneath the top material.***

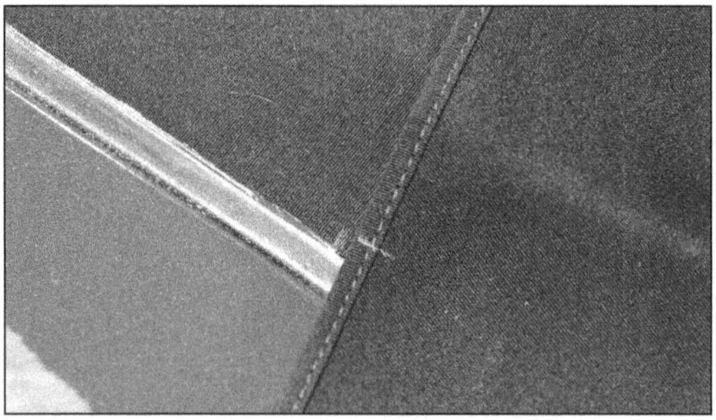

2 ***At the rear of the top, and with the rail still bolted in place, we positioned the two distinct creases in the top material on either end of the rear bow, making sure the window opening perfectly framed the rear window. We then marked both how far down the top material extends and the side-to-side location where we wanted the top to end up.***

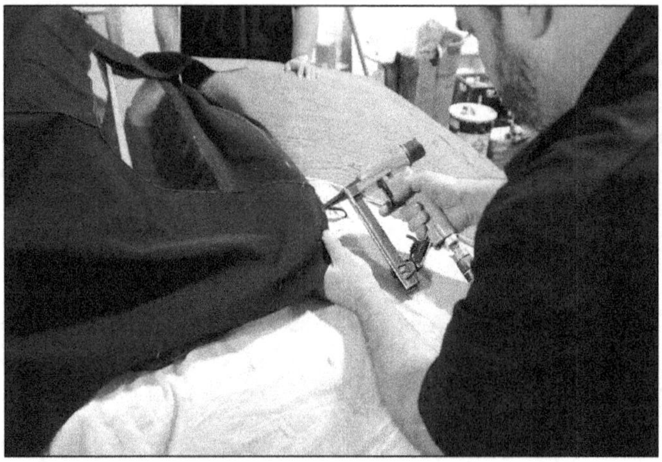

3 ***Next, we removed the rail and, based on those marks, lightly stapled the top material to the rail. After test fitting the rail, we made any adjustments in the same manner as before, then permanently stapled the top to the rail.***

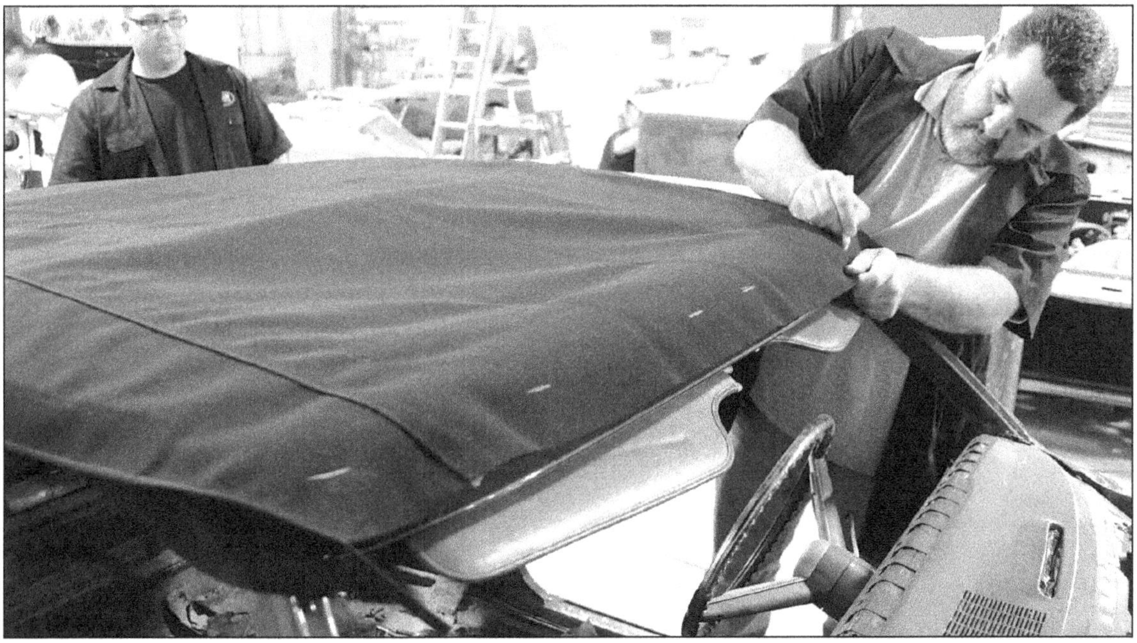

4 ***With the top anchored at the rear, we secured the front of the top. We raised the top again and pulled the top material forward, leaving a little slack. We marked the top at the leading edge of the header.***

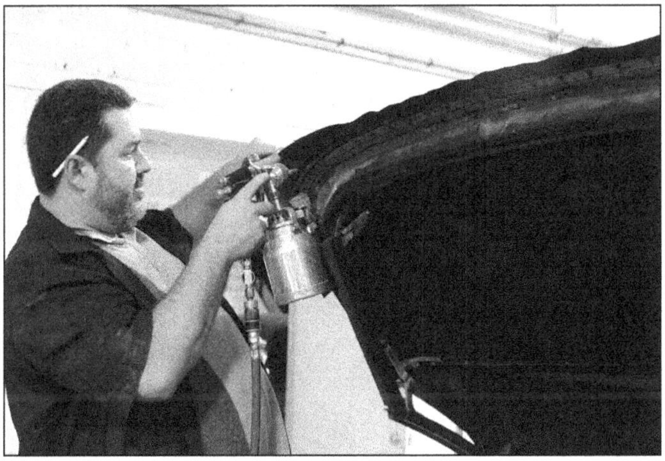

5 ***We put the top at the halfway position to make it easier for the next couple of steps, starting with some adhesive sprayed on the underside of the top material and on the header surface to which the top material will mate.***

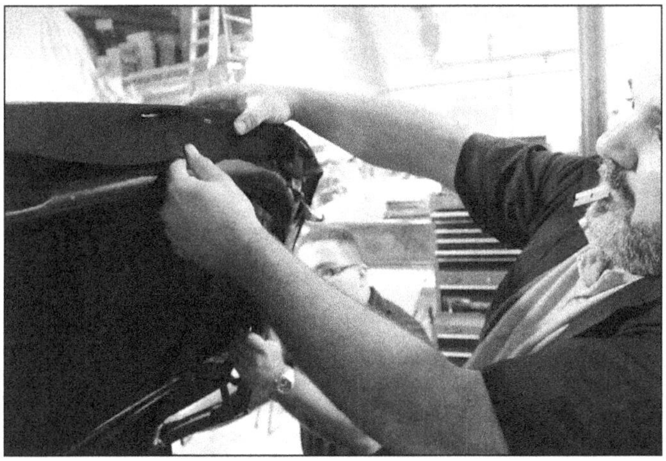

6 ***When the adhesive set up, we pulled the top material forward until our chalk marks just crested the lip of the header. We secured the top material in that position with several staples.***

creases in the convertible top, located above each corner of the window opening, laid on the rear bow.

Once again we unbolted the rail and, following both our alignment marks and the ARO 2000 alignment marks, we stapled the top to the rail, with additional staples—about half a dozen—to secure the two creases at the edges of the top material. As before, we didn't put too many staples into the convertible top material until after we bolted in the rail to make sure the rear window piece and the convertible top squared up nicely.

On this particular top, everything did indeed square up nicely the first time around, which was a bit unusual. Most times, it takes two or three attempts to get the top adjusted just right. Adjusting the convertible top requires essentially the same process as adjusting the rear window piece: Establish the trim line, pinch the material, mark the distance it needs to extend, then pull the staples and stretch it that distance.

Fitting the New Top *CONTINUED*

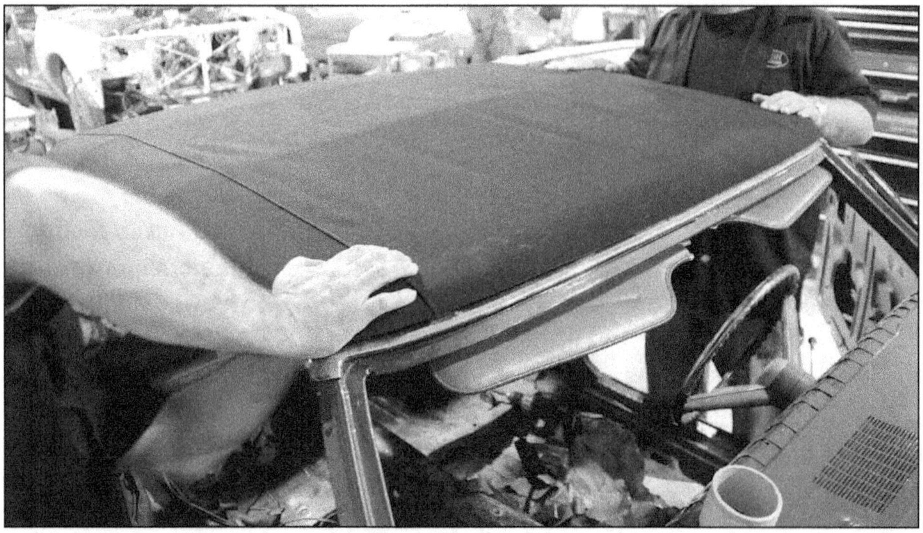

7 *By pulling the top just far enough forward, the slack in the top disappeared on its own when we latched the top in its up position. No hand-stretching, no pulling, and no damage to the top material.*

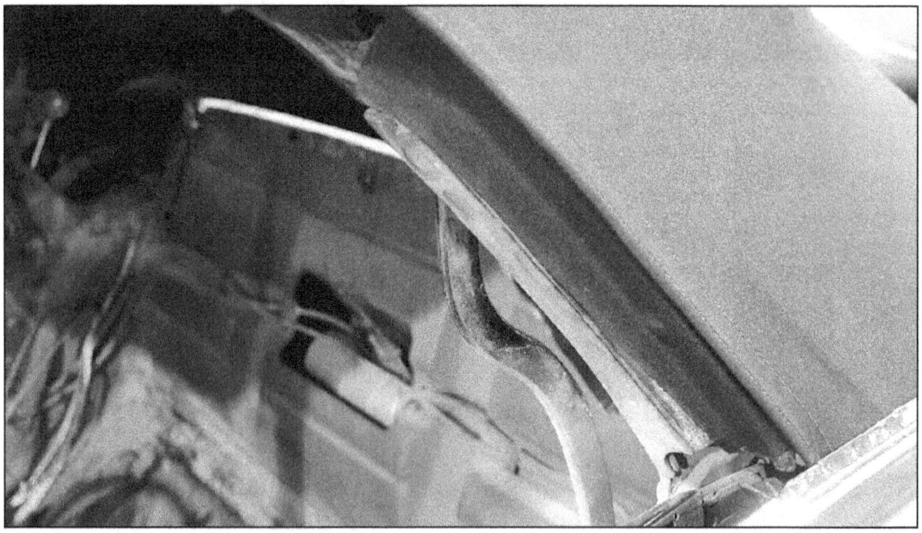

8 *For the final edge of the top, on the sides just behind the quarter-windows, the top material includes a flap that glues to a flat spot in the top frame. A piece of weather stripping will later screw to this flat spot in the frame.*

9 *We then moved to the rearmost bow. Another flap attached to the underside of the top (hidden in this picture by the top itself), which serves to keep water from creeping in between the top material and the rear window piece, needs to be pulled forward and stapled between the top material and the rear bow.*

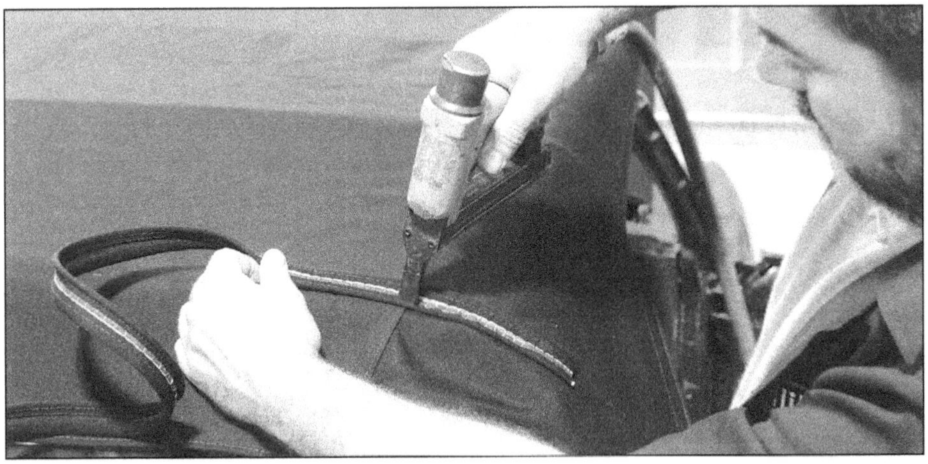

10 *The new wire-on is then stapled to the rear bow. This simply hides the staples holding the top material to the rear bow. To cover the staples holding the wire-on down, the wire-on was stapled with its presentable side down, and off-center, with most of the wire-on's width forward of the staple.*

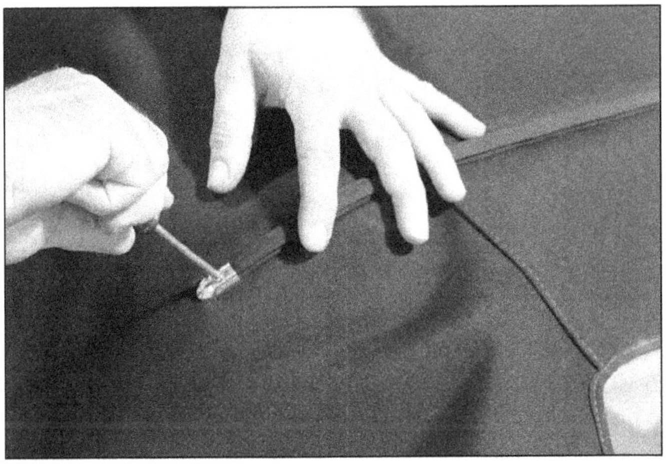

11 *We then folded the wire-on over on itself and tapped it shut with a hammer. Next, we located the screw holes in the rear bow for the end caps, trimmed the wire-on to length, and screwed down the end caps.*

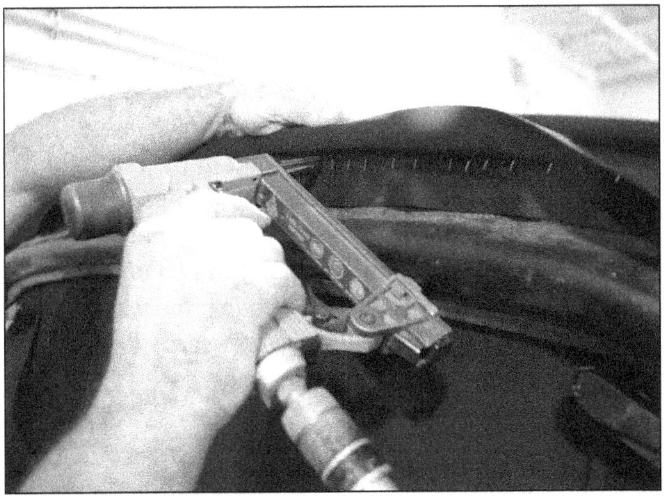

12 *The windlace, a simple piece of cloth folded and stitched over a length of soft cord, was stapled to the underside of the header. With the top up, this windlace simply keeps wind from entering the cabin between the header and the windshield frame.*

We next turned our attention to the leading edge of the top, still unattached to the header and hanging loosely. We let the header rest atop the windshield, then gently pulled the top material forward, not so that it was taut, rather so that it still hung a bit loose between the bows. We then marked the top material at the leading edge of the header, but didn't yet begin to secure the material to the header.

Instead, we lifted the top to its halfway position to remove all slack from the material, and sprayed the underside of the top material as well as the underside of the header with contact cement. With the top still in its halfway position, we pulled the material forward until the marks we made just a moment ago rounded the leading edge of the header. We then pressed the two glued surfaces together, always making sure the leading edge of the top material remained parallel to the header. Adding a brace of staples into the tack strip on the underside of the header made sure everything stayed put while the glue dried.

This technique effectively forces the top to stretch itself taut when it is fully up and latched. As long as we pulled the marks just far enough forward of the leading edge of the header, the top won't end up overly tight or flapping-in-the-breeze loose. And indeed, when we later put the top up and latched it, the material was stretched perfectly.

With the glue gun, we glued down the flaps at the rear of the quarter-window openings directly to the top frame. Once the glue set, we then trimmed the flaps and reattached the sections of weather stripping that screwed into the frame through the flaps.

Fitting the New Top *CONTINUED*

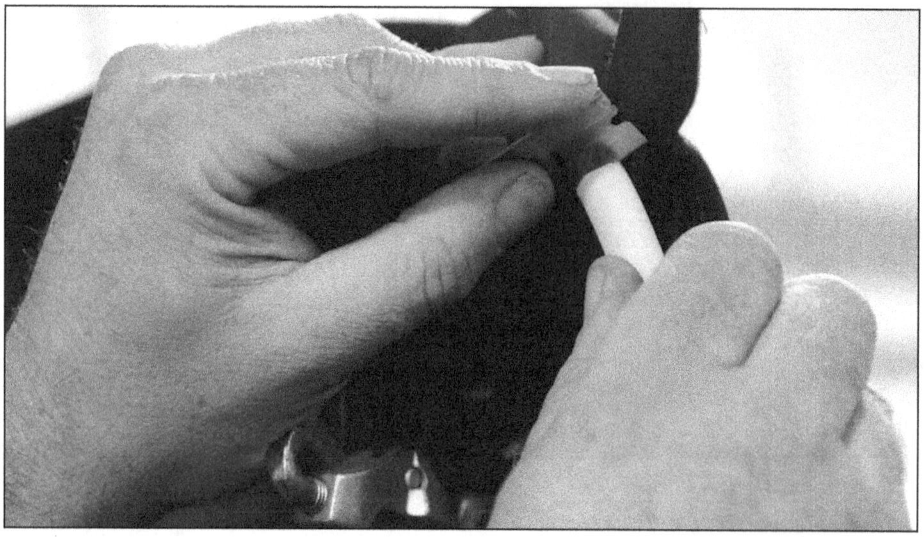

13 *At either end of the windlace, we trimmed the cord to the appropriate length, but did not trim the cloth over the cord. Instead, we folded it over on itself to conceal its own edges, then stapled it to the header.*

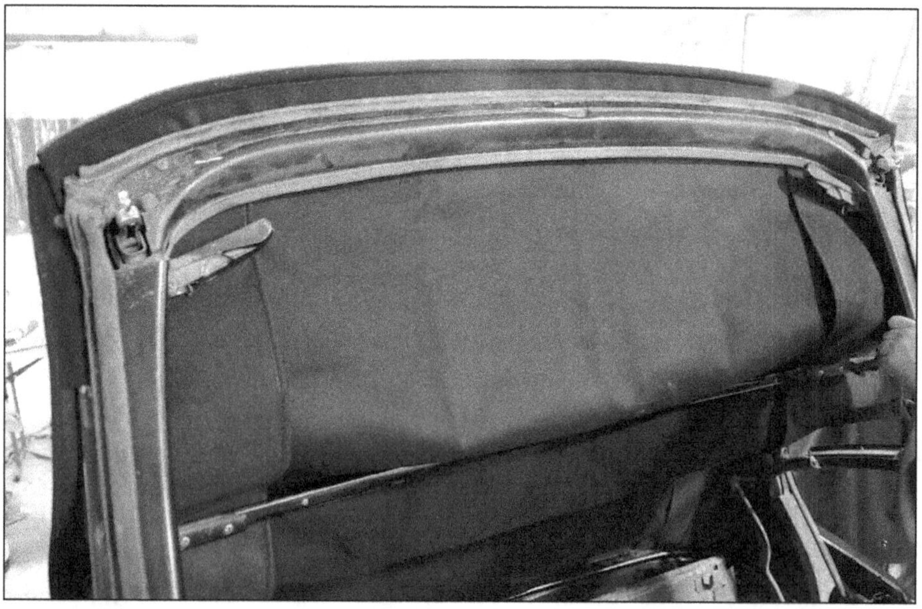

14 *At this point, we trimmed the edges of the top material away from mounting holes and reinstalled all of the weather stripping pieces we removed earlier.*

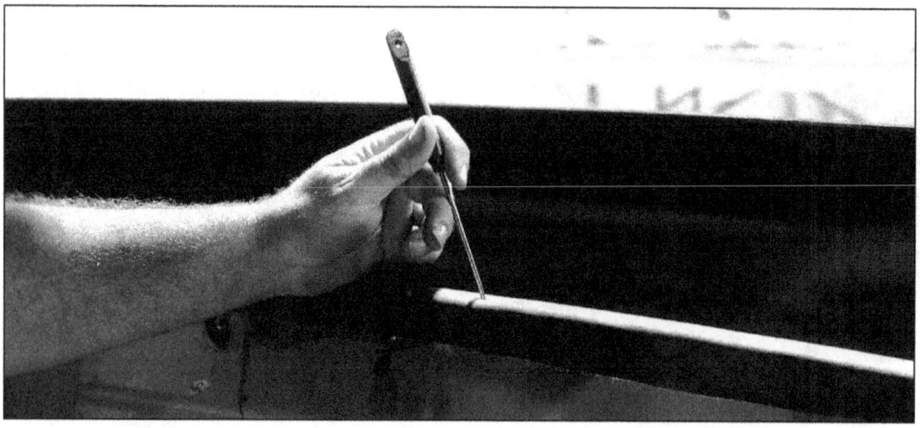

15 *One of the last details involves the well liner, which is both glued and screwed to the rear bulkhead, the structure that the rear seat rests up against. We let the edge of the liner overhang the lip of the bulkhead by a couple inches. We then located the screw holes with an awl and tightened the screws.*

16 ***The top should now be left up for at least a week to sufficiently stretch out. Those wrinkles you see in the middle of the top are actually packaging creases and should smooth out over time, though putting the Firebird in the sun would help stretch out the wrinkles quicker.***

With the top stretched, we shot a few staples through the top material into the rear bow. We made sure to place a pair of flaps, which prevent water from leaking in between the top material and the rear window piece, between the top material and the rear bow before stapling.

Functionally, these staples help force the rear window to fold as the top goes down; aesthetically, they break up the desired smooth black surface of the top. For that reason, a special strip called a wire-on needs to be stapled to the rear bow next. The wire-on contains a lattice of thin wires that go back and forth between two parallel cords, all covered in the same black fabric as the top material.

We stapled the wire-on belly up and off-center, closer to the rearmost cord than the front cord. Once we stapled it all down, we turned up the rearmost cord forward over the staples, then bent the forward cord back over the rearmost cord and lightly tapped shut the wire-on with a hammer.

Once we had trimmed the wire-on to the correct length, we then screwed in the chrome bullets that cap off its ends. And voilà, no staples visible from the outside.

Moving back to the header, we trimmed the excess material ahead of the staples only enough to expose the holes for the weather stripping that we removed earlier. We then stapled one final cord called a windlace to the header. Instead of straight-trimming the ends, we just cut the stitches and removed the cord within the windlace's sheath past this trimming point, then folded the empty strip of material back on itself and stapled that to the header. We then reinstalled the weather strip piece along the underside of the header.

Our last task for the installation was to attach the leading edge of the well liner to the bulkhead. We glued the liner so that it extended over the front edge of the bulkhead by 1 inch or so, then found the screw holes with an awl and inserted the screws to secure the liner to the bulkhead. The back of the rear seat will then cover the leading edge of the well liner.

Perhaps the most important part of the top installation comes here, at the very end. Whenever they put a new top on, most restorers leave it in the up position for at least a week to stretch it out and seat it to the car. Though the top starts out tight and stiff, after a few days it settles into position on the car. During this time any folds or wrinkles in the top material—left over from its time spent packaged up—relax and give way to a perfectly smooth top.

Oh, and by the way, most professional upholsterers warn owners of convertibles to never store the car with the top down. Doing so can lead the top to shrink, which then leads to an incorrect fitting, and possibly to damage. A convertible with its top stored in the down position also provides a cushy nesting ground for mice.

In all, the removal of the old top and installation of the new top took about 6 hours, including a 1-hour lunch. Some manuals call for about 9 hours for the same job, but having the proper tools, the right workspace, and all the necessary materials will make the job go much quicker.

UPHOLSTERY REPAIR, RESTORATION AND REPLACEMENT

Of all the components of an interior, none takes more abuse than the seats. Let's face it, the older we get, the heavier we get, and that's a lot of abuse on those seats, probably more than what the manufacturer suspected they'd have to support. Springs sag over time (that is, if they don't outright break), foam cushions go flat (if the mice don't ruin them first), and seat covers become stained, ripped, and torn (regardless of the materials used in their construction). Before long, you're sitting on seats no more comfortable than a swift kick in the rear.

Just as putting a cheesy, big-box parts-store dash cover over your dashboard won't address the real problems underneath the dash skin, putting a cheesy big-box parts-store seat cover over your buckets won't repair the damage done by 35-plus years of abuse. That means you'll have to strip down the seats and rebuild them with new foam and new seat covers. The seat frame should be free of any cracks, twists, bends, or severe rust. If it is, a simple sandblast and repaint will be sufficient to prepare it for new padding and covers.

If the seat frames exhibit severe damage, they should be replaced—refurbished and reproduction seat frames are available for some of the more popular muscle cars, while less popular muscle cars require a search for good, used seat frames. Fortunately, for most muscle car owners, it's simply a matter of picking up the phone or logging on to the Internet to order brand-new reproduction seat covers, foam seat buns, and even the springs and internal seat mechanisms. Even if your car isn't that widely supported by the aftermarket, it's still possible to repair and refurbish it using simple techniques and commonly available materials.

But first, you should identify the materials used in the construction of your muscle car's seats. Remember the swatch books we mentioned in Chapter 1? Here's where they come into play. You can hold them up against your seats to determine the correct patterns of the cloth or the correct grains of the vinyl. You may find that the sun has faded the colors on the seats; to find the original color, you may have to disassemble the seats at least partially to find a spot that hasn't seen the sun since the Age of Aquarius.

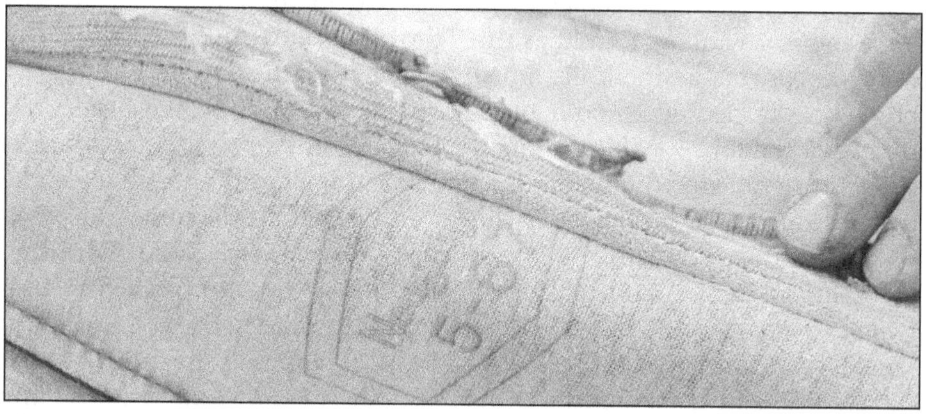

Naugahyde is a common vinyl product, which is actually made from vinyl polymer coated plastic. Many people consider it the premium product of its kind.

Installing New Seat Covers

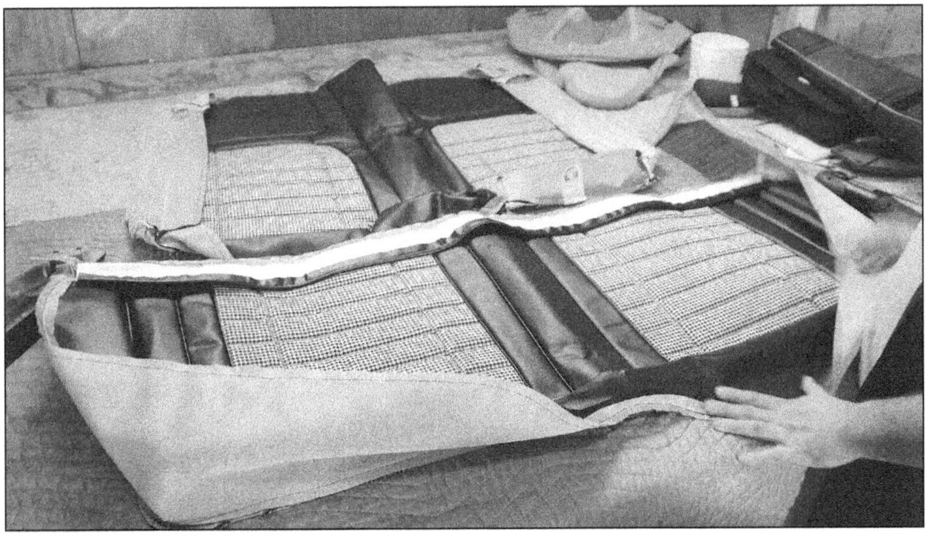

1 ***Though not stock to this 1968 Camaro, the houndstooth-pattern vinyl and cloth seat covers will look much nicer than the raggedy, plain-vinyl seat covers in the Camaro now. New seat cushions to match the covers were ordered at the same time.***

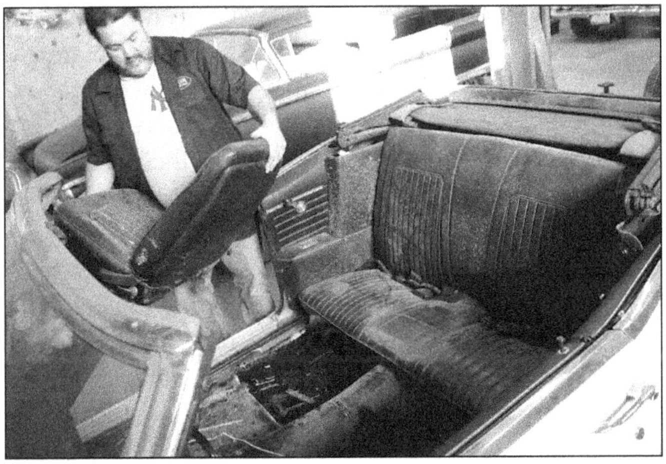

2 ***You can see how extensive the mildewing had become. Though it could be cleaned up now, you won't be sure all traces of mildew or the source of the problem is gone, until you've removed and/or replaced the entire interior.***

3 ***Oooh, money! Another benefit to replacing or refurbishing your interior is that you find all sorts of change and neat stuff. Of course, if you lost it in the first place, you're not really ahead of the game, are you?***

A quick note here on the different terms you'll hear for vinyl. Naugahyde, for instance, is similar to most other cloth-backed vinyls used in automotive interiors. It only refers to the company that produces it, which took its name from its initial home in Naugatuck, Connecticut. The material is completely artificial and is not made from the hides of the mythical Nauga creature.

If you're into Pontiacs, you'll hear about Morrokide. If you're into Oldsmobiles, you'll hear about Lansing's version, called Morocceen. Both are also cloth-backed vinyls, though they're rather renowned for their durability and longevity.

Leather is out of the scope of this book, if only because, quite frankly, muscle cars didn't come with leather upholstery. For the same reason, I won't discuss bench seats. However, many of the same techniques that are used to restore vinyl upholstery can also apply to leather upholstery, and in fact, many restorers note that leather is often easier to work with than vinyl.

So before ordering new seat covers—or before taking the old covers to an upholstery shop to have them replicated—note not only the material type, but also the construction methods. Does the seat back have a plastic shell, or does the seat material extend all the way down? How are the seat inserts configured? Will you need to replace any trim on the seats? Are the stitches at the seams actual stitches, or are they molded, imitation stitches?

Keep in mind that the width of the back seat will be narrower in a convertible than in a hardtop. And check to make sure whether your seat covers were standard for your car or if they were a deluxe or optional item; sometimes the entire seat construction, down to the foam padding, changes between standard and deluxe interiors.

Installing New Seat Covers

For the seat cover replacement process, we went back to our 1968 Camaro, which had a pair of standard vinyl seat covers on the original buckets. However, the Camaro's owner wanted a full set of houndstooth vinyl-and-cloth seat covers, manufactured by PUI Interiors and supplied by Classic Industries. The buns for the seats—the foam padding that will go between the springs and the seat cover—were ordered from American Cushion Industries. You can also sometimes buy buns from Dashes Direct.

To save money, you may be tempted to order just the seat covers and skip the buns, but it's a bit ridiculous not to replace the old, squished, dirty, and possibly mouse-chewed foam while the seat's all apart anyway.

We started by removing the seats, both front and back, and inspecting them to make sure the new covers will fit. These seats showed extensive mildewing, just like the door and interior panels in Chapter 6. The mildew could be removed with either Simple Green or Spray Nine and a soft brush (a potato brush from the local kitchen store works well). However, mildew usually comes on the heels of excessive moisture, which can warp and damage more than just the seat covers. Besides, these seats also exhibited some rips, and as we turned over the rear seat back, we found a substantial mouse nest, reasons enough to put new covers on the seats.

Installing New Seat Covers *CONTINUED*

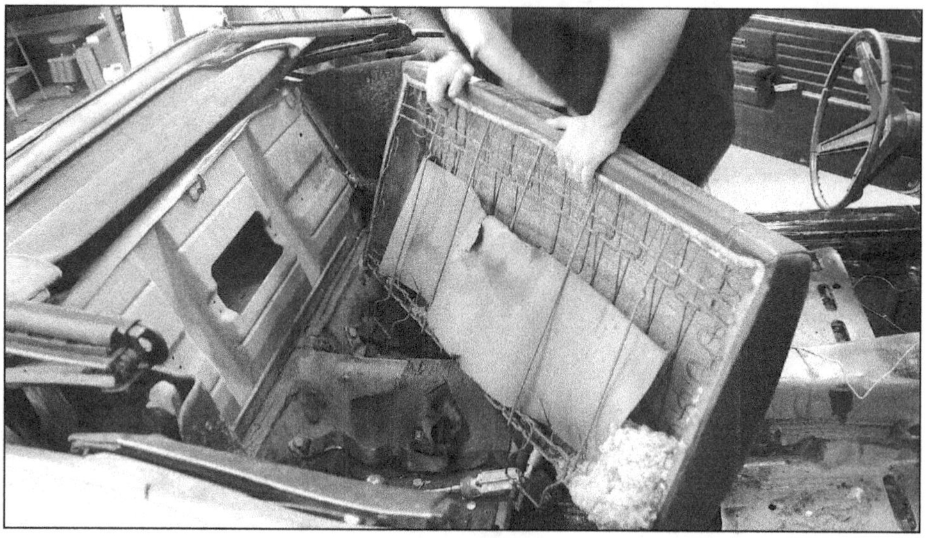

4 ***This Camaro was full of surprises; when we removed the rear seat back we discovered a mouse condo in one corner. It's for this reason that you should probably wear a respirator, or at the very least a dust mask, when disassembling your interior.***

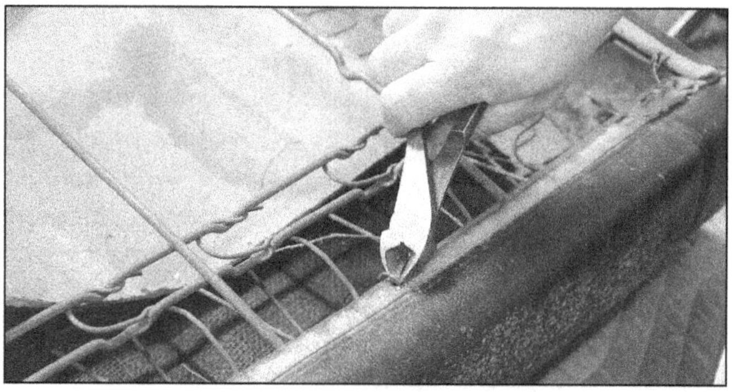

5 ***With a pair of side cutters (also called diagonal cutters or electrician's snips), we began removing the hog rings from the rear seat back. Rather than cut the rings, however, we used a twisting motion that removed them just as quickly and with less strain on our hands. This is an important consideration because a typical seat will have two or three dozen hog rings.***

6 ***With all the hog rings removed from one side of the seat, we removed the rod from the listing. Cleaning the rust from the rods now will help them slide into the listing in the new seat covers later.***

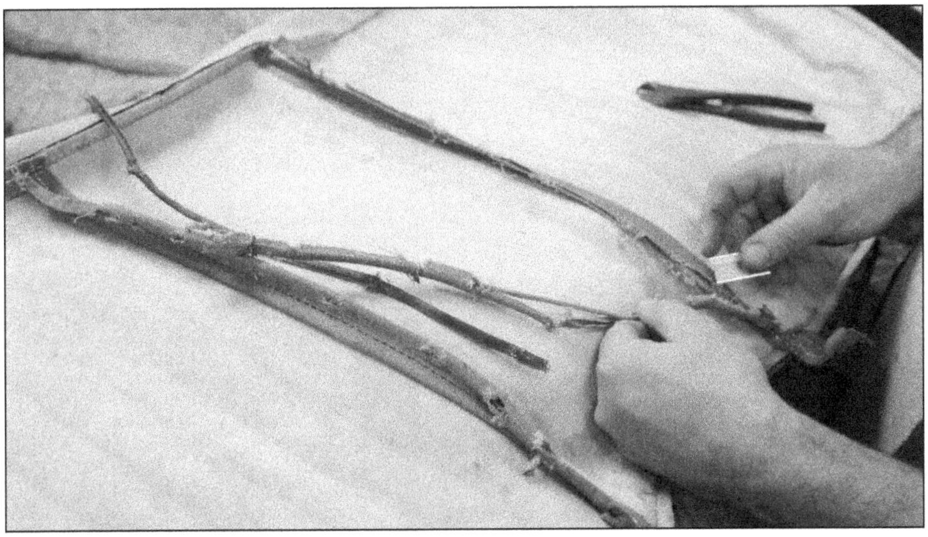

7 ***If the rods do not easily slide out of the listing, as with these rods from the back seat cushion, you may have to cut them from their listing with a razor blade. Just be sure to cut only the listing and not the seat material, which you may need for reference later on.***

8 ***With all four rods removed from all four sides, the seat cover will pull away from the seat frame just as easily as it will go back on later in the process, so there should be no need to cut the seat cover apart just to separate it from the frame.***

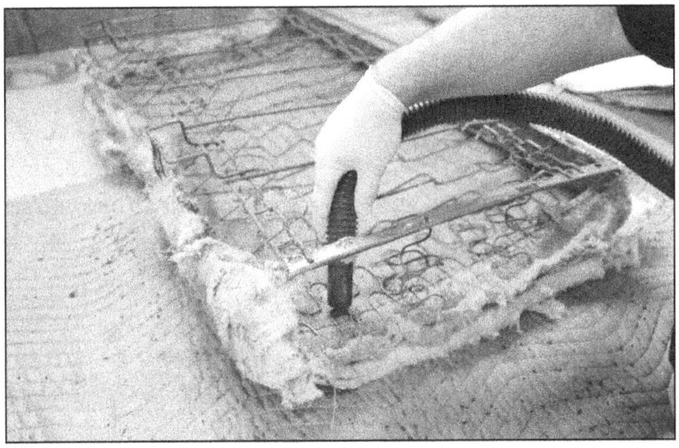

9 ***Vacuum the remains of the mouse nest. This is also a good time to continue stripping the frame down to bare metal to rid it of rust, and to paint it to deter further rust.***

Beginning with the rear seat back, we began removing all the old hog rings holding the seat cover to the frame. Where the hog rings didn't go through pre-stamped holes in the frame, we noted what seat springs or other seat-frame structures they attached to. Rather than cut the hog rings with side cutters, we employed a twisting technique—using the seat frame as leverage—that removed the hog rings without hand fatigue and without sending sharp pieces of hog ring flying across the room.

With all the hog rings removed, we then removed the stiff metal rods from loops of fabric (the technical term for the loops is *listing*) around the perimeter of the seat cover. Usually, the factories built seats with one rod for each side of the seat, so in this case, the seat back used one rod for the left side, one for the right side, another rod at the top, and another rod at the bottom.

We came across some exceptions to that rule as we did the rest of the seats in this Camaro. If the rods didn't easily slide out, we cut them out of the listing with a razor blade. The rods are usually rusty, so now would be a good time to clean them up and paint them. Note that sometimes the factory wrapped the rods in paper, which can help them slide into and out of the listing.

Next we removed the cover from the seat back, being careful not to disturb the cotton filler under the cover. (The seat back is unique in that it doesn't use foam padding and instead relies on the springs and a thin layer of cotton for cushioning.) The owner of the Camaro wanted to save a few bucks, so we didn't strip down the seat any farther than it needed to be stripped, which means we simply left the cotton and springs in place and vacuumed out the remains of the mouse nest.

Anybody doing this step at home, however, can certainly take a more thorough approach and remove the cotton in order to attack any rust on the springs and frame, and then repaint them before applying a fresh layer of cotton.

The cotton, by the way, is simple craft-store cotton that comes off a roll; it can be torn apart with the hands rather easily to fit the seat frame and springs. Higher-grade cottons aren't necessary here. Unfortunately, the cotton also usually soaks up the smell of mouse urine, so if you find that you just cannot get rid of that acrid, ugly smell, you may have to replace the cotton.

For this Camaro, we added a little extra cotton to make up for the compression that the old cotton suffered over the decades. Adding extra cotton also makes the seat covers a little tighter, and most upholsterers aim for a tighter fitting seat cover rather than a loose one, which has more potential to slide around on the seat.

We then laid the cover over the seat with the correct orientation, making sure it was generally centered on the seat. The cover should come with the sides folded up—as if it were inside-out—which makes it easier to pull the sides down over the frame.

By inserting a hand into the pocket created by the turned-up sides at the corners of the cover, we were able to flip the corner down and snug it over the corner of the frame, repeating the process at each corner. Though we pulled the sides down by hand, if you feel you can't get a good grip on the seat cover or if

Installing New Seat Covers *CONTINUED*

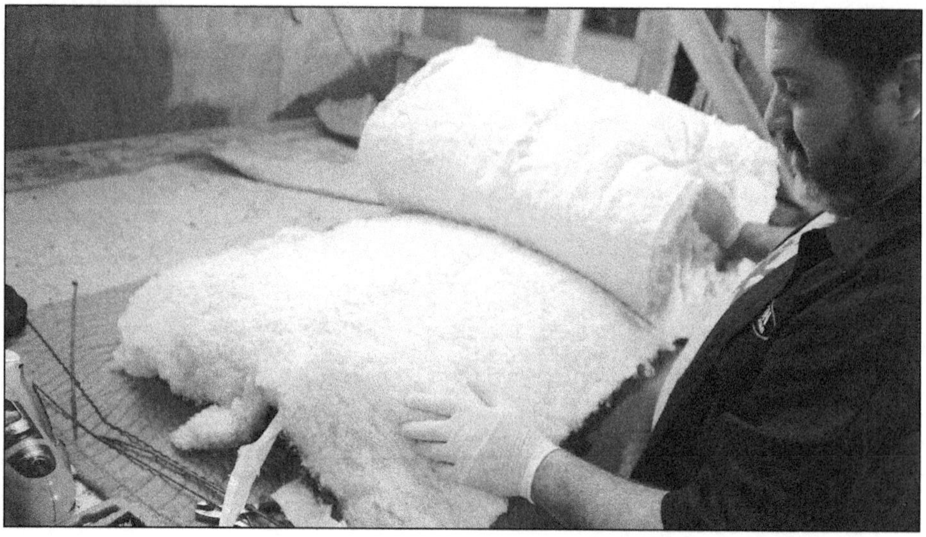

10 ***Rather than remove the cotton padding and burlap spring cover from the seatback, we instead rolled out another layer of cotton. The old cotton, flattened over the decades, wouldn't fill out the new seats on its own, and would leave the seat covers loose on the seat back.***

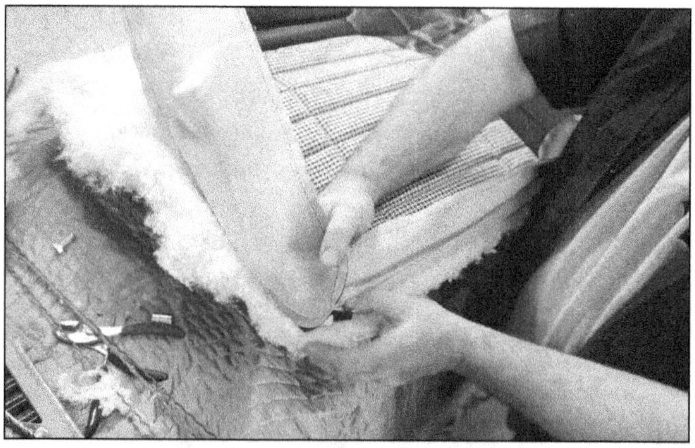

11 ***With the cotton trimmed to size (it pulled apart easily by hand), we centered the seat cover over the frame and flipped its edges over the seat frame, starting at the corners. The last two corners are sometimes difficult to pull over the frame, but will eventually make it.***

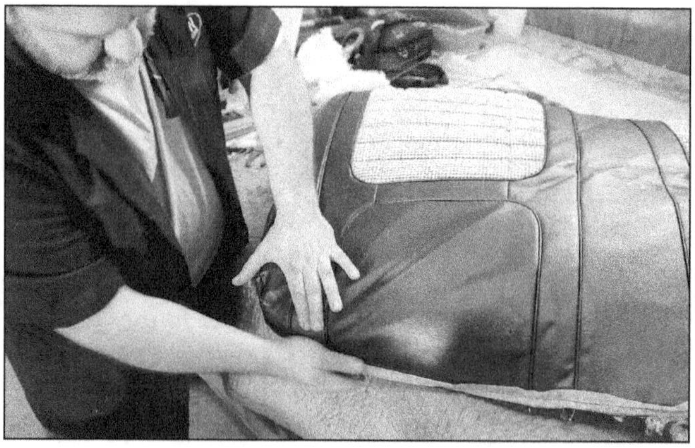

12 ***After pulling all four corners over the frame, we checked to make sure the cover had remained centered. A bit of gentle tugging from either side brought the cover back to the correct position.***

13 *The listing on the new seat covers may need to be cut open at the ends, as with the covers for our Camaro. Note the holes stamped into the inner edges of the frame; the hog rings will attach here momentarily. If no such holes exist, the hog rings will have to attach to the seat springs.*

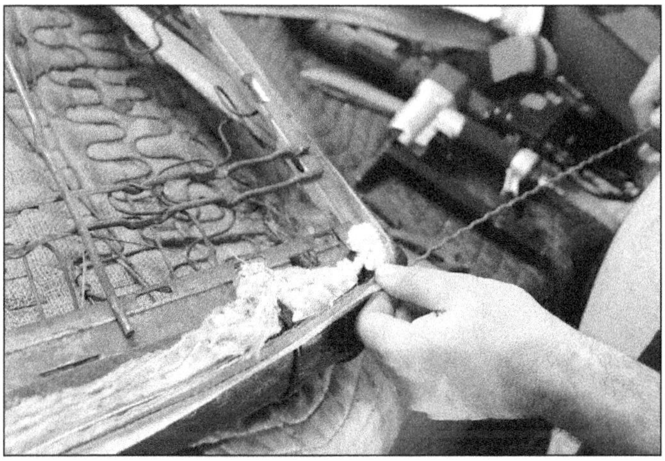

14 *We inserted the rods that we removed earlier into the new seat cover's listing. For the longer rods, we often had to hold the listing straight to force the rods to slide in without catching the sides of the listing.*

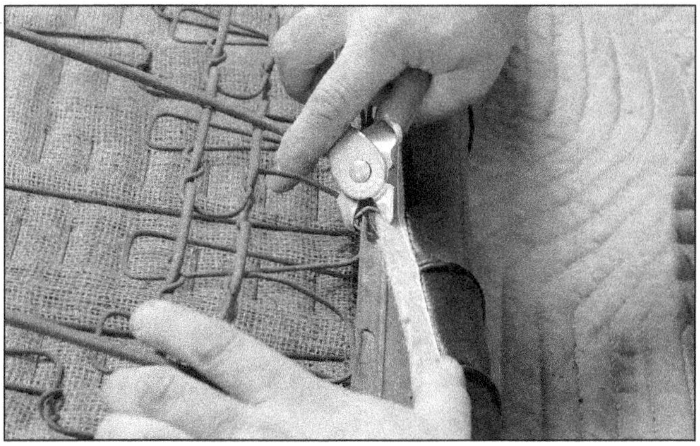

15 *These hog ring pliers are a bit simpler than the ones we discussed in Chapter 1. These require loading the hog ring into the pliers manually, but the concept is the same. Here, we used the sharp end of the hog ring to pierce the listing behind the rod, and hooked both ends of the ring around the stamped holes in the frame.*

you can't stretch it enough by hand, it may be necessary to pull the sides down with a pair of stretching pliers. Vinyl is notorious for being hard to stretch, but it also is capable of resisting damage while stretching it.

It's a good idea to start stretching the cover down at the corners, which will show you if the cover fits tight or if it needs more cotton. If it's too tight, you can either take some cotton out of the seat or use a heat gun to soften and stretch the areas that are too tight.

The listing on the new seat cover wasn't open at both ends (which is not uncommon), which forced us to cut a small slit in one end so we could slide the rods into the listing. Here's where cleaning up rusty rods helps reassembly—painted (or paper-coated) rods slide easier through the listing than rusted rods.

With the rods inserted into the listing, we then loaded up our hog ring pliers. Starting at the center of each side, we poked one end of the hog ring through the listing, making sure to hook the rod within the listing. We then poked the other end of the ring either through a pre-stamped hole or around the seat structure noted earlier. With a squeeze of the pliers, the hog ring collapses, securing the rod (and thus the listing and thus the seat cover) to the seat frame.

Unless pre-stamped holes in the seat frame dictate how much space to put between the hog rings, you can leave about 3 or 4 inches maximum between hog rings. Secure them to the seat springs if necessary.

After we finished hog ringing the top and bottom of the seat cover, we double-checked that the seat cover remained centered on the frame, then hog ringed the sides of the seat

Installing New Seat Covers *CONTINUED*

16 *We tackled each side of the seat back by cinching the hog ring closest to the center first, then working out from there. The stamped holes told us how to space the hog rings, but in the absence of stamped holes, we usually placed a hog ring about every 2 to 3 inches.*

17 *With all four sides hog ringed, we flipped over the seat back to examine our work. Wrinkles in the vinyl were easily smoothed out with heat or steam.*

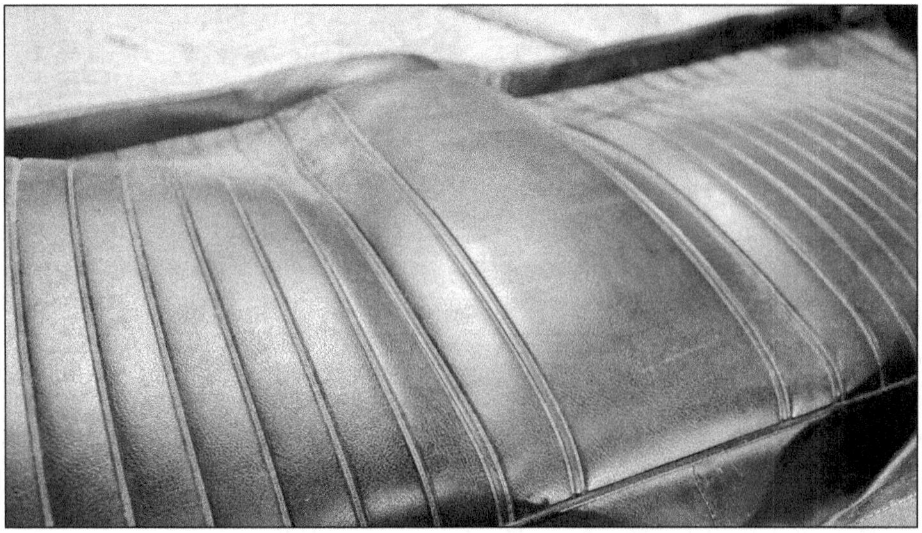

18 *For the cushion of the rear seat, the process is nearly the same as for the seat back, except the cushion has this center hump, created by two additional rods inserted in two additional pieces of listing on either side of the hump.*

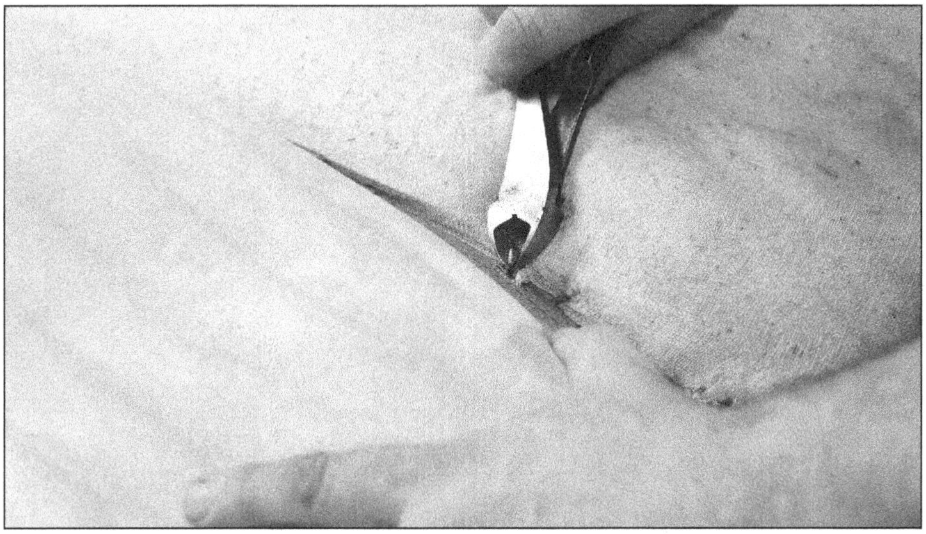

19 ***After removing the hog rings and four rods from the underside of the cushion, we flipped over the cushion back and folded back the seat cover to the first defining rod, to reveal the hog rings that hold that rod to the seat frame.***

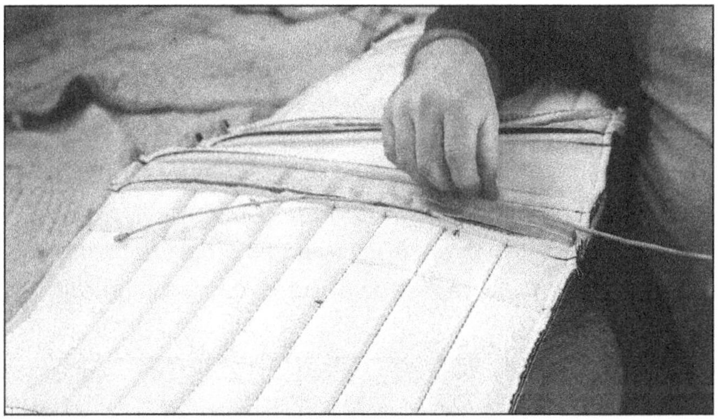

20 ***With both of those defining rods removed, we transferred them to the new seat cover before stretching the seat cover over the frame. The listing for the defining rods is occasionally stitched in the wrong place, so it's a good idea to check the new seat cover against the old one to make sure the listing is in the same place.***

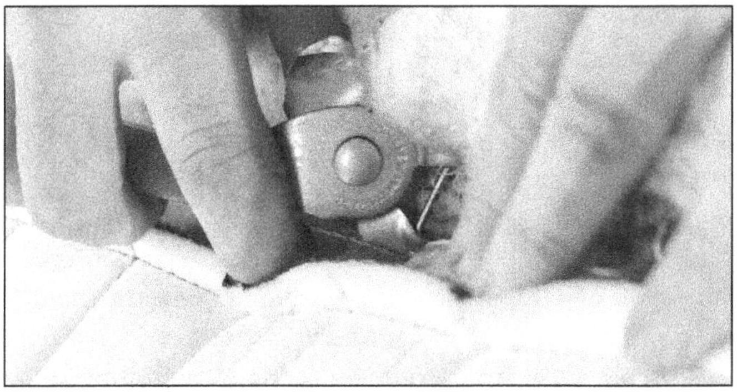

21 ***Usually, the defining rods are hog ringed straight to the seat springs, but you should double-check to see where exactly they attach. The hog ringing process is the same as for the rods on the perimeter of the seats, save for the fact that you have to negotiate the hog ring pliers into a somewhat more cramped space.***

cover. We then flipped over the seat back. Where we saw any loose spots or wrinkles in the seat cover, we either manually stretched that area of the seat cover or applied some heat to smooth it out.

Some restorers recommend using steam in such a case, which works well on cloths and vinyls, but will shrink and stiffen leathers. However, it's not really worth the time to fire up a steam machine (which many resto shops have) or even to boil a pan of water if you're only doing one or two seats. A heat gun will accomplish the same thing with less hassle.

The bottom of the back seat (called the cushion) is constructed largely the same, with cotton over springs instead of foam padding. It does, however, have two additional rods and pieces of listing running from front to back toward the center of the cushion, hog ringed to the seat springs. These help define the rear seat cushion into distinct sections for each passenger. The old hog rings here should be removed after the old hog rings around the perimeter of the cushion. The new hog rings here should be installed before the new perimeter hog rings. The easiest way to reach them is to just flip over the seat cover with it laying on the seat, which will give you access to the listing and the valley through the cotton padding where the hog rings attach to the seat springs.

The transmission and driveshaft tunnel will also likely intrude into the rear seat cushion, but you'll notice that the cushion only uses one rod for the front and one rod for the back, both bent to conform around the tunnel. Before inserting these rods into the new listing,

Installing New Seat Covers *CONTINUED*

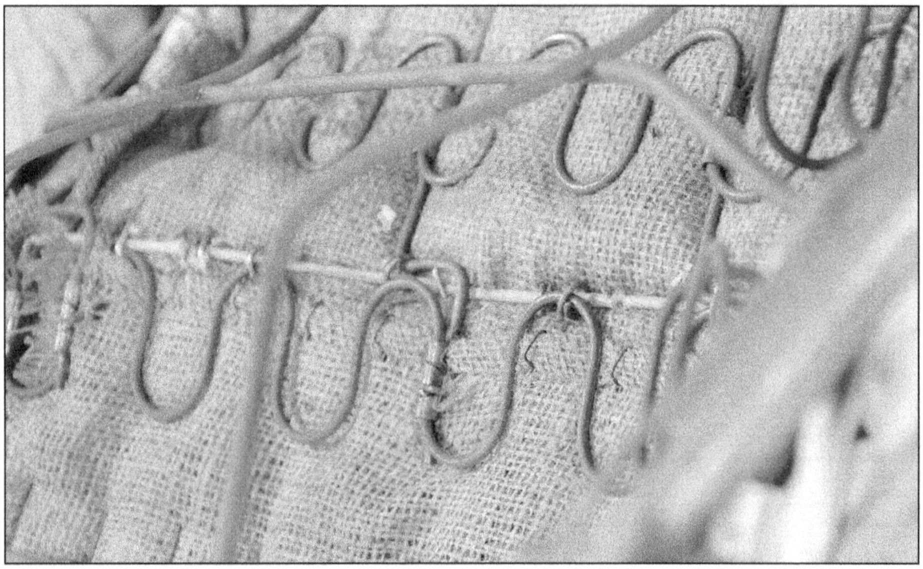

22 *From the underside, you can see exactly where the hog rings attach to the springs.*

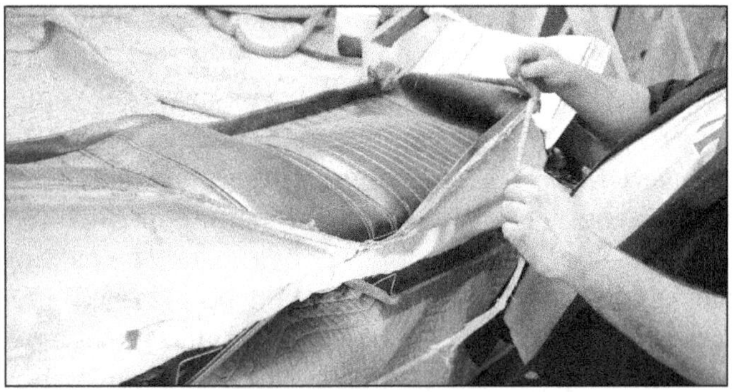

23 *Only one rod secures the front of the seat cover to the cushion around the driveshaft tunnel, and that rod bends around the tunnel while in the listing. Simply straighten the rod before inserting it into the new listing (it goes in a lot easier when straight) and then hog ring it exactly as it was hog ringed in the old listing. The driveshaft tunnel will bend it back into its previous shape.*

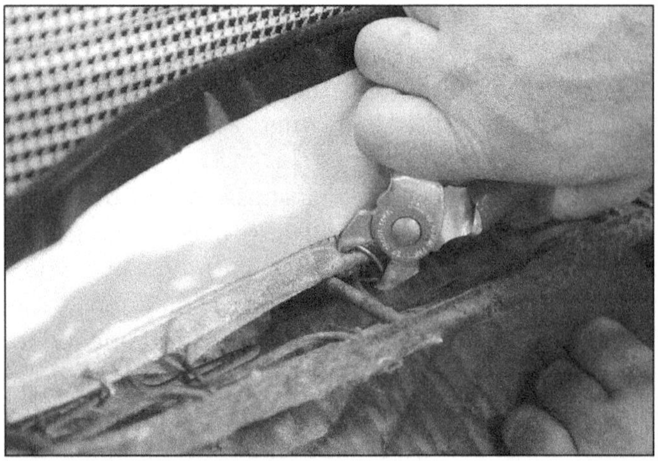

24 *At the back of the seat cushion, the rod is actually hog ringed just forward of the back of the frame, so don't try to pull the seat cover back too far. A flap of material aft of the listing will cover the back of the seat frame.*

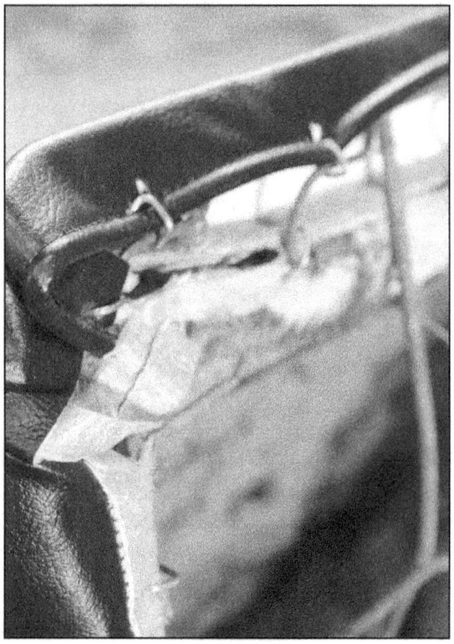

25 *Hog rings secure that flap of material as well, though without the benefit of rods and listing. At the corners, fold over the excess material and hog ring it down. Even the topside of this area won't be visible once the cushion is installed in the car, but folding over the edge will prevent that excess material from getting snagged during assembly.*

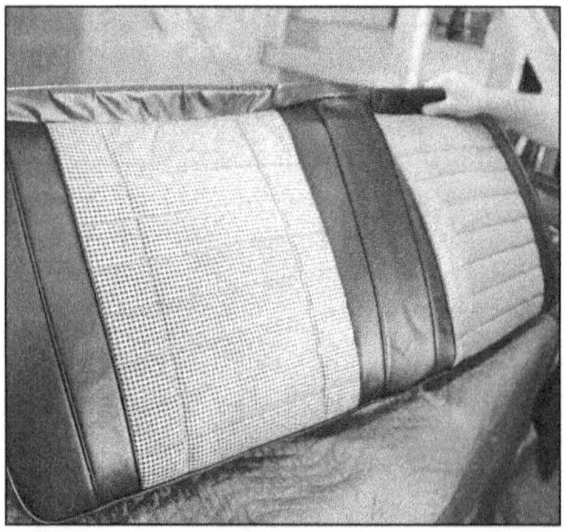

26 *Again, you may have to smooth out some wrinkles with the heat gun, but just for a moment, congratulate yourself on a job well done. You're making some good progress.*

27 ***You'll have to spend a little more time disassembling the front seats before you are able to remove the seat covers. For example, our Camaro uses hard plastic shells to cover the back of the bucket seats and the latch assembly. If possible, work on one bucket seat at a time to avoid confusing parts.***

28 ***If you can't work on one bucket seat at a time, it helps that most of the bucket seat parts are marked L or R, such as this bracket for the seat latch. Also, make sure you have the right covers for the right seat, and that you're installing the left covers on the left bucket seat.***

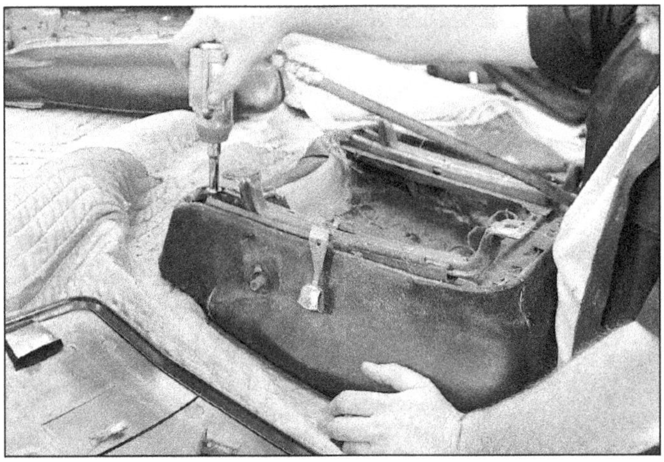

29 ***Separate the seat back from the cushion and remove the seat tracks. Now is a good time to de-rust and paint the seat tracks. Make sure to grease the tracks thoroughly before reassembly.***

straightening them will help them slide in. Attach the hog rings as you normally would. They will then bend around the transmission tunnel according to the placement of the hog rings.

Also, pay attention to how the back of the seat cushion is constructed. On this Camaro, the rod isn't hog ringed to the far back edge of the seat frame. Instead, it reaches down to the springs just forward of the back edge of the frame. A flap rearward of the listing stretches over the back edge of the frame. Hog rings pierce that flap, assisted by a cord stitched into the flap. This trailing edge tucks in under the seat back, so wrinkles in the flap here don't show when the rear seat is in the car. For this reason, though, the flap covers the trailing edge of the frame and protects the seat back from that raw metal edge.

Front bucket seats are a little more complicated, but the overall process remains very similar. Take care during disassembly to note not only which side each seat track goes on, but also how the seat latch operates and the location of any hardware or trim that attaches to the seats. Doing one bucket seat at a time helps reduce parts confusion, and allows a seat to remain assembled for reference.

After removing the trim and separating the seat back from the cushion, we focused on the cushion. General Motors F-bodies, such as this Camaro, use only a few hog rings around the seat perimeter, at the back of the seat. The rest of the perimeter relies on a plastic piece stitched into the seat cover material that clips directly into the seat frame. Rather than fight with the tension of the plastic clip, we cut it free from the seat cover with a razor blade. Most other muscle cars use hog rings to attach the seat cover to the frame, but such plastic clips are not uncommon.

The Camaro's bucket seat uses hog rings to hold down the foam buns and to attach the rods that define the center of the seat to the springs (similar to the rear cushion's defining rods). The hog rings that hold down the foam buns go straight through the buns rather than through any listing, though the hog rings do attach through areas that are lightly reinforced by a listing-like material bonded to the foam.

If the foam is damaged and no reproduction buns are available, it's easy enough to repair the foam by cutting out the damaged sections with an electric carving knife, then buying new foam at any craft store and using contact cement to bond the new foam to the old foam. Similarly, some reproduction seat buns come as universal blocks of foam, which then need to be shaped with an electric carving knife to match the original shape.

Even the shaped reproduction bun for this Camaro required a slight alteration. The cushion used three rods to define the shape of the cover—two running longitudinally and one running latitudinally. The bun had two pre-cut valleys for the longitudinal rods, but no pre-cut valley for the latitudinal rod. For that reason, we had to mark the location of the latitudinal rod using the listing on the seat cover as a reference, then slice open a valley with a razor blade. Although our new valley extended to the other two valleys, it didn't go all the way through the foam, which left enough bun for the hog rings to grasp.

Installing New Seat Covers *CONTINUED*

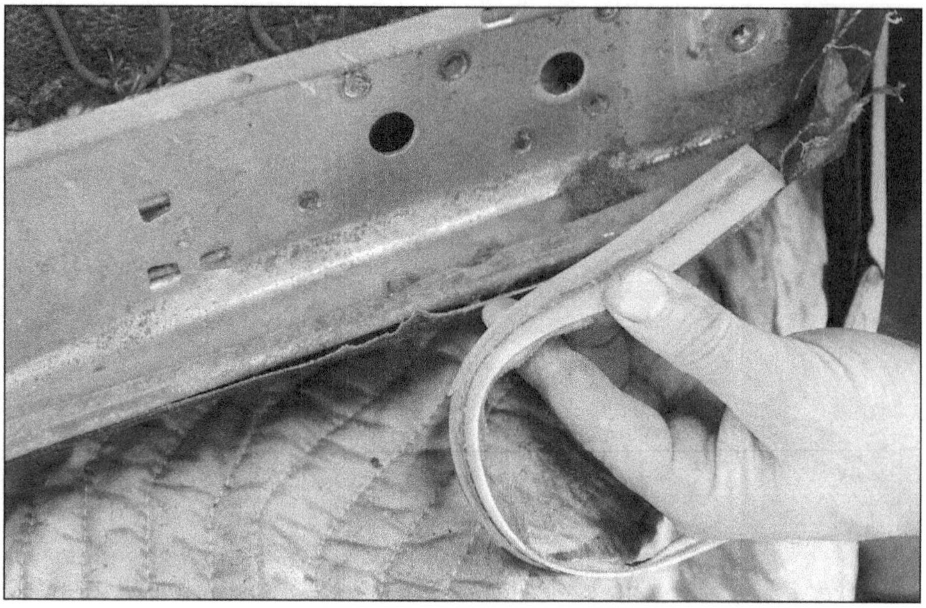

30 ***On first-generation Camaro and Firebird seats, the covers for the front cushions are held down with plastic clips that fasten to the seat frames (not with hog rings). The easiest way to remove these clips is to simply slice them to release the tension, letting the clips fall away from the seat frames.***

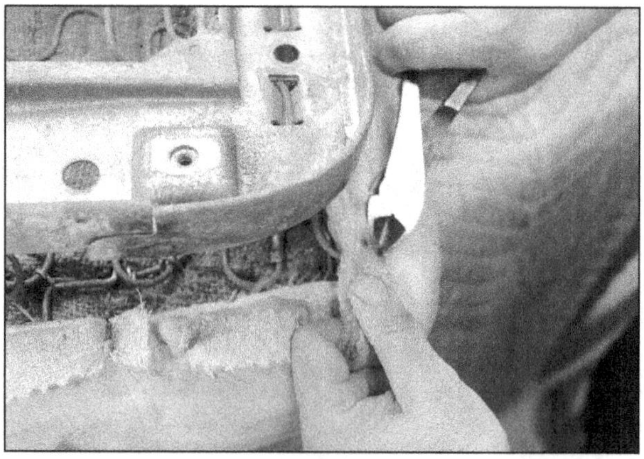

31 ***It's not that first-generation Camaro and Firebird cushions don't use hog rings at all; it's just that GM decided to use hog rings to secure the foam buns to the frame instead of the covers. They also used hog rings to secure the defining rods in the center of the cushion.***

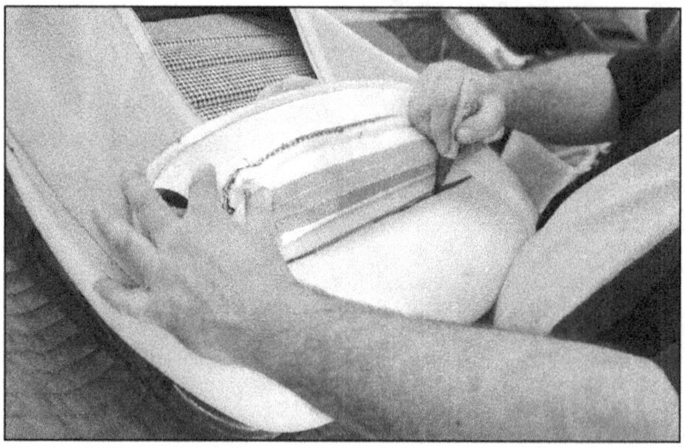

32 ***Speaking of those defining rods, the new buns should have three valleys for three defining rods. Unfortunately, these buns came with just two valleys, so we laid the new seat cover over the new bun and marked the position of the listing.***

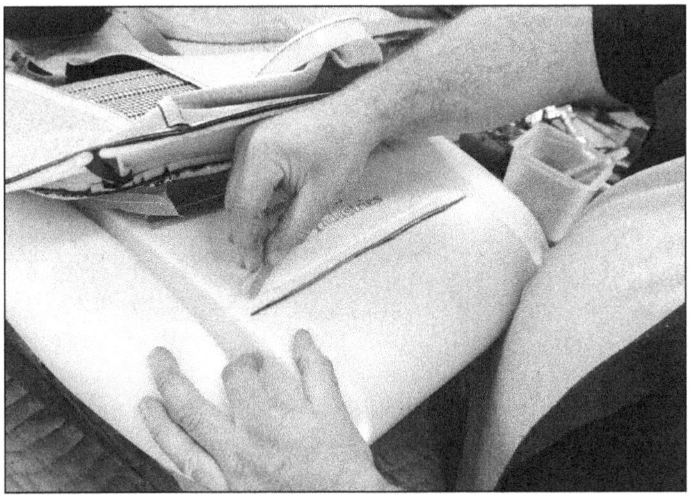

33 *We cut out a new valley along the marked line, careful not to cut entirely through the bun.*

34 *Before installing the seat cover and the bun, however, we checked the seat frame for any damage to the springs. We also checked the burlap and the thin layer of cotton atop the springs, and found that the mice that built that little condo in the back seat must not have needed to nibble on the front seat innards.*

After we removed the old bun from the seat, we checked the springs to make sure they didn't require repair or replacement. Of all the seats in a car, the driver's seat sees the most use, followed by the front passenger seat. Thus, the driver's seat is the one most likely to suffer a broken spring or other maladies. Broken springs usually occur right at the edges of the seat, where they are secured to the frame, and can easily be replaced with new spring material.

Bulk spring material comes on a roll from upholstery supply houses such as Albany Foam and Supply or through reproduction parts houses.

Restoring Seat Mechanisms

At a minimum, your front bucket seats have a pivot and latch assembly for folding the seat forward to allow access to the rear seats (if they don't, your seats likely came from a four-door). Buck seats become more complicated if they have reclining features, fore and aft adjustment, and power mechanisms. Either way, with the seats apart, now is an ideal time to make sure those features all work as they should, lube them up, and repair them where necessary.

You'll notice that many of the manual adjustments use ratchets and springs in certain configurations to operate. Just as the springs in the seat cushions can fatigue and break over time, springs in these mechanisms can fatigue and break also. You should consider replacing springs–even the ones that haven't yet broken–with reproductions.

The ratchet mechanisms in most fore-and-aft sliders tend not to wear out, but the ratchets in the recline adjusters do, thanks to the weight placed on the seat back (and the force of big-block launches pushing you back in your seat). You obviously don't want that ratchet to let go at inopportune times, so make sure the teeth in the ratchet aren't worn down.

For the fore-and-aft sliders as well as for any power motors, make sure to lube them as thoroughly as you would the window mechanisms discussed in Chapter 6. Check all plastic sliders, rollers, and gears for wear or cracking, and replace those as necessary.

Sometimes, you'll find that all your seat mechanisms really need is a thorough disassembly, sandblasting to remove any rust, a fresh coat of paint, and a reassembly with careful attention to details and plenty of lubrication.

Installing New Seat Covers *CONTINUED*

35 ***Had the seat springs busted, we could have replaced them with new springs cut from a roll, available at any interior or upholstery supplier.***

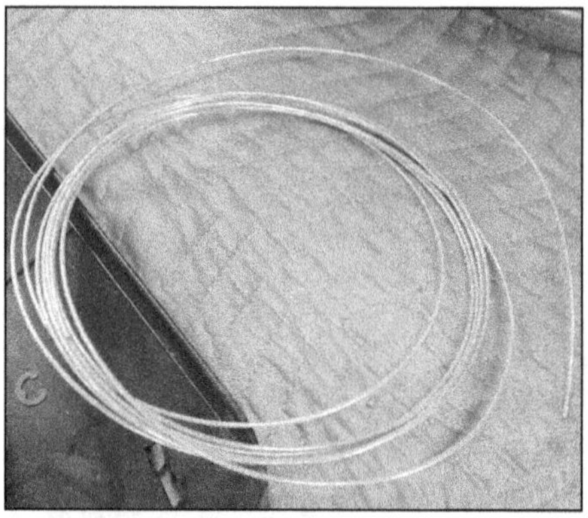

36 ***Where we couldn't use an original rod, or when the car's owner didn't supply us with the original rod, we found that 16-gauge wire from the local hardware store made a decent substitute. It was stiff enough to hold the listing in place, but was still pliable with pliers or side cutters.***

Heated Seats

We all know how muscle cars can soothe the tire-frying gearhead's soul, but it's possible for muscle cars to soothe the body as well, and let's face it, a full day at the races or walking the rows of a car show can take its toll on a gearhead, and he could use some body-soothing when he's done.

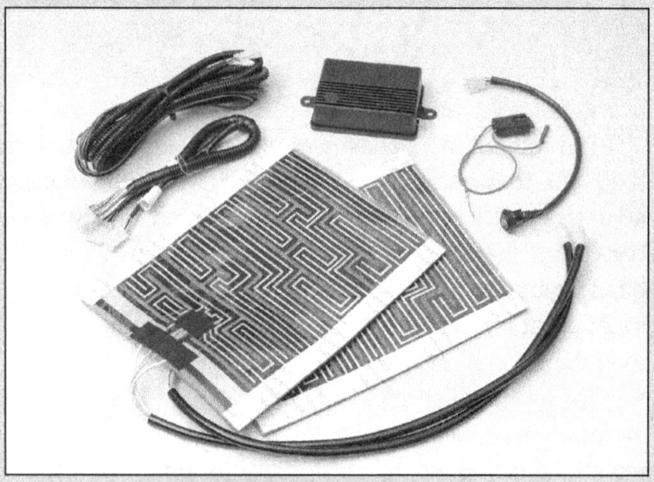

Rostra supplies a pair of heated seat kits to a number of retail outlets, including Summit Racing. When installed, they're all but invisible, save for the three-position switch. If heated seats are on your car's resto plan, it's a no-brainer to install them at the same time you replace the seat covers.

Many modern cars have optional seat warmers, and it's possible to add those to your muscle car's seats to provide a little warmth to your backside while driving. You can add heated seats in one of three ways: Option one is to buy those cheesy heated pads from the mall that plug in to your cigarette lighter and slip over your seat covers. But those are bulky and screw up the look of your muscle car's interior. Option two is to buy a heated seat setup from the junkyard, but then you'd be on your own for figuring out the wiring.

Option three is to buy an aftermarket kit such as the one offered by Rostra. The kits are nearly universal and only require two or three wire connections. They warm up to 130 degrees F and include temperature monitors and two temperature settings. Also, they are advertised as safe for vinyl, cloth, and leather interiors.

The heating elements simply slip in between your seat cover and the foam bun. This means they need to be mounted where they won't contact any metal seat structure, including the hog rings and the wires that go through the listings.

Best of all for the kit option is that the heating elements and wiring are completely concealed, and only the switch–that can easily be hidden out of sight with some creativity–reveals the presence of the seat warmers. And if you're installing new seat covers anyway, adding seat warmers takes almost no effort at all.

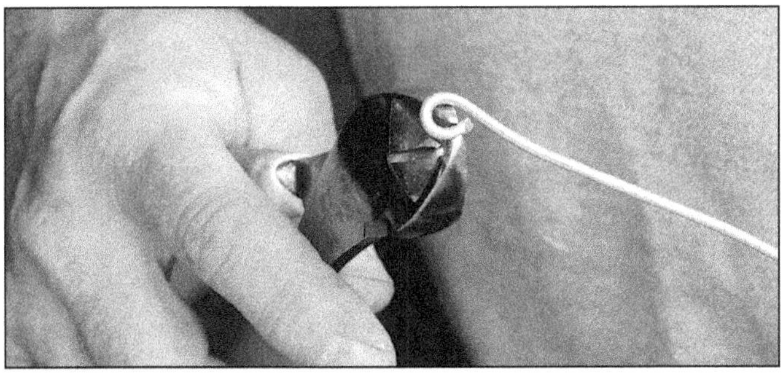

37 *To fashion a replacement rod, we first cut and straightened a piece of 16-gauge wire at a length slightly longer than the listing. We then curled each end into a loop to make the wire slide through the listing a little easier.*

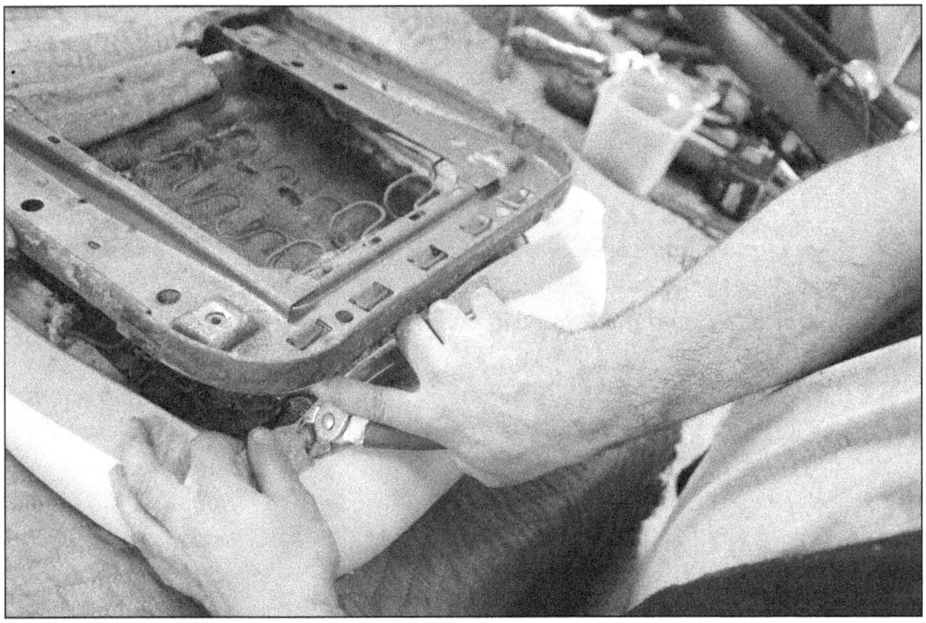

38 *When hog ringing the bun to the seat frame, we didn't have the benefit of the stiff rods in the listing that we had with the seat covers, so we made sure to insert the hog rings through the reinforced section of the bun.*

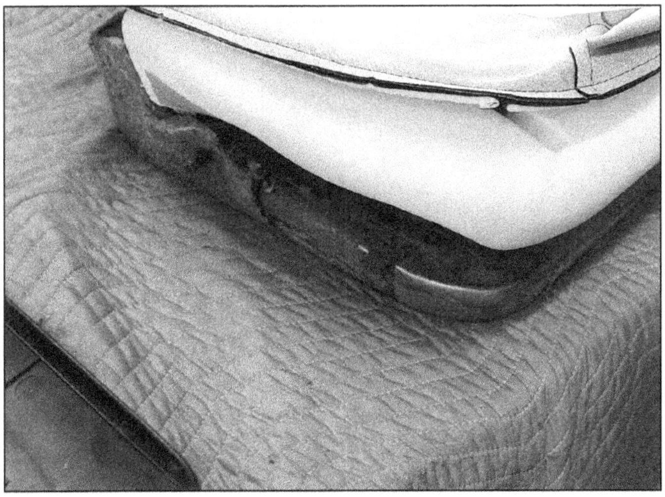

39 *To make sure the seat cover slid over the bun, which can often grab at the cover material when new, we hit them both with a shot of silicone spray. We gave the seat a good dose to get the cover to stretch all the way down to the seat frame.*

Some upholsterers like to use actual coil springs, also available through upholstery supply houses, to assist the stock corrugated springs. Coil springs last longer, but they require some creativity to figure out how to mount them to the seat frame.

Burlap is also a commonly available item; heck, check with your local feed supply store. It serves two functions when it's laid over the springs. First, it suppresses the noise of the springs. So if you hear your seat springs creaking as you drive down the road, your burlap is probably shot. Second, it covers the raw metal edges of the seat frame and prevents the seat frame from damaging the foam buns. Some restorers like to use heavy canvas instead of burlap, simply because it doesn't disintegrate as easily as burlap.

We found that a couple of the original rods from the Camaro's bucket seats couldn't be reused, a common malady due to extensive rust, original rods snapping in half, or car owners misplacing the rods. Some reproduction seat covers come with rods already inserted into the listing, and sometimes rolls of prestitched listing come with the rods already inserted.

No such luck in this case, so we took a roll of 16-gauge wire—available in any hardware store and usually labeled for use in drop ceiling installations—and cut a length just slightly longer than the section of listing. After straightening the length of wire, we then bent the ends of the wire into a loop, which made it easier to slide the wire through the listing. The loops also prevented the wire from sliding past the hog rings once installed. The corrugation of the original rods served the same purpose.

Some reproduction seat covers come with flimsy cardboard inserted into the listing and intended to take the place of the metal rods. Unfortunately when the cardboard is hog ringed, it pulls in toward the hog ring only around the hog ring instead of along the entire length of the rod. The effect is less than pleasing and less than durable, so whenever possible, it's a good idea to replace the cardboard insert with a wire insert.

After setting the center hog rings into place and hog ringing the bun, we sprayed some silicone on the upturned sides of the cover and the bun itself. The silicone helps the cover slide down over the foam (which doesn't slide well on its own), as we stretched it toward the seat frame. One warning about silicone: Do not spray it anywhere near where you'll be doing bodywork or painting. You'll end up with plastic filler that won't stick to the metal, and fisheyes in your paint.

Some people like to use plastic grocery bags to slide the seat cover over the bun. But if you can't remove the bag afterward, the seat crinkles and crunches like your grandma's plastic couch cover.

Whatever slipping agent you use, be sure to use plenty. You'll need to pull the cover tight to either hog ring it to the frame or attach the plastic clip on the new seat cover to the frame.

At this point, the cover should look stuffed, but not overstuffed. Many times, an overstuffed seat is the result of an overlooked wire in listing that needs to be hog ringed down. Nor should the seat look understuffed and flat—to puff it back out, layer the buns underneath the covers with cotton until the voids between the bun and cover are filled.

Installing New Seat Covers *CONTINUED*

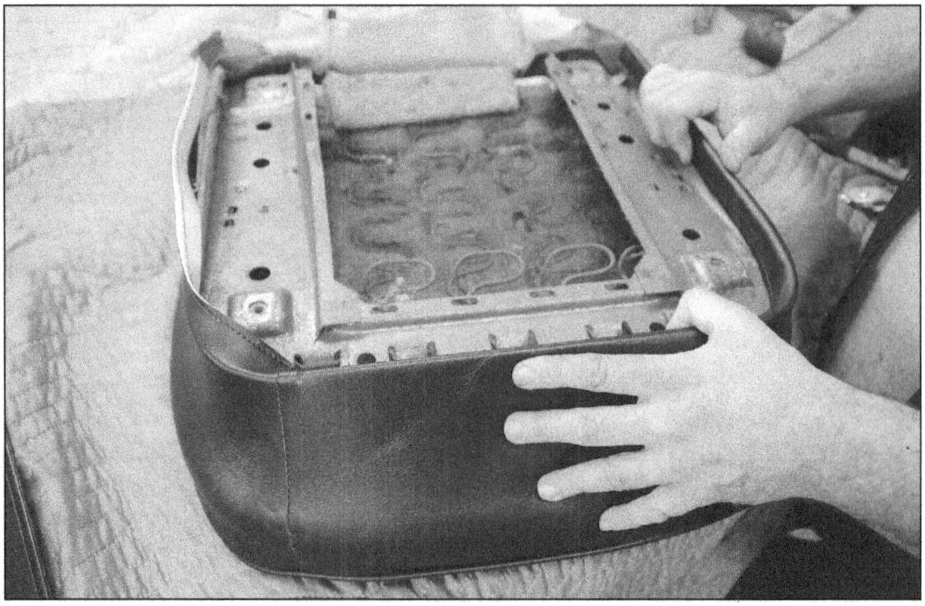

40 ***Slipping the seat cover over the frame is only half of the job with these F-body seats. We next had to flip over the plastic clip already stitched into the seat cover, and hook the clip over the lip in the seat frame.***

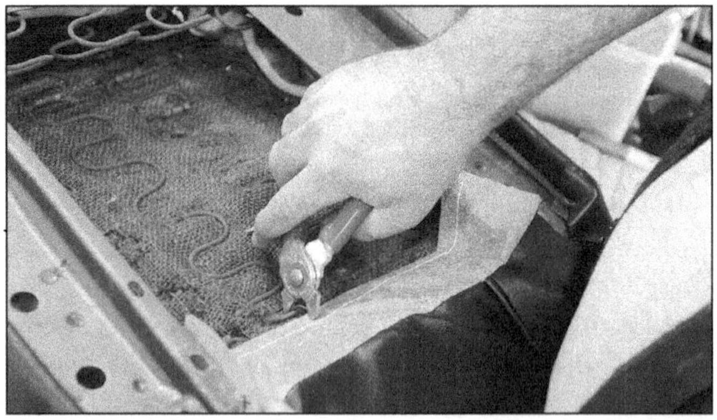

41 ***The back of the cushion needs to be hog ringed to the springs in the conventional method.***

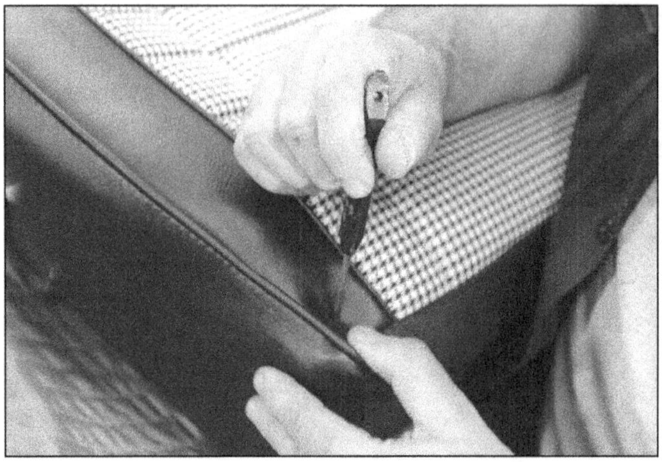

42 ***With the seat cover secured, it was time to reassemble the bits that came off the cushion during disassembly. To find screw and bolt holes, we first felt around for the depressions, then poked a starter hole with an awl.***

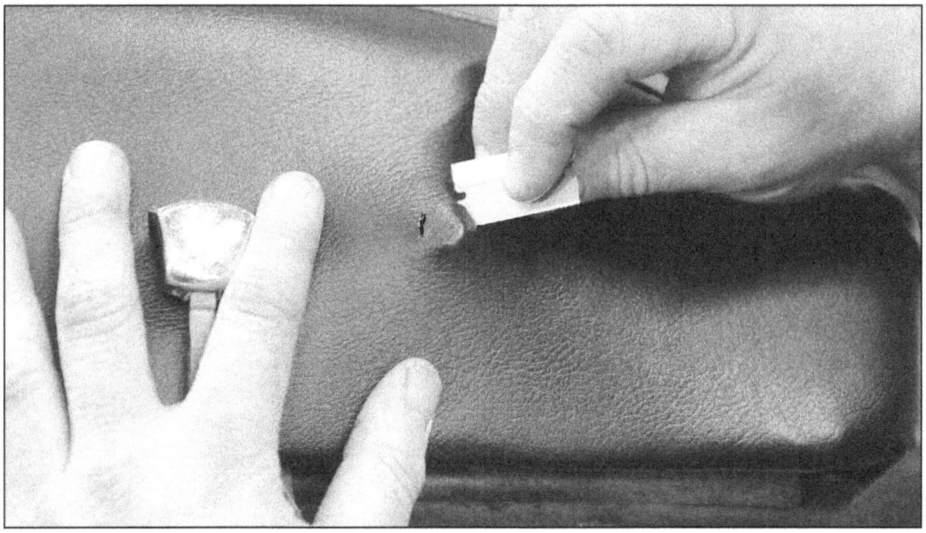

43 ***Holes for the seat back pivot posts can be cut in a variety of ways. We used the most straightforward method of just cutting around the post. We already knew that a piece of plastic trim would slide over the post later on, covering any hole that we cut.***

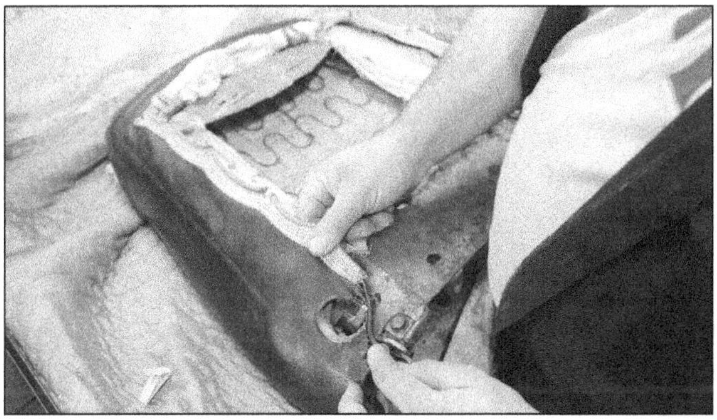

44 ***As mentioned before, make sure the seat back covers are not mixed left-to-right, so the hole for the latch handle will end up on the correct side of the seat back.***

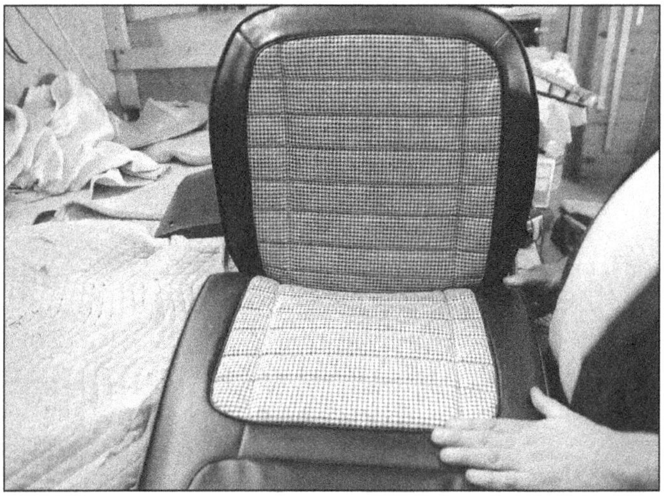

45 ***With the seat back recovered and the two halves of the bucket rejoined, we can see how the two covers don't quite match up. A difference like this would definitely be noticeable with the bucket installed in the car, but lesser differences may not be visible.***

With the seat cover secured, we used an awl to find the screw and bolt holes for the various brackets that we removed earlier, using the old seat covers as reference. A variation of the leave-the-screws-threaded method (see Chapter 5) would have also worked well in this case. For the posts on either side that the seat back pivots on, we took a razor blade and pressed an X in the top of either post, which allowed us to push the seat cover down around the post. Some upholsterers also like to tap a hammer lightly around the edge of the post's top, effectively punching out a perfect-sized hole for the post. Just as long as the hole cut for the post isn't too large, any hole will do. The factory used a plastic disc to cover the material around the post.

For the seat back, the process is nearly the same as for the cushion, except the seat cover is fastened with hog rings around the back. Oh, and the seat back covers are often different—left versus right—due to the location of the handle for the latch, so it's important to make sure you have the driver's side seat back cover on the driver's side seat back, and vice versa.

With both covers on, reattach the seat back to the cushion to make sure the two seat covers line up. Sometimes they do, and sometimes they don't, depending on the quality of the seat covers. The houndstooth pattern on these seat covers also made any misalignment between the two very evident. If the covers don't line up, you'll have to separate the seat back from the cushion again and adjust one or the other or both by pulling on the covers until they slide into position.

In all, and without including any time for sandblasting and painting, it

Installing New Seat Covers *CONTINUED*

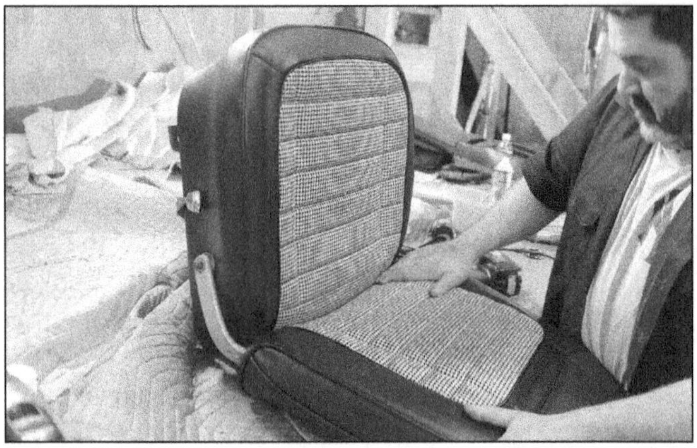

46 ***Rather than separate the two halves of the bucket and rework both halves to make the seat covers match up, we gently tugged at the seat covers until they lined up.***

47 ***This looks much better than the mildew-and-mouse-nest state in which we found it. As for the continued mismatch between the seat covers, perhaps this head-on perspective makes it more noticeable than the angled perspective you'll have when the seat is installed in the Camaro.***

48 ***With our new seats plopped into the Camaro, resting atop new carpet (see Chapter 5) and beside new door panels (see Chapter 6), the Camaro certainly looks a few thousand dollars better. Not bad for a few hours of work, right?***

took us about 1½ to 2 hours to finish each cushion and seat back set. So for both buckets and the rear seat, set aside about 6 hours total. It's maybe not a project for one night in the garage, but perhaps for a weekend, or a string of three or four nights.

Vinyl Repair

So maybe you don't have the dough to spring for new seat covers, or your existing seats aren't ratty enough to warrant total replacement. But there's a rip or a cigarette burn in the original seat cover that's bugging you, and you know it will become major damage sooner or later.

If the damage is in a cloth section of the seat cover, you're looking at a seat cover replacement. Those iron-on fabric patches might cut it for elementary-school fashion, but not for our discerning (yet some might say still juvenile) muscle car palates. But if the damage is in a soft vinyl section, you're in luck and can repair the damage without removing the seat cover.

Permatex offers a kit that does just that, and it's usually available at your corner parts store. The kit seems to be good for damage up to about the diameter of a tennis ball, and can be implemented in a day.

As with most other repair processes, the first step requires you to clean the area with denatured alcohol, and to remove the loose threads or chunks of vinyl from the damaged area. If the material is charred, bubbled, melted, distorted,

Vinyl Repair

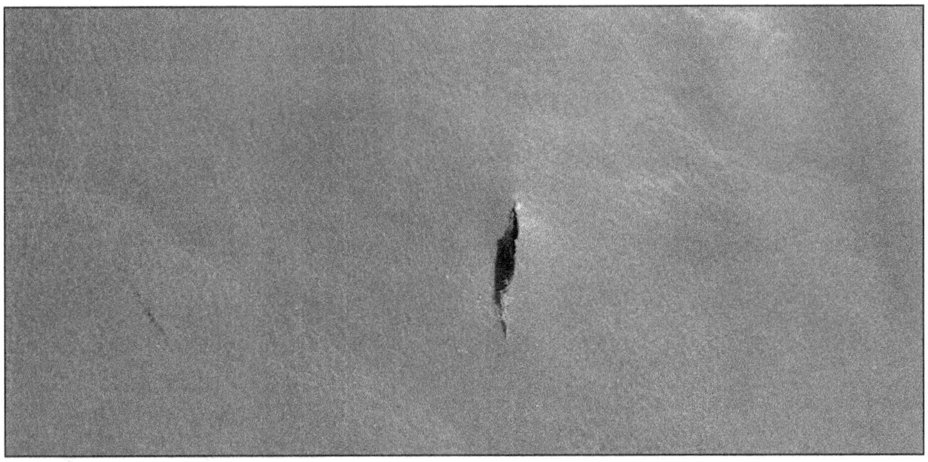

1 *This small tear in the back of our otherwise decent bucket seat's cover didn't warrant replacing the entire seat cover, but we still didn't want the tear there, nor did we want it to expand beyond its current size. We found a vinyl repair kit at our local parts store that promised to do the trick.*

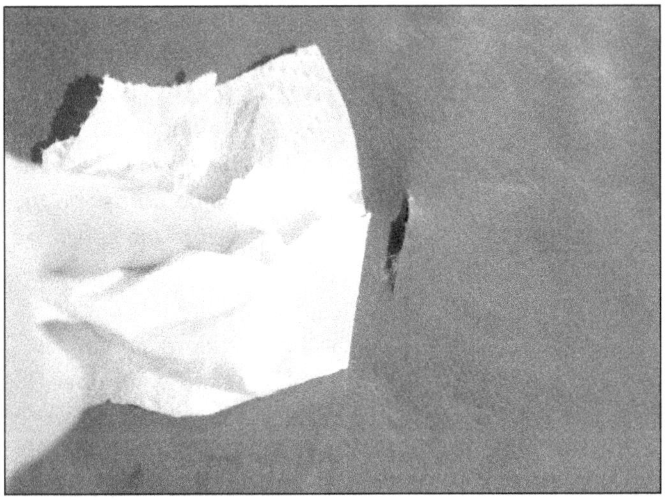

2 *We began the repair process by cleaning the area surrounding the tear with denatured alcohol to remove grease and grime from the vinyl surface. It's funny how a surface like this looks rather clean and uniform until you get up close to it.*

3 *We probably didn't need to cut off a section of the backing cloth for a repair this small, but we noticed that the fibers behind the tear had already started to come out, so we thought we'd play it safe. For larger repair areas, you should definitely use the backing cloth.*

or otherwise heat damaged, remove the entire damaged area with a razor blade.

Included in the kit is a swatch of plain muslin cloth. Cut a piece of the cloth slightly larger than the damaged area itself, then place the cloth behind the damaged area, pushing it through with a dull instrument. Use the spatula included in the repair kit, or even a popsicle stick will work.

Next, use the adhesive/filler included in the kit to fill in the damaged area until it becomes level and smooth against the surrounding undamaged vinyl. If repairing a cut or tear in the vinyl, lift the edge of the tear and dab a small amount of adhesive between the vinyl and the backing cloth before applying the adhesive/filler to the tear itself. Try to use as little of the adhesive as possible—it spreads quickly and doesn't easily come off a vinyl surface, so it can make a rather large mess in a short amount of time.

Though the adhesive/filler sets up quickly, it should dry for about 4 hours. Drying time can be reduced drastically, however, by aiming a hair dryer or heat gun set on low at the repair for about 15 minutes. Keep the heat moving; concentrating it in one place for too long will melt the vinyl.

While the adhesive's drying, it's a good time to do a couple things. First, you need to match the vinyl grain pattern to one of three samples included in the kit. Most vinyls should come awfully close to one of those three, if they don't match the grain patterns outright.

Second, you need to match the color of the vinyl to the colors on the card supplied in the kit. We found that by cutting off the white border of the color card, we could see which color matched the vinyl better.

Vinyl Repair *CONTINUED*

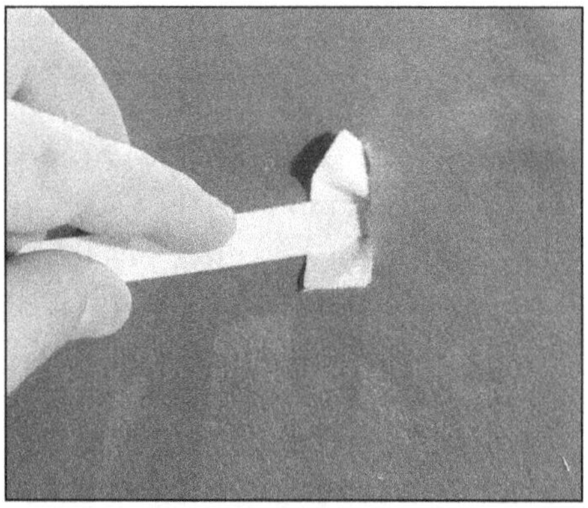

4 *Using the provided spatula, we shoved the small section of backing cloth into the tear and made sure it laid flat behind the vinyl. It quickly became apparent that all we were really doing here was replicating the cloth-backed composition of the vinyl seat covers.*

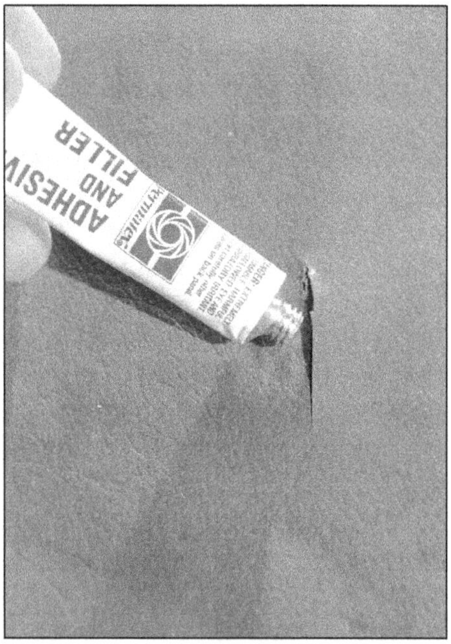

5 *A tube of adhesive and filler is supplied to actually make the repair to the vinyl cover. A little of this stuff goes a long way, so we squeezed out a dab and used the provided spatula to smear it up and down the length of the tear, then let it sit overnight.*

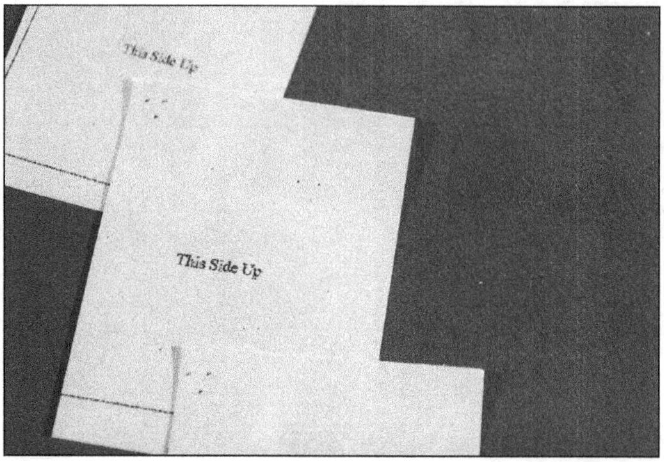

6 *The kit included three pieces of grain paper, each with different grains that would replicate the pattern embossed in the seat cover. None of them were spot on, but we chose the one that seemed closest. In actuality, it was much further off than we suspected, but it's the best we could do.*

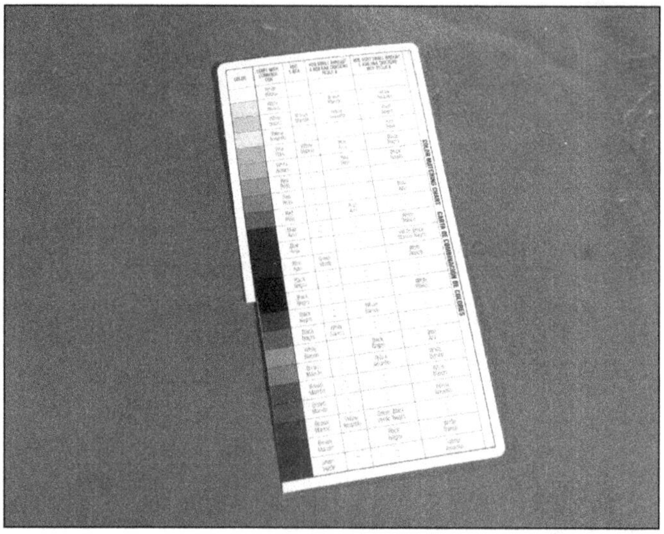

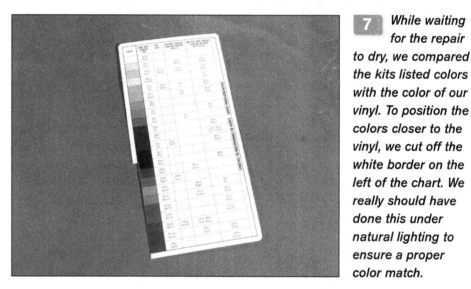

7 *While waiting for the repair to dry, we compared the kits listed colors with the color of our vinyl. To position the colors closer to the vinyl, we cut off the white border on the left of the chart. We really should have done this under natural lighting to ensure a proper color match.*

8 *Following the instructions on the chart, we mixed up what was supposed to be the correct color. We tried several batches to come up with a good match, keeping in mind that the white lightens the color, while the yellow brightens it, and the black darkens it.*

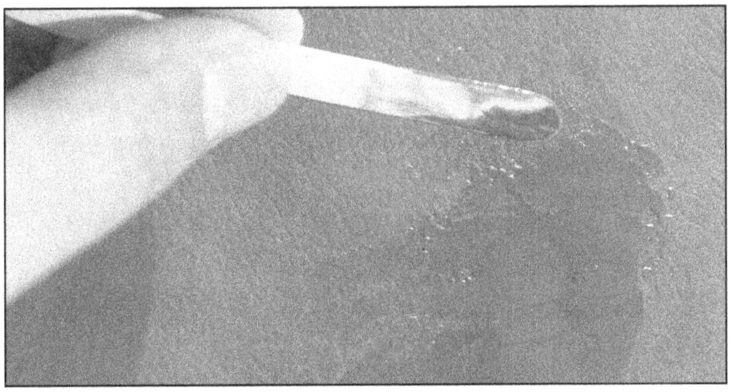

***9* We found a combination that seemed to work, so once the adhesive dried, we spread a section of the color paste over the repair area. The kit's instructions suggest you feather the color paste over the surrounding areas, but we later found that the feathered areas flaked away from the vinyl.**

***10* Using the piece of grain paper we selected earlier, we laid it over the repair area. The color paste sticks to the grain paper until it has been heat cured, so once you set the grain paper in place, you can't make adjustments without making a mess.**

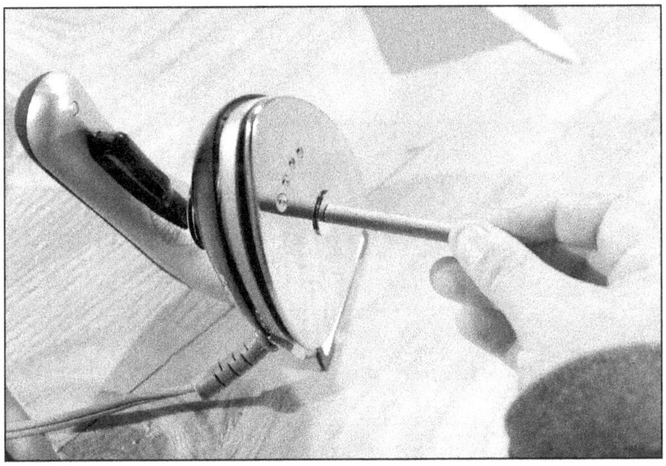

***11* Following the instructions, we placed the metal tip of the supplied dowel against a hot iron. The heat from the iron should transfer to the metal tip, which is supposed to immediately transfer to the grain paper.**

Find a clean surface on which to mix the colored pastes provided in the kit and follow the mixing directions on the color card. Experiment now—the kit provides plenty of colored paste material—to make the color mix as close as possible to the color of your vinyl. Here's where it pays to have a black vinyl interior—one color of paste and you're done!

Keep in mind that the paste will darken in the next step, so experiment through the next step on a scrap piece of vinyl. If you find it difficult to match the exact color of your vinyl, consider as an alternative using simple white paste and then hitting the area with a matching vinyl dye at the end of the repair process.

The colored paste only sets up with heat, becoming a somewhat pliable rubbery substance, so you have plenty of time to work with it, apply it, and shape it on the vinyl. Spread the mixed paste on the repair area, just enough to cover the dried adhesive/filler, and make it as smooth and consistent as possible.

Here, I'm going to depart from the kit's instructions. The instructions recommend feathering the edges of the paste over the undamaged vinyl, but that only results in edges that bubble and don't fully adhere to the vinyl. I recommend you keep a sharp edge all around the paste and wipe away excess paste with a clean popsicle stick or spatula edge.

As for applying heat, the kit directions recommend laying the grain paper over the color paste and using the metal tip of a wooden dowel to transfer heat from a household iron through the grain paper onto the color paste. That method, quite simply, sucks. It takes forever and the results are messy. Sure, it covers the repair, but the results then need their own repair.

A better method involves hitting the bare paste with the low setting on a heat gun. Once you start to see a little white smoke come from the color paste, it has started to set. At that exact second, remove the heat, apply the grain paper to the still-hot color paste and apply pressure to the grain paper (not with your bare hands; use the metal-tipped wooden dowel). The paper should impress enough of a grain on the color paste and any surrounding area that might have gone soft from the heat. Slowly peel the grain paper away from the vinyl once the area has cooled.

As long as the grain and the color of the paste match your existing vinyl, you should have a seamless repair. Running your hand along the repair, you shouldn't be able to feel a ridge as long as you didn't use too much adhesive or color paste. Making the color and grain correct is the most difficult part of this repair, so time should be spent making sure the right color is mixed and the right grain is selected. If possible, practice the repair on a junkyard seat or on seat covers that you're going to replace anyway.

Seat Belt Restoration and Replacement

The National Traffic and Motor Vehicle Safety Act was passed by Congress and signed by President Lyndon Johnson on September 9, 1966. It requires all new vehicles sold in the United States to have, among other safety items, head rests, shatter-resistant windshields, and energy-absorbing steering columns. The Act also mandates seat belt installation on all new cars, which is why you will not see a car without seat belts from the 1967 model year on.

Of course, seat belts had been around for decades before that, and installing seat belts was nothing new for the factories. Since the 1950s they'd been installing belts (or at least the mounting points for optional or dealer-installed belts) in many of their cars. So the structures and the seat belts exist for most 1966 and older muscle cars. Studies show that a three-point belt offers a significant increase in safety over a two-point belt, so if the mounting holes exist allowing an upgrade to a three-point seat belt, converting is highly recommended. In the rare case you have a car not originally designed for seat belts, the street rod market—specifically companies such as Juliano's and RetroBelt—offer seat belt retrofit kits.

Vinyl Repair CONTINUED

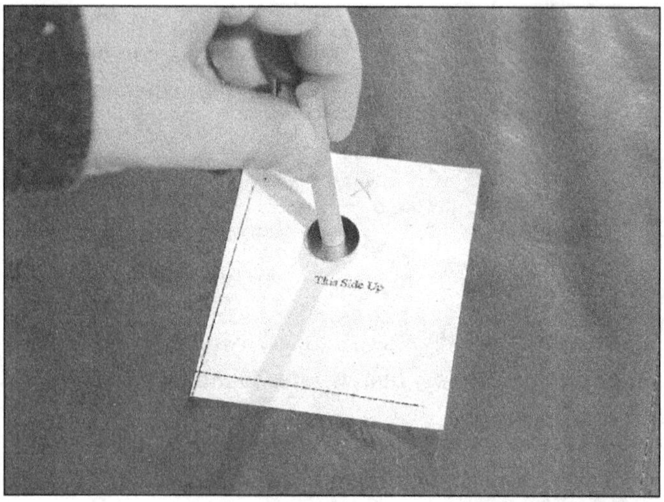

***12** The heat is then supposed to transfer through the grain paper to the color paste and cure it with the grain pattern of the paper embossed into it. You can understand how this takes quite a while, and doesn't really work as advertised.*

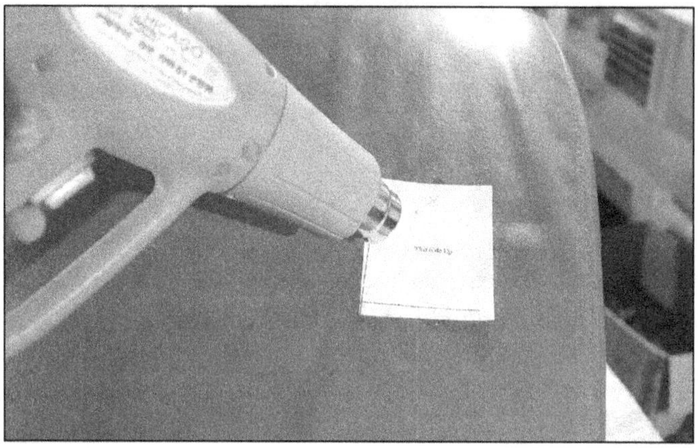

***13** We decided to leave the grain paper and bust out the heat gun, moving it quickly over the entire section. This cured the color paste in record time and embossed the paper's grain into the paste.*

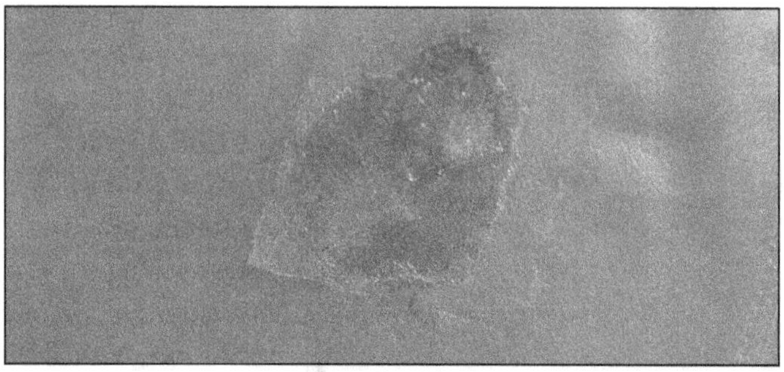

***14** However, the instructions failed to mention that the color paste darkens as it cures, leading to a blob of mismatched color. Also, we were a little overzealous with the heat gun on the left side, as evidenced by the parting lines from the grain paper. But at least you can't see any evidence of the tear. If we found the right shade of vinyl dye, we could eliminate the mismatched colors. This is why we're sticking with black vinyl interiors from now on.*

Seat belts are unique in that their primary function is not for aesthetics, comfort, or control of the car. Instead, it's for safety, with aesthetics a distant secondary function, so any thought of seat belt restoration must keep safety at the forefront of even the most minor decision.

Anybody with serious racing experience knows that the SFI Foundation, which issues and administers racing equipment standards, not only specs out racing seat belt and harness standards, but also tests and certifies racing belts. These standards stipulate that seat belts should be inspected and replaced or re-webbed every two years, largely because studies show that nylon webbing—the main component in seat belts—loses half its strength in a year with outdoor exposure. After two years, webbing loses more than 80 percent of its strength. Recall one more time the study mentioned in Chapter 2 regarding UV exposure on plastics; same concept with seat belts.

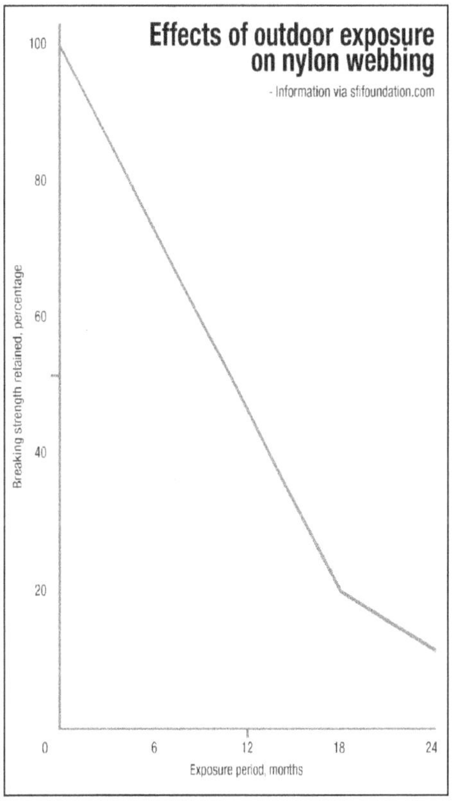

The seat belts in your 40-year-old muscle car may not seem much weaker than the ones on your wife's late-model daily driver, but research has shown that UV exposure and exposure to the weather play a big part in weakening the nylon webbing of the seat belts.

Sure, a typical muscle car nowadays doesn't see race speeds, and the seat belts do not have constant outdoor exposure. Nor do we see any campaigns by safety advocates to replace seat belts in everyday street-driven cars every two years. On the other hand, if the rest of your 40-year-old muscle car's interior has seen enough UV exposure to significantly weaken and stress the dashboard and other plastic components, then perhaps it's seen enough exposure to significantly weaken the seat belts as well.

The very-fine-threaded bolts securing the seat belts to the floor of your muscle car tend to require a star bit and an awful lot of force to make them budge, especially if your muscle car has been undercoated or has a good amount of rust on the underside. If you can't find new reproduction belts, companies such as Ssnake-Oyl provide seat belt restoration services that involve re-webbing the original belts.

You should also replace your seat belts if you know the muscle car has been in a collision or if you see even the slightest amount of damage. Either circumstance weakens the seat belt enough so that you might as well not be wearing one in a collision.

If you trust your life to 40-year-old seat belts and simply find them a bit dirty or stiff, some restorers recommend soaking the belts in a solution of Simple Green or other mild cleaner for a couple hours, then scrubbing them with a very soft-bristled brush before rinsing them off and hanging them up to dry. Unless they're severely rusted, stainless or chromed buckles can usually be cleaned up with 0000 steel wool.

As for the retractor and latch mechanisms, ensure that they are in proper working order. That means checking to see that the pendulum in the retractor moves freely and contacts the lockbar. Also be sure that the lockbar engages the entire tooth on the sprocket, not just the tip of the tooth. It may be necessary to apply a little white grease to the retractor mechanism for smooth operation.

With our seat belt retractor out of the car, we could easily see how the pendulum (with the black weight) contacts the lockbar, and thus locks the teeth of the retractor mechanism. To check for proper operation, set the retractor assembly upright on a level surface, and the seat belt should extend and retract normally. Next, tilt the retractor mechanism, and the pendulum should activate the lockbar, preventing the seat belt from extending. Be sure to replace malfunctioning retractors.

Albany Foam and Supply
Upholstery supplies and tools
1355 Broadway
Albany, NY 12204
800-235-0888
www.ausinc.net

American Cushion Industries
Reproduction foam seat buns
890 West Golden Pheasant Rd.
Shelton, WA 98584
360-427-1725
www.americancushionindustries.lbu.com

ARO 2000
Convertible tops and related materials
145 Orange Ave.
Walden, NY 12586
845-778-1314
www.aro2000.com

Auto Custom Carpets
Reproduction molded carpet sets
1429 Noble St.
Anniston, AL 36202
800-352-8216
www.accmats.com

AutoLoc
Power window conversion kits and accessories
201 SE Oak St.
Portland, OR 97214
800-651-1970
www.thehoffmangroup.com/autoloc

Au-ve-co
Interior clips and fasteners
100 Homan Dr.
Cold Spring, KY 41076
800-354-9816
www.auveco.com

Bob Johnson's Auto Literature
Factory service manuals and fabric swatch books
92 Blandin Avenue
Framingham, MA 01702
800-334-0688
www.autopaper.com

Caswell Inc.
Home replating kits
7696 Route 31
Lyons, NY 14489
315-946-1213
www.caswellplating.com

Classic Industries
Reproduction parts, retailer
18460 Gothard St.
Huntington Beach, CA 92648
800-854-1280, ext. 5-210
www.classicindustries.com

Conrad's Radio Service
Digital radio conversions
4 Red Wing Lane
Worcester, MA 01605
508-852-3974

C.S. Osborne
Upholstery hand tools
125 Jersey St.
Harrison, NJ 07029
973-483-3232
www.csosborne.com

Dashes Direct
Reproduction seat foams and dashboard covers
4201 E. Lone Mountain Rd.
North Las Vegas, NV 89081
800-761-0225
www.dashesdirect.com

DonJer Products
Flocking kits
13142 Murphy Rd.
Winnebago, IL 61088
800-336-6537
www.donjer.com

Dynamic Control
Dynamat and Dynaliner
3042 Symmes Rd.
Hamilton, OH 45015
513-860-5094
www.dynamat.com

Eastwood
Automotive finishes and repair tools
263 Shoemaker Rd.
Pottstown, PA 19464
800-345-1178
www.eastwood.com

Electric Life
Power window conversion kits and accessories
5990 N. Northwest Hwy.
Chicago, IL 60631
800-548-2168
www.electric-life.com

Gillin Custom Design
Upholsterers
75 Wisner Ave.
Middletown, NY 10940
845-857-2734
www.gillincustomdesign.com

Grain-It Technologies
Woodgraining services, tools, and supplies
334 Commerce Ct.
Winter Haven, FL 33880
863-299-4494
www.woodgraining.com

Hancock Fabrics
Fabrics and sewing supplies
877-322-7427
www.hancockfabrics.com

Insulshield Technology
Noise and heat reduction materials
781-749-4971
www.insulshield.net

Juliano's
Replacement seat belts
100 Windermere Ave.
Ellington, CT 06029
800-300-1932
www.julianos.com

Just Dashes
Dashboard restoration and customization; door panel restoration
5941 Lemona Ave.
Van Nuys, CA 91411
818-780-9005
www.justdashes.com

Legendary Auto Interiors
Reproduction seat covers, door panels, and interior trim
121 West Shore Blvd.
Newark, NY 14513
800-363-8804
www.legendaryautointeriors.com

Master Upholstery
Upholsterer, trimmer
185 Halsey Rd.
Newton, NJ 07860-9530
973-383-6622

McLellan's Automobile Literature
Factory service manuals and fabric swatch books
9111 Longstaff Dr.
Houston, TX 77031-2711
713-772-3285
www.mclellansautomotive.com

McMaster-Carr
Industrial supply warehouse
200 Aurora Industrial Pkwy.
Aurora, OH 44202-8087
330-995-5500
www.mcmaster.com

Newburgh Auto Glass
Automotive glass replacement
155 Orange Ave.
Walden, NY 12586
845-778-7117

Novus
Acrylic polishing compounds
12800 Hwy. 13 South, Suite 500
Savage, MN 55378
952-944-8000
www.novuspolish.com

Original Auto Interior
NOS interior fabrics and vinyls
7869 Trumble Rd.
Columbus, MI 48063-3915
586-727-2486
www.originalauto.com

Original Parts Group
Reproduction parts
1770 Saturn Way
Seal Beach, CA 90740
800-243-8355
www.opgi.com

Permatex
Automotive adhesives and sealants
10 Columbus Blvd.
Hartford, CT 06106
877-376-2839
www.permatex.com

Plastex
Plastic repair kits
P.O. Box 18308
Reno, NV 89511
775-852-4066

PUI Interiors
Reproduction door panels, seat covers, and other interior items
2801 Interior Way
LaGrange, KY 40031
800-342-0610
www.puiinteriors.com

RetroBelt
Seat belt installation kits
13831 Roswell Ave., Suite J
Chino, CA 91710
909-364-1372
www.retrobeltusa.com

Rostra Precision Controls
Seat warmer kits
2519 Dana Dr.
Laurinburg, NC 28352
910-276-4853
www.rostra.com

Ssnake-Oyl
Seat belt restoration services
114 N. Glenwood
Tyler, TX 75702
800-284-7777
www.ssnake-oyl.com

Super Bright LEDs, Inc.
Automotive LED bulbs
100 Washington St.
Florissant, MO 63031-5921
314-972-6200
www.superbrightleds.com

Terminal Supply Co.
Electrical terminals and components
1800 Thunderbird
Troy, MI 48084
800-989-9632
www.terminalsupplyco.com

YearOne
A full range of restoration products
1001 Cherry Drive, Suite 1
Braselton, GA 30517
1-800-YEARONE extension 223
www.yearone.com

American Chevelle Enthusiasts Society
615-773-2237
www.chevelles.com

American Motors Owners Association
1615 Purvis Ave.
Janesville, WI 53548
608-752-8247
www.amonational.com

Buick Club of America
P.O. Box 360775
Columbus, OH 43236-0775
614-472-3939
www.buickclub.com

Buick GS Club of America
625 Pine Point Cir.
Valdosta, GA 31602
229-244-0577
www.buickgsca.com

Buick Performance Group
1150 W. 5th St.
P.O. Box 614
Marysville, OH 43040-0614
937-642-2026
www.buickperformancegroup.com

Corvette Club of America
P.O. Box 9879
Bowling Green, KY 42102
866-482-1191
www.corvetteclubofamerica.com

Cougar Club of America
757-587-5498
www.cougarclub.com

Fairlane Club of America
340 Clicktown Rd.
Church Hill, TN 37642-6622
423-245-6678
www.fairlaneclubofamerica.com

First Generation Monte Carlo Club
864-296-9624
www.firstgenerationmontecarloclub.com

Instrument Specialties, Inc.
65 Foliage Dr.
North Kingstown, RI 02852
401-267-0055

National American Motors Drivers and Racers Association
P.O. Box 987
Twin Lakes, WI 53181-0987
262-843-4326
www.namdra.org

National B-Body Owner's Association
216-12th St.
Boone, IA 50036-2019
515-432-3001
www.wwnboa.org

National Corvette Restorers Society
6291 Day Rd.
Cincinnati, OH 45252-1334
513-385-8526 or 513-385-6367
www.ncrs.org

National Impala Association
5400 43rd Ave. S.
Minneapolis, MN 55417
612-727-2404
www.nationalimpala.com

National Monte Carlo Club
204 Shelby Dr.
Greensburg, PA 15601-4974
850-457-2945
www.montecarloclub.com

National Nostalgic Nova
P.O. Box 2344
York, PA 17405
717-252-2383
www.nnova.com

Oldsmobile Club of America
P.O. Box 80318
Lansing, MI 48908
517-663-1811
www.oldsclub.org

Plymouth Owners Club
P.O. Box 416
Cavalier, ND 58220-0416
www.plymouthbulletin.com

Pontiac GTO Association of America
P.O. Box 213
Timnath, CO 80547
www.gtoaa.org

Pontiac Oakland Club International
P.O. Box 68
Maple Plain, MN 55359
877-368-3454
www.poci.org

Shelby American Auto Club
P.O. Box 788
Sharon, CT 06069
860-364-0769
www.saac.com

Shelby Dodge Auto Club
P.O. Box 3759
Centerline, MI 48015
586-759-6160
www.sdac.org

The Dodge Charger Registry
P.O. Box 79
Meherrin, VA 23954
434-223-1305
www.dodgechargerregistry.com

Thunderbolt Owners Association
www.thunderboltowners.com

WPC Club
P.O. Box 3504
Kalamazoo, MI 49003-3504
www.chryslerclub.org

More Information for Your Project ...

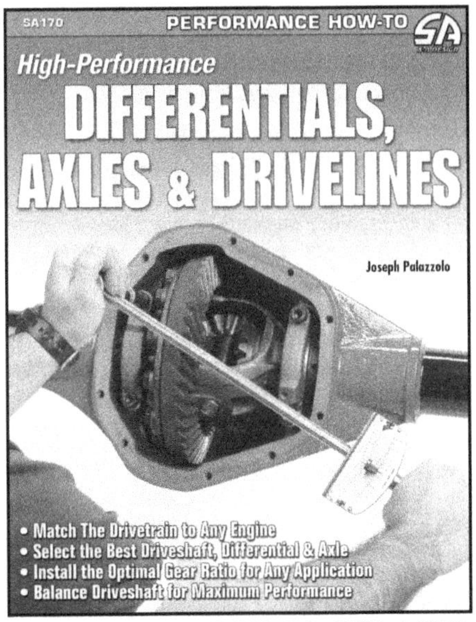

HIGH-PERFORMANCE DIFFERENTIALS, AXELS & DRIVELINES *by Joseph Palazzolo* This book covers everything you need to know about selecting the most desirable gear ratio, rebuilding differentials and other driveline components, and matching driveline components to engine power output. Learn how to set up a limited-slip differential, install high-performance axle shafts, swap out differential gears, and select products for the driveline. This book explains rear differential basics, rear differential housings, rebuilding open rear differentials, limited-slip differentials, and factory differentials. Ring and pinion gears, axle housings, axle shafts, driveshafts, and U-joints are also covered. Softbound, 8-1/2 x 11 inches, 144 pages, approx. 400 color photos. ***Item #SA170***

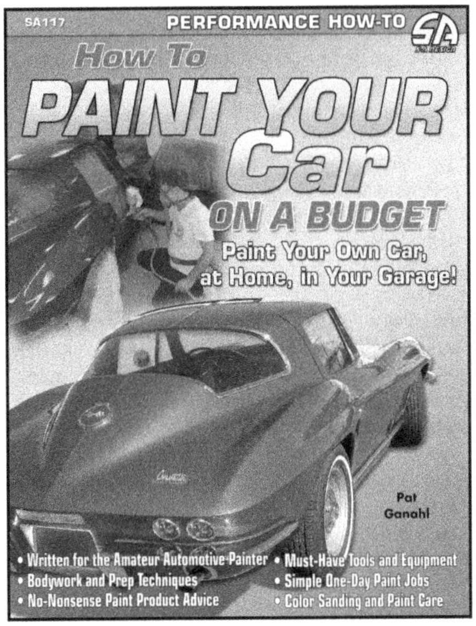

HOW TO PAINT YOUR CAR ON A BUDGET *by Pat Ganahl* If your car needs new paint, or even just a touch-up, the cost involved in getting a professional job can be more than you bargained for. In this book, author Pat Ganahl unveils dozens of secrets that will help anyone paint their own car. From simple scuff-and-squirt jobs to full-on, door-jambs-and-everything paint jobs, Ganahl covers everything you need to know to get a great-looking coat of paint on your car and save lots of money in the process. Covers painting equipment, the ins and outs of prep, masking, painting and sanding products and techniques, and real-world advice on how to budget wisely when painting your own car. Softbound, 8-1/2 x 11 inches, 128 pages, approx. 400 color photos. ***Item #SA117***

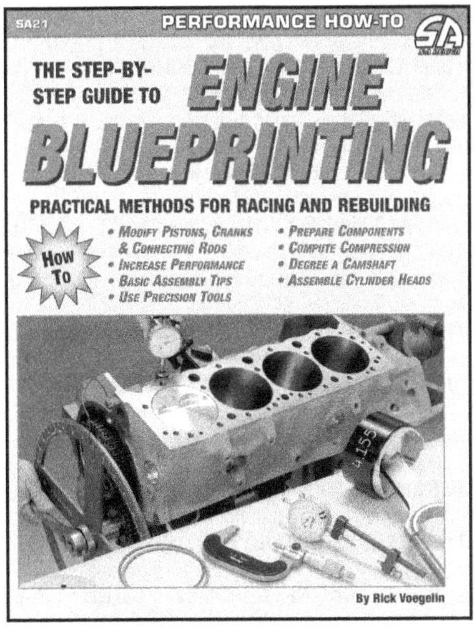

THE STEP-BY-STEP GUIDE TO ENGINE BLUEPRINTING *by Rick Voegelin* this book is simply the best book available on basic engine preparation for street or racing. Rick Voegelin's writing and wrenching skills put this book in a class by itself. Includes pro's secrets of using tools, selecting and preparing blocks, cranks, rods, pistons, cylinder heads, selecting cams and valvetrain components, balancing and assembly tips, plus worksheets for your engine projects, and much more! Softbound, 8-1/2 x 11 inches, 128 pages, over 400 b/w photos. ***Item #SA21***

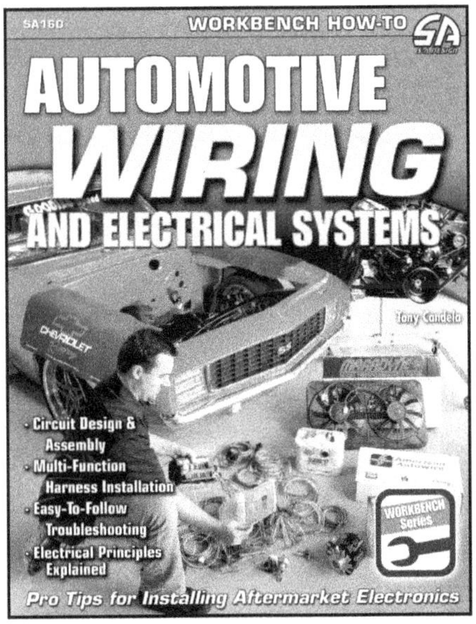

AUTOMOTIVE WIRING AND ELECTRICAL SYSTEMS *by Tony Candela* This book is the perfect book to unshroud the mysteries of automotive electrics and electronic systems. The basics of electrical principles, including voltage, amperage, resistance, and Ohm's law, are revealed in clear and concise detail, so the enthusiast understands what these mean in the construction and repair of automotive electrical circuits. Softbound, 8-1/2 x 11 inches, 144 pages, approx. 350 color photos. ***Item #SA160***

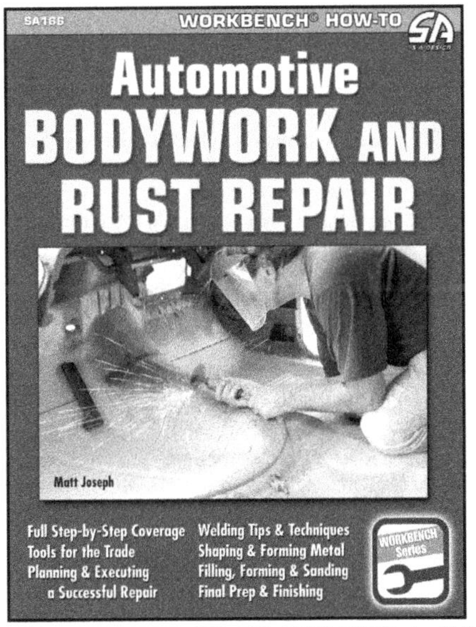

AUTOMOTIVE BODYWORK AND RUST REPAIR *by Matt Joseph* This book shows you the ins and out of tackling both simple and difficult rust and metalwork projects. This book teaches you how to select the proper tools for the job, common-sense approaches to the task ahead of you, preparing and cleaning sheet metal, section fabrications and repair patches, welding options such as gas and electric, forming, fitting and smoothing, cutting metal, final metal finishing including filling and sanding, the secrets of lead filling, making panels fit properly, and more. Softbound, 8-1/2 x 11 inches, 160 pages, 400 color photos. ***Item #SA166***

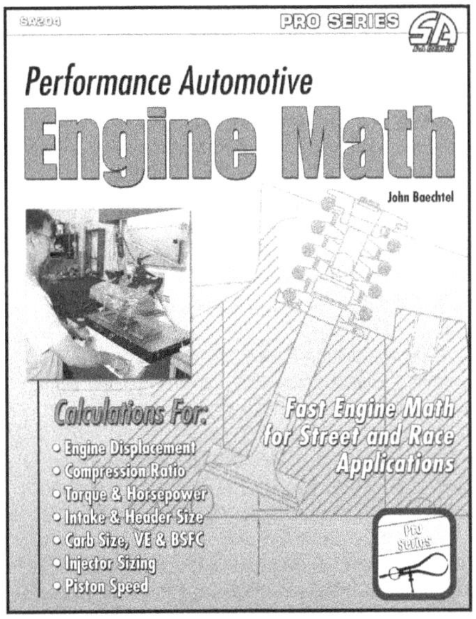

PERFORMANCE AUTOMOTIVE ENGINE MATH *by John Baechtel* When designing or building an automotive engine for improved performance, it's all about the math. From measuring the engine's internal capacities to determine compression ratio to developing the optimal camshaft lift, duration, and overlap specifications, the use of proven math is the only way to design an effective high performance automotive powerplant. This book walks readers through the wide range of dimensions to be measured and formulas used to design and develop powerful engines. Includes reviews the proper tools and measurement techniques, and carefully defines the procedures and equations used in engineering high efficiency and high rpm engines. Softbound, 8.5 x 11 inches, 160 pages, 350 photos. ***Item #SA204***

www.cartechbooks.com or 1-800-551-4754